PRAISE FOR *DOLLAROCRACY*

"With this book, John Nichols and Bob McChesney invite Americans to examine in new ways the challenges facing America, and to fully recognize the threat that the combination of Big Money and big media poses to the promise of self-government. They paint a daunting picture, rich in detail based on intense reporting and groundbreaking research. But they do not offer us a pessimistic take. Rather, they call us, as Tom Paine did more than two centuries ago, to turn knowledge into power. And they tell us that we can and must respond to our contemporary challenges as a nation by rejecting the Dollarocracy and renewing our commitment to democracy." —United States Senator Bernie Sanders

"Incisive. . . . [A] fervent call to all citizens." —*Publishers Weekly*

"An alarming, not-incorrect diagnosis." —*Kirkus Reviews*

"John Nichols and Bob McChesney make a compelling, and terrifying, case that American democracy is becoming American dollarocracy. Even more compelling, and hopeful, is their case for a radical reform agenda to take power back from the corporations and give it to the people." —Naomi Klein

"This is the black book of politics-as-industry, an encyclopedic account of money's crimes against democracy. The billionaires have hijacked our government, and anyone feeling complacent after the 2012 election should take sober note of Nichols' and McChesney's astonishing finding: It's only going to get worse. *Dollarocracy* is an impressive achievement." —Thomas Frank

"*Dollarocracy* gets at what's ailing America better than any other diagnosis I've encountered. Plus it prescribes a cure. What else could a reader—or a citizen—ask? To me, it's the book of the year." —Michael J. Copps, FCC Commissioner, 2001–2011

"*Dollarocracy* is the most important political book of the year, maybe of our times. Nichols and McChesney provide an original and painstakingly researched account of how corporations and billionaires have come to dominate the political process, as well as the contours of what they term the 'money-and-media election complex.' Although I study politics for a living, I learned more about how political advertising works, the crucial role of media corporations, and dreadful election journalism than I would have ever imagined possible. In the smartest treatment I have seen, *Dollarocracy* also details how the Internet is being incorporated into the system; its fantastic potential to empower citizens to battle big money has been effectively neutered. Most important, Nichols and McChesney provide a roadmap to a better and more just election system, built on the foundation of establishing the right to vote. It is an optimistic response to a disturbing analysis. This is exactly the book every concerned American needs to read, because the process of understanding what exactly is going on and taking America back from the corporations starts here." —Thom Hartmann

"I hope *Dollarocracy* reaches a large audience, not just among journalists but among the citizens who will produce the next journalism, so we can all move toward a more open, competent, and trustworthy press." —Bill Kovach, former Washington Bureau Chief of the *New York Times*, and former editor of the *Atlanta Journal Constitution*

"As Nichols and McChesney's new book shows, the robber barons of the late 19th century were pikers compared with today's moneyed interests. They have hijacked our elections at all levels, and nothing short of the sweeping reforms called for in *Dollarocracy* can fix the problem. The book is a must-read for anyone who cares about the integrity of our democratic system." —Thomas E. Patterson, Bradlee Professor of Government and the Press, Harvard Kennedy School

"U.S. representative democracy is built on four pillars: independent journalists, informed and engaged citizens, fair and free elections, and responsive and re-sponsible government. These pillars have been eroded by what Nichols and McChesney label 'the money-and-media election complex,' an incestuous and self-interested marriage of big media and big money. The result is a 'dollaroc-racy' resting on four new pillars: media corporations, disenchanted and manip-ulated citizens, elections that go to the highest bidder, and government that is only responsive to and responsible for the needs of the privileged class. Read this book, then go to your window and shout 'I'm mad as hell and I'm not going to take this anymore!'" —Michael X. Delli Carpini, Dean, Annenberg School for Com-munication, University of Pennsylvania

"*Dollarocracy* tackles the most important problem in American public life today in a highly readable and truly insightful fashion. Americans know generally that they live in a money-driven political system, but the book is still likely to shock and dismay them. It's particularly good on how the press plays into money pol-itics, making the whole far worse than the sum of the parts." —Thomas Ferguson, Professor of Political Science at University of Massachusetts, Boston, Senior Fellow, Roosevelt Institute

"Votes should matter more than dollars. Unfortunately, too many politicians and pundits forget this basic American value. John Nichols and Bob McChesney provide a vivid reminder of why we cannot allow our country to become a Dol-larocracy. And they inspire us to make the reforms that are needed to realize the full promise of democracy." —Congressman Mark Pocan, D-Wisconsin, Sponsor, "Right to Vote Amendment"

"The billionaires are buying our media and our elections. They're spinning our democracy into a dollarocracy. John Nichols and Bob McChesney expose the culprits who steered America into the quagmire of big money and provide us with the tools to free ourselves and our republic from the corporate klepto-crats." —Lisa Graves, Executive Director, Center for Media and Democracy

"If we want America to be a democracy—and we do—we must guarantee the right of all Americans to vote. John Nichols and Bob McChesney recognize this, and their groundbreaking book makes a compelling case for placing the right to vote at the center of our urgent struggle to protect and extend democracy." —Rob Richie, Executive Director, FairVote: The Center for Voting and Democracy

"Those of us who have been fighting at the grassroots against the corporate influence on both major parties have for years been waiting for an uncompromising, unrelenting exposé of how big money shouts down the voices of citizens. This is it! Nichols and McChesney reveal how billionaires and corporations are buying our media, buying our elections. But Nichols and McChesney don't stop there. They outline an agenda that is bold enough to make this country a real democracy. If you want to build a movement that gives power to the people, you must read this book." —Tim Carpenter, Executive Director, Progressive Democrats of America

"John Nichols and Bob McChesney reveal that the 2012 election cycle had a price tag of $10 billion. They show us who the money came from and how it was spent. But, most important, they explain why this cannot go on if we are to have fair elections and honest government. With its breakthrough reporting and incisive analysis, *Dollarocracy* gives us the foundation we need to make the case for fundamental change like a constitutional amendment to overturn our system of unlimited campaign spending and restore democracy to the people." —John Bonifaz, Co-Founder and Executive Director, Free Speech For People Founder, National Voting Rights Institute

"Nichols and McChesney strike again! And, as usual, these two experienced and effective fighters for common sense and the common good are right on target with *Dollarocracy*. The truth might not 'make you free,' but it can make you move into action to free our great nation from the political stranglehold of big money. So read . . . and let's get moving!" —Jim Hightower, bestselling author, nationally syndicated columnist and radio commentator, and editor of the Hightower Lowdown

"This is the book that says it all: It gets right at everything that we know is wrong with politics in America." —Lila Garrett, Host, "Connect the Dots with Lila Garrett," KPFK-FM (Los Angeles)

DOLLAROCRACY

Also by **John Nichols** and **Robert W. McChesney**

It's the Media, Stupid (2000)

Our Media, Not Theirs (2002)

*Tragedy and Farce: How the American Media Sell Wars,
Spin Elections, and Destroy Democracy* (2005)

*The Death and Life of American Journalism:
The Media Revolution That Will Begin the World Again* (2010)

DOLLAROCRACY

How the Money-and-Media Election
Complex Is Destroying America

JOHN NICHOLS
AND ROBERT W. McCHESNEY

NATION
BOOKS
New York

Hardcover first published in 2013 by
Nation Books, A Member of the Perseus Books Group
116 East 16th Street, 8th Floor
New York, NY 10003

Paperback first published in 2014 by Nation Books
Nation Books is a co-publishing venture of
the Nation Institute and the Perseus Books Group.

Books published by Nation Books are available at special discounts for bulk
purchases in the United States by corporations, institutions, and other organizations. For more information, please contact the Special Markets Department
at the Perseus Books Group, 2300 Chestnut Street, Suite 200, Philadelphia, PA
19103, or call (800) 255-1514, or e-mail special.markets@perseusbooks.com.

Designed by Pauline Brown

The Library of Congress has cataloged the hardcover as follows:

Nichols, John.
  Dollarocracy : how the money-and-media election complex is destroying
America / John Nichols and
Robert W. McChesney.
    pages cm
  Includes bibliographical references and index.
  ISBN 978-1-56858-707-3 (hardcover) — ISBN 978-1-56858-711-0 (e-book)
  1. Campaign funds—United States. 2. Elections—United States. 3. Mass
media—United States—Forecasting. 4. Democracy—United States.
  I. McChesney, Robert Waterman, 1952- II. Title.
  JK1991.N54 2013
  324.7'80973—dc23
                                                              2013009813
  ISBN 978-1-56858-953-4 (paperback)

10 9 8 7 6 5 4 3 2 1

For Whitman,
Amy, and Lucy

I speak the password primeval,
I give the sign of democracy;
By God! I will accept nothing which all cannot have their counterpart of
    on the same terms.

WALT WHITMAN, *SONG OF MYSELF*

CONTENTS

FOREWORD

United States Senator Bernie Sanders

More than a decade ago, in April 2002, I opened a crowded meeting at the Unitarian Church on Main Street in Montpelier, Vermont, by announcing, "I want to welcome you to what I believe is the first congressional town meeting ever organized to address the issue of corporate control of the media." For the next several hours, John Nichols, Bob McChesney, and I had the remarkable experience of talking with and listening to citizens who were ready to engage in a serious discourse about the role of a free press in sustaining democracy. The people got it, as they almost always do. Even then, they could see what we saw: a decline in the amount and quality of journalism and a parallel rise in the influence of Big Money in our politics.

The media reform movement that Nichols and McChesney have done so much to foster—as the authors of four books on media policy, as advocates for independent media, and as cofounders of the nation's media reform network, Free Press—has always sought to address that concern. I've been proud to work with them on media issues and proud of the successes we have had in pushing back against consolidation of media ownership and in supporting public and community broadcasting and maintaining net neutrality.

But Nichols and McChesney have always argued that realizing the full promise of a free press in America must be seen as the founders saw it: as a way of providing the information and ideas that sustain democratic discourse and enable citizens to cast informed votes. And the past decade has, unfortunately, been rough on democratic discourse and on democracy itself. Local newspapers have closed or been downsized. Coverage of statehouses and even of Washington, DC, is declining. Although there is hope for online journalism, resources are few. For tens of millions of Americans, an information void has developed. And it is being filled by political advertising and public relations spin.

The simple truth is that we cannot govern our own affairs when our national, state, and local debates are bought and sold by billionaires, who use thirty-second commercials to shout down anyone who disagrees. Democracy demands a rich, robust discourse about ideas, not a spending spree that demeans those ideas, diminishes honest debate, and turns voters off to the political process. Yet this is the threat we now face. In this book, Nichols and McChesney, pioneers in explaining the relationship between media and democracy, step up to address the great challenge of our time: the replacement of democracy with what they describe as Dollarocracy.

This is not a casually chosen term. They suggest that with the decline of independent journalism as a primary source of information about elections and governing, and its replacement by now-omnipresent political advertising, especially since the Supreme Court's *Citizens United v. FEC* ruling, we have seen the development of an electoral equivalent to the self-perpetuating military-industrial complex that Dwight Eisenhower warned us about. The money-and-media election complex, producing a slurry of negative ads, spin, and obstruction, is not what the founders intended.

That's one reason that I was proud to introduce a Saving American Democracy amendment to the U.S. Constitution that says corporations are not persons with constitutional rights equal to real people, corporations are subject to regulation by the people, corporations may not make campaign contributions or any election expenditures, and Congress and the states have the power to regulate campaign finances. In this book, Nichols and McChesney make a powerful case for why it is necessary to amend the Constitution to tackle the Money Power that the Progressive reformers of a century ago warned would replace democracy with plutocracy.

But they do not stop there. They recall the Progressive Era and argue that America is ripe for a new age of reform that focuses on renewing democracy and that takes as its foundational premise an understanding that the essential act of democracy, voting, must be protected and made meaningful by legislation, statutes, and amendments. Nichols and McChesney are not doctrinaire; they recognize that many reforms can and should be entertained and that not every American will agree on every proposal. But, they argue, the energy that has been seen in popular protests on behalf of labor rights; in campaigns to defend public education and public services; in the movements to save Social Security, Medicare, and Medicaid; in the Occupy movement's challenge to income inequality; and in the town meetings of my home state of Vermont, which have called for amending the Constitution to address corporate abuses of the political process constitutes evidence of a rising call for reforms that will allow American democracy to work for all Americans, not just a privileged and powerful few.

This is an exciting prospect and one with deep roots in American history. The wisest of the founders recognized that America would evolve and change with time, and they rested great power in the people to assure that the evolution might serve the common good. With this book, John Nichols and Bob McChesney invite Americans to examine in new ways the challenges facing America and to fully recognize the threat that the combination of Big Money and big media poses to the promise of self-government. They paint a daunting picture, rich in detail based on intense reporting and groundbreaking research. But they do not offer us a pessimistic take. Rather, they call us, as Tom Paine did more than two centuries ago, to turn knowledge into power. And they tell us that we can and must respond to our contemporary challenges as a nation by rejecting Dollarocracy and renewing our commitment to democracy.

BURLINGTON, VERMONT
FEBRUARY 2013

PREFACE

O, let America be America again—
The land that never has been yet—
And yet must be

LANGSTON HUGHES, "LET AMERICA
BE AMERICA AGAIN," 1936

There comes a point, sometime after the last election campaign, when a politician becomes a statesman or a stateswoman. And it is at that point when he or she begins to speak the deeper truth, what Walt Whitman described as the "password primeval" of our American experiment.[1]

The truth these statesmen and stateswomen tell today is a harrowing one.

Bemoaning "a dangerous deficit of governance" that has left critical issues unaddressed, former vice president Al Gore argued in his 2013 book, *The Future,* that "not since the 1890s has U.S. government decision making been as feeble, dysfunctional, and servile to corporate and other special interests as it is now."[2] From across the aisle, 2012 Republican presidential contender Jon Huntsman decried deficits of leadership and confidence and declared that, corrupted by special-interest money and corroded by the crude cynicism of negative politics, "the system is broken."[3] But the most damning delineation of the Zeitgeist came from the most senior of our nation's former presidents, Jimmy Carter, who looked out across the American political landscape in the midst of the 2012 election campaign and saw a political process "shot through with financial corruption" and witnessing "a total transformation of America into a negative campaigning process."[4]

Describing the 2010 U.S. Supreme Court ruling in the case of *Citizens United v. FEC* as "a major victory for big oil, Wall Street banks, health insurance companies and the other powerful interests that marshal their power every day in Washington to drown out the voices of everyday Americans," Carter declared—as the planet's most famous election observer—that "we have one of the worst election processes in the world right in the United States of America, and it's almost entirely because of the excessive influx of money."[5]

Imagine if the internationally renowned, Nobel Peace Prize–winning former president of any other country were to say that his homeland suffered under "the worst election processes in the world." We would, as Americans, be justifiably skeptical of claims that the country in question met the basic standards of democratic governance. We might even threaten to cut off foreign aid until fundamental reforms were initiated. Yet like the frog in the pot that is slowly coming to a boil, we do not always respond with the same urgency to indications of a crisis at home.

This book argues for a conclusion that is obvious and unavoidable to anyone paying attention to the likes of Gore, Huntsman, and Carter: that with democracy itself so threatened, citizens must, as they have before, respond with the boldness appropriate to maintain the American experiment. In a country where, as Huntsman noted, millions of Americans decide not to vote because they think the political process is "rigged" to produce the results desired by contemporary robber barons, the time for debating whether a crisis exists is long past. It is no longer rational, let alone permissible, to neglect the crisis of our political process, which goes far beyond the challenges posed by corporate cash and the renewal of the Money Power that the last century's Progressives took on in a battle for the soul of the nation.

This is a radical book in the best sense of that term. It reminds the American people, who, polling suggests, are well aware of the crisis and are searching for solutions, that the Reverend Martin Luther King Jr. said in his wisdom, "When you are right you cannot be too radical."[6] It is not just right but also necessary to reach a radical recognition of the scope of the crisis, to understand that a discussion of a "broken system" must identify the points of rupture: special-interest influence on our politics, to be sure; but also the collapse of a journalism sufficient to name and shame the influence peddlers; the abandonment of basic premises of democracy by partisans who are willing to win at any cost; and the rise of a consulting class that makes "win at any cost" politics possible by shaping a money-and-media election complex every bit as dismissive of the popular will as the military-industrial complex is.

The high-stakes partisanship of the moment causes even the best of those who are in power to be cautious in their responses to the crisis. A perfect example came when President Barack Obama delivered his fourth State of the Union address in February 2013. He delivered a stirring defense of the right to vote—a right that this book argues must be explicitly protected by our Constitution. But then, against all the evidence of a need for a bold response to explicit disenfranchisement and to the broader dysfunction of the system, President Obama proposed merely to appoint a commission to reflect on the challenge. Worse yet, the commission the president named for the purpose of improving "the voting experience in America" was to be chaired by the most rigid of partisans: the top election lawyer for the Democrats and the top election lawyer for the Republicans.[7]

The president likes to say that with regard to the challenges posed for voters, "We have to fix that." We agree, but it has to be the right fix, not just in the details but also in the character and the scope of its ambition.

We do not mean to be cynical, but we are certain that any improvement of "the voting experience in America" that is proposed and implemented by partisans of the current process, any insider "fix," will be insufficient to address the pathologies inherent in "one of the worst election processes in the world."

The change must come, as it always has, from the people. It must go beyond partisanship and ideology, beyond the narrow confines of a discourse that too frequently sustains, rather than challenges, that "broken system." This book invites the reader to embrace what is best about America: a bold willingness to subvert the dominant paradigm and to begin the world over again. Our history tells us that Americans can reclaim their country and chart a democratic course toward a future that is not only better than this moment but also better than the best moments of our past. America is a progressive nation, and it is time, once more, for it to progress.

OUR CONFIDENCE in this prospect comes from the people who helped to make this book possible, in particular Katrina vanden Heuvel, the editor and publisher of *The Nation* magazine, who, in the aftermath of the High Court's *Citizens United* ruling and the 2010 election campaign's beginning revelation of the fullness of the crisis at hand, invited us to write an article on the development of a money-and-media election complex. Almost as soon as the article appeared, we found ourselves entertaining conversations with publishers, which is a nice place to be, especially when you have our terrific agent, Sandra Dijkstra, and her team sorting things out. Ultimately, we ended up with Nation Books, working again with our friend and comrade editorial director Carl Bromley. Carl is the hero of this book. At a critical point in the writing process, he recognized with us that the timeline was wrong; instead of anticipating the 2012 election, we needed to cover it and incorporate into the book an understanding of where the process is now.

Carl was not the only patient supporter of the long reporting and writing process. John Nichols was cheered on along the way by Roane Carey, Peter Rothberg, Betsy Reed, Richard Kim, Emily Douglas, Liliana Segura, and everyone else at *The Nation,* as well as Dave Zweifel, Judie Kleinmaier, Lynn Danielson, and all the folks at the *Capital Times* in Madison. Many of the ideas contained in this book were explored in media appearances by John on MSNBC, with Ed Schultz, Chris Matthews, and Chris Hayes, among others, and the MSNBC crew of Rich Stockwell, Querry Robinson, Arianna Jones, Gregg Cockrell, Sheara Braun, Jen Zweben, and so many others. James Holm and Diane Shamis deserve special mention as friends and colleagues, as do Brent, Wendy, and all the folks who work with Ed Schultz's radio show. Conversations with Amy Goodman, Juan González, Nermeen Shaikh, and the *Democracy Now!* crew were invaluable. And the same goes for on-air and off-air discussions with Shihab Rattansi for Al Jazeera English, as well as the folks with BBC and RTE-Radio Ireland and, of course, Wisconsin Public Radio. And a special shout-out to Thom Hartmann, brilliant radio and television host and author of groundbreaking books on corporate power. Tim Carpenter, Steve Cobble, and all the people associated with Progressive Democrats of America have hosted many events at which John has appeared to debate and discuss all the issues addressed in this book, as have RoseAnn DeMoro, Michael Lighty, Chuck Idelson, Jean Ross, and everyone else with National Nurses United.

John also owes thanks to Mark Janson, Ed Garvey, Lisa Graves, Rob Richie, Jeff Clements, Doug Clopp, Michael Briggs, John Bonifaz, the Reverend Jesse Jackson, Congressman Keith Ellison, Congressman Mark Pocan, David Panofsky, Pat Smith, Sharon Lezberg, Brian Yandell, Susan Stern, Kitty Nichols, Cary Featherstone, Meredith Clark, all the activists in Wisconsin (especially those in Spring Green and Burlington!), campaigners across the country for Move to Amend and Free Speech for People, and too many other friends and comrades to name who helped wrestle with these issues.

Bob owes particular thanks to David Tewksbury, his chair in the Department of Communication at the University of Illinois, and everyone in the department and at the university who bent over backward to make this research possible. Bob is extremely fortunate to have such a supportive environment for research. Some material in this book overlaps work Bob did for his 2013 book *Digital Disconnect: How Capitalism Is Turning the Internet Against Democracy* (New Press). Bob thanks both publishers for their collegiality.

Bob also owes thanks to Bruce Ackerman, Scott Althaus, Patrick Barrett, Lance Bennett, Paul Buhle, Sundiata Cha-Jua, Vivek Chibber, David Cobb, Jeff Cohen, Diana Cook, Michael Copps, Michael Delli Carpini, Frank Emspak, Thomas Ferguson, John Bellamy Foster, Lew Friedland, Peter Hart, Amy Holland, Steve Horn, Kathleen Hall Jamieson, Shanto Iyengar, Van Jones, R. Jamil Jonna, Marty Kaplan, Jed McChesney, Michael McDonald, Mark Crispin Miller, Alan Nasser, Sarah Niebler, Molly Niesen, Tom Patterson, Victor Pickard, Travis Ridout, Joel Rogers, Allen Ruff, Ron Salmon, Josh Silver, Norman Stockwell, Inger Stole, Mandy Troger, Katherine Cramer Walsh, Mark Weisbrot, Rob Weissman, Darrell West, Bruce Williams, and Kristina Williams. Each of them helped Bob with researching and developing the arguments. In some cases, such as those of Jamil Jonna, Mandy Troger, Amy Holland, and Kristina Williams, the assistance was extraordinary. The book could not have been written without their assistance.

And from both John and Bob, a special thanks to Matt Rothschild and Ruth Conniff of *The Progressive,* who have embraced and published our work for almost two decades. Likewise, thanks to the terrific staff at Free Press, especially Craig Aaron, Derek Turner, and Josh Stearns, who had smart answers for every question we threw at them. When we helped launch Free Press in 2003, we had no idea what an extraordinary organization it would become, owing entirely to Craig, Derek, Josh, and the other exceptional staff members.

Special thanks, too, to our dear friend and our senator, Bernie Sanders, who has been fighting on these issues for decades and whose conversations with us have been invaluable. We are honored beyond words that he has written the Foreword to this book.

Then there are those closest to our hearts. For Bob, his "keeping it real" dawg posse: Chubby Boy, Juicer, Hambone, and the Bear; and his family: Lucy, Amy, and Inger. For John, Mary Bottari, the wisest of them all, who put it all in perspective, as did Whitman Genevieve Bottari Nichols, who continues to advocate for a kids' version. And, of course, to Whitman's grandmother, Mary Nichols, who demands only that the progressive flame remain well and truly lit.

JOHN NICHOLS
ROBERT W. McCHESNEY
MADISON, WISCONSIN
MARCH 2013

DOLLAROCRACY

INTRODUCTION

Privilege Resurgent

> At many stages in the advance of humanity, this conflict between the men who possess more than they have earned and the men who have earned more than they possess is the central condition of progress. In our day it appears as the struggle of freemen to gain and hold the right of self-government as against the special interests, who twist the methods of free government into machinery for defeating the popular will. At every stage, and under all circumstances, the essence of the struggle is to equalize opportunity, destroy privilege, and give to the life and citizenship of every individual the highest possible value both to himself and to the commonwealth. That is nothing new.

> THEODORE ROOSEVELT, 1910

It is, of course, nothing new.

America has from its founding struggled along a narrow arc of history toward an end never quite reached: that of sincere and meaningful democracy. We have made massive progress, evolving from a nation of privileged elites that espoused lofty ideals about all men being created equal and then enslaved men, women, and children into a nation where the descendants of those slaves have taken their places as governors, senators, and Supreme Court justices. Yet as the great champion of American advancement, the Reverend Martin Luther King Jr., reminded us in a time of historic change, "Human progress is neither automatic nor inevitable."[1]

What was gained in the Progressive Era when Teddy Roosevelt championed radical reform and across the years of unsteady but genuine democratic progress that followed was written into the Constitution and the statutes of the land. Witness amendments eliminating poll taxes and extending the franchise to women and eighteen- to twenty-year-olds, the Civil Rights and Voting Rights acts, and, finally, the National Voter Registration Act of 1993.

But this progress never quite assured that the great mass of people would gain and hold the right of self-government as against the special interests. The U.S. Constitution contains no guarantee of a right to vote, and this lack of definition is constantly exploited by political hucksters who would make America a democracy for the few, and a plutocracy in essence. The malefactors of great wealth continue to twist the methods of free government into the machinery for defeating the popular will. And scarcely one hundred years after Roosevelt identified his central condition of progress, they have reversed it, with court rulings and practices that are contributing to the destruction of the American electoral system as a tool for realizing the democratic dreams that have animated American progress across two centuries. U.S. elections have never been perfect—far from it—but the United States is now rapidly approaching a point where the electoral process itself ceases to function as a means for citizens to effectively control leaders and guide government policies. It pains us, as political writers and citizens who have spent a combined eighty years working on and/or covering electoral campaigns, to write these words. But there can no longer be any question that free and fair elections—what we were raised to believe was an American democratic birthright—are effectively being taken away from the people.

In this book we examine the forces—billionaires, corporations, the politicians who do their bidding, and the media conglomerates that facilitate the abuse—that have sapped elections of their meaning and of their democratic potential. "The Money Power," as Roosevelt and his contemporaries termed the collaboration that imposed the will of wealth on our politics, achieves its ends by flooding the electoral system with an unprecedented tidal wave of unaccountable money. The money makes a mockery of political equality in the voting booth, and the determination of media companies to cash in on that mockery—when they should instead be exposing and opposing it—completes a vicious circle.

This is not an entirely new phenomenon, as we note in the historical chapters of this book. But it is an accelerating phenomenon. The U.S. Supreme

Court's 2010 *Citizens United* decision allowing unlimited corporate campaign spending confirmed the court-ordered diminution of democratic processes that over four decades has renewed the political privileges of the elites. "The day before *Citizens United* was decided," Lawrence Lessig wrote, "our democracy was already broken. *Citizens United* may have shot the body, but the body was already cold."[2]

Economic elites are now exercising those privileges with an abandon not seen since the era of the robber barons that Roosevelt decried. To enhance the influence of their money, billionaires, corporations, and their political pawns began in the run-up to the 2012 election to aggressively advance policies designed to limit the voting rights of those Americans who are most disinclined to sanction these elites' continued dominance of the political process. They are grasping for total power, and if they did not succeed in choking off the avenues of dissent in 2012, they will surely return—with increased determination and more insidious tactics—in 2014 and 2016 and beyond. "There's been almost a shameless quality to it," says former U.S. senator Russ Feingold of the pressure on politicians to raise and spend exponentially more money since the *Citizens United* decision. "It has grossly altered our system of government. We don't have the kind of elections that most of us grew up seeing."[3]

The moneyed interests are confident, even in the face of temporary setbacks, that they will be able to continue their initiative because they are well served by the rapid decline of the news media as a checking and balancing force on our politics. Our dominant media institutions do an absolutely dreadful job of drawing citizens into public life, especially elections. The owners of media corporations have made their pact with the new order. For the most part, they do not challenge it, as the crusading editors and publishers of another age did. Rather, advertising departments position media outlets to reap windfall profits through the broadcasting of invariably inane and crudely negative political campaign advertising, which is the lingua franca of American electioneering in the twenty-first century. The corporate media are the immediate financial beneficiaries of our increasingly absurd election system—and the primary barriers to its reform. To talk about the crisis of money in politics without addressing the mess that the media have made of things is the equivalent of talking about the deliberate fire without discussing the arsonist.

We term the combine that has emerged the "money-and-media election complex." It has become so vast and so powerful that it can best be understood as an entity unto itself. This complex is built on a set of commercial and institutional relationships involving wealthy donors, giant corporations, lobbyists, consultants, politicians, spinmeisters, corporate media, coin-operated "think tanks," inside-the-beltway pundits, and now super-PACs. These relationships are eviscerating democratic elections and benefit by that evisceration. The complex has tremendous gravitational power, which increases the degree of difficulty for those wishing to participate in elections outside its paradigm. The complex embraces and encourages a politics defined by wealthy funders, corporate media, and the preservation of a new status quo; it is the modern-day reflection of the arrangements that served the robber barons of the late nineteenth and early twentieth centuries.

2012: THE END OF THE BEGINNING

In the days and weeks following the 2012 election, the winning side predictably announced that the problem of money in politics was overrated because, after all, this side won. Imagining that all was well because the darkest possible scenarios did not immediately play out, the *Christian Science Monitor* declared, "Despite concerns that huge amounts of money spent by political action committees would skew the results, many candidates backed by large PAC-financed advertising campaigns did not win their races. Money was less influential than expected. Voters thought for themselves."[4] So there you have it. Or maybe not.

While Republicans and their allied super-PACs did spend billions to defeat President Barack Obama and the Democrats, it is not as if the Democrats failed to return fire with fire. As the *New York Times* concluded, "The president and his allies appear to have matched or exceeded Mr. Romney and his allies in the number of advertisements that aired." As the dust cleared after the election, it became obvious that the Democrats were very much part of the system, with their own dependence upon big money in countless areas. "The president's re-election does not presage a repudiation of the deregulated campaign financing unleashed by the Supreme Court's 2010 Citizens United decision," political correspondent Nicholas Confessore of the *Times* wrote. "Instead his victory most likely reinforced the practice."[5]

This is the truth of 2012: money beat money.

To believe otherwise is naïve, just as it is naïve in the extreme to imagine that the money-and-media election complex ground to some kind of halt in November 2012. To the contrary, it has not yet built up to full force. That's a daunting prospect, but it is also good news. Before it becomes the status quo, we may have an opportunity to intervene. But for that to happen, we must understand how we got to this point, how this system operates, what the consequences are, where it appears to be heading, and what Americans can and must do to get their nation back on the democratic grid. That is the purpose of this book.

The immediate effect of the money-and-media election complex is to encourage election campaigns, like those in 2012, that do not even begin to address the societal pathologies afflicting the people of the United States. The trillion dollars spent annually on militarism and war is off-limits to public review and debate. Likewise, the corporate control of the economy and the corporate domination of government itself get barely a nod. Stagnation, gaping economic inequality, growing poverty, and collapsing infrastructure and social services—major issues all—are accorded nothing more than the market-tested drivel candidates say to get votes. The existential threats posed by climate change and nuclear weaponry are virtually off-limits as campaign-season issues; whole debates that are supposed to go to the heart of domestic and global concerns pass by without mention of them. The drug war, which has created a prison-industrial complex so vast that the United States has a greater percentage of its population imprisoned than any other nation in history, is not to be mentioned—except when obviously engaged and concerned citizens force the issue onto the ballot via the initiative process.

The United States, like much of the world, is in a period of crisis, not unlike the 1930s or the Progressive Era of Teddy Roosevelt and Robert M. La Follette. But now the stakes are higher. Mainstream politics, following elections, seems increasingly irrelevant to addressing these grave, even existential, challenges. As a result, they are untended and grow more severe. Something has to give; this can't go on forever, or even very much longer. It is in all our interests that these problems be addressed by democratic governance and sooner rather than later. The alternative is an ugly picture, one that is entirely unnecessary.

As the subsequent chapters will demonstrate, widespread popular disillusionment with contemporary elections and the political system is anything but irrational. The type of society we have is far better understood as a Dollarocracy than as a democracy. We have a system that is now defined more by one dollar, one vote than by one person, one vote. We live in a society where a small number of fabulously wealthy individuals and giant corporations control most of the dollars—and by extension have most of the political power. They buy election results that give them control over the government, and they hire lobbyists to fine-tune that control so that the distribution of wealth and income continually skews to their advantage. This is not a mystery. Polling shows that more than 60 percent of Americans understand that the nation's economic structure is "out of balance" and that it favors a "very small portion of the rich" over everyone else.[6] And they despair that political structures are so skewed and corrupted that nothing will change this circumstance. As political scientist Jeffrey A. Winters characterized American governance circa 2012, "Democracy appears chronically dysfunctional when it comes to policies that impinge on the rich."[7]

To be clear, elections are not entirely worthless—especially on the handful of issues where the wealthy do not necessarily have a horse in the race. Popular forces can prevail, even against increasing odds, and we admire and respect numerous politicians who enter and occasionally succeed in the electoral arena. Elections will remain among the main playing fields for politics in the visible future. Our argument is simply that the degree of difficulty that citizens confront when they seek to use the election process to effectively control government policies is vastly higher than it has been in memory. And it will only get worse unless Americans do something about it. A difficult truth lurks not far in the future: if our elections get appreciably more corrupt, extending the trajectory they were already on in 2012, the use of the term "democracy" to describe the United States will be inaccurate in even the weakest sense of the term. The point, then, is not to abandon elections, but to make them viable and credible.

To do that, however, we all must recognize that Robert F. Kennedy Jr. is right when he describes the *Citizens United* ruling as ushering in the completion of "a hostile takeover of our government" by corporations and billionaires. "We are now in a free fall toward old-fashioned oligarchy; noxious, thieving and tyrannical," he writes. "America, the world's premier template for democracy and a robust middle class, is now listing toward oligarchy and corporate kleptocracy. America today is looking more and more like a colonial economy, with a system increasingly tilted toward enriching the wealthy 1 percent and serving the mercantile needs of multinational corporations with little allegiance to our country."[8]

We are not interested in promoting cynicism; we believe it is possible to change the world for the better. And we believe there is a way out of the current crisis: in a reform moment focused on the bold new voting rights movement that we outline in Chapter 9. But we do no one any favors by sugarcoating the reality around us. Our optimism in the midst of the wreckage we describe in this book is fueled by our recognition that the forces of reform have the numbers on their side. If America were to hold truly fair elections where the preponderance of Americans vote, where there is credible journalism, we are certain there would be progressive results. The dollarcrats get that too, which is why they battle so hard to see that fair elections with credible journalism never come to pass. It is why they are not satisfied with overwhelming financial advantages and media that are sympathetic to their demands on society. They seek to restrict the franchise and rig election laws in a manner than can only be described as obscene.[9] All the once-common rhetoric about the importance of expanding the rate of voter participation to join the rest of the civilized world has been shelved by the dollarcrats. They know that their policies and their privileges could never survive democracy.

Our motivation in writing this book is to encourage Americans to demand the electoral democracy they deserve and require. We take as our foundational premise the understanding of the franchise explained in 1957 by the Reverend Martin Luther King Jr. when he wrote, "So long as I do not firmly and irrevocably possess the right to vote I do not possess myself. I cannot make up my mind—it is made up for me. I cannot live as a democratic citizen, observing the laws I have helped to enact—I can only submit to the edict of others."[10] King was merely restating the longstanding American democratic tradition. As Benjamin Franklin put it, "They who have no voice nor vote in the electing of representatives, do not enjoy liberty, but are absolutely enslaved to those who have votes."[11] In the twenty-first century, it is offensive to us that many Americans do not believe that they firmly and irrevocably possess the right to vote—either because they encounter barriers to their participation or because they believe their vote has been rendered meaningless by the overwhelming influence of the Money Power. It is our faith that the vast majority of our fellow citizens take similar offense, and this faith tells us that radical reform is possible.

In order to address the crisis of elections in the United States, this book chronicles the rise and functioning of the money-and-media election complex as a cornerstone of Dollarocracy.

In Chapter 1 we take a longer look at the nature of Dollarocracy in the contemporary United States. Americans enjoy what is at best a "weak" democracy. But the problems confronting the nation today are not new with regard to governance, particularly the democratizing of elections. This chapter traces this important and mostly overlooked history.

How much does Dollarocracy cost? In Chapter 2 we take a look at the 2012 election and chronicle the billionaires and very-nearly billionaires who put up the lion's share of this money and what they will get in return for their investments. This was a $10 billion election, almost double what was spent in 2008 and ten times what was spent a generation ago, even allowing for inflation. We assess how this shadowy underworld of big money is institutionalizing and operating and why notions that the dollarcrats were vanquished for all time in 2012 are untenable. At current patterns, 2012 may be remembered nostalgically a few election cycles down the road.

How is Dollarocracy made possible? In Chapter 3 we look at the U.S. Supreme Court and the long path it took from the 1970s to the *Citizens United* case and beyond. With a judicial activism that is unwarranted and arguably unprecedented, the current Court has overturned nearly all efforts by elected officials or even public referenda to limit the ability of big money to buy elections. The chapter describes how this process was no fluke. One of the primary Supreme Court champions of unleashing corporate and billionaire campaign spending was Lewis Powell, the person responsible for the 1971 U.S. Chamber of Commerce memo that was central to igniting the campaign by large corporations and the wealthy to aggressively enter the political realm and establish Dollarocracy.

How does Dollarocracy warp our politics? In Chapter 4 we examine the history and nature of political advertising, especially television political advertising. We describe how it shares attributes found in product advertising—including a loose connection to factual accuracy or context—but also how it has one overriding difference: it tends increasingly to favor negative advertising, where the point of the exercise is to discredit the opponent by any means necessary. Negative advertising now dominates campaigns and is a signature contribution of Dollarocracy.

Who gets rich from Dollarocracy? In Chapter 5 we examine the corporate media, especially the firms owning TV stations and cable channels that are raking in money hand over fist. Political advertising has been manna from the heavens for local broadcasters, now sometimes accounting for as much as 25 or 30 percent of total revenues. As these revenues have skyrocketed over the past two decades, broadcasters have all but abandoned fulfilling their legal obligation to provide campaign coverage. Moreover, we chronicle how, unlike many other democracies, the United States has no credible public broadcasting to fill the breach. This chapter also describes the grisly story of how corporate media have become to campaign finance reform what the National Rifle Association is to efforts to restrict the sale and use of assault weapons.

How do news media cover Dollarocracy? Won't they provide a check to campaign propaganda? In Chapter 6 we take a look at the important and necessary role the news media have played in the election system in American history. In particular, we examine how professional journalism's campaign coverage became obsessed with "horse-race" issues, which allowed campaign spin and advertising to set the terms of public debate. The news media, far from being the people's sentinel, have come to fan the flames of the idiocy of election campaigns.

But wait, it gets worse. In Chapter 7 we chronicle two of the great news media trends of recent times. First, there is an absolute and sharp decline in the resources going to journalism as commercial interests no longer find the news profitable. This means that most races get no coverage whatsoever and what little coverage exists otherwise is mostly gossipy fluff. As a result, the balance of power shifts decisively to big money to set the agenda of election campaigns. Second, the void has been filled by the rise of right-wing partisan media, like Fox News, that effectively front for Dollarocracy at every turn. We describe the decided effect this has on the political culture.

Won't the Internet solve most or all of these problems? Won't social media provide an inexpensive way for people to communicate with each other and undermine the power of Big Money? In Chapter 8 we take a hard look at how the Internet has evolved from its romantic origins to where it is today. We look at how political campaigns used the Internet in 2012 and how digital advertising is a very different, and far more invasive, enterprise than TV or newspaper advertising ever was. Far from overturning the money-and-media election complex, the Internet may be perfecting it.

So where does this leave matters? Should people look for the nearest ledge to jump off of? Hardly. In fact, there are workable solutions to all these problems, both in American history and in the experiences of other democratic nations. In Chapter 9, the conclusion, we address these options and begin to describe the political process necessary to make reform. Spoiler alert: the historical evidence demonstrates that the money-and-media election complex can be successfully dismantled only as part of a broader popular wave leading to the democratic reform of our core institutions. Likewise, no successful democratic reform movement can possibly succeed without fundamental election and media reform. Such reforms have to be in the center of *any* credible reform program to rejuvenate American democracy. But we go beyond that in Chapter 9 to argue that it is imperative that there be a guiding vision that enlivens and empowers the entire range of campaigns for democratic renewal such that the whole will become immeasurably larger than the sum of its parts; in our view it must be a campaign for a constitutional commitment to a right to vote for all citizens, with all that entails.

With a certain amount of irony, concerned citizens will have to work through, as well as around, the existing electoral and media systems to generate the necessary reforms. Difficult? Yes. Impossible? No, at least if the history of the American experiment is to be believed—and extended.

1

THIS IS *NOT* WHAT DEMOCRACY LOOKS LIKE

These damned consultants come in and say, "This is how you have to run," and it's always the same: raise money, spend it on television, don't say anything that will offend anyone.

SENATOR BERNIE SANDERS OF VERMONT, 2012

During the course of 2011, the United States experienced the largest and most widespread public demonstrations in many decades. To the surprise, even shock, of politicians, pundits, and news media, countless Americans were so dissatisfied with the growing inequality in American life and with the corruption of a political system—and elections—that they were willing to take to the streets. They were standing up to protest a world dominated by the wealthy and by gigantic corporations. They were looking at a future that seemed to belong to a privileged few rather than the great mass of Americans, and they were declaring that they wanted another future—one that worked for everyone. As these often-heterogeneous crowds gathered and demanded attention, their self-referencing slogan was "This Is What Democracy Looks Like." It was a direct challenge to the prevailing wisdom of those in power and the pundits who were so busy hailing America, circa 2011, as the greatest, freest, and most democratic nation in the world that they missed the evidence of political stagnation and democratic decline.

Suddenly, the politicians weren't writing the script. The people were, or, at the very least, they were trying. This surprised the elites that imagined an "end to history" had occurred with the fall of the Berlin Wall more than two decades earlier. Even more surprising to the punditocracy was how it seemed that a significant percentage of Americans were sympathetic to the protestors and thought they were making accurate and important points.[1] When the demonstrations subsided, the politicians, pundits, and journalists went back to sleep. They returned to regurgitating their bromides, but the sleeping giant of American democracy had let its presence be known. And it is this unruly mass, which wants democracy in reality not just in clichés, that most petrifies the proponents of Dollarocracy.

Nowhere is this lack of effective political democracy more apparent than in the election system. The United States, unlike most democracies, does not make an explicit guarantee of the right to vote in its Constitution. And the disregard for voting rights, as well as implicit and explicit efforts by the political class to suppress participation, has risen to crisis levels in many states. Americans see that crisis. Fifty-nine percent of those surveyed in 2012 polling by the Rasmussen Reports group believe our elections are rigged to produce results that are invariably beyond the control of mere voters. Rasmussen polling in 2011 found that 45 percent, a solid plurality, believe the U.S. Congress would be better chosen through random selection of members from the pages of a phone book than via the current election process. More than 70 percent are certain that the system has degenerated to such an extent that members of Congress trade votes for cash or campaign contributions. And the old trust that citizens once placed in their own representatives, the elected officials whom they knew and respected, has disappeared: 56 percent of those surveyed say their representatives and senators would sell them out for a campaign-contribution check.[2] Two-thirds of Americans say their "trust in the political system has been weakened by the recent developments in political financing," said Vidar Helgesen, head of the International Institute for Democracy and Electoral Assistance.[3]

Americans have lost faith in the process. Voter turnout among eligible adults has plummeted since the second half of the nineteenth century, when a 75 percent turnout on Election Day was routine, and when the numbers pushed past the 80 percent level several times. Today, anything approaching a 60 percent turnout for a presidential election—a level not achieved since the 1960s—gets the pundits shouting for joy.[4] The 2012 turnout fell to around 52 percent of American adults. This was down from a 58 percent turnout in 2008.[5] (By comparison, in ten of the other twelve largest democratic nations in the world in terms of GDP, the voter turnout rate in the most recent national elections ranged from 61 to 81 percent; the laggards are Canada at 54 percent and India at 56 percent.)[6] For America's congressional "off-year" elections— the actual equivalent to many countries' national elections, which do not have direct elections of the chief executive—turnout is a lot closer to 35 percent of all adults.

In the elections for the local school boards, county commissions, and city councils that frequently have a more definitional role in our lives than the federal government does, turnout goes from disappointing to dismal, as many communities report participation rates below 20 percent. It's so bad that the U.S. State Department assures the world that "2011 U.S. State, Local Elections Important Despite Low Turnout."[7] If there were broad rejection of the franchise equally across all classes, races, and regions, that would be a subject of profound concern. But it should be even more profoundly concerning that disengagement from the process tends to be concentrated in particular populations—those frequently targeted by voter suppression initiatives of the politically and economically powerful.[8] And voting is defined by class: people in the wealthiest one-sixth of the population vote at nearly double the rate of people in the poorest one-sixth.[9] Not surprisingly, Pew Research polled nonvoters before the election in 2012 and found that by a 5–2 margin those at the lower end favored Obama over Romney.[10]

These figures reveal the extent to which popular support for current government policies in the United States is overrated. Even in 2008, with the highest voting turnout percentage since 1972, the median voter was in the sixtieth percentile for annual household income—meaning, 59 percent of Americans had *lower* incomes than the average voter—while the median nonvoter was in the fortieth percentile for annual household income.[11] As far back as the 1970s, research by scholars such as Walter Dean Burnham lent credence to the notion that if Americans voted across income levels at the same rate as most Europeans did, the nation would be electing governments with far greater sympathy toward social democratic policies.[12] Research also demonstrates—

despite the repeated claims of conservative pundits and mainstream media commentators about the United States becoming a "center-right nation"—that Americans have not moved to the right on a battery of core political issues since the 1970s. Indeed, they may have become more progressive.[13]

Dollarocracy reigns in practice, as is well outlined in a series of recent trailblazing research projects by leading political scientists. These independent studies and analyses reach a stunning consensus that the interests and opinions of the great bulk of Americans unequivocally have no influence over the decisions made by Congress or executive agencies today, at least when they run up against the interests of either a powerful corporate lobby or wealthy people as a class. When the opinions of the poor, working class, and middle class diverge from those of the very well off, the opinions of the poor, working class, and middle class cease to have any influence. While there is a high likelihood that politicians will adopt the positions of their very wealthiest constituents, research confirms with eerie consistency that politicians will generally take the *opposite* position of those favored by the poorest third of their constituents.[14] Dollarocracy, indeed.

Understood this way, the fact that tens of millions of poor and working-class Americans still vote is a testament to just how deep-seated democratic ideals are in this nation.

In discussing what ails American elections, we must recognize the structural challenges that go beyond money and media. For example, the two-party system itself contributes a good deal to political disengagement. The two parties have rigged the system—in a manner that has nothing to do with the U.S. Constitution—so that it is virtually impossible to launch a credible third party.[15] This means, as former Republican governor of New Mexico and 2012 Libertarian presidential candidate Gary Johnson put it, that in American elections many—perhaps most—Americans "cast their votes for a candidate who doesn't really reflect their views."[16]

Indeed, polling tells us that there are about as many "independents" as there are Democrats or Republicans, and the ranks of the politically unaffiliated are swelling. Pundits suggest that these folks are "swing voters," bouncing back and forth between the big parties. But tens of millions of Americans swing out of the process altogether. They are not having a hard time choosing between the Democrats and the Republicans. They've made their choice: they don't like either major party. But they have nowhere else to go.

The two parties also gerrymander (draw district boundaries) so that most congressional and legislative districts are one-party estates and only a minority are competitive, except in rare landslide years.[17] In 2012, Democrats received 500,000 *more* votes in House races than Republicans did, but thanks to aggressive redistricting following the 2010 election and effective targeting of spending by Karl Rove and others, the Republicans maintained a whopping landslide-caliber 34-seat advantage.[18] Why? "The Republican Party has a significant structural advantage in U.S. House elections," explained FairVote's Rob Richie and Devin McCarthy. "That advantage was the most important reason why the GOP kept a comfortable majority of 54% of seats in the House despite Democratic candidates having an overall 4% advantage in voter preference over their Republican opponents."[19] Following the 2012 election, Mark Karlin explained the extraordinarily undemocratic consequences of modern gerrymandering, when a single party can draw the district lines with the aid of sophisticated datasets:

> Take Pennsylvania, for instance, the Democrats received 2,710,827 votes for congressional candidates; the Republicans, 2,642,952. Although it was a slim victory, the Dems won the popular vote in Pennsylvania as far as electing representatives to Congress.
>
> Astonishingly, however, due to gerrymandering from the Tea Party tsunami election of 2010, which left the Pennsylvania legislature and governor in full control of the GOP, only 5 Democratic reps to Congress were elected in 2012, while the Republicans will send 13 reps to DC![20]

"In a normal democracy," *The Economist* observed, "voters choose their representatives. In America, it is rapidly becoming the other way around."[21]

As a rule, more than 90 percent of House members are in districts that have been gerrymandered to be "safe seats." They rarely face a tough reelection battle, despite the strong generic unpopularity of Congress. In many states, the only federal races that are remotely in play are hyperexpensive statewide contests for Senate seats, where gerrymandering is impossible. And at the presidential level, there remains the Electoral College, which effectively renders moot the votes of the vast majority of citizens who do not live in a shrinking number of "swing" states.[22]

With so little competition, it is logical to ask, why do the wealthy care so much about elections? The answer, of course, is that elections are of singular importance because they remain the one brief shining moment when everyone in our political system is closest to being equal. They provide the fleeting moment when we can hope that the person earning minimum wage scrubbing toilets on the graveyard shift has the exact same power as Bill Gates, the heirs to the Wal-Mart fortune, or the CEO of Goldman Sachs. They are the one moment when the people can theoretically go in a different direction and reform society to the liking of a majority. For those wealthy and corporate interests that dominate the American political economy, elections are the one direct threat to their dominance of government and policymaking. Minimizing the capacity of elections to damage their privileges is of the utmost importance.

Elections take on greater significance because the rest of our democratic life has been so diminished.

We can gain some sense of how hollowed out American democracy has become by looking at the ways in which the notion of voting has changed. In democratic theory, and in more successful democracies, voting is a given, the ante to admission to the life of a free person and a citizen. As Thomas Jefferson put it, merely voting for representatives is far from sufficient. "Every day," he wrote, a citizen must be a "participator in the government of affairs."[23] Today the act of voting is the epitome of civic engagement, and once the election has past, citizens are invited to return to their couches while the wealthy and privileged resume their central role in guiding the government and its policies, mostly in the dark. This, the contemporary American practice, is what political scientists politely call a "weak democracy."

The wealthy well understand that democracy poses the great existential—and potentially practical—threat to extreme economic inequality. There is nothing new about this conflict. Indeed, the core problem was understood at the very beginning of democracy in Athens some 2,500 years ago. "Democracy is when the indigent, and not the men of property, are the rulers," Aristotle observed in his *Politics*. "If liberty and equality are chiefly to be found in democracy, they will be best attained when all persons share alike in government to the utmost."[24] This prospect has always horrified those with immense amounts of property; in Greece and later in Rome the powerful were able to quash existing variants of democratic rule.[25]

In the United States, this conflict is a story as old as the nation itself. If there is one constant in the history of the American experiment, it is the struggle over the question placed at its founding by the author of the Declaration of Independence. Which would these United States be? Democracy or plu-tocracy? And as the United States became a corporate capitalist economy, the ruling elite became defined increasingly in terms of money wealth, or as a Dollarocracy. The battle to establish a credible system of "one person, one vote" instead of "one dollar, one vote" has been a running theme in American history. The stakes have always been the same: the less democratic our elections, the more corrupt and irresponsible our governance.

THE AMERICAN BATTLE

The tension between democracy and plutocracy from the beginning has re-volved around the franchise: who is permitted to vote and who is not. The framers of the Constitution—many of whom had considerable property hold-ings and were upper class—struggled to balance their desire for a republic that could prevent the tyranny of a monarch on the one hand with their concern on the other about excessive popular rule in a society where the poor constituted a majority and would likely challenge the prerogatives of property owners. Although Benjamin Franklin and Thomas Paine forcefully advocated universal male suffrage, theirs was a minority position. Even for white males alone, James Madison was dubious about universal suffrage, while John Adams was downright hostile. If men without property could vote, Adams stated, "an im-mediate revolution would ensue."[26]

John Jay, the first chief justice of the Supreme Court, was hardly outside the mainstream when he stated—in what could be regarded as Dollarocracy's guiding principle—that "those who own the country ought to govern it." This was a recurring battle. At the founding of the Republic, members of Congress were chosen by a tiny elite of the wealthy, white, and male. An epic contest for Virginia's Fifth Congressional District seat in the first Congress of the United States pitted the man who would be the fourth president, James Madi-son, against the man who would be the fifth president, James Monroe. Yet it attracted barely 2,000 voters.[27] The definitional presidential election of 1800, between Thomas Jefferson and John Adams, was decided by a total of 68,000 voters in a country where the census of that year counted a population of 5.3 million. Even those who voted found themselves frequently disenfranchised, as in 1800 when the legislatures of Georgia, Massachusetts, New Hampshire, and Pennsylvania rejected the popular vote and simply appointed representatives to the Electoral College.[28] And the constrained and convoluted processes of selecting House members and presidents stood out as marvels of democratic enterprise when compared to the selection of senators, which was entirely by legislative fiat in a process defined by bribes, backroom deals, intimidation, and a fair measure of physical violence.

By 1824, for example, nearly fifty years after the Declaration of Independence declared that all men are created equal, only 27 percent of voting-age white males cast ballots in the presidential race.[29] Requirements that white men own property in order to cast ballots remained on the books in many states at that point. The rules would change radically in the subsequent decades, but universal adult suffrage did not become the rule until the Voting Rights Act of 1965.

Even as the franchise has been extended, however, the nation's economy increasingly has come to be dominated by large national and multinational corporations and wealthy individuals. Thus, the tension between democracy and plutocracy has continued to be influenced by the power of money. Reform has come in fits and starts. Andrew Jackson broke the patterns of a paternal elite that handed the presidency from one wealthy family to the next: of the first six presidents, three were neighbors from the plantation country around Charlottesville, Virginia (Thomas Jefferson, James Madison, James Monroe), and two were father and son (the Adamses of Quincy, Massachusetts). Jackson beat an Adams, John Quincy, in 1828, and then had to battle the Bank of the United States, which spent an unprecedented $40,000 to try to defeat him in 1832.[30] The seventh president beat the latter challenge by establishing a patronage system that filled government posts with political allies, who showed their appreciation by kicking back campaign money.

The wealthy made their comeback in the 1850s, when a Pennsylvania railroad and banking magnate named Simon Cameron came up with the "Pennsylvania Idea," a model for financing campaigns that encouraged banks and large corporations to steer a portion of their profits toward the project of maintaining Republican control of the state legislature. With that control, Cameron was able to have himself and his son named to the U.S. Senate (in an era when senators were selected by legislators rather than the people), to draw election district lines, to guide the selection of members of the Electoral College, and to eventually position himself to become Lincoln's first secretary of war. Cameron was so crooked that he was soon bounced from the Lincoln administration, but he quickly engineered his return to the Senate, where he brought a measure of realism to that chamber's deliberations by suggesting that "an honest politician is one who, when he is bought, will stay bought."[31] Cameron and his generation of corporate contributors bought plenty of top-shelf candidates.

In 1873, as the rot of what came to be described as the "Gilded Age" was becoming evident, the incoming chief justice of the Wisconsin Supreme Court, Edward Ryan, told the graduating class of the University of Wisconsin Law School that "the accumulation of wealth [is] the handmaiden of disaster" for all civilizations. He further asserted that the democratic promise of a revolution launched almost a century earlier was being squandered by those who failed to recognize that economic liberty—freedom from want, a level playing field, a fair distribution of the wealth—was the essential underpinning of political freedom.

"There is looming up a new dark power," Ryan warned. "The accumulation of individual wealth seems to be greater than it has been since the downfall of the Roman Empire. The enterprises of the country are aggregating vast corporate combinations of unexampled capital, boldly marching, not for economic conquest only, but for political power," the aging patriot declared. "For the first time in our politics money is taking the field of organized power. The question will arise, and arise in your day, though perhaps not fully in mine, which shall rule—wealth or man; which shall lead—money or intellect; who shall fill public stations—educated and patriotic free men, or the feudal serfs of corporate wealth?"[32]

The targets of Ryan's attack were the robber barons, who ran wild in the Gilded Age and made presidents, senators, governors, and mayors their errand boys. William Vanderbilt famously declared, "The public be damned!" His father, Cornelius, is reputed to have mused, "What do I care about the law? Ain't I got the power?"[33] The Gilded Age's political "genius," the man who connected corporate dollars to political dominance, was Mark Hanna of Ohio. "There are two things that are important in politics," the legendary Republican kingmaker explained in 1895. "The first is money and I can't remember what the other one is."[34] Hanna, a hero of Karl Rove, has come to symbolize the politics of that age. But his abuses were a symptom of the broader disease.

By 1887, the retired nineteenth president of the United States, Rutherford B. Hayes, observed:

> It is time for the public to hear that the giant evil and danger in this country, the danger which transcends all others, is the vast wealth owned or controlled by a few persons. Money is power. In Congress, in state legislatures, in city councils, in the courts, in the political conventions, in the press, in the pulpit, in the circles of the educated and the talented, its influence is growing greater and greater. Excessive wealth in the hands of the few means extreme poverty, ignorance, vice, and wretchedness as the lot of the many.

Playing off of Lincoln's stirring defense in the Gettysburg Address of the Civil War's appalling carnage as being justifiable only if it protected democracy, Hayes further wrote, "This is a government of the people, by the people, and for the people no longer. It is a government by the corporations, of the corporations, and for the corporations."[35] Several decades later, as the crisis continued, Justice Louis Brandeis of the Supreme Court argued in a similar vein, "We can have democracy in this country, or we can have great wealth concentrated in the hands of a few, but we can't have both."

Over time, the demands that the Money Power placed on America became so great that America pushed back. Edward Ryan's speech inspired "the righteous reformer," Robert M. La Follette of Wisconsin, to fight as a governor, senator, and founder of the Progressive movement against this power. Alarmed by revelations regarding the human wreckage left in the wake of the Gilded Age—evidence of which was detailed in the pioneering reports of muckraking journalists such as Lincoln Steffens, Upton Sinclair, Ida B. Wells, Ida Tarbell, and Jacob Riis—an outcry from a new generation of progressive reformers, socialists, and social-gospel Christians rose against what Theodore Roosevelt described as "every evil man whether politician or business man, every evil practice, whether in politics, in business, or in social life."[36] La Follette and Progressives enacted groundbreaking reforms that would for a time make real the promise that "the will of the people shall be the law of the land."[37]

Historians of the Progressive Era focus much of their attention on the consumer and labor reforms of the time—food and drug protections, regulation of wages and hours, workplace-safety initiatives, and the banning of child labor. But there also was an early and ongoing recognition that the corruption of politics by corporate elites represented the most critical of all threats posed by the "grave evils" that Roosevelt said could be found lurking in "the body politic, economic and social."

So it was that the reformers focused on electoral reforms—secret ballots, voter registration programs, suffrage for women—and, above all, on getting corporate money out of politics. Roosevelt, who had initially played the political game as it was set up by Hanna and the broad network of corporate donors he used to control elections and elected officials, broke with the Republican machine and announced in his 1905 message to Congress that "contributions by corporations to any political committee or for any political purpose should be forbidden by law." Roosevelt was proposing a sweeping challenge to the Money Power, declaring that "not only should both the National and the several State Legislatures forbid any officer of a corporation from using the money of the corporation in or about any election, but they should also forbid such use of money in connection with any legislation save by the employment of counsel in public manner for distinctly legal services."[38]

La Follette, now a senator, and Senator Ben Tillman of South Carolina took up the fight, with the Wisconsin legislator traveling across the country to rally the masses in support of legislation that would make it

> unlawful for any national bank, or any corporation organized by authority of any laws of Congress, to make a money contribution in connection with any election to any political office. It shall also be unlawful for any corporation whatever to make a money contribution in connection with any election at which Presidential and Vice-Presidential electors or a Representative in Congress is to be voted for or any election by any State legislature of a United States Senator. Every corporation which shall make any contribution in violation of the foregoing provisions shall be subject to a fine not exceeding five thousand dollars, and every officer or director of any corporation who shall consent to any contribution by the corporation in violation of the foregoing provisions shall upon conviction be punished by a fine of not exceeding one thousand and not less than two hundred and fifty dollars, or by imprisonment for a term of not more than one year, or both such fine and imprisonment in the discretion of the court.[39]

The resulting Tillman Act was passed by the House and Senate and signed into law by Roosevelt in 1907. Its reach would be extended by the Publicity

Act of 1910 and by 1911 amendments to both measures that were intended to address corporate manipulation of party primaries. Unfortunately, the lack of effective enforcement mechanisms and the existence of loopholes meant that corporations merely gamed the system by directing officers and employees to make personal campaign contributions to favored candidates and then providing bonuses to these officers and employees in the amount of their contributions.

The battle against the power of money over elections and politics was carried on by countless Americans across the nation. Consider Burton K. Wheeler, a crusading Montana district attorney and legislator who chased the money-lenders from the temples of American politics a century ago. Wheeler framed his activism as a patriotic and moral crusade. "Gentlemen," he declared, "we stand only to place humanity above the dollar."

Wheeler, an epic political figure of twentieth-century public life, was a senator, as well as a vice presidential candidate and a seriously considered presidential prospect, who wrangled mightily with Republican and Democratic presidents, battled corporate titans, and defended the Constitution across the most difficult decades of the century. As La Follette's running mate on the independent Progressive presidential ticket of 1924, he helped to shape the outlines of the New Deal. He went on to work with, and sometimes battle with, FDR through the entirety of its implementation. But Wheeler's defining moment came decades earlier, in the mining country of Montana, where he risked his life, his fortune, and his political prospects to join in organizing a victorious initiative in 1912 that forever banned corporate contributions to Montana candidates and political parties, thereby breaking the stranglehold of corporate cash on the government of a western state that had been ceded to the copper barons.[40]

"We are opposed to private ownership of public officials," announced Wheeler and the reformers who ended the dictatorial reign of the Anaconda Copper Mining (ACM) Company over Montana politics. "If elected, I will not put the ACM out of business. But I will put it out of politics." Wheeler and his compatriots, battling across decades and against the threat of violence in a region where labor leaders and Progressives were jailed, assaulted, and lynched for their activism, finally prevailed. They did not completely close the spigots of the Money Power. But they tightened them enough to open a new era of clean government in Montana.

By the time La Follette and Wheeler ran on the Progressive Party ticket in 1924, the party's platform announced:

The great issue before the American people today is the control of government and industry by private monopoly. For a generation the people have struggled patiently, in the face of repeated betrayals by successive administrations, to free themselves from this intolerable power which has been undermining representative government.

Through control of government, monopoly has steadily extended its absolute dominion to every basic industry.

In violation of law, monopoly has crushed competition, stifled private initiative and independent enterprise, and without fear of punishment now exacts extortionate profits upon every necessity of life consumed by the public. The equality of opportunity proclaimed by the Declaration of Independence and asserted and defended by Jefferson and Lincoln as the heritage of every American citizen has been displaced by special privilege for the few, wrested from the government of the many.[41]

La Follette's was the most successful third-party run against the Money Power in American history. It certainly contributed to slowing the march of the plutocrats, but it did not prevail. Over the next fifty years, lawmakers, jurists, and presidents would wrestle with this power. They could briefly gain the political advantage, as when Franklin Roosevelt denounced the "economic royalists" and pledged to do battle with "the privileged princes of these new economic dynasties, thirsting for power, [who have] reached out for control over government itself."[42]

THE PENDULUM SWINGS TOWARD DEMOCRACY

From the 1920s to the 1960s, the Federal Corrupt Practices Act was the nation's primary law regulating the financing of elections. It looked good on paper—requiring the reporting of campaign contributions and spending, regulating political parties and committees, limiting spending in congressional races with a $5,000 cap on House runs and a $25,000 cap on Senate campaigns. But as Lyndon Johnson famously observed with regard to the federal statute that governed his politicking from that first special-election campaign for a Texas congressional seat in 1937 to his landslide victory over Barry Goldwater in the 1964 presidential election, it was always "more loophole than law."[43]

The next, and last, great reform wave began in the 1960s and culminated in the early 1970s. It was provoked by the escalation in campaign costs attributable mostly to the emergence of TV advertising by the 1960 election.

Shortly after taking office, President John F. Kennedy bemoaned the "great financial burdens" on campaigns due largely to the costs of television advertising. It meant that candidates' chances were largely "governed by their success as fundraisers."[44] "The cost of conducting campaigns has become astronomical," Democratic National Committee chairman John M. Bailey stated at the same time, citing "soaring outlays for television."[45]

The great problem was that rank-and-file voters were unaccustomed to making campaign contributions; that had been the role of political parties. And soaring costs put enhanced pressure on politicians to seek funds from the wealthy. "I couldn't begin to finance my campaign on the offerings of small contributors," Senator Frank Church, an Idaho Democrat who kept alive the western populism of Burton K. Wheeler and his kind, complained in 1962. "I discovered what every candidate for Congress learns, that big contributors are essential."[46] For Church, like countless others from less-populated and rural states, that meant fat-cat out-of-state contributors. Long gone were the days of Harry Truman, who even as a presidential candidate in 1948 once paused on a whistle-stop campaign trip to pass the hat and raise the money needed to get to the next train stop.

Church noted that Americans had reason to be justifiably proud that "cash bribes are about extinct as a method of attempting to influence votes in the United States Congress." But the new unsolved problem was how to deal with the "heavy" influence over politicians achieved through large campaign contributions. "There is always the danger that a certain bias, favorable to the big contributor, will weigh upon the judgment of even the most objective legislator." To Church, it "isn't what we do in Congress but how we get into Congress that accounts for the lingering suspicion in the public mind."[47] And it was only going to get worse, much worse, unless Congress intervened.

President Kennedy appointed a nine-person bipartisan commission on campaign costs in 1962 to make recommendations specifically for the presidential campaigns.[48] Although Kennedy was in favor of free airtime for candidates and extensive televised candidate debates, the commission's recommendations centered on capping donation amounts and giving significant tax credits to encourage small donors, Such changes would, in effect, sharply reduce large contributions and institute a public subsidy for small campaign contributions.[49] The report met with the enthusiastic support of former presidents Truman and

Dwight Eisenhower and former presidential candidates Thomas Dewey, Adlai Stevenson, and Richard Nixon.[50]

The resulting legislation never got very far. Some critics thought it was not sweeping enough and should cover congressional races as well. Others were already adjusting to the new politics of money. But most did not see the crisis that was coming. The *New York Times* editorialized that the commission's recommendations "seem to have dropped into a bottomless void."[51]

To give some sense of the crisis that did come, consider this: the total amount of TV and radio political ad spending in 1960 that so alarmed Kennedy, Church, and many of the leading politicians in both parties was around $14 million. With inflation factored in, that number translates into $109 million in 2012. That is around 2 percent of what was spent on TV political advertising in the 2012 election cycle.[52]

If there is one thing we have learned from our study of money in politics, it is this: those who fail to initiate reforms when they are first proposed always come to regret their inaction. Money makes things worse. Fast. Lyndon Johnson recognized this after the 1966 election, which saw a dramatic increase in television advertising in congressional and state races.

In 1967, LBJ sought to establish a public-financing system for elections, with the goal of assuring that "radio and television, newspaper and periodical advertising" by the parties and their presidential candidates would be paid for with federal funds rather the private donations that, in an era of "skyrocketing" campaign costs, "were creating a potential for danger—the possibility that men of great wealth could achieve undue influence through large contributions."[53] The *Wall Street Journal* sympathized with LBJ's concerns, as did many Republicans. Even though it did not embrace the whole of the president's proposal, the *Journal* editorialized that it "would not be averse to a law requiring broadcasters to 'pay' for use of the free public airwaves by donating free time to major political candidates."[54]

Although LBJ was unable to get his public-financing plan approved, Congress did create Medicare, launch a "war on poverty," and pass a civil rights act. It also approved a voting rights act. In the mid-1960s, democracy was on the march in America, voting rolls were expanding, and electoral politics was reforming. On the heels of the civil rights movement, the vote for eighteen-year-olds, the peace movement, and the women's movement, signs suggested the United States might continue moving in a more social democratic direction in the 1970s.

Emboldened by the times, the labor movement (in a manner that has been underappreciated) was also being rejuvenated by a new generation of activists.[55] By the end of the 1960s and the beginning of the 1970s, Richard Nixon and his fellow Republicans were busy enacting numerous measures—such as creating the Environmental Protection Agency (EPA) and the Occupational Safety and Health Administration (OSHA), passing sweeping Clean Air and Clean Water acts, expanding public housing—that were well to the left of anything Bill Clinton would advocate in the 1990s or Barack Obama would pursue in the 2010s.

A more concrete sense of the change in the political culture is found in the career of consumer advocate Ralph Nader. In the 1960s and early 1970s, Nader and his activist gaggle of "Nader's Raiders"—whom he would eventually organize into the Public Citizen infrastructure that remains to this day—were able to win a stunning series of legislative and regulatory victories for consumer rights, open governance, and environmental regulation.[56] The accomplishments of this revitalized consumer movement are still recognized today in scores of groundbreaking laws, such as the Freedom of Information Act and the seminal 1966 National Traffic and Motor Vehicle Safety Act, and in enforcement agencies such as the EPA and OSHA. Not for nothing is it said that Ralph Nader has saved more lives than any American except Dr. Jonas Salk. Nader was arguably the most popular living American during the era of his greatest agitation. He stood for honest and effective government and against monopolistic and corrupt crony capitalism. He encouraged a generation of young people to take an optimistic view that organized political activity was capable of positive outcomes and that public service was an honorable life's work. To this day, his acolytes are among the republic's greatest legislators, regulators, journalists, and activists.

In making this argument, we do not mean to romanticize U.S. politics of the 1960s or 1970s. This was an extraordinarily turbulent period, and a remarkably large portion of Americans thought social inequality, militarism, racism, and poverty, even political corruption, were so severe at the time that they required radical solutions. The 1972 Democratic presidential candidate, George McGovern, argued passionately that "at no time have we witnessed official corruption as wide or as deep as the mess in Washington right now."[57]

While some of the economic and social problems of those days seem almost quaint by comparison with today's Dollarocracy, the important point is simply that the political culture at the time was better equipped to deal with popular dissent; it even allowed a progressive like McGovern to gain the nomination of a major political party. Not since McGovern has a Democrat or Republican, liberal or conservative, who was not in bed with the moneyed interests been able to take the lead of one of the two dominant parties. It was still very much an uphill battle, as McGovern's eventual defeat in his 1972 race with Nixon illustrated. There were deep frustrations, to which the demonstrations and riots of the period attest. But organized people were more serious players in U.S. politics than they have been subsequently, and radical reformers, such as Congressman Ron Dellums of California and Congresswoman Bella Abzug of New York, actually walked the corridors of power. Detroit even elected a Marxist judge, Justin Ravitz, and Alaska elected the nation's first Libertarian legislator, Dick Randolph.[58] It was a freer and more fluid time politically.

As those election results illustrate, the social movements of the 1960s were quick to put the election system in their sights. But the reformers of that era did not merely compete for power; they also exposed power, with a fury not seen since the days of the muckrakers in the early years of the century. By the time Lyndon Johnson's career wound down, a new generation of muckrakers was exposing the commoditization of American politics with books such as Joe McGinniss's *The Selling of the President 1968* and Mark Green and Michael Waldman's *Who Runs Congress?*

The pressure for meaningful campaign finance reform was such that Democrats and Republicans attached their names to reform measures. No less a partisan than President Nixon signed the Federal Election Campaign Act of 1971, with its unprecedented campaign donation and spending disclosure requirements, its spending limits calculated with a ten-cents-per-voter multiplier, and its fines for violating candidates and contributors. The *New York Times* imagined the ushering in of "a revolution in American political financing."[59]

Barely six months after Nixon signed the new law, with high praise and a promise of full Republican compliance, however, Nixon's lawyers were contending in court that a key provision of the measure—public disclosure of the identity of campaign contributors—was an unconstitutional invasion of privacy. Campaign donors, the lawyers for Nixon's reelection campaign claimed, had a "fundamental right" to remain anonymous in their political associations. Remarkably, the lawyers for Nixon were asking the courts to allow the campaign to keep secret the names of contributors to a $10-million slush fund that had been reported in federal filings only as "cash on hand," and that the Federal Bureau of Investigation eventually determined had been used by the head of Nixon's campaign, Attorney General John Mitchell, for an ambitious campaign of political spying and sabotage that was organized to harm the president's political foes and ensure his reelection.[60]

Within months of Nixon's landslide reelection in 1972, investigative journalists had brought the Watergate scandal into full view, shocking the American people and Congress into action. By the summer of 1973, the *New York Times* announced that, with a Senate vote to impose a $3,000 limit on donations to federal campaigns, prospects were good for the establishing of "the first effective curbs in American political history on the influence of the rich in government." A year later, Congress seemed to realize the promise by voting overwhelmingly to amend the Federal Election Campaign Act to

- limit contributions to candidates for federal office;
- require the disclosure of political contributions;
- provide for the public financing of presidential elections;
- limit expenditures by candidates and associated committees;
- limit independent expenditures to $1,000;
- limit candidate expenditures from personal funds; and
- create a federal election commission (FEC) as an independent regulatory agency charged with disclosing campaign finance information, enforcing provisions of the law such as limits and prohibitions on contributions, and overseeing the public funding of presidential elections.[61]

The political pendulum had swung, or so it seemed. The enthusiasm for a cleaner politics was widespread. In the final vote for FECA, 75 percent of House Republicans and 41 percent of Senate Republicans supported the law.

The major resistance on the Hill came from Representative Wayne Hays, a powerful old-school pol and Ohio Democrat, who "loathed campaign finance reform" as an impediment to his modus operandi.[62] The mood was sufficiently optimistic that former secretary of health, education, and welfare John Gardner—a Republican—could speak, as he did in launching Common Cause, of the American people not merely "revitaliz[ing] politics and government" but also "rebuilding the nation."[63]

HERE COMES DOLLAROCRACY

America did not continue for long on the progressive path of revitalizing politics and government. Beginning in the mid-1970s, the campaign trail began bending back toward privilege and the gains of the previous era began to be wiped away. Those rules, regulations, and enforcement agencies that could not be shuttered came under sustained attack. And a new generation of politicians, trained to recognize and respect the Money Power, swept away the old reformers.

In a single election, that of 1980, McGovern and Church were ushered out of the Senate, as were Gaylord Nelson, a great environmentalist; Birch Bayh, who had championed the Voting Rights Act and organized congressional approval of the amendment that lowered the voting age to eighteen; and Mike Gravel, who partnered with Nader and others in fights for freedom of information and open government. The modern age of reform, such as it was, had ended. Under the leadership of newly elected President Ronald Reagan and the Republican senators who replaced McGovern, Church, Nelson, Bayh, and Gravel, government returned to the old calculus of doing no more than was absolutely necessary for citizens and absolutely everything that could be done for the wealthy and big business.

This did not just "happen." Corporations and wealthy individuals organized politically as never before. They responded to a situation where, as political scientist David Vogel put it, "from 1969 to 1972, virtually the entire American business community experienced a series of political setbacks without parallel during the postwar period. . . . For the first time since the 1930s, business found its political influence seriously challenged by a new set of interest groups."[64] By the early 1970s, corporations were also arguably at or near their low ebb to date in public esteem, regarded as rather unsavory actors.[65]

This elite response was not simply a "right-wing" countermovement. It drew from both parties and had congressional supporters who identified themselves as liberal "reformers." What unified the players was a strong commitment to having corporations and the wealthy return to playing a preeminent and unquestioned role in the governance of the United States. Consider *The Crisis of Democracy,* a report prepared in 1975 by Harvard's Samuel Huntington and two other prominent academics for the Trilateral Commission, a group of establishment—some even self-described "liberal"—political, academic, and corporate leaders founded by David Rockefeller in 1973.

The report imagined the contemporary crisis of democracy in 1975 America precisely in Tom Paine's or La Follette's terms, except that the Trilateral Commission was on the other side. "The essence of the democratic surge of the 1960s was a general challenge to existing systems of authority, public and private. . . . People no longer felt the same compulsion to obey those whom they had previously considered superior to themselves in age, rank, status, expertise, character, or talents."

The report noted that the percentage of people who regarded the government as being "run for the few big interests" rather than for "the benefit of all" increased from 17 percent in 1958 to 53 percent in 1972. The percentage of Americans expressing confidence in large corporations fell by half between 1966 and 1973, to 29 percent, a larger drop than that experienced by any other institution. In the view of the report, the problem stemmed from an "excess of democracy"—with people having unrealistic expectations that the system could never satisfy.[66]

The "logic" of the report was plain to see: it was time for corporations and their supporters to organize politically and do their best to undermine the effectiveness of the organizations that opposed them or made "unrealistic" demands upon them. Citizens had to learn their place and be happy with it. The "crisis" of democracy was that there was too much democracy. The report concluded that "the effective operation of a democratic political system usually requires some measure of apathy and noninvolvement on the part of some individuals and groups."[67] It was time for suddenly involved minorities, poor people, students, militant workers, and women to return to the lower decks of their galleys and let the traditional rulers again steer the ship of state.

As we explain in Chapter 3, a future Supreme Court justice, Lewis Powell, provided corporate America with a plan of action. The organizations spawned by this new corporate campaign for power would spend hundreds of millions, eventually tens of billions, of dollars to shift the political culture dramatically to the right and undo the gains of the preceding fifty years. Organized labor, business's nemesis, would lose much of the status and strength it had gained during the New Deal era and then seemed to solidify during the Truman and Eisenhower years. By the 1990s, corporations and their congressional hirelings would be passing free-trade deals, deregulating whole industries, and eliminating Glass-Steagall protections against banking industry abuses. As Warren Buffett acknowledged when he looked back across the years in which the son of a Republican congressman from Omaha became a billionaire, "There's class warfare, but it's my class, the rich class, that's making war, and we're winning."[68]

To win the war, the dollarcrats did not merely champion their own agenda. They also demonized any and all who might question it. Nader became Public Enemy No. 1 for the champions of Dollarocracy, if only because job one for the dollarcrats was to eliminate the notion of the government as a progressive force on behalf of an informed and engaged citizenry. (Job two was to eliminate the notion among the young of public service as a worthy career goal.) In the 1970s, the corporate community organized to limit or terminate Nader's influence and, by extension, the myriad of activist groups that he, along with the women's, student, labor, and civil rights movements, had inspired to influence public policy by grassroots organizing.[69]

When President Jimmy Carter began to organize his administration, he consulted with Nader and appointed Naderites to top positions. By the 1980s, the corporate campaign had succeeded to such an extent that Nader and his fellow reformers were cast into the wilderness, as there was no place for their work under Dollarocracy. Nader turned to the next stage of his career as a prophetic voice against corruption and corporate power and as a periodic presidential protest candidate. He was sometimes referred to as "bitter." But it was not bitterness that motivated the man; it was anger at the obscuring of America's democratic vistas. That anger would come to be shared by millions of Americans who recognized that they were losing more than elections. They were losing democracy itself.

Since the 1970s, money has become extremely well organized as a political force, while the great mass of nonwealthy people has lost much of its organizational capacity to influence politics. The result has been the rise of Dollarocracy. The Republican Party effectively purged its liberals and then the few remaining moderates, becoming by the 1990s a political home for the Dollarocracy.[70] There was no longer any room in the Grand Old Party for reform. Senator Mitch McConnell of Kentucky, who once had advocated for meaningful campaign finance rules, became the leading champion of money in politics.[71] And the refusal of McConnell and his kind to compromise on issues of concern to corporations did not isolate the GOP. It created a new pole in politics to which an unsettling number of Democrats were attracted. To be sure, there were, and are, Democrats who refuse to play by the rules of the money-and-media election complex. But they reside on the margins of the party, not at its core and certainly not at the top.

The most powerful Democrats may still talk a populist line, especially as Election Day approaches. But when it comes time to govern, too many of them choose to switch rather than fight. The party of Franklin Roosevelt has come with each ensuing election to sound more and more like the party of Dwight Eisenhower and Richard Nixon. "New Democrats" such as Bill Clinton, who presented themselves as determinedly probusiness, came to dominate the party in the 1990s. Clinton taught his fellow Democrats to "triangulate": moving to the right in order to appeal to corporate interests while keeping a working-class and liberal voting base because the base had no alternative and was terrified by the extreme social conservatism and market fundamentalism of the Republicans.

The die was cast. Democrats would compete with Republicans for the middle rather than seek to expand the electorate by mobilizing poor people and people of color with "Rainbow Coalition"–style mass mobilization. The Reverend Jesse Jackson and some of his labor allies tried throughout the 1980s and 1990s to sell the Democratic Party on mobilization strategies and the progressive populist approaches that would inspire and empower them. But this was an exercise in frustration.

By 2002, political observers were noting that "today neither party makes much effort to mobilize the tens of millions of poorer and less well educated Americans who are not currently part of the electorate."[72] A whole consultant class rose up to tell Democratic politicians that the only way to win was to tack to the middle, or even the right, especially on economic issues. "For the life of me, I can't figure out why progressives listen to consultants. Building movements, making progress on progressive issues—you have to talk to people, educate people, organize people," says Vermont senator Bernie Sanders, an independent who caucuses with Democrats but rarely takes advice from anyone in Washington.[73]

Barack Obama's 2008 campaign broke the pattern to some extent, especially when it came to the demographics of a winning coalition, by exciting young people and African Americans to turn out in higher numbers for a candidate who seemed to promise not just historic progress but also "change we can believe in." When the change did not materialize, however, all that was left was a tired, centrist, and business-friendly Democratic Party that could not reenergize the base in 2010 and that prevailed in 2012 largely by scaring the wits out of Americans who did not expect much from the Democrats but were genuinely frightened by Republicans who threatened Social Security, Medicare, and Medicaid. This was lesser-evilism raised to high art. Dollarocracy perfected. "The Republican Party is accurately defined as a party that looks out for the interests of the very wealthy," wrote former *New York Times* columnist Bob Herbert. "The Democratic Party less so, but I think they look out for the interests of the wealthy, too, before they look out for the interests of working Americans."[74]

Herbert nailed it. The dollarcrats had succeeded not by beating the Democrats but by subsuming them. Dollarcrats feared the Democratic Party's existing and potential voting base but were comfortable with the party's political leaders, whom the system had for all intents and purposes domesticated.

There were many elements to the corporate campaigns to remake American politics and governance launched in the 1970s. These included massively increasing lobbying activity; hectoring the news media to be more sympathetic to business, eventually creating procorporate news media; making universities more procorporate; creating think tanks and other venues to generate extensive public relations on the virtues of "free enterprise" and "markets" and the duplicity of anything that stood in their way; and getting the courts to be more friendly toward business concerns.[75] But no area was of greater concern than rendering the election system more susceptible to business influence and more likely to produce outcomes satisfactory to the wealthy. The confirmation that the project has succeeded came not in the overinflated rhetoric of the Republican Party but in the constrained and compromised language of the Democrats. If the point of refashioning the political process was to make it easier for corporations to call the shots, then this was the truest measure of success: a titular two-party system in which every debate revolved around which party was best for business.

To be sure, there remain real differences between the Republicans and the Democrats. They are stark on issues such as abortion rights and gay rights. And we do not seek to deny or diminish the distinctions. But corporations do not worry much about reproductive health or marriage equality. They worry about their bottom lines. And the bottom line of American politics has in recent decades come to reflect the demands of the wealthiest Americans and the corporations they control. The differences between Republicans and Democrats on issues of consequence to corporations are now matters of degree, not the deep distinction that is found on social issues. "The Obama position is: The super-rich have to pay a little more. The Romney position is: They don't have to pay anything," said Thomas Ferguson. "That's it, folks, that's the party difference in American politics."[76] As the long 2012 campaign wore on, it became quite clear that Mitt Romney and Barack Obama despised each other. Yet one of the most common phrases when the two men debated policy was "I agree."[77]

The people do not happen to agree. Poll after poll confirms that they prefer a far more potent politics, that they want a Democratic Party that will stand up to corporations, and that they would like the Republican Party to do the same. Ninety percent of Americans now agree that there's too much corporate money in politics, with a clear majority—51 percent—"strongly agreeing" with that statement.[78]

Nice sentiments and in a democracy we might expect that the system would reflect those values. Instead, under Dollarocracy, the electoral system works on entirely different principles, shaped and fueled by big money. To understand the depth of the crisis, it is time to take a look at what Dollarocracy has wrought: the election of 2012.

2

THE $10 BILLION ELECTION

....

What It Looks Like When
Billionaires Start *Spending*

> I don't cry when I lose. There's always a new hand coming up. I know
> in the long run we're going to win.
>
> **SHELDON ADELSON, DECEMBER 5, 2012**

For the first time in the history of the United States, the 2012 campaign to
elect a president was covered—for the most part—as a business story. That
was fine by business, which had been newly freed by the Supreme Court's
Citizens United decision to invest in the emerging market of American politics.
That was fine by the politicians who could jet off to Vegas, have lunch with
a billionaire casino mogul, and come away with "a $100 million investment"
in the campaign.[1] And that was just fine by American mainstream media, as
most editors and publishers, hosts and programmers had long before accepted
as gospel Calvin Coolidge's false premise that "after all, the chief business
of the American people is business."[2] Not citizenship. Not democratic engagement. Not justice. Not the construction of a shining city on a hill. Nor
the illuminating of a light unto the nations. No need for any of that romantic
mumbo jumbo. America was, as Coolidge famously suggested, all about "producing, buying, selling, investing and prospering."[3]

And if that was so, then, surely, every American story could be a business story: the Hollywood box office receipts could shape our culture, commodity prices could tell us all we need to know about eating, and the Christmas spirit could surely be got from reports on folks lining up Thanksgiving night for "Black Friday" shopping. Mr. Potter, not George Bailey, was triumphant. Donald Trump was right: it was all about "the art of the deal."[4] So why not consider the competition for power as the biggest "deal" of all? Why not go all in on the fantasy that government should be "run like a business" and turn campaigns to control the government into the political equivalent of Trump's *The Apprentice*?

Trump was certainly willing to oblige. The nation's most identifiable rich guy—with the possible exception, by campaign's end, of Mitt Romney—was the Hamlet of the 2012 melodrama, wrestling with the existential angst of a Republican presidential run. He jetted up to New Hampshire for an almost-announcement, ranted and raved about Barack Obama's birthplace on any Fox News show that would have him, published a manifesto (*Time to Get Tough: Making America #1 Again*), and made major announcements via a Web site dubbed "Trump HQ."[5] By April 2011, The Donald was leading in polls of likely Republican voters and running close to even with Obama.[6] A month later, Trump took himself out of the race, announcing, "I will not be running for president as much as I'd like to" because he was committed to a higher goal: preparing for the next season of his new NBC show, *Celebrity Apprentice*.[7] Within weeks, he was back in the news, saying of his almost-party, "If they pick a loser, I may very well run as an independent."[8] That never happened. In fact, nothing about Trump—not even his planned moderation of a December 2011 debate among the actual Republican candidates just prior to the Iowa caucuses—happened.

Jon Stewart's *Daily Show,* Stephen Colbert's *Colbert Report,* and *The Onion* all recognized the absurdity of the Trump talk and treated the rich guy as a political punch line. Unfortunately, the joke was on the America people. Trump's ridiculous approach to politics, with its "birther" obsessions, fiscal fantasies, and talk about self-financing his campaign by pouring "a large chunk of his $270 million in liquid assets into a presidential bid," was perfectly in synch with the 2012 Zeitgeist.[9] Except for the part about the $270 million. That would not have done the deal.

Not by a long shot.

If Trump had spent all $270 million—more than four times the $63 million that Ross Perot, the last serious independent contender, slathered on a wildly extravagant 1992 media campaign—he would have been at an 8 to 1 disadvantage into trying to break into the presidential race.[10] Yes, 8:1. Barack Obama, Mitt Romney, and their backers spent more than $2.3 billion competing for the presidency in 2012. They may even have spent a lot more because the reported figures ($1,112,041,699 for the Obama campaign, the Democratic Party, and outside groups for the president versus $1,246,902,432 for Romney et al.) do not include hundreds of millions of dollars in unaccounted and unaccountable dark money spending by "charities" that sought to influence the contest.[11]

Even Donald Trump would have had to go begging to compete in 2012, just as Obama and Romney did, for the largesse of the billionaires who invest in campaigns not to advance ideals or to elect the best candidate but to make a cold, calculated business arrangement. "You have to spend money to make money" is the motto for the relative handful of wealthy Americans and businesses that provide most of these funds. And those are the Americans that campaigns, be they Democratic or Republican, take most seriously. Put another way: for candidates wishing to succeed, fund-raising is about big-game hunting. Much is made of the 3 million small donations the Obama campaign generated in 2012, and even of the more than 350,000 Americans who wrote small checks to aid the campaign of quarter billionaire Mitt Romney.[12] But the truth is that small donations are small potatoes in the overall scheme of things.

Consider this: Romney's 350,000 small donors as of mid-October gave $70.8 million. That was barely one-third of what fewer than forty major donors had given to outside groups by the same date.[13] In the end, which call does the candidate or the consultant take: the billionaire industrialist with millions to spread around or the grandmother on a fixed income who just wants to do right by her country? Americans know the answer to that question.

That's the single best explanation for why roughly 87 percent of Americans make no contributions to federal or state political campaigns.[14] In the twenty-five most hotly contested 2012 House of Representative races, for example, donors giving $200 or less provided only 12.5 percent of Democratic candidate funds and 18.3 percent of Republican candidate funds. Had it not been for

Allen West, the Tea Party favorite who attracted national grassroots support, the figure for Republican candidates would have plummeted to 7.6 percent.[15] These small donors, the ones who contribute largely to promote their values and to be good citizens, are bit players in the game. Only one out of every four hundred Americans gives more than $200 to a congressional campaign, and this is where you start if you want to know where the action is.[16]

Even one in four hundred seems downright egalitarian as the scope of the emerging corporatization of our politics becomes evident. This is about a lot more than *The Selling of the President* or even *The Art of the Deal*. This is about the whole shebang. The 2012 election, which decided contests not just for president but also for Congress, dominance of statehouses, control of units of local government across the country, and the very definition of the agenda via initiative and referendum votes, saw more than $10 billion in spending by candidates, parties, wealthy individuals, corporate in-kind donors, super-PACs, and shadowy dark money groups. For five decades, the central goal of campaign finance reformers from John F. Kennedy to John McCain was to have small donors—those who invest for principles and citizenship—increase in numbers and provide the lion's share of funds. By 2012, that gambit was dead and buried. Small-time donors increasingly came to play the role of chumps, manipulated by focus-group-tested buzzwords and bandied about to show a candidate's populist credentials but having virtually no influence over candidates once in office. It is difficult to imagine that these donors will not continue to diminish as their impotence becomes increasingly and depressingly apparent. "There will be huge scandals," McCain said, "because there's too much money washing around . . . and we don't know who's behind it."[17]

RETHINKING THE 2012 ELECTION

This chapter looks at that $10 billion figure to help explain the transformation of our politics, and of our governing processes, that has taken place since the U.S. Supreme Court began redefining the rules of engagement in order to facilitate unlimited spending by the wealthiest American and corporations, and since major U.S. media began to cash in on the phenomenon. Americans know about money in politics, and we would be wasting our time here if we simply set out to remind them of a crisis that they see every night on television—not

explanation for why President Obama laid an egg in the first presidential debate was not that he was too busy doing his duties as chief executive and commander in chief to prepare; instead, it was that he had spent the entire Friday before the debate doing three private fund-raising events with big game rather than preparing for the debate, as candidates had done in the past.[27] Kantar Media's Elizabeth Wilner, one of the sharpest observers of the business of elections, explained the importance of this fund-raising: Had Obama "been outspent by a wider margin, we might well be writing today about how the outside groups helped win the air war for President-elect Romney."[28]

Many older Republicans quietly lamented the fact that Mitt Romney lacked the political courage, people skills, and focus displayed by his father, former Michigan governor and Nixon Cabinet secretary George Romney. Likewise, when Seymour Hersh returned to spend significant time on Capitol Hill in the early 2000s, after having been mostly absent for several decades, he was struck by how the intellectual and ethical caliber of members had plummeted.[29] It has become increasingly common for observers to bemoan the unwillingness of individuals of great talent and integrity to enter public life. These transformations are all but unavoidable under Dollarocracy. Being a politician today means engaging in endless fund-raising—hours every day spent backslapping, glad-handing, butt-kissing, begging, and, ultimately, offering deals to very rich people for donations. This comes at the expense of actual public service or even traditional politicking. We admire those friends of ours who have worked hard to have successful careers in Congress, but after the 2012 election cycle we can see that many of them might have never entered public life decades ago if they knew this would be their fate. For a generation of idealistic and principled young Americans eager to serve, electoral politics is not a viable career option. Electoral politics is an arena that will attract people on the make, whose only principle is to take care of number one, which means taking care of those with deep pockets.

When the Democrats prevailed—winning the presidency, 55 of 100 Senate seats, a solid plurality of votes for U.S. House seats, as well as the vast majority of gubernatorial races—they were still hamstrung by a money-defined politics that had Obama and his fellow partisans curtailing their victory celebrations in order to begin the next stage of wrangling over "fiscal cliffs," "debt ceilings," and a host of other crises manufactured by Republican politicians and interest groups that had just been defeated. Despite the election numbers, that struggle was all about imposing precisely the austerity measures that voters had rejected overwhelmingly on November 6. And despite epic unpopularity, enough to fuel much of the antipathy toward Romney, Wall Street, with its record campaign donations split between both parties, was still in the catbird seat.[30] So it was that, even when money got "beat," money won, as casino magnate Sheldon Adelson well recognized on his "victory lap" visit to Washington after the 2012 election. The vanquished billionaire did not look like a beaten man; he looked like someone who had experienced some setbacks but who was already hard at work calculating for the next election cycle and an eventual victory.

That's how the money-go-round goes round. Sometimes you are up; sometimes you are down. But if you have the money to buy a ticket on the carousel, when you are down, you know that you will eventually be up. "Obama's victory was just a blip in the master plan measured in decades, not election cycles," *Forbes*'s December 2012 profile of billionaire right-wing donors Charles and David Koch noted. "We're going to study what worked, what didn't work, and improve our effort in the future," David Koch said. "We're not going to roll over and play dead."[31]

What changed in 2012 was the price of that carousel ticket. It went way, way up—to more than $10 billion.

That number provides our place of beginning. Let's consider what $10 billion bought in 2012 and what it is still buying as you read these words.

THE NEW MATH

The $10 billion total figure we use here, which is merely a baseline, is a good deal greater than the estimated fund-raising figures reported around Election Day 2012. "Total Cost of Election Could Be $6 Billion," read the *New York Times* headline.[32] "Election Costs to Exceed $6 Billion in 2012," announced *Businessweek*.[33] "Did That $6 Billion in Campaign Spending at Least Help the Economy?" *Time* magazine asked after the election.[34] Even campaign finance reformers declared, "After $6 Billion Election Campaign, Movement to Get Money Out of Politics Starts a 'Prairie Fire.'"[35]

Everyone seemed to agree that $6 billion, more than had ever been spent in an American election season, more than had ever been spent in any election season anywhere, was astronomical. And everyone was right. The figure was roughly $2 billion over the amount spent in 2004, the last election cycle where an incumbent president was seeking reelection.[36] The fund-raising for the Obama-Romney race alone was ten times the level seen in 1996, the previous cycle where a young Democratic president was challenged by a senior Republican. We happen to think that multibillion-dollar spending spikes and tenfold increases in the amount of money raised are consequential.[37] It's just that the spending was more astronomical than the headlines suggested. The $6 billion figure was based on an estimate by the ablest analysts of federal election spending, the folks at the Center for Responsive Politics, who released the number in an October 31, 2012, report that had the group's executive director, Sheila Krumholz, declaring, "In the new campaign finance landscape post–*Citizens United,* we're seeing historic spending levels spurred by outside groups dominated by a small number of individuals and organizations making exceptional contributions." Krumholz was absolutely right in that regard, as she was when she added, "One thing we can say for certain is that the transparency the Supreme Court relied upon [in its *Citizens United* ruling] to justify this new framework has been sorely lacking."[38]

Another certainty is that the regulatory agency tasked with overseeing elections, the Federal Election Commission (FEC), is worthless. "Virtually from the beginning," Thomas Ferguson, Paul Jorgensen, and Jie Chen wrote, "dark forces of law and politics have combined to render the agency almost impotent as a regulator."[39] Today, the FEC's "powers" are "so weak that for most offenses it can only ask political groups to enter a voluntary process in which they bargain to agree to a monetary settlement," as the *Washington Times* reported. "But campaigns have learned not to fear the body, and even those fines are often simply ignored."[40] This lack of enforcement means that accurate reporting of donations and spending is not a life-and-death concern. Likewise, it means the Supreme Court's call for independent super-PAC money not to be coordinated with a candidate's campaigns has been routinely and effectively flouted.[41] The *New York Times* noted that "the result is a striking degree of symmetry" between campaigns and the "independent" groups supporting them.[42] Even the Internal Revenue Service (IRS) has exhibited little interest in making sure the various relevant nonprofit groups play by the rules. *Politico*'s examination of the IRS's role concluded the service had a "feeble" grip on big political cash and was a "toothless tiger."[43] The metaphor widely used is that this is a wild, wild west environment where people shoot first and worry about the legal niceties later, much later, if ever. And there is no sheriff on the horizon.

Accordingly, the Center for Responsive Politics report from late October 2012 acknowledged, "What remains unknown—and may never fully be accounted for—is how much money secretive 'shadow money' organizations spent, with some investing massive sums on ads, but also on unreported and purportedly 'non-political' activities, as the election neared. It may take years to determine how much they spent. Furthermore, it likely will never be known who provided the vast majority of this money, which includes at least $203 million in the last two months."[44] *Bloomberg Businessweek* wrote that "a Cayman Islands–style web of nonprofit front groups and shell companies . . . are increasingly being used to protect the identity of donors who want to get involved in politics in big ways without leaving a trace."[45] Thanks to a leak to the Center for Public Integrity, we know the pitch made to donors by one such shadowy group, Colorado's American Tradition Partnership (ATP). It led a successful fight to overturn Montana's one-hundred-year ban on corporate money in elections (a topic we explore in Chapter 3) and promised its prospective funders that "no politician, no bureaucrat, and no radical environmentalist will ever know you helped."[46]

As the Center for Media and Democracy, which tracked what has variously been referred to as "shadow money" or "dark money" more closely than any group in 2012, explained it:

> Unlike PACs or Super PACs formed exclusively for electoral purposes and which report all of their expenditures to the Federal Elections Commission (FEC), "dark money" groups are officially organized as social welfare nonprofits under section 501(c)(4) of the tax code or as trade associations under section 501(c)(6). Because these groups are supposed to primarily advance some sort of social welfare, or in the case of a 501(c)(6) the interests of a particular industry, they need only report their *electoral* expenditures to the FEC, rather than all of their spending.[47]

But—and this is a Grand Canyon–sized "but"—

electoral activities have been narrowly construed to only require reporting of expenditures on ads that explicitly call for the election or defeat of a candidate, allowing these groups to avoid disclosure by running "issue ads" that criticize a candidate on issues like taxes or healthcare but stop short of explicitly telling viewers to vote for or against. The omission of an explicit call for a candidate's defeat or victory allows the groups to claim with a wink-and-a-nod the ads were about "issues," despite clearly being intended to influence the election.[48]

So it is that the roughly $44 million that Karl Rove's Crossroads GPS spent between January 2011 and June 2012 on issue ads scorching President Obama and Democratic candidates for the U.S. Senate went unreported on most formal measures of political activity. Elaborate schemes cloak the identity of donors. A loophole, upheld by a federal appeals court, allows dark money groups to hide the movement of money not expressly given to fund specific issue ads. Donors who wish to remain anonymous simply give to the general fund. Similarly, transfers of money among supposedly independent groups, party committees, and candidate-tied super-PACs are "governed" by so many different sets of "rules" that campaign activity can be shielded from even minimal accountability during the course of an election season, as well as for months, even years, afterward.[49] Perhaps forever.

What we do know is that in 2012 "outside money" overtook traditional campaigns and political parties as the main source of election funding and that within the category of outside money, the entirely secretive dark money groups were a significant factor. The dark money total discussed in late October media reports—$203 million—kept rising after major media outlets seized on the $6 billion figure for "total" spending. By mid-November, Center for Media and Democracy executive director Lisa Graves was noting, "At least $400 million, *and probably much more than that,* was spent by groups organized as 'nonprofits' that do not disclose their donors or report many of their electoral expenditures, so little is known about who funds them, who is really calling the shots, and whether or not they are illegally coordinating with candidates."[50]

What did Graves mean by "probably much more"? Hundreds of millions more, she told us. And she was right.

Only after the 2012 election, and after the media had fixated on the $6 billion figure, did we learn that Sheldon Adelson had spent "far more" on his various political charities than had been imagined. How much more? On the eve of the election, the boldest estimate of his campaign giving put the figure at $52.2 million.[51] One month later, in early December 2012, $150 million in campaign spending by Adelson and his wife had been identified. And that number was all but certain to rise.[52] Because he approached the campaign with such billionaire bravado, Adelson was one of the more transparent, easily identified big donors. Others, for instance those who worked at the state and local levels to shift control of legislatures and school boards as part of long-term strategies to privatize education, by design flew well under the radar. But not so far under that the real cost of unlimited spending cannot be detailed.

Let's look at the data. And in so doing, let's go deeper. Let's look at how money is gathered and spent to influence every nook and cranny of American public life. We're going to introduce you to a lot of numbers because, as former president Bill Clinton famously said during the 2012 campaign, it is about "the math." But our point in detailing where the $10 billion was collected and where it went is not to provide an accounting of dollars and cents. Our point is to provide a sense of how the money-and-media election complex is fueled. And why.

We are more than happy to accept the Center for Responsive Politics' well-calculated $6 billion figure for relatively transparent spending on the 2012 federal races as a baseline. We also accept the well-reasoned assessments of the researchers and analysts who track the no-man's-land of campaign finance abuse when they say that dark money spending in 2012 was "much more" than $400 million. How much more is the question, and when we consulted with analysts from the Center for Media and Democracy, they replied that the number could easily exceed $1 billion. Very easily.[53] This dark money is overwhelmingly, though not exclusively, Republican.[54] Liberal dark money that ran ads for a Libertarian candidate in the 2012 Montana Senate race may well have contributed to Democrat Jon Tester's narrow re-election.[55] But this is an area ideally suited for billionaires and corporate interests to operate surreptitiously, and it shows all signs of growing in importance.

By pulling the dark money discussion into the sunlight, and by acknowledging the immense amount of in-kind support that elected officials, political parties, business associations, and unions provide to candidates in organized but essentially unaccountable dark aid, we can reasonably assert that the federal elections figure for 2012 exceeded $7 billion.

STATE ELECTION SPENDING

But federal elections were not the only ones on which Big Money was spent in 2012. The 2012 election cycle saw unprecedented spending at the state and local levels of government and on state and local recalls, referendums, and initiatives. In other words, if there was an election in 2012, there was Big Money spent on it—often, though not always, by the same wealthy individuals and corporations seeking to influence the direction of the presidential race and of congressional contests.

Much of the real power to influence public expenditures and policies rests in the statehouses, and some of the biggest spenders in American politics have recognized this fact. For instance, the Koch brothers may have started as big players on the federal level. But they long ago recommitted to a state-based strategy of funding gubernatorial and legislative campaigns in order to elect not just conservatives but also lockstep supporters of their antiunion, anti-public-education, antigovernment agendas. And they have coupled this money with huge amounts of structural support for the American Legislative Exchange Council (ALEC), in which representatives of major corporations participate in the drafting of "model legislation" that can then be forwarded on for introduction and passage by allied legislators.[56]

Similarly, billionaire Dick DeVos, an heir to the Amway door-to-door retailing fortune, and his wife, Betsy, both longtime leaders of the Michigan Republican Party, once bragged about their role in national politics. Betsy wrote in 1997:

> [My] family is the largest single contributor of soft money to the national Republican Party. . . . I have decided, however, to stop taking offense at the suggestion that we are buying influence. Now, I simply concede the point. We expect to foster a conservative governing philosophy consisting of limited government and respect for traditional American virtues. We expect a return on our investment; we expect a good and honest government. Furthermore, we expect the Republican Party to use the money to promote these policies, and yes, to win elections.[57]

In the years since Dick DeVos spent $41 million on a losing Michigan gubernatorial race, however, they shifted more and more of their substantial giving to groups that work to elect state legislative supporters of school privatization schemes.[58] And it was a significant shift. In 2007, Dick and Betsy DeVos were fined $2.6 million each, for a total of $5.2 million, for illegally funneling $870,000 from a Virginia-based political action committee into the Ohio affiliate of their All Children Matter operation. The transfer was eighty-seven times higher than that allowed under Ohio law and amounted to one of the most blatant assaults on campaign-finance limits in the state's history. The fines were imposed accordingly—amounting, as reported by the Ohio Elections Commission, a bipartisan grouping that unanimously imposed the sanctions, to "easily the largest fine the Ohio commission has levied."[59]

When the outsized players in national politics wade into state and local politics, it is no longer possible, let alone appropriate, to see contests for state senate seats in Ohio or school board posts in Milwaukee as footnotes to stories about campaign spending. Those races need to be seen as part of a whole. A big part. There are now networks of wealthy donors who, freed from much of the oversight provided by the campaign-finance laws that the U.S. Supreme Court has scrapped, pour money into state and local races, writing checks to gubernatorial and mayoral candidates every bit as furiously as they do to presidential contenders.

The 2012 election season in the states began with historic recall elections in Wisconsin, where Governor Scott Walker and his state senate allies were targeted for removal from office by labor and progressive groups infuriated by the governor's assault on collective bargaining rights and his implementation of a Greek- or Spanish-style austerity program of deep cuts to public service and education funding, combined with de rigueur rounds of additional tax cuts for millionaires, billionaires, and corporations. Walker did not mount a traditional fight back, with appeals to Wisconsin's conservative contributors. He "went national," jetting around the country for meetings with the same right-wing donors who funded presidential and congressional races: folks like Texas homebuilder Bob Perry, who drew national attention in 2004 when he wrote $4.45 million in checks to fund the Swift Boat attack campaign against Democratic presidential nominee John Kerry. Perry, who gave $7 million to help Karl Rove get his American Crossroads combine started in

2010 (and another $6.5 million to keep it going in 2012), wrote a $250,000 check to support Walker as the recall fight got started. A few weeks later, he chipped in another $250,000. And at $500,000, Perry was not even Walker's biggest donor. Or all that uncommon. Thirty-seven individuals, the vast majority of them from outside Wisconsin, each gave the embattled governor contributions of more than $50,000.[60] Walker took advantage of a loophole in Wisconsin election law that created precisely the sort of no-holds-barred campaign circumstance proposed by Mitt Romney and other defenders of the Supreme Court's rulings in cases such as *Citizens United*. As the Wisconsin Democracy Campaign explained, "Walker drew massive contributions above the usual $10,000 calendar year limit on individual donations because state law allows recall targets to collect unlimited cash to pay bills that come in before a recall election is approved."[61]

Before the June 2012 vote, Walker's personal campaign committee raised and spent $36.1 million—three times the largest amount ever previously spent on a gubernatorial candidate in the state and more than had ever been spent by all the candidates in any previous gubernatorial campaign. According to the Wisconsin Democracy Campaign's study of the spending, "Nearly $22 million or 64 percent of the individual contributions he raised since January 2011 and spent mostly on the recall came from out-of-state banking, manufacturing, construction, real estate and other powerful special interests hailing from Florida, Texas, New York, Missouri, Nevada, Wyoming and New Jersey, among other states." But that was only the first wave of the national money that flowed into the state. Another $22.6 million was spent on Walker's behalf by party organizations and so-called independent groups that backed him, bringing the total spending on the governor's behalf to $58.7 million.[62]

In contrast, the campaign of Walker's Democratic challenger, Mayor Tom Barrett of Milwaukee, spent $6.6 million, while party organizations and independent groups that explicitly backed Barrett spent in the range of $10 million.[63] Walker's money advantage was always dramatic, and it was especially large in the early stages when the direction of the fight was defined. No serious observer doubted that Walker's money, most of it from out of state, made it possible for the controversial governor to prevail with 53 percent of the vote in June 5. But for our purposes here, let's add the Walker and Barrett spending, as well as the spending for the post of lieutenant governor and for four

Wisconsin state senate races that played out on the same date. What do we get? A cool $93.5 million.[64] And that's one state. By the end of 2012, other states with closely contested gubernatorial races had seen similarly dramatic spending: roughly $50 million in Washington State, roughly $30 million in Missouri, roughly $25 million in North Carolina, and roughly $25 million in tiny New Hampshire.[65] In a dozen states during the course of 2012, the candidates alone spent more than $200 million on gubernatorial races.[66]

Moreover, independent groups often equaled or exceeded candidate spending. Clearly partisan organizations such as the Republican Governors Association (RGA) consistently top the lists of *federal* super-PAC donors. How? "The Republican Governors Association's appearance on a list of top donors to super PACs—which were formed to spend money on federal races—at first glance appears to be a mistake. But a close look at the Washington, D.C.-based 527 organization's disclosure filings shows it is using super PACs to funnel funds into state races," explained a Center for Public Integrity examination of how the group operates. "The recipient of the RGA's generosity is a super PAC called 'RGA Right Direction PAC.' The super-PAC takes the money it receives from the RGA—which as a 527 can accept unlimited funds from corporations and wealthy individuals—and spends it on state races." Via the RGA in 2012, million-dollar corporate donations flowed on a regular basis to gubernatorial candidates in states that were still trying to maintain some limits on the size of donations and on corporate dominance of their elections. Similarly, groups such as the Republican Lieutenant Governors Association, the Republican Attorneys General Association, the Republican Secretaries of State Association, the Republican Legislative Campaign Committee, and the Republican State Leadership Committee (RSLC) joined the RGA in moving tens of millions of dollars from corporations and wealthy individuals into state contests.

Indeed, these groups bragged about the money they moved into the states. After the Republican State Leadership Committee celebrated the fact that it had raised almost $40 million for the 2012 election cycle, *Politico* explained in late October:

> RSLC's political spending has increased 36 percent over last cycle—even more than the group's overall fundraising.

RSLC is among the Republican independent groups that have risen in prominence in an age of looser campaign finance rules and Democratic control of the
White House. Along with its Democratic counterpart, the Democratic Legislative
Campaign Committee, and the Republican and Democratic Governors Associations, RSLC has channeled new levels of national money into state campaigns.

Matt Walter, the RSLC's political director, predicted the heavy national investment in state races would continue past 2012 and "heading into 2014, when
the focus returns much more significantly to the state level."

"I think people have bought into that in part because of the lack of action in
Washington, at the federal level, but there is also an increased interest and po-
larization, in general, in the political process," Walter said. "It's difficult to see
that trajectory changing."[67]

In our discussions with dozens of candidates, party operatives, and consultants working at the state and local levels, the consistent response was
that these are the real "growth" areas for campaign spending in the *Citizens
United* era. Corporations and wealthy individuals seeking to influence policy
can be talked into writing checks for state races. And not just the high-
profile gubernatorial contests. Democratic state attorneys general—notably
but not exclusively New York attorneys general Eliot Spitzer and Eric
Schneiderman—have been in the forefront of fights to hold Wall Street traders,
credit card companies, polluters, agribusiness giants, and gun manufacturers
to account.[68] So it should not come as much of a surprise that the Republican
Attorneys General Association has been collecting big-dollar donations from
corporations such as Aetna U.S. Healthcare, Brown & Williamson, Microsoft
Corporation, SBC Communications Inc., and, of course, the National Rifle
Association. Indeed, as the *Washington Post* revealed after a study of internal
fund-raising documents, Republican state attorneys general have engaged in
the solicitation of contributions from corporations and trade groups that have
been the subject of lawsuits and regulations by their states.[69]

After the 2012 election, the Republican state-based groups declared, "In
West Virginia, we unseated a five-term incumbent Attorney General."[70] Darrell
McGraw, a Democrat who over five terms in office had "consistently drawn
the ire of industry groups for his office's consumer protection litigation,"[71]
did indeed lose by a 51–49 margin to Republican Patrick Morrisey. A lawyer
with a politically connected Washington, DC, law firm, Morrisey bragged during the campaign that he had assisted states challenging the federal Affordable

Care Act (Obamacare) and that he "continues to counsel Members of Congress on strategies to repeal the law." But he obtained his license to practice law in West Virginian only four days before he filed papers to seek the state's chief law-enforcement position.[72] Morrisey's candidacy would have been absurd by traditional measures of credible candidates in West Virginia. But he had an advantage: virtually unlimited—and unaccountable—outside money. More money from outside the state poured into Morrisey's race for attorney general than into races for governor or potentially competitive congressional seats.[73]

One group alone, the Virginia-based Center for Individual Freedom, poured at least $1.6 million into anti-McGraw television ads that aired before the election. As the *Charleston Daily Mail* noted, "The Center got its start as a front group for the tobacco lobby and now funds conservative candidates and causes. It does not report its donors, though former Bush political operative Karl Rove's political action committee has given money to the Center, according to spending information made public by Rove's Crossroads GPS."[74] Another group, the Des Moines, Iowa–based American Future Fund, spent almost $600,000 in ads that benefited Morrisey.[75] The organization, which registers with the IRS under laws governing charitable institutions as a nonprofit, runs something called the "AG Project" for the purpose of "bringing attention to the important constitutional issues facing our state and federal courts, as well as identifying and supporting those candidates for states attorney general who defend the constitutional principles that founded our nation."[76] Left unmentioned was the project's essential purpose: the movement of huge amounts of money into the states for the purpose of electing law-enforcement officials who would take their cues from corporate special interests and national conservatives rather than from their constituents.

In addition to the West Virginia race, the American Future Fund made itself a big player in Missouri, where the group bought $250,000 in advertising to attack the state's Democratic attorney general, Chris Koster. A former Republican who was rated "100 percent pro-gun" by the National Rifle Association, Koster was no liberal. But he was targeted all the same, and in a common reaction, Koster ramped up his fund-raising to more than $5 million. It was part of a spending spree on down-ballot races in Missouri, where initial reports on formal spending by the committees of candidates for state posts totaled more than $65 million.[77] Add on the known interventions by outside groups, and the spending pushed well past $70 million, roughly the combined amount spent by the campaigns of Republican presidential candidates Rick Santorum, Newt Gingrich, and Ron Paul on their races for the party's 2012 nomination.[78]

The pattern was the same in state after state, where spending records were met and exceeded by candidates, party organizations, and independent groups. Many of them were funded by national donors who did not even know where their money was going or whom it was being spent for or against. In California, there were no statewide contests, just races for the legislature. But the fund-raising by candidates for the state Assembly and Senate still topped $102 million, with at least $23 million spent by outsiders.[79] So that's, very conservatively, $125 million for California legislative races. In Texas, legislative candidates raised $93 million. In Florida, it was $60 million. Just the formal fund-raising by state legislative candidates and their committees, according to the National Institute on Money in State Politics, totaled $800 million.[80] Couple that figure with the independent expenditures of outside groups playing on issues ranging from abortion rights to farm policy to labor rights and, above all, privatization of education, and there is little question that the money flowing in and around the contests for the 7,382 state legislative seats that were chosen in 2012 exceeded $1 billion. Even the most conservative estimates of candidate and party spending on gubernatorial and down-ballot statewide races exceed $300 million. Add on outside spending and the state-based equivalents of dark money in those contests and legislative races, and the overall figure for state races surpasses $1.4 billion. With federal spending, transparent and dark, that takes us to around $8.5 billion.

LOCAL ELECTION SPENDING

And, no, we're not done. Beneath the state level are the county and local levels of government, where thousands of officials were chosen in 2012 elections. The influence of Big Money on local races can be dramatically greater than at the federal and state levels, since it doesn't take that much money to change the character of a race for a county commission, a mayor's post, a town council, or a school board. Yet local government often decides where and how and even whether a corporation can develop a mine, turn a public park into a private condominium development, or take money from hard-pressed public schools into order to fund the speculative fantasies of charter-school enthusiasts.[81]

More than four hundred cities, from Anchorage, Alaska, to Wheeling, West Virginia, elected mayors in 2012, and almost invariably the campaigns saw "unprecedented," "unrivaled," and "explosive" spending. Cities where mayoral contests had historically been local affairs fought out "at the doors" witnessed media extravaganzas, where tens of millions of dollars were spent on contests that recreated all the pathologies of the presidential election.[82] In San Diego, for instance, a frenzied contest between Democrat Bob Filner, a liberal congressman with strong ties to organized labor, and Republican Carl DeMaio, a councilman who was a favorite of downtown developers, cost at least $13 million.[83] And remember that the Filner-DeMaio runoff on November 6 was merely the end of a yearlong process; a primary in June had included other candidates and had cost millions more. There was significant spending for city council races and other local fights, including a June referendum to roll back pensions for public employees. When all was said and done, spending on San Diego's local elections in 2012 cost in the $20 million range—the kind of money that used to be considered "excessive" in high-stakes gubernatorial and U.S. Senate races.

It wasn't just mayoral races. Local races that were once thought of as classic grassroots contests were transformed in 2012 into hyperexpensive battles where traditional grassroots politics was overwhelmed by outside money. Take, as an example, the District 8 city council contest in San Jose. The city was wrestling with questions about how to maintain and fund public employee pensions. The incumbent, Rose Herrera, and her challenger, Jimmy Nguyen, had different views on those questions, which they ably articulated. But independent groups that were unaffiliated with the candidates, and that got the overwhelming majority of their money from outside the working-class district, wanted to have their say as well. So groups like the San Jose Silicon Valley Chamber of Commerce started writing checks for more than $100,000.[84] Ultimately, the contest for a single council seat in a midsized American city featured television ads, radio ads, and stacks of mass-mailed communications that ended up costing well in excess of $500,000. It probably does not need to be explained that the candidate of the San Jose Silicon Valley Chamber of Commerce, Herrera, won. But she did. And so did the four Las Vegas–area county commissioners who accumulated $1.6 million for their 2012 re-election races.

One of the biggest donors to the commissioners was Bill Walters, a developer who was in the process of turning a golf course on county land into a business park. Walters, whose money flowed in increments of $20,000 and $25,000 to the various contenders, told the *Las Vegas Review-Journal* that "he doesn't call his contributions 'donations,' instead viewing them as 'investments' in good candidates." He explained, "The bottom line is, if you own a business in Las Vegas, if you have employees in Las Vegas . . . the most important people in the world to you are the people who run local government."[85]

A lot of wealthy donors came to that conclusion in 2012. Across the country, there were hundreds of examples of local contests where, using the tactics and tools of the new *Citizens United* era, wealthy developers and business owners—and, in some communities such as San Jose, the unions representing the public employees who were targeted by those outside interests—paved over the grassroots and erected a Dollarocracy on Main Street. Our calculations, based on a study of reports from across the country, suggest that spending for thousands of municipal, school board, local judicial, and county races across the country can easily be placed in the $500 million range and could well exceed that figure.

That brings us into the $9 billion range for baseline spending on races where voters had to pick a candidate. So where do we find the last billion on the way to the $10 billion figure? On the part of the ballot that makes no mention of parties' candidates, except in judicial races.

Welcome to the new frontier of the money-and-media election complex.

INITIATIVES, REFERENDUMS, AND JUDICIAL RACES

If you were looking for extreme spending in 2012, for the spending that produced the most ads on television stations in states such as California and Maryland, you would have to pay attention to the campaigns for and against initiatives and referendums. According to *State Legislatures* magazine, 174 ballot measures were considered by the electorates of thirty-eight states on November 6, 2012.[86] That figure does not include the hundreds of local school and public-services spending referendums considered in states across the country; almost all of these referendums saw substantial spending. How substantial? Add up the numbers from all the ballot measures—from liquor law changes in Chicago precincts, where local bar owners ponied up their thousands, to the $55 million fight over labeling of genetically modified food in California[87]—and the total easily exceeds $1 billion.

In many statewide "issue" votes around the country, the spending went beyond "substantial." The proper word is "extreme" or, arguably, "obscene." Consider this: in California, spending on statewide initiatives was at least $450 million. In Maryland, it was $100 million. In Michigan, the initial spending reports pointed to total spending easily in excess of $150 million.[88] The Michigan figure is instructive, as the *Detroit News* explained in a *preelection* report that summed up the extent to which initiatives and referendums trumped all other politics in a number of major states:

> The high-profile ballot issues alone total $149.5 million—and counting—of the campaigning to amend the constitution, a whopping 85 percent of all spending on state races.
>
> Ballot proposal spending dwarfs the $107 million spent in 2010 on all state races for governor, attorney general, secretary of state, the Legislature and courts.
>
> "This is really all about the ballot stuff—that's what's carrying the whole thing," said Rich Robinson, executive director of the Michigan Campaign Finance Network, which tracks money in state politics.
>
> Campaigns to amend the state constitution or thwart those changes are being largely funded by a handful of wealthy individuals, labor unions and organizations bundling millions in anonymous donations, a *Detroit News* analysis of spending data shows.
>
> Some of the donors are more traceable than others.
>
> The most widely known financier of ballot issues is billionaire Ambassador Bridge owner Manuel "Matty" Moroun, whose companies have dumped $33.1 million into a campaign to pass Proposal 6, requiring statewide votes for new public bridges, and another $3.5 million for Proposal 5, seeking a two-thirds voting threshold for the Legislature to raise taxes.
>
> In the Proposal 2 fight over a union-led effort to enshrine collective bargaining in the constitution, members of the DeVos family in Michigan have contributed $1.58 million to a campaign to defeat the initiative while billionaire Las Vegas casino mogul Sheldon Adelson and his wife have chipped in another $2 million to the cause.[89]

Hey, not *that* Sheldon Adelson? Not the guy whose $150 million in contributions to Republican candidates and causes made him the most notorious campaign donor of the super-PAC era? The very same. Like most of the major donors to candidates, including the privatization-obsessed DeVos family,

Adelson moved his money into referendum and initiatives campaigns that gave him a chance to achieve his ends.[90]

A century ago, in the Progressive Era, initiatives, referendums, and recalls ("IRRs," as the old campaigners described it in the shorthand of the day) were seen as democratizing tools—like the direct election of U.S. senators—that would take politics out of the back rooms and give people the power to set agendas, frame policy, and hold elected officials to account. Throughout much of the twentieth century, in states from California to Maine, this was the case. With the rise of Dollarocracy, however, IRRs have been co-opted by the Money Power.

The same goes for judicial elections. Just as the Progressives of a century ago sought to battle corruption by handing more authority over policy-making to the voters via direct-democracy initiatives, and just as they sought to take the power to select senators away from state legislators and give it to the people, they battled to move authority over the selection of state and local judges out of the back rooms and into the hands of the voters. There are now thirty-nine states where the voters, as opposed to the politicians and their Big Money backers, choose justices and judges in elections that, until recently, served the purpose the Progressive reformers of the past intended. The relative integrity of the justice system for much of the twentieth century makes it easy to forget just how corrupt the process was only one hundred years ago. In recent generations, there was minimal funding of these judicial races: American Bar Association ratings, newspaper recommendations, experience and reputation in the community, and party affiliations went a long way toward determining the outcomes. As recently as 1990, total campaign spending for all state Supreme Court races nationwide was estimated at $3 million.

That is no longer the case. Over the past two decades, corporate interests and funders like the Koch brothers and the U.S. Chamber of Commerce have zeroed in on judicial elections as a cost-effective way to buy control of the court system. By the mid-1990s, the spending on state Supreme Court races increased fivefold from 1990; it then tripled again by 2000, according to a 2012 study by the Center for American Progress (CAP). "Since then," the CAP reports, "corporate America's influence over the judiciary has grown. The U.S. Chamber of Commerce, in particular, has become a powerful player in judicial races. From 2001 to 2003 its preferred candidates won 21 of 24 elections. The chamber spent more than $1 million to aid the 2006 campaigns of two Ohio Supreme Court justices, and in the most recent High Court election in Alabama, money from the state's chamber accounted for 40 percent of all campaign contributions."[91] That does wonders when it comes to reducing corporate liability in civil cases, among other things.[92]

The most dramatic recent example of the payoff provided for corporate interests that set out to buy state court elections comes from West Virginia. The A. T. Massey Coal Company—yes, the same Massey Energy Company responsible for the worst American mining disaster since 1970, killing twenty-nine West Virginia miners in 2010—took an interest in West Virginia court contests in 2002 when a West Virginia jury ordered Massey to pay out $50 million to plaintiffs. As the matter went through the appeals process, then CEO Don Blankenship spent $3 million of his own money in the 2004 election cycle to unseat a justice on the state Supreme Court and gain the seat for his ally, Brent Benjamin. Well, Benjamin won, and when Massey's appeal got to the state's highest court, Benjamin joined the majority in a 3–2 vote to overturn the award.[93]

The process accelerated in 2012, as tens of millions of dollars in money, much of it from outside the targeted states, poured into judicial contests. The spending shattered records and produced tens of millions in spending and some of the crudest campaigns of the season.[94] With spending for down-ballot state judicial posts, as well as circuit, county, and municipal judgeships, added in, the total spending is certainly in the range of $50 million. Most of that money was targeted to win control of the top courts, since they have the power to overrule the lower courts. And a substantial portion of the spending on High Court races paid for advertisements designed to discredit and defeat sitting justices. According to the Justice at Stake Campaign, a record-breaking $29.7 million was spent on more than 51,000 television ads seeking to influence 2012 state Supreme Court contests.[95] Ten states saw television advertising exceed $1 million: Alabama, Florida, Illinois, Louisiana, Michigan, Mississippi, North Carolina, Ohio, Texas, and, yes, West Virginia. And the money came from familiar groups, such as the American Future Fund, the shadowy organization that pumped money into the West Virginia attorney general contests. Talk about coming at a "problem" from all sides—the American Future Fund was picking prosecutors *and* judges.[96] But that's just one reason that "investing" in judicial contests is probably the best investment to be found in American electoral politics. Because there is scant press coverage of judicial races, and because in some states judicial candidates are limited in what they are allowed to talk about during the campaign, judicial candidates who are seen as insufficiently procorporate tend to be easy pickings. A barrage of negative attack ads is often enough to do the trick.

The entire process has made a mockery of the justice system. As retired U.S. Supreme Court justice Sandra Day O'Connor put it, "When you enter one of these courtrooms, the last thing you want to worry about is whether the judge is more accountable to a campaign contributor or an ideological group than to the law."[97] "Every litigant," said the CAP's Billy Corriher, "is supposed to be equal in the eyes of the law. But this principle is less true with each passing judicial election."[98] Indeed, a new Justice at Stake survey finds that 76 percent of Americans believe campaign contributions have at least some impact on the decisions made by justices and judges in their courtrooms.[99] So much for the integrity of the bench.

Of course, this is exactly as might be expected under Dollarocracy. And, notably, it is in the judicial competition that the promise of Dollarocracy is being realized for corporate donors—far more rapidly and far more clearly than in contests for top-of-the-ballot partisan posts or referendum votes. In a number of states, once the moneyed interests control the High Court, increasingly no one even makes a serious attempt to challenge their dominance. In Alabama in 2012, for instance, the Democrats fielded a candidate in only one of the five open Supreme Court races. Just the threat of money is sufficient to keep challengers at bay.[100]

Maybe this is how Dollarocracy solves the problem of too much money in elections: just stop having meaningful and competitive elections.

THE BIGGEST LOSER?

Arguably, the dominant meme among the pundits in the weeks following the 2012 election was that Big Money lost and Adelson was the biggest loser of them all. Along with his wife, the twelfth richest man in the world, and the seventh richest in the United States, poured tens of millions into helping Newt Gingrich get beat in the Republican primaries; then he poured tens of millions, and tens of millions and tens of millions more, into helping Mitt Romney get beat in the November election. They spent tens of millions more, directly and indirectly, to influence U.S. House and Senate contests. Major publications and Web sites took a certain glee in noting, as *Politico* did in December 2012, that "Adelson's massive amounts of cash largely went toward supporting candidates who lost."[101] "Sheldon Adelson Had a Bad Night," read the *Salon* headline on the morning after the November 6 election. But Adelson, media outlets noted with the fascination reserved for coverage of the emotional state of the rich and famous, did not seem all that upset. Perhaps because, while he might not have been winning high-profile races, he was winning contests for "causes close to Adelson's heart"—and his pocketbook.[102]

In Michigan, the heartland of the United Auto Workers union and a key base of strength for unions nationally, organized labor sought to protect collective bargaining rights with a constitutional amendment. Antiunion interest from across the country rushed in to defeat the referendum, knowing that its success might create a model for prounion ballot initiatives across the country. Adelson and his wife wrote some of the biggest checks, and they were not just "interested observers." Just weeks before the Michigan vote, the Adelsons poured $2 million into the coffers of Protecting Michigan Taxpayers, one of several shadowy groups that flooded Michigan airwaves with ads that, literally, sought to suggest that collective bargaining guarantees would make it impossible to remove child molesters from schools.[103]

It was an antiunion fantasy, but Adelson has few passions to rival his antilabor stance. His Venetian hotel is the Las Vegas Strip's only hotel-casino that is not unionized. The billionaire says he started backing the Republican Party in the 1990s because it was more consistently antiunion. And union activists like Yvanna Cancela, the spokeswoman for the Culinary Workers Union in Las Vegas, know that. For all the speculation about Adelson's motivations for donating huge amounts of money in 2012, the casino king's disdain for organized labor still topped the list. "It is a shame that we have a political system that allows for one person to essentially buy elections," said Cancela after the election. But wait . . . didn't all the headlines say Adelson lost?[104] Well, he won in Michigan. The measure that would have provided a clear constitutional protection for collective bargaining rights was defeated.[105]

The *New York Times* headline two days after the election read, "In Michigan, a Setback for Unions." It was also an opening for those "causes close to Adelson's heart."[106] Barely a month after the voting was done, the Michigan legislature passed so-called right-to-work legislation, the most virulent of all antilabor initiatives. In one week, basic protections for all workers were dramatically weakened and the ability of billionaires like Sheldon Adelson to rake in ever-greater profits with the prospect of paying lower wages and benefits to employees was increased.[107] And crushing labor is a twofer, because as unions decline in power, so does their ability to pry the Democrats away from dollarcrat policies, not to mention win elections for them.

This is the best way to understand the role that Big Money plays in our politics in the emerging Dollarocracy. The Money Power may win or lose a race, even an election year. But its authority is not conveyed via an election result. Its authority comes from its permanent presence. The Money Power is constant and, ultimately, definitional. Its purpose is not just to prevail on a particular election day. Its purpose is to create a politics where temporary setbacks are just that: temporary. It is their permanence that gives the biggest spenders their power. Adelson knows this. Maybe 2012 wasn't all that great an election year for him. But it finished with a great big win on one of his most vital issues in a key state, and that win set the stage for new fights filled with promise for Adelson. After all, if the unions that played such a critical role in thwarting Adelson's ambitions in 2012 could be beaten down in Michigan, the heartland of the labor movement, how hard will it be to beat them down in Nevada, the heartland of Sheldon Adelson's empire? And if the ability of unions to function as effective political forces can be undermined in enough states, then Adelson's election year "investments" will go a whole lot further.

Maybe that's why Sheldon Adelson was smiling when he jetted into Washington a few weeks after the 2012 election in which he was supposedly the biggest loser. Adelson met with congressional leaders and power players. He was startlingly blunt about why the doors opened for him. "Mr. Adelson, 79 years old, said he has many friends in Washington," wrote the *Wall Street Journal,* which quoted the billionaire as saying, "but the reasons aren't my good looks and charm. It's my 'pocket personality.'" He was, explained the *Journal,* "referring to his donations." And Adelson had a message for those who might have thought he was rethinking his political investment strategies:

"Mr. Adelson's 2012 donations were double what he spent in 2008, and looking ahead, he said, he was ready to again 'double' his donations," reported the *Journal*. "'I'll spend that much and more,' he said in his first extensive post-election interview. 'Let's cut any ambiguity.'"[108]

It's cut.

NO COUNTRY FOR RICH MEN?

Big donors like Sheldon Adelson were just getting started in 2012. And for every showman like Adelson, there are hundreds of other billionaires, centimillionaires, and CEOs waiting in the wings who prefer anonymity but, like Adelson, demand results. With the institutions, professionals, and PACs they bankroll, they will be back. With more money. And better strategies. "Independent groups have cemented their status as permanent fixtures in the political firmament," noted the *Los Angeles Times*. "The center of the strategic universe has shifted from parties to the PACs," said former George W. Bush strategist Mark McKinnon in the same *LA Times* article.[109]

In fact, they never left. Issue advertising is projected to hit $2 billion in 2013, almost double the figure for 2009.[110] The megafunders and their PACs are already chomping at the bit about the 2014 election, as it is a midterm with a much lower turnout, especially among traditionally antidollarcrat voters. "A lot of these groups may have much better impact on the money spent on the House and Senate," just as they did when they dominated the 2010 election, said Bill Allison of the Sunlight Foundation.[111] "Once seasonal affairs, campaigns from the presidential race down to the House contests are becoming longer and more intense," said Confessore, "driven by deep-pocketed donors eager to see incumbents pummeled throughout the political cycle."[112] In short, thanks to Big Money, says Elizabeth Wilner, "we are in the era of the permanent campaign."[113]

The "investors" bankrolling permanent campaigns don't worry about silly notions like "throwing good money after bad." For them, political investments come from the petty-cash drawer. What does $150 million mean to Adelson, a man with a net worth of $20.5 billion?[114] If Sheldon Adelson donated $10 million to political campaigns *every single day* from January 1, 2013, until Election Day, November 1, 2016, he would wake up on November 2, 2016, with a net worth of $6.6 billion and still be among the 50 or 60 richest people in the United States. Hell, Adelson could spend $150 million on politics—his epic contribution total for 2011–2012—every single day for four months and still be a billionaire twice over and one of the 250 wealthiest persons in America. The Koch brothers could spend $150 million on political campaigns *every single day for a full year,* and each of them would still remain among the 120 richest Americans.[115] Their heirs and their heirs' heirs and on and on would still have lives of unimaginable leisure. But that won't happen, because if Adelson and the Koch brothers spend money, it will have the effect of increasing their net worths; that is the whole point. This is the problem with how so much of the media covered the explosion of campaign spending in 2012. There was the assumption, writ large across the reporting, that millionaires and billionaires were desperately spending their fortunes down in order to "buy" an election. That's silly. A David Koch, a Dick DeVos, a Sheldon Adelson does not spend until it hurts on politics. They're making investments, not high-end consumer purchases, and those investments are small in the scheme of things.

They are smaller still for what big banks or insurance or agribusiness or energy interests can get on their relatively small "investments"; hence the risk is well worth it. For decades, scholars have posited that campaign spending by big business and the wealthy was actually quite low in view of the immense returns they could gain by writing laws, tax codes, and regulations and having access to the government trough.[116] Now corporations and the billionaires who own them have been set free. They have no romantic illusions about politics. When they write checks, they are putting their money into a business enterprise, run increasingly by a money-and-media election complex that they are perfecting. Adelson admitted as much after the election when he acknowledged that he was in favor of "socialized medicine," abortion rights, stem-cell research, and the welcoming of immigrants to America. "Look, I'm basically a social liberal," explained the billionaire, as he ticked off the list of issues on which he disagreed with the party and the candidates he lavishly funded in 2012. Yet the billionaire dismissed any suggestion that he might be in the wrong party. He is, he said, a political pragmatist. "Look, nobody agrees with 100 percent of their planks," he remarked of the GOP platform. What he's interested in, what so many big donors are interested in, is a politics that serves their business interests. And they can buy it.

Like other members of the American 1 percent who have over the past fifty years seen their personal wealth grow to 288 times the personal wealth of the median American household, simply maintaining the status quo is a pretty good deal. And for the superrich, there's even more at stake. In Adelson's case, there was, as *Politico* noted, the matter of "self-defense": "Adelson's Las Vegas Sands Corp. is being scrutinized by federal investigators looking into possible money-laundering in Vegas, and possible violation of bribery laws by the company's ventures in China, including four casinos in the gambling mecca of Macau. (Amazingly, 90 percent of the corporation's revenue is now from Asia, including properties in Macau and Singapore.)" But there was also the potential for enormous personal gain. An analysis by Seth Hanlon, the director of fiscal reform for the Center for American Progress Action Fund, estimated that Adelson stood "to receive a potential tax cut from the Romney tax agenda of more than $2 billion—an exponential return on a $100 million investment."[117] And he was hardly alone. As former labor secretary Robert Reich noted:

> If and when they eventually win, these billionaires will clean up. Their taxes will plummet, many laws constraining their profits (such as environmental laws preventing the Koch brothers from more depredations, and the anti-bribery Foreign Corrupt Practices Act that Adelson is being investigated for violating) will disappear, and what's left of labor unions will no longer intrude on their bottom lines.
> And they have enough dough to keep betting until they eventually win. That's what it means to be a billionaire political investor: You're able to keep playing the odds until you get the golden ring.[118]

Reich is essentially correct. We would quibble with him only on the question of whether there is a "golden ring" at the end of the calculus or something greater. Our sense is that what took shape in 2012, from the lowliest city council races to the lofty presidential competition, was not so much about grabbing for a precious jewel as it was about creating a monopoly politics where those who own the golden rings will never have to worry about losing them—in the way that a working family might lose a home—because questions about their dominant position will forever be settled.

Of course, this reshaping of the political process to a "heads I win, tails you lose" duopoly requires the same constant commitment that McDonald's brings to hamburger sales, that Starbucks brings to coffee peddling, that Wal-Mart brings to the unloading of cheap goods. No one in business questions the wisdom of taking steps to corner the market. That's how to understand what we saw in 2012. It was not a transitory explosion of spending. It was a new model for how those who already possessed immense wealth and power will corner the market unless they are stopped by political challenges and then laws. They will do so by continually engaging in variations on what *Politico* described in an article on the 2012 electoral machinations of Charles and David Koch: an "ambitious expansion of the billionaire brothers' political operation that includes the recruitment of new donors and fundraisers into their network by a development team."[119]

This "ambitious expansion," with its "recruitments" and its "development teams," is not beginning. It is well under way. And it has as its goal not a thing but a definition.

If our politics is always about money, as it was in 2012, it will always default to a position—not an ideal but a rather lowly and easily manipulated position—that will make sense for Sheldon Adelson and David Koch. If all that is needed is a little more money, or a smarter investment strategy, then they have that. And they can adjust until our politics, our very governance, adjusts to them. This is, as Donald Trump explained it, the art of the deal.

That's what $10 billion bought in 2012: a politics that makes sense to the folks who have $10 billion and are willing to spend it to achieve their ends. We didn't get a Donald Trump as a president or even as a nominee. But we got a Mitt Romney. Money, not merit, bought the Republican presidential nomination in 2012. Republicans did not want Romney as their nominee; they were so desperate that they entertained the notion of nominating the likes of Herman Cain, Newt Gingrich, and Rick Santorum before finally accepting—thanks to the dramatic spending advantages of the Romney campaign and the pro-Romney Restore Our Future super-PAC—that this was not a free market of ideas or a meritocracy. This was a Dollarocracy.

Once Romney secured the nomination, Barack Obama's supporters used early financial advantages and skillful messaging to define their opponent as the doltish plutocrat that his own errors confirmed. And they closed the campaign with a final flurry of spending that equaled that of their foes. Yes, Romney and the Republicans spent a little more. But when both major candidates for president and their backers are mounting billion-dollar campaigns, the price of admission has been redefined. This is Dollarocracy.

When a veteran attorney general whose only "crime" is his determination to defend the rights of consumers is defeated by a challenger who got his license to practice law in the state four days before launching a campaign that flooded the airwaves with out-of-state money, this is Dollarocracy.

When the race for a city council is so "awash in money" that supposedly independent business interests are paying $20 a vote to secure a win that will allow them to take away the pensions of public employees, this is Dollarocracy.

When a billionaire can "invest" $2 million in the causes close to his heart and gain the "return" of diminished rights for workers and a discourse where the voice of organized labor is weakened, this is not democracy. This is Dollarocracy.

Political systems do not arrive fully formed. They take shape over time, defined by structural changes and interventions, pressured and influenced by powerful forces. America is not a complete Dollarocracy. But it is Dollarocracy in the making. Democracy did not fall in 2012; it held its own in some places against the withering assault of a $10 billion campaign. But the billionaires who paid for that campaign—to a far greater extent than our media revealed—have established their beachheads. And they are on the march.

3

THE ARCHITECTS OF DOLLAROCRACY

Lewis Powell, John Roberts,
and the Robber Baron Court

Elections are not to turn on the difference in the amounts of money that candidates have to spend. This seems an acceptable purpose and the means chosen a common sense way to achieve it. The Court nevertheless holds that a candidate has a constitutional right to spend unlimited amounts of money, mostly that of other people, in order to be elected. The holding perhaps is not that federal candidates have the constitutional right to purchase their election, but many will so interpret the Court's conclusion in this case. I cannot join the Court in this respect.

JUSTICE BYRON WHITE, DISSENT FROM
THE SUPREME COURT'S *BUCKLEY V. VALEO* DECISION, 1976

In 1973, when the U.S. Senate voted to amend the Federal Election Campaign Act not only to address the obvious abuses of the Watergate moment but also to stall the slide toward Dollarocracy, the *New York Times* celebrated the establishment of "the first effective curbs in American political history on the influence of the rich in government."[1] A year later, over the veto of President Gerald Ford, the amended law was put into place. For a brief shining moment, it looked as if the United States might actually mark its bicentennial by finally realizing Thomas Jefferson's last hope for the republic: "that the mass of mankind has not been born with saddles on their backs, nor a favored few booted and spurred, ready to ride them legitimately, by the grace of God."[2]

Unfortunately, the U.S. Supreme Court, as it has so frequently throughout its history, rode in, "booted and spurred," to defend the Money Power. Before the bicentennial of 1976 and, more ominously, before the first presidential or congressional primary contest of that definitional political year, the court's landmark decision in the case of *Buckley v. Valeo*—which rejected federal limitations on campaign expenditures, on expenditures by a candidate from personal funds, and on independent expenditures by individuals and special-interest groups—began a dismantling of the law.[3] Over the next thirty-five years, at every critical turn, the Court would reverse and undermine effective curbs on the influence of the rich on the government of the United States.

How has money prevailed upon the electoral process? How has the United States ended up with what can only be described as a corrupt and corrupting election system? The answers to these questions are almost as depressing as the nature of the money-and-media election complex itself. The dramatic changes in the election system over the past forty years, which accelerated by 2012, did not result from the will of the people expressed through deliberation and debate by their elected representatives. Instead, the decisions were made by a sectlike group of highly partisan, unelected, and unaccountable judges. They declared bluntly and with relish that Americans do not have a constitutionally defined or protected right to vote. They routinely overthrew laws established by elected bodies to promote fair elections; in doing so, the Supreme Court singlehandedly rewrote election law in what is arguably the most overt, opportunistic, and brazen example of judicial activism in American history. We tell the story of democracy not just denied but assaulted in this chapter.

IT STARTED LONG BEFORE *CITIZENS UNITED*

It is the nature of explorations of political patterns to look for recent developments to explain a bad turn; as such, much attention has been and will be paid to the Supreme Court's dramatic decision in the 2010 case of *Citizens United v. FEC*. To be sure, the *Citizens United* case is a big deal, and we focus on it. But an honest examination of the current crisis must run deeper, to the late 1960s and early 1970s, when it seemed that a reform moment was at hand. And to the *Buckley v. Valeo* decision, which interrupted that moment. With its majority opinion gutting key elements of the Federal Election Campaign Act, the Supreme Court did not merely reject recently enacted limits on campaign contributions and expenditures. It asserted the fantasy that money is speech, declaring:

> The Act's contribution and expenditure limits operate in an area of the most fundamental First Amendment activities. Discussion of public issues and debate on the qualifications of candidates are integral to the operation of the system of government established by our Constitution. The First Amendment affords the broadest possible protection to such political expression in order to assure unfettered exchange of ideas for the bringing about of political and social changes desired by the people.[4]

Back in 1976, the Court offered a (soon-to-disappear) measure of deference to the view that First Amendment freedoms might be preserved in tandem with limits on individual contributions to political campaigns and candidates. After all, if the First Amendment could survive restriction against someone yelling "Fire" in a crowded theater, then it could survive with campaign rules and regulations that were broadly viewed as necessary to maintain the "integrity of our system of representative democracy." But the Court's interpretation of that word "integrity" was excruciatingly narrow. The Court did not recognize that removing all limits on campaign spending by the wealthy tipped the balance so that future election results could be bought, rather than won in contests of ideologies and partisanships. Rather, the "integrity" on which the majority was focused consisted merely of preventing the unscrupulous practice of wealthy donors delivering contributions in suitcases full of cash—rather than in envelopes containing checks.[5]

The Court was made up of veteran political players, such as William Rehnquist, an Arizona Republican Party operative who had served as a legal advisor and speechwriter for Barry Goldwater's 1964 Republican presidential campaign. Rehnquist's résumé included a controversial turn with the right-wing Operation Eagle Eye project, which set up "voter harassment teams" in the mid-1960s to challenge the citizenship, literacy, and ability of African American voters to interpret the U.S. Constitution. Rehnquist was a jurist who calculated not for the maintenance of representative democracy but for political advantage.[6]

This was what his political benefactors in the Nixon administration intended when they vetted him politically before his appointment to the High Court.[7] In 1971, when Rehnquist was being considered as a replacement for Justice John Marshall Harlan II, Henry Kissinger, Nixon's national security advisor, raised the issue. "Rehnquist is pretty far right, isn't he?" asked Kissinger. White House chief of staff H. R. Haldeman, whose crude political gaming earned him the moniker "the president's son-of-a-bitch," responded, "Oh, Christ! He's way to the right of Buchanan"—a reference to the most rigidly right-wing of Nixon's aides, Patrick J. Buchanan.[8]

Jurists often evolve during their tenures. This was the case with Rehnquist, who over time would grow increasingly ill at ease with the extremism favored by the corporate elite. In 1976, however, the Nixon appointee was determined to halt the tide of reform that had swept his benefactor from office—and that seemed in the aftermath of the Democratic sweep of 1974 congressional elections to be shifting the United States dramatically to the left.[9]

In the intense behind-the-scenes wrangling on the High Court over the *Buckley* case, Rehnquist argued with considerable success for the rejection of restrictions on "independent expenditures" on behalf of candidates and parties, of the limitation on expenditures by candidates from their own personal or family resources, and of the limitation on total campaign expenditures. The theory, pushed by Rehnquist, was that, even though individual contributions to candidates might foster corruption, free spending by the wealthy was protected speech. While others on the High Court were more cautious, Rehnquist threw down the money-is-speech gauntlet, arguing, "A restriction on the amount of money a person or group can spend on political communication during a campaign necessarily reduces the quantity of expression by restricting the number of issues discussed, the depth of their exploration, and the size of the audience reached."[10]

Even that was not enough for Chief Justice Warren Burger, who was so determined to overturn the entire campaign-finance reform enterprise that he dissented from the Court's decision, arguing that *any* limit on contributions— even those going directly to candidates—was at odds with the First Amendment.[11] Burger's extreme view, later adopted by future justices Antonin Scalia and Clarence Thomas, was mainstreamed in the years following the *Buckley v. Valeo* decision by Court rulings such as the 1978 *First National Bank of*

Boston v. Bellotti decision. Ruling in a case that arose after Massachusetts attempted to limit corporate campaign contributions, the Court's 5–4 decision in *Bellotti* effectively extended the money-is-speech protection to corporations, declaring that campaign spending could not be limited "simply because its source is a corporation."

This was too much even for Rehnquist, who argued that the whole notion of corporate personhood was "artificial," not "natural" in the sense that the founders had believed human beings were endowed with "natural rights." "A state grants to a business corporation the blessings of potentially perpetual life and limited liability to enhance its efficiency as an economic entity. It might reasonably be concluded that those properties, so beneficial in the economic sphere, pose special dangers in the political sphere. . . . Indeed, the states might reasonably fear that the corporation would use its economic power to obtain further benefits beyond those already bestowed," wrote Rehnquist, who observed a long history of state and federal limitation on the ability of corporations to participate in politics. He concluded, "The judgment of such a broad consensus of governmental bodies expressed over a period of many decades is entitled to considerable deference from this Court."[12]

Despite Rehnquist's wise counsel, that deference was not paid. A series of decisions, most of them little noted outside legal and campaign-finance circles, not only undid existing reforms but also erected barriers to future attempts to control the Money Power.

LEWIS POWELL'S MASTER MANIPULATION

The *Bellotti* ruling, which laid the formal groundwork for the *Citizens United* ruling thirty-two years later, was not written by Burger, however. The author, Lewis Franklin Powell Jr., was a jurist who aggressively promoted not just the legal fantasy of corporate personhood but also the remarkable political infrastructure that would come to assert corporate political power.[13]

Media assessments of Powell's tenure on the High Court frequently portrayed him as a centrist, and few journalists ever described him as an activist. But this view had everything to do with the narrow, frequently listless coverage of the Court, which usually begins and ends with discussions of so-called social issues, such as reproductive rights and protections for lesbians and gays.[14] However, when it came to using the Court to extend the reach of corporate power—in the workplace, the media, and politics—Powell was one of the most determined judicial activists in the history of the Supreme Court.[15]

A Virginia lawyer who made a national name for himself in the mid-1960s as the president of the American Bar Association, Powell specialized in corporate law. He served on the board of eleven major corporations, including Philip Morris, and became a legal point man for the tobacco industry in the 1960s, when the Federal Communications Commission (FCC) began cracking down on cigarette advertising on television and radio. After Congress approved the Public Health Cigarette Smoking Act in 1970, which banned advertising for cigarettes, it became increasingly clear to Powell that as the American political process opened up, and as democracy itself extended to include previously disenfranchised groups, corporations were having a harder time dominating the national agenda. It wasn't just that Ralph Nader—whom Powell derided in what he presumed were secret communications as "perhaps the single most effective antagonist of American business"[16]—was forcing the auto industry to make cars safer, or that liberal Senator Gaylord Nelson of Wisconsin was leading a crackdown on the abuses of the food and drug industries. Even Richard Nixon, who was supposed to be Wall Street's man in the White House, was signing landmark environmental legislation and, in the summer of 1970, using an executive order to create the Environmental Protection Agency.[17]

In 1971, after his tobacco industry clients had been banished from the all-powerful arena of TV advertising, where it had proven profoundly easy to create new generations of tobacco addicts, Powell pondered the political moment where the commercial interests of big business could be so thoroughly upended by regulators. He took two extraordinary steps. One was very public, the other very private. Together, they would redefine the politics and policy-making of America and provide the set of circumstances that led us to write this book.

In 1969, Powell had turned down Nixon's offer of a nomination to serve on the Supreme Court; Powell did not want the scrutiny, or presumably the pay cut, and his family was opposed to the move from Richmond to Washington. Yet less than two years later, as it became clear that two senior justices (Hugo Black and John Marshall Harlan) would be stepping down, Powell expressed his openness to being nominated. Nixon was thrilled; he desperately wanted to appoint southerners to the High Court, especially old-school southern Democrats like Powell, whose nomination would highlight the president's "southern strategy" of making what was once a "solid south" for the Democrats into a Republican stronghold. And Powell, who did not have a record as a judge and who had a reputation as a moderate, would easily pass muster with the American Bar Association he had so recently led. Nixon, himself a former corporate lawyer, dismissed suggestions that Powell at sixty-four was too old, declaring that "10 [years] of him is worth 30 of most."[18]

The Senate Judiciary Committee, which was grilling Nixon's other High Court nominee of the moment (Rehnquist), agreed. After what the *New York Times* described as a "friendly five hours" of questioning, most of which related to the multimillionaire Powell's arrangements to sell off his extensive portfolio of corporate stocks and bonds, his nomination was approved and sent to the full Senate. A month later, Powell was confirmed by an 89–1 vote. Senator Fred Harris of Oklahoma, a populist whose politics and rhetoric harkened back to the great struggles to rein in the robber barons, cast the sole opposing vote. Powell, complained Harris, was "an elitist" who "has never shown any deep feelings for little people."[19]

Fred Harris could not have known how very right he was.

Less than two months before President Nixon nominated him to serve on the Supreme Court, Powell completed the drafting of a confidential memorandum that, when its full contents were eventually revealed, would come to be known as "a corporate blueprint to dominate democracy"—to borrow a phrase from corporate watchdog Charlie Cray. Author Jeff Clements and Michael Waldman, the executive director of the Brennan Center for Justice at New York University's School of Law, would cite Powell's memo as an essential inspiration for the forty-year campaign to redefine the First Amendment as a "free-market" statement that treated corporate spin as the equal of speech by citizens.[20] Powell's memo was written in secret and delivered to his friend Eugene Sydnor Jr., a former Virginia legislator who chaired the education committee of the U.S. Chamber of Commerce. Sydnor would circulate the memorandum, titled "Attack on American Free Enterprise System," among the chamber's leadership immediately, as befit the sense of urgency underpinning a document that opened with a warning: "The American economic system is under broad attack" by consumer activists, environmentalists, civil rights campaigns, and labor unions engaged in a "frontal assault . . . on our government, our system of justice, and the free enterprise system."[21]

"There always have been some who opposed the American system, and preferred socialism or some form of statism (communism or fascism). Also, there always have been critics of the system, whose criticism has been wholesome and constructive so long as the objective was to improve rather than to subvert or destroy," Powell continued. "But what now concerns us is quite new in the history of America. We are not dealing with sporadic or isolated attacks from a relatively few extremists or even from the minority socialist cadre. Rather, the assault on the enterprise system is broadly based and consistently pursued. It is gaining momentum and converts." Note the word "us." Powell was identifying himself as a combatant, or at the very least a strategist, in what he hoped would be a counterattack by the most powerful corporations in the United States. His plan urged an across-the-board response "to the chorus of criticism . . . from perfectly respectable elements of society: from the college campus, the pulpit, the media, the intellectual and literary journals, the arts and sciences, and from politicians."

The corporate lawyer who would in just a matter of months don the robes of a Supreme Court justice did not hesitate to get into the down-and-dirty politics of identifying pressure points that the nation's business elites could attack. "The campuses from which much of the criticism emanates are supported by (i) tax funds generated largely from American business, and (ii) contributions from capital funds controlled or generated by American business. The boards of trustees of our universities overwhelmingly are composed of men and women who are leaders in the system," wrote Powell. "Most of the media, including the national TV systems, are owned and theoretically controlled by corporations which depend upon profits, and the enterprise system to survive."[22]

Bluntly declaring that corporations needed to get a whole lot more political, Powell argued:

> The first essential—a prerequisite to any effective action—is for businessmen to confront this problem as a primary responsibility of corporate management. The overriding first need is for businessmen to recognize that the ultimate issue may be survival—survival of what we call the free enterprise system, and all that this

means for the strength and prosperity of America and the freedom of our people. The day is long past when the chief executive officer of a major corporation discharges his responsibility by maintaining a satisfactory growth of profits, with due regard to the corporation's public and social responsibilities. If our system is to survive, top management must be equally concerned with protecting and preserving the system itself. This involves far more than an increased emphasis on "public relations" or "governmental affairs"—two areas in which corporations long have invested substantial sums. A significant first step by individual corporations could well be the designation of an executive vice president (ranking with other executive VP's) whose responsibility is to counter—on the broadest front— the attack on the enterprise system. The public relations department could be one of the foundations assigned to this executive, but his responsibilities should encompass some of the types of activities referred to subsequently in this memorandum. His budget and staff should be adequate to the task.[23]

Powell's proposal to position corporations as political players was only the beginning. He outlined plans to retake the academy, with proposals that corporations demand "equal time" on campuses and use their resources and influence to pressure colleges and universities to hire corporate-friendly professors. The campaigning, Powell wrote, must extend even into the nation's high schools. And into the media. The soon-to-be Supreme Court justice counseled:

> The national television networks should be monitored in the same way that textbooks should be kept under constant surveillance. This applies not merely to so-called educational programs (such as "Selling of the Pentagon"), but to the daily "news analysis" which so often includes the most insidious type of criticism of the enterprise system. Whether this criticism results from hostility or economic ignorance, the result is the gradual erosion of confidence in "business" and free enterprise. This monitoring, to be effective, would require constant examination of the texts of adequate samples of programs. Complaints—to the media and to the Federal Communications Commission—should be made promptly and strongly when programs are unfair or inaccurate. Equal time should be demanded when appropriate. Effort should be made to see that the forum-type programs (the Today Show, Meet the Press, etc.) afford at least as much opportunity for supporters of the American system to participate as these programs do for those who attack it.[24]

Ultimately, however, none of this would be sufficient, explained Powell. To reassert corporate power, the chamber and its members would need to enter what the soon-to-be justice referred to as "the neglected political arena." He advised:

In the final analysis, the payoff—short of revolution—is what government does. Business has been the favorite whipping-boy of many politicians for many years. But the measure of how far this has gone is perhaps best found in the anti-business views now being expressed by several leading candidates for President of the United States. It is still Marxist doctrine that the "capitalist" countries are controlled by big business. This doctrine, consistently a part of leftist propaganda all over the world, has a wide public following among Americans. . . .

Yet, as every business executive knows, few elements of American society today have as little influence in government as the American businessman, the corporation, or even the millions of corporate stockholders. If one doubts this, let him undertake the role of "lobbyist" for the business point of view before Congressional committees. The same situation obtains in the legislative halls of most states and major cities. One does not exaggerate to say that, in terms of political influence with respect to the course of legislation and government action, the American business executive is truly the "forgotten man."[25]

As implausible as that construction was at the time, and as manifestly absurd as it is today, Powell's assessment struck a chord with the board of the chamber, which discussed his memorandum in detail a day after Powell delivered it. The board quickly appointed executives of ABC and CBS (ironically, stewards of the so-called liberal media), Amway, General Electric, General Motors, Phillips Petroleum, 3M, and U.S. Steel to a task force that would develop strategies for implementing the Powell plan within the apparatus of the Chamber of Commerce and far beyond its headquarters in Washington, DC. Central to the project was a recognition that, while "the educational programs" outlined in the memorandum would

enlighten public thinking . . . one should not postpone more direct political action, while awaiting the gradual change in public opinion to be effected through education and information. Business must learn the lesson, long ago learned by labor and other self-interest groups. This is the lesson that political power is necessary; that such power must be assiduously [sic] cultivated; and that when necessary, it must be used aggressively and with determination—without embarrassment and without the reluctance which has been so characteristic of American business.

"As unwelcome as it may be to the Chamber," Powell concluded, "it should consider assuming a broader and more vigorous role in the political arena."[26]

Powell was not the first conservative to make a case for development of concerted, long-term strategies for challenging liberal elites. Barry Goldwater had run for the presidency in 1964 as a sworn foe of "the eastern liberal establishment," and conservative writer M. Stanton Evans published *The Liberal Establishment: Who Runs America . . . and How* in 1965.[27] But Powell, with his legal acumen and combination of corporate and political connections, was able to convince CEOs who dismissed right-wing ideologues.[28] A Democrat who would be appointed to the High Court by a Republican, he did not speak to the corporate class as a partisan. He spoke as a member of the inner circle. And he was convincing—so convincing that, in the words of political scientists, he inspired the most powerful economic players in the nation to unleash "a domestic version of Shock and Awe."[29]

The chamber's members "heard" Powell in a way that it had not heard others preaching that corporations needed to step up when it came to producing propaganda and political outcomes. Barely noted as a political player in 1970, and still inclined at that time toward a bipartisanship that emphasized connections to both major parties, the U.S. Chamber of Commerce would transform itself into a political machine over the next forty years. In the late 1960s, the Chamber of Commerce had named Ralph Nader to its list of "outstanding young men."[30] It convened a series of local meetings around the nation between businesses and consumers to address areas of consumer discontent.[31] When a team of Nader's activists produced a widely publicized report in January 1969 critical of how feebly the Federal Trade Commission operated and how subservient it was to business, the chamber and much of the business community responded with "mild admissions of culpability and the need for responsible business practices."[32] Those days and that approach were quickly put in the rearview mirror and forgotten. The time for peaceful negotiation was over; it was war.

Lewis Powell was a learned man who, after receiving his law degree from Washington and Lee University, went on to obtain his master's degree from Harvard Law School. It is doubtful that he was familiar with Edward Ryan's 1873 warning about "the enterprises of the country . . . aggregating vast corporate combinations of unexampled capital, boldly marching, not for economic conquest only, but for political power."[33] But Powell's 1971 memo outlined a plan for exactly the march Ryan anticipated. Indeed, any definition of "irony" should have as its example the fact that precisely a century after Ryan spoke, the U.S. Chamber of Commerce was putting the finishing touches on a program of political and educational engagement designed to realize the full promise of the Powell memo. The chamber would triple its budget over the next six years as an infrastructure of procorporate think tanks and advocacy groups took shape.[34]

VAST RIGHT-WING NETWORKS WITH CORPORATE CLOUT

Frequently cited as "the inspiration" for the remaking of the foundations of old right-wing families—the Coors, the Olins, the Bradleys, the Scaifes, the Kochs—as new-right political powerhouses, the Powell memo made the case for the recommitment of resources that would usher into existence in 1973 the Heritage Foundation and the American Legislative Exchange Council, which framed the conservative agenda in the form of proposed bills and resolutions at the national and state levels.[35] Then came the ramping up of Accuracy in Media, after Richard Mellon Scaife, an heir to the banking fortune associated with his middle name, began to pour money into the group in 1977. The Cato Institute formed in 1977. The Manhattan Institute came into being in 1978. In 1982, the Federalist Society began to take shape as a force for countering a perceived "liberal bias" in the nation's law schools; it would eventually become one of the most potent forces in defining the nation's judiciary, encouraging the rise of members such as Chief Justice John Roberts and Justices Antonin Scalia and Samuel Alito.[36]

There was more: the Koch-brothers-funded Citizens for a Sound Economy (which would eventually evolve into the defining force behind the supposedly grassroots Tea Party movement, Americans for Prosperity) swung into operation in 1984. In 1985, Accuracy in Academia, a group that channeled Powell's proposal not just for "educational programs" but also for a relentless assault on academics who did not follow the corporate line, was created. Two years later, the American Tort Reform Association stepped into the fray and began to establish a nationwide network of state-based liability "reform" coalitions that have succeeded in dramatically undermining the constitutionally protected right to petition for the redress of grievances in civil courts. And in 1987, there arrived the Media Research Center, which channeled conservative Bradley, Olin, and Scaife foundation money into the Powell-inspired project of proving "through sound scientific research—that liberal bias in the media does exist and undermines traditional American values" and moving to "neutralize its impact on the American political scene."[37]

But the whole point of all these exercises was to reshape the political system so that it would be far less likely to generate policies contrary to the interests of large corporations and wealthy investors. Following the Powell memo, corporate political action committee spending on congressional races increased "nearly fivefold" during the late 1970s and early 1980s.[38] But even more importantly, Powell argued that corporate America needed to forcefully enter and dominate the political process—a crucial idea the chamber and its members embraced. In 1971, according to David Vogel, only 175 U.S. corporations had registered lobbyists in Washington, DC. A decade later, there were 2,500. By the mid-1970s, most of the industrial trade associations not already located in Washington had moved there. The key to trade association hires became knowing politics rather than knowing the industry the group represented.[39] In the late 1960s, there were about 100 corporate public affairs offices in Washington; by 1978, there were more than 500.[40]

A whole industry was born of lobbying shops, primarily serving corporate clients, to such an extent that the term K Street came to symbolize an industry in a manner similar to Wall Street or Madison Avenue. Suddenly, Washington and especially Capitol Hill were crawling with tens of thousands of very-well-paid representatives of industry trade associations and specific corporations or the lobbying firms that served them.

Where did corporate America find talented people who could greatly influence members of Congress and maneuver effectively around regulatory agencies? Former government employees—regulatory agency personnel and congressional aides and the like—provided a tried-and-true supply of labor, and there was a longstanding tradition of the "revolving door" already in place. But for the big job of dominating the commanding heights of Congress, corporate America needed middle-of-the-order home-run hitters. Where better to find people who could influence Congress than Congress itself? *In the early 1970s, 3 percent of retiring members became lobbyists; that quickly changed, and by 2012 the figure had grown to the 50 percent range.*[41] The annual incomes for these postcongressional jobs generally start at mid six figures and are not infrequently seven figures. The days of stepping down from Congress and taking a college teaching job or just simply retiring were over. "The dirty secret of American politics," the Roosevelt Institute's Matt Stoller noted, "is that, for most politicians, getting elected is just not that important—what matters is post-election employment."[42]

"Corporate headhunters are sizing up the K Street prospects of the retiring members of the 112th Congress," *The Hill* reported in 2012, "and they like what they see." "We are doing a mock draft with some of our clients," Ivan Adler, a principal at K Street's McCormick Group, said. "As a retiring class goes, this is a valuable class. A lot of these members are marketable and will be welcomed by K Street with open arms." The going rate for former senators in 2012 was between $800,000 and $1.5 million in annual salary; for ex-House members the range was between $300,000 and $600,000.[43]

Of course, to be eligible for this lucrative life, members have to prove while in Congress that they are willing to advance industry's agenda. This provides powerful implicit incentives for them to embrace specific priorities and to temper their criticisms of specific interests; if members play their cards right, they can cash in serious chips in their next job. This calculus applies, we regret to say, across lines of partisanship and ideology. Sure, someone as principled as Dennis Kucinich on the antiwar left or Ron Paul on the libertarian right might be immune to the pressures. But liberal partisans who imagine that only conservative corporatists cash in are fooling themselves. When Connecticut liberal Democrat Chris Dodd left the Senate in 2011 after five terms, he was recruited by ten firms before he finally accepted a $1.5 million annual salary to run the motion picture industry lobby in Washington.[44]

In the process of building up their lobbying armada, corporations and trade associations changed the way members of Congress regarded their own careers and injected the concerns, needs, and dictates of big business into the bone marrow of government, regardless of the party in power, as never before. Politicians did not always need to be pressured to vote against the interests of their constituents; they could simply be encouraged to watch out for themselves—and for the lucrative payouts available at the end of legislative careers. If the whole point of Powell's memo had been to get corporations focused on the work of influencing the people who make up the government, the K Street hiring hall became a key part of the process. Barely a year after the soon-to-be jurist had argued that "business must learn the lesson . . . that political power is necessary; that such power must be assiduously cultivated; and that when necessary, it must be used aggressively and with determination," the National Association of Manufacturers responded as directed with an announcement that it was decamping from Manhattan to

Washington: "We have been in New York since before the turn of the century, because we regarded this city as the center of business and industry. But the thing that affects business most today is government. The interrelationship of business with business is no longer so important as the interrelationship of business with government. In the last several years, that has become very apparent to us."[45]

This "K Street" carrot has served Dollarocracy well for decades, and in the new post–*Citizens United* era it has taken on a new dimension. Republican governors like Scott Walker in Wisconsin, Rick Snyder in Michigan, and Rick Scott in Florida no longer need to concern themselves with the popularity of a particular policy—say, eliminating collective bargaining rights for workers— as they toss out decades of legal precedent and practice to create a brave new world. They have no incentive to compromise with Democrats or the few remaining "moderates" in their own party. They know that mega–campaign donors—Sheldon Adelson, the Koch brothers, and countless others—will provide unlimited funds for the next election if they place the demands of those donors ahead of the interests of their constituents. Moreover, even if they might lose reelection, politicians of modest means, like Walker, are well aware that they are the new "made men" of Dollarocracy. They can rest assured that they will always be taken care with high six- and seven-figure incomes in the heavily financed world of right-wing think tanks, institutes, and lobbying groups for the rest of their working lives. Serving Big Money never stops paying off big, as Senator Jim DeMint of South Carolina learned when he leapt in late 2012 from the Capitol, where he earned $175,000 a year, to the other side of Capitol Hill, where he would earn more than $1 million annually as the new head of the Heritage Foundation.[46]

Looking backward, we can easily recognize the outlines of Powell's project and its trajectory. But that was not the case when it mattered. While Powell was busy circulating his memorandum with CEOs and wealthy political donors even as his Supreme Court confirmation hearing approached, he did not bother to share the document with members of the Senate Judiciary Committee or the full Senate. A year after Powell's confirmation, his memorandum was leaked to syndicated columnist Jack Anderson, who wrote a series of articles in which he suggested that the justice "might use his position on the Supreme Court to put his ideas into practice . . . in behalf of business interests."[47]

Anderson's suggestion was hardly unreasonable. In the document that Powell had neglected to share with senators was a section that argued:

> American business and the enterprise system have been affected as much by the courts as by the executive and legislative branches of government. Under our constitutional system, especially with an activist-minded Supreme Court, the judiciary may be the most important instrument for social, economic and political change. Other organizations and groups, recognizing this, have been far more astute in exploiting judicial action than American business. Perhaps the most active exploiters of the judicial system have been groups ranging in political orientation from "liberal" to the far left. The American Civil Liberties Union is one example. It initiates or intervenes in scores of cases each year, and it files briefs amicus curiae in the Supreme Court in a number of cases during each term of that court. Labor unions, civil rights groups and now the public interest law firms are extremely active in the judicial arena. Their success, often at business' expense, has not been inconsequential. This is a vast area of opportunity for the Chamber, if it is willing to undertake the role of spokesman for American business and if, in turn, business is willing to provide the funds. As with respect to scholars and speakers, the Chamber would need a highly competent staff of lawyers. In special situations it should be authorized to engage, to appear as counsel amicus in the Supreme Court, lawyers of national standing and reputation. The greatest care should be exercised in selecting the cases in which to participate, or the suits to institute. But the opportunity merits the necessary effort.[48]

Just think what could happen if the chamber had a friend, a really good friend, on the Court.

On January 6, 1972, less than five months after he explained "the vast area of opportunity for the Chamber" were it to engage more actively with the courts, corporate lawyer Lewis Powell became Justice of the Supreme Court Lewis Powell. Three years later, his votes would begin the shredding of the Federal Election Campaign Act, with the *Buckley v. Valeo* decision, a ruling political philosopher John Rawls, a great defender of political fairness and democracy, warned "runs the risk of endorsing the view that fair representation is representation according to the amount of influence effectively exerted."[49]

Powell took that risk in 1978 when he stepped forward to write the opinion in the *First National Bank of Boston v. Bellotti* case, which struck down a Massachusetts law that gave corporations broad leeway to spend money on issues "materially affecting" their own operations, but that limited the ability of corporations to spend freely to achieve political goals. The state's attorney general, Francis X. Bellotti, used the law to challenge efforts by banks to influence the outcome of a 1976 referendum on establishing a graduated tax on the income of individuals.

Bellotti argued that the banks were overstepping their bounds, and lower courts agreed with him. But Powell led a Supreme Court majority that effectively dismissed any debate about whether corporations enjoy the same rights as citizens. "The proper question therefore is not whether corporations 'have' First Amendment rights and, if so, whether they are coextensive with those of natural persons," wrote Powell. "Instead, the question must be whether [the statute] abridges expression that the First Amendment was meant to protect. We hold that it does."[50]

Asserting the right of corporations to spend as they choose to achieve political ends, the former corporate lawyer who had encouraged corporations to engage in politics explained that the Court majority could

> find no support in the First or Fourteenth Amendment, or in the decisions of this Court, for the proposition that speech that otherwise would be within the protection of the First Amendment loses that protection simply because its source is a corporation that cannot prove, to the satisfaction of a court, a material effect on its business or property. The "materially affecting" requirement is not an identification of the boundaries of corporate speech etched by the Constitution itself. Rather, it amounts to an impermissible legislative prohibition of speech based on the identity of the interests that spokesmen may represent in public debate over controversial issues and a requirement that the speaker have a sufficiently great interest in the subject to justify communication.[51]

Powell was making a case for corporate speech that suggested it was protected at least in part because citizens needed input from multinational corporations when deciding whether to fund after-school programs or repair potholes on Main Street. But what if the corporations, with their access to vast amounts of money, did not merely provide information but instead overwhelmed the electoral process in a way that might dictate results?

Powell had an answer for that concern. "Appellee advances a number of arguments in support of his view that these interests are endangered by corporate participation in discussion of a referendum issue," the justice wrote.

> They hinge upon the assumption that such participation would exert an undue influence on the outcome of a referendum vote, and—in the end—destroy the

confidence of the people in the democratic process and the integrity of government. According to appellee, corporations are wealthy and powerful and their views may drown out other points of view. If appellee's arguments were supported by record or legislative findings that corporate advocacy threatened imminently to undermine democratic processes, thereby denigrating rather than serving First Amendment interests, these arguments would merit our consideration. . . . But there has been no showing that the relative voice of corporations has been overwhelming or even significant in influencing referenda in Massachusetts, or that there has been any threat to the confidence of the citizenry in government.[52]

"THE POLITICAL ACTIVITY OF BUSINESS CORPORATIONS"

Three decades later, the people themselves say that they have lost confidence in the democratic process and the integrity of government. This view emerges in poll after poll, in election results that evidence a desperation for fundamental change, and in rapid growth of popular movements on the right and the left. Citizens are taking to the streets to express frustration and fury with a system in which political corruption plays a "major role" in the nation's economic distress, according to 82 percent of Americans surveyed. Long before the rise of the Occupy Wall Street movement, 85 percent of voters surveyed told Hart Research pollsters that corporations have too much influence over the political process. In that same 2010 survey, 93 percent of Americans questioned said average citizens have too little influence.[53]

Yet far from embracing Powell's suggestion that threats to democracy would merit reconsideration of the role of corporate money in politics, the Supreme Court has moved beyond Powell and far, far beyond William Rehnquist, who in his 1978 dissent from the *Bellotti* decision wrote:

The question presented today, whether business corporations have a constitutionally protected liberty to engage in political activities, has never been squarely addressed by any previous decision of this Court. However, the General Court of the Commonwealth of Massachusetts, the Congress of the United States, and the legislatures of 30 other States of this Republic have considered the matter, and have concluded that restrictions upon the political activity of business corporations are both politically desirable and constitutionally permissible. The judgment of such a broad consensus of governmental bodies expressed over a period of many decades is entitled to considerable deference from this Court. I think it quite probable that their judgment may properly be reconciled with our controlling precedents, but I am certain that under my views of the limited application of the

First Amendment to the States, which I share with the two immediately preceding occupants of my seat on the Court, but not with my present colleagues, the judgment of the Supreme Judicial Court of Massachusetts should be affirmed.[54]

"Early in our history," noted Rehnquist, "Mr. Chief Justice Marshall described the status of a corporation in the eyes of federal law: 'A corporation is an artificial being, invisible, intangible, and existing only in contemplation of law. Being the mere creature of law, it possesses only those properties which the charter of creation confers upon it, either expressly, or as incidental to its very existence. These are such as are supposed best calculated to effect the object for which it was created.'"

Rehnquist held to the view that "it cannot be disputed that the mere creation of a corporation does not invest it with all the liberties enjoyed by natural persons," and he argued further that limiting the role corporations play in politics is a desirable goal. "A State grants to a business corporation the blessings of potentially perpetual life and limited liability to enhance its efficiency as an economic entity. It might reasonably be concluded that those properties, so beneficial in the economic sphere, pose special dangers in the political sphere," explained Rehnquist.

> Furthermore, it might be argued that liberties of political expression are not at all necessary to effectuate the purposes for which States permit commercial corporations to exist. So long as the Judicial Branches of the State and Federal Governments remain open to protect the corporation's interest in its property, it has no need, though it may have the desire, to petition the political branches for similar protection. Indeed, the States might reasonably fear that the corporation would use its economic power to obtain further benefits beyond those already bestowed. I would think that any particular form of organization upon which the State confers special privileges or immunities different from those of natural persons would be subject to like regulation, whether the organization is a labor union, a partnership, a trade association, or a corporation.[55]

Rehnquist was an old-school conservative, as opposed to a corporatist, and we recount his thinking at length because it is vital to recognize that there is no simple liberal-versus-conservative split over campaign-finance issues. The debate over how to control or unleash the Money Power is not a battle of ideas. The calculus, as Texas populist Jim Hightower told us, "isn't about left versus right; it's about top versus bottom." Rehnquist, with his roots in Barry

Goldwater's Arizona and Barry Goldwater's movement, believed that right-wing ideas would prevail in a fair fight, and we hope there are still many conservatives like him.[56]

Rehnquist was a flawed champion, to be sure. But after his nomination by Ronald Reagan in 1986 to serve as the sixteenth chief justice of the U.S. Supreme Court, he would maintain an imperfect but real balance when it came to the regulation of campaign spending. Powell, who left the High Court in 1987, had succeeded with the *Bellotti* decision in extending the reach of corporations into the political sphere. But *Bellotti* dealt with a narrow question of spending on referendums, and despite Powell's attempt to define the issue more broadly, there was a caution during the Rehnquist era about reopening the broader question of whether money really equals speech.

With the replacement of Rehnquist in 2005 by John Roberts, the balance was tipped toward Wall Street. Roberts, a corporate lawyer with a background as a hyperideological member of the steering committee of the Washington, DC, chapter of the conservative Federalist Society, was a committed partisan who had traveled to Tallahassee, Florida, following the 2000 election to advise Governor Jeb Bush on how to manage the recount process that would eventually make Jeb's brother the president. Roberts was appointed by George W. Bush first to the District of Columbia Circuit of the United States Court of Appeals in 2003 and then two years later to the most powerful judicial post in the land.[57]

When it came to questions of corporations and politics, Roberts would not follow in Rehnquist's tradition. Roberts was a Lewis Powell man, and then some. "Almost from the moment Chief Justice John G. Roberts Jr. joined the bench five years ago," observed the *Washington Post* in 2010, "the court's conservatives have acted systematically on their deep skepticism of campaign spending restrictions. They have repeatedly questioned the ability of Congress to regulate the role of wealth and special interest involvement in elections without offending the First Amendment guarantee of unfettered political speech."[58]

Under Roberts's leadership, the High Court would implement what the *Post* described as "game-changing decisions on campaign finance reform."[59] On paper, and in practice, that is true. Roberts's manipulations to position the Court as not merely a defender but also a champion of corporate influence in politics were every bit as unseemly as Powell's, and far more aggressive. They began immediately with interventions such as the Court's ruling in the 2007 case of *Federal Election Commission v. Wisconsin Right to Life,* which Nate Persily, director of the Center for Law and Politics at Columbia Law School, argues with some validity "opened [the] floodgates" by eliminating restrictions on the airing of so-called issue ads during the peak campaigning seasons before primary and general elections.[60]

It became clear very early in Roberts's tenure as chief justice that he had his eye out for the case that would give the Court an opportunity to overturn any remaining rules governing advertising by groups that—because they were supposedly commenting on issues rather than campaigns—could steer corporate money into the thick of election fights. And, ultimately, to do a whole lot more.

Roberts found his opening with a case involving a relatively obscure right-wing group known as Citizens United, which nurtured a scorching disdain for former president Bill Clinton and Senator Hillary Rodham Clinton—along with the United Nations, the American Civil Liberties Union, and filmmaker Michael Moore, to name but a few Citizens United "targets." As Hillary Clinton prepared to bid for the 2008 Democratic presidential nomination, Citizens United produced a "documentary" titled *Hillary: The Movie,* which it sought to promote with Clinton-bashing television commercials. There was never any real doubt about what was going on. The commercials, which were aggressively anti-Clinton, were set to air on television stations in states that were key to her presidential candidacy. The U.S. District Court for the District of Columbia recognized as much, ruling in January 2008 that the commercials violated provisions of the McCain-Feingold Bipartisan Campaign Reform Act of 2002. Specifically, the court held that the supposedly nonpartisan commercials represented precisely the sort of "electioneering communications" that McCain-Feingold barred thirty days before primaries.[61]

This was the opportunity Roberts had been looking for. The Supreme Court grabbed the case. But after the oral argument on March 24, 2009, proved to be too narrow in the view of the more activist of the justices, the High Court issued an order directing that the case be reargued on September 9 of that year. Justice John Paul Stevens, the senior member of the Court, recognized that something untoward was afoot. He noted that the Court could easily have decided the case along the narrow grounds that both parties had argued it; instead, he would eventually charge, Roberts and his allies "changed the case to give themselves an opportunity to change the law."[62] Stevens's blunt assessment was correct. By January 2010, it was clear the Court was going to make a dramatic decision. And so it did, holding that legal prohibitions on independent expenditures by corporations, associations, and unions were, in any meaningful sense, invalid and could not be applied to spending of the sort that *Citizens United* had engaged in.[63]

Justice Anthony Kennedy, a Reagan appointee who replaced Lewis Powell, wrote the opinion for the five justices who formed the majority, arguing, "If the First Amendment has any force, it prohibits Congress from fining or jailing citizens, or associations of citizens, for simply engaging in political speech." But it was Chief Justice Roberts, obviously concerned about the judicial activism on display, who attempted to defend the ruling's rejection of a century of lawmaking and judicial rulings—of virtually all precedent, save that of Powell's rulings in the 1970s—on the grounds that "there is a difference between judicial restraint and judicial abdication." Effectively, Roberts was claiming that there was an urgent need for the Court to go even further than the lawyers for Citizens United had initially argued—or imagined.[64]

Justice Stevens, who was joined by Justices Ruth Bader Ginsburg, Stephen Breyer, and Sonia Sotomayor, not only wrote but also read aloud from the bench a ninety-page dissent. "At bottom," argued the eighty-nine-year-old jurist,

> the Court's opinion is thus a rejection of the common sense of the American people, who have recognized a need to prevent corporations from undermining self-government since the founding, and who have fought against the distinctive corrupting potential of corporate electioneering since the days of Theodore Roosevelt. It is a strange time to repudiate that common sense. While American democracy is imperfect, few outside the majority of this Court would have thought its flaws included a dearth of corporate money in politics.[65]

Stevens, who had joined the court thirty-five years earlier as a Republican appointee, warned that the *Citizens United* ruling "threatens to undermine the integrity of elected institutions across the Nation." He would be proven right with all the immediacy and force of the political moment *and* the media moment in which we live.

A flurry of initial speculation by media pundits—especially cynical conservatives who rather liked their prospects in the new political order, but even from some liberals who apparently needed to confirm that they really did not "get it"—advanced "much ado about nothing" defenses of the Court's majority's activism. They tried to foster the fantasy that corporations and unions were equally matched players on the field of political battle, that corporations didn't really want to spend money to achieve political ends, and that CEOs and their lawyers would be cautious about leaping into the political fray. "With last week's ruling, the justices granted corporations (and implicitly unions) a constitutional license to explicitly urge voters to support or oppose candidates in all communications, while interring the remains of the McCain-Feingold restrictions on ads," mused Stephen Weissman in the *Los Angeles Times*. "Yet this decision is unlikely to change the political situation on the ground very much."[66]

In fact, it would change things a lot. Before the year was done, the prominent political player who most passionately embraced the new politics of the *Citizens United* era, Karl Rove, was celebrating victories that were beyond the wildest imagination of Lewis Powell. Rove's Republicans had been badly beaten in the congressional races of 2006 and 2008, losing the Senate and House to the Democrats, but they stormed back, narrowing the Democratic majority in the Senate and retaking the House with a 63-seat gain—their biggest pick-up in seventy-two years.[67] Rove's decision to take immediate advantage of the opening created by the *Citizens United* ruling paid off handsomely. Of 53 competitive House districts where Rove and his compatriots backed Republicans with "independent" expenditures that exceeded those made on behalf of Democrats—often by more than $1 million per district, according to Public Citizen—the Republicans won 51. Roughly three-quarters of all GOP House gains came in districts where independent expenditures by groups like the Chamber of Commerce and Rove's American Crossroads gave to Republican candidates, some of them virtual unknowns until the outside money flowed in, dramatic advantages. American Crossroads wasn't resting on its laurels, however, "It's a bigger prize in 2012, and that's changing the White House," said Robert Duncan, a Rove lieutenant at American Crossroads. "We've planted the flag for permanence, and we believe we will play a major role for 2012."[68]

John Roberts's Supreme Court was making sure of that.

Even as the term *"Citizens United"* came to be understood as the shorthand phrase for massive judicial intervention in the political process, the chief justice and his allies were still busy legislating from the bench. Very busy.

SILENCING DISSENT

In the summer of 2012, the Court kicked the legs out from under the unions.

Traditionally, major corporations and major unions have both sought maximum flexibility when it comes to political spending. Much of the media has covered corporations and unions as equal players. That was never really the case. And it was even less so in 2012. Corporations, freed by the Court to spend as much as they chose from their treasuries on political campaigns, had much more money at their disposal than the unions.[69] One investment house, Goldman Sachs, spends more annually to pay just its top employees than the combined available assets of the nation's major unions. Indeed, as RoseAnn DeMoro, the savvy executive director of the National Nurses United union, said, "Equating what unions and working people could spend on campaigns (as compared to corporations) would be like comparing a toy boat to an aircraft carrier. Corporate influence peddling in politics already distorts and prevents our democracy and political system [from functioning]."[70]

But the Roberts Court was not satisfied just to empower corporations. The majority was determined to make it a good deal harder for unions to work on political issues with the people they represent—especially nonmembers in organized workplaces—and to support candidates and mount campaigns.

In a barely noted June 2012 ruling in the case of *Knox v. Service Employees International Union (SEIU) Local 1000,* the High Court's hyperpartisan, hyperactivist majority—Roberts and Associate Justices Antonin Scalia, Anthony Kennedy, Clarence Thomas, and Samuel A. Alito—moved to restrict the flexibility of unions in election fights. Unions that represent large numbers of workers often establish political structures so that they can move quickly to address unexpected electoral and public policy threats; these structures usually involve gaining advance permission from represented workers to act on their behalf. The ruling—in a California case where a public-sector local of the Service Employees had made a special dues assessment in order to fund a fight to preserve collective bargaining rights[71]—took away much of that flexibility and imposed cumbersome new bureaucratic demands on organized labor groups seeking to raise their voices in the public sphere. Indeed, the ruling was so sweeping in its assault on the ability of unions to represent their members, so adventurous in its politics, that Justice Sonia Sotomayor (joined by Justice Ruth Bader Ginsburg), objected. She asserted, "I cannot agree with the majority's decision to address unnecessarily significant constitutional issues well outside the scope of the questions presented and briefing. By doing so, the majority breaks our own rules and, more importantly, disregards principles of judicial restraint that define the Court's proper role in our system of separated powers."[72]

Justice Sotomayor fretted about the Court creating a "new world of fee collection" that is ill defined and that will necessarily have an impact on all workers, members and nonmembers, represented by a union. She was right to worry. Justice Alito explicitly rejected definitions of political work by unions that is directly related to the protection of worker pay, benefits, and rights and to the maintenance of collective bargaining:

> Public-employee salaries, pensions, and other benefits constitute a substantial percentage of the budgets of many states and their subdivisions. As a result, a broad array of ballot questions and campaigns for public office may be said to have an effect on present and future contracts between public-sector workers and their employers. If the concept of "germaneness" were as broad as the SEIU advocates, public-sector employees who do not endorse the unions' goals would be essentially unprotected against being compelled to subsidize political and ideological activities to which they object.[73]

But aren't fights over salaries, pensions, and other benefits, as well as the ongoing ability of a union to fight on behalf of represented workers, germane to those workers—whether they are union members or not? The court said no. What would happen, however, if its standard were applied to the corporations that, with the *Citizens United* ruling and related decisions, the Court has done so much to empower politically? Corporations do not currently have to seek the approval of stockholders to direct money into political campaigns. Indeed, shareholders get far less communication from corporations about political activity than union members or represented nonmembers get from their unions. And, in most unions, workers have far more say about political choices than do shareholders. So what if the Court were to say that shareholders had to affirmatively approve corporate expenditures on behalf of candidates, parties, or ballot measures?

Let's go a step further. Millions of Americans own pieces of corporations through pension plans, investment funds, and other vehicles that hold stock. Yet these Americans get no information from corporations about political activities. What if the Court were to require corporations to get affirmative approval from these owners? Or even from the managers of pension plans or funds? Corporate CEOs and their amen corner in the media would scream about the "bureaucratic nightmare" imposed on them by the Court, and their lawyers would portray it as an infringement of their free speech "rights." Yet a court that had spent much of the previous decade removing barriers to corporate "speech" imposed just such a bureaucratic nightmare burden on unions.

"[This] Supreme Court says you cannot do anything to hamper the First Amendment rights of corporations," argued AFL-CIO president Richard Trumka following the issuance of the *Knox* decision. "But when it comes to workers, they haven't seen a detriment to the First Amendment that they haven't liked yet." Trumka had figured out how this game was going to be played.

The Roberts majority on the Supreme Court does not operate as a referee. The chief justice has a side in this fight, as do the justices who have aligned with him.

The U.S. Supreme Court may still retain some familiarity with the Constitution when it comes to deciding the nuances of cases involving immigration policy or lifetime incarceration or even health care financing. But when it comes to handing off control of American democracy to corporations, this is now Lewis Powell's Court. It can, and will, reject the intents of the founders and more than a century of case law to assure that CEOs have the upper hand in American politics.

Make no mistake: this is not a "free speech" or a "freedom of association" stance by the Court's Republican majority. Roberts and his colleagues are narrowing the range of debate. They are picking winners. The same Court that in January 2010 ruled with the *Citizens United* decision that corporations can spend freely in federal elections—enjoying the same avenues of expression as human beings—has been meticulous about extending the reach of that decision. It did so by restricting the ability of unions to try countering corporate spending. And, even more ominously, it did so by barring states from even trying to level the political playing field. States like Montana.

Within days of the Court's clampdown on unions, it determined that states would no longer have the ability to guard against what historically has been seen as political corruption and the buying of elections. The Court's June 25, 2012, ruling in a case dealing with the Montana law Burton K. Wheeler and his colleagues had enacted a century before, *American Tradition Partnership v. Bullock* (which we discuss in Chapter 1), was little noticed amid the intense focus on the Court's June 28, 2012, ruling on the constitutionality of health care reforms contained in the federal Affordable Care Act. On hearing the Supreme Court had agreed to take the case, the *New York Times* hoped the move would mean the Court had come to its senses and would reject the flawed logic of the *Citizens United* decision: "A factual record would show unlimited independent expenditures can have a corrupting effect, without qualifying as quid-pro-quo bribery. It's hard to see how the court's conservative majority could contend that these expenditures pose no threat to American democracy."[74]

No such luck. Instead, the 5–4 decision on the Montana matter has the potential to be every bit as definitional.[75]

The Court significantly expanded the scope and reach of the *Citizens United* ruling by summarily striking down state limits on corporate spending in state and local elections. "The question presented in this case is whether the holding of *Citizens United* applies to the Montana state law," the majority wrote. "There can be no serious doubt that it does." Translation: if Exxon Mobil wants to spend $10 million to support a favored candidate in a state legislative or city council race that might decide whether the corporation is regulated, or whether it gets new drilling rights, it can. But why stop at $10 million? If it costs $100 million to shout down the opposition, the Court says that is fine. If it costs $1 billion, that's fine, too.

What of the opposition? Can groups that represent the public interest push back? Can labor unions take a stand in favor of taxing corporations like Exxon Mobil? Not with the same freedom or flexibility that they had from the 1930s until 2012. The Court's ruling in the *Knox* case, establishing a requirement that unions get affirmative approval from workers they represent before making dues assessments to fund campaigns countering immediate threats to the livelihoods and security of those members, made sure of that.

How might it work? If Wal-Mart wanted to support candidates who promised to eliminate all state or local taxes for Wal-Mart, the corporation could spend unlimited amounts of money to do so. It would not need to gain stockholder approval. It could, the Court has confirmed, just go for it.

But if a public-employee union such as the American Federation of State, County, and Municipal Employees wants to counter Wal-Mart's argument by saying that eliminating taxes on out-of-state retailers will save consumers very little but ultimately will undermine funding for schools and public services, the union will have to go through the laborious process of gaining permission from tens of thousands, perhaps hundreds of thousands, of workers. And even then, the union will face additional reporting and structural barriers imposed by the Court.

Prior to the ruling in the Montana case, campaign-finance reformers had held out hope that states might be able to apply some restrictions on corporate spending, as Montana did with its one-hundred-year-old law barring direct corporate contributions to political parties and candidates. That law, developed to prevent the outright buying of elections by "copper kings" and "robber barons," was repeatedly upheld by jurists. In the very case that the U.S. Supreme Court considered, the Montana Supreme Court had warned that overturning restrictions on corporate spending would create a circumstance where "candidates and the public will become mere bystanders in elections."[76]

That was the point of the 1912 law. Well understood. And well maintained. Until June 2012.

With the Montana law's rejection by the Roberts court, said Marc Elias, one of the nation's top experts in election law, "to the extent that there was any doubt from the original *Citizens United* decision [that it] broadly applies to state and local laws, that doubt is now gone. . . . To whatever extent that door was open a crack, that door is now closed."[77]

The man who held the Montana Senate seat from which Burton K. Wheeler had once decried the Money Power explained to the Senate what the ruling meant. "At the turn of the last century, one of the world's wealthiest men literally bought himself a seat in the U.S. Senate. His name was William Clark. And because of him, Montana passed a law in 1912 limiting the influence of wealthy corporations over our elections," said Senator Jon Tester. "The Supreme Court's decision means we're back where we were in the past—when seats in Congress were up for sale."[78]

Tester's colleague Bernie Sanders, the chamber's most ardent defender of the populist ethic that inspired the radical reformers of the previous century, spoke as Wheeler would have. "In his famous speech at Gettysburg during the Civil War, Abraham Lincoln talked about America as a country 'of the people, by the people and for the people,'" recalled Sanders. "Today, as a result of the Supreme Court's refusal to reconsider its decision in *Citizens United*, we are rapidly moving toward a nation of the super-rich, by the super-rich and for the super-rich."[79]

When billionaires can "spend hundreds of millions of dollars to buy this election for candidates who support the super-wealthy, this is not democracy," said Sanders. "This is plutocracy."[80]

Or as we term its current variant, Dollarocracy.

Call it "plutocracy." Or call it "Dollarocracy." But don't doubt that this is the reassertion of the Money Power that the Progressives of another age so feared. And don't doubt that the Money Power is paying not just for a new politics but also for a new media system, as Chapters 4 and 5 illustrate.

4

THE BULL MARKET

....

Political Advertising

It's still the nuclear weapon.

DAVID AXELROD ON THE ROLE OF
TELEVISION ADS IN CAMPAIGNS, 2011

To help explain the brave new world of politics in which Americans now reside, we'd like to introduce readers to Bridget McCormack.[1] She's pretty impressive. A distinguished professor of law and associate dean at the University of Michigan, McCormack earned international recognition and a mantle full of awards and honors as the founder and codirector of the Michigan Innocence Clinic, a pioneering project to address the distinct challenges that arise when individuals are wrongfully convicted in cases where there is no DNA evidence. She's also helped to launch and expand a mediation clinic, a low-income-taxpayer clinic, an international transactions clinic, a human trafficking clinic, a juvenile justice clinic, and an entrepreneurship clinic.[2]

Like a number of the nation's top lawyers, Democrat and Republican, liberal and conservative, she volunteered on a project organized by the Center for Constitutional Rights, which sought to obtain civil trials for suspects illegally detained by the U.S. government at Guantánamo Bay in Cuba. As the *New York Times* noted, the "goal was not to 'free terrorists,' but to ensure that American prisoners were entitled to the rights and representation provided

97

under international and American law. The Supreme Court affirmed those rights on more than one occasion." McCormack's involvement with the project was slim, as the prisoner she sought to represent was released by a military tribunal under a process developed by the Bush administration.

Fast-forward five years to 2012, when an opening occurred on the Michigan Supreme Court. Nominated by the Democratic Party to seek the seat in the November election, McCormack ran a classic judicial campaign, emphasizing her qualifications and promising to put the rule of law ahead of partisanship and ideology. In the final days of the race, however, she found herself under attack as a legal ally of terrorism. A slick television advertisement featured the mother of Joseph Johnson, a Michigan soldier killed in Afghanistan, saying, "My son is a hero and fought to protect us. . . . Bridget McCormack volunteered to help free a terrorist. How could you?"[3]

The woman in the ad did not pay for it. Nor does it appear did anyone else in Michigan. It was paid for by a Washington-based conservative group called the Judicial Crisis Network. There was no evidence to suggest that the Judicial Crisis Network had a bone to pick with McCormack; rather, the group in all likelihood shared the concern of Michigan conservative and corporate interests about whether the High Court would retain its conservative majority. To the ad's question of "How could you?" the *Times* replied, "That's easy to answer. She didn't. Ms. Johnson may not know that, but the Republican activists who paid for the ad surely do."

The attack on McCormack was so inappropriate that the nation's newspaper of record decried it with a lengthy editorial that declared, "Without that legal representation, there can be no justice, no system of democratic values to defend against terrorism. An attack on lawyers willing to defend Guantanamo detainees is an attack on that system. Those lawyers aren't helping our enemies; they're deeply patriotic."[4] A few Michigan papers wrote about the ad as well, although they did so with headlines that only compounded the damage, including one reading "Michigan Supreme Court Candidate Defends Against Terrorism Claim."[5]

On those screens in Michigan homes, however, it kept running on television stations that made little or no effort to clarify that Bridget McCormack was being unfairly attacked for defending the rule of law. The television stations merely pocketed an estimated $1 million in checks from the Judicial Crisis Network, as McCormack's campaign scrambled to raise the money needed to counter the negative image of the candidate by raising more money to pay for more ads that would further enrich the very same television stations.[6] McCormack won her election, in part because of her own TV ad featuring the cast of *The West Wing* promoting her virtues.[7]

But not every candidate has a sister who played the deputy national security adviser on *The West Wing*'s final three seasons and can call on Hollywood to counter dishonest attack ads.

Unfortunately, that's the option that candidates who are lied about are left with.

The uglier, the crueler, the more distorted and dishonest campaigns become, the richer local television stations across the country become. As rackets go, it's a lucrative one.

And it is this racket that has come to define American politics.

🏛 🏛 🏛

SINCE THE 1970s, there is little or no evidence of a seriously contested campaign for a consequential political office costing less than the previous campaign for that post. This is not a matter of inflation. Even in jurisdictions where population growth is stagnant, even as new technologies have made campaigning more efficient, campaign costs have risen at dramatic rates. It's not because candidates are saying more, not because their message is getting any more elegant or deeper. Indeed, as campaigns grow ever more expensive, they grow more deliberately absurd and thuggish.

What's happening here? After a brief interlude of Watergate-era campaign-finance controls, which might reasonably be thought of as the electoral equivalent of a nuclear arms control treaty, the courts began tearing up the rules and regulations, creating a political no-man's-land. That land is not the border between two belligerent states. It is the American living room. The living room war that began in the 1970s has become the costliest political conflict in the history of the world. And no one has the courage to lay his or her arms down. So it is that for forty years political campaigns have raised ever-increasing amounts of money to spend on television advertising campaigns that have become the electoral equivalent of the old Cold War concept of "mutually assured destruction." Candidates no longer raise the relatively modest amount of money needed to communicate their messages to voters. They raise the amount of money required to match or, ideally, surpass the spending of opponents.

Outside of war, there is no equivalent for the equation that adds up campaign costs. Economies of scale are rejected, along with simple logic. Candidates spend more time raising money in almost every election cycle. As in the Cold War, this has led to the formation of a multifaceted industry that favors not just the combatants but also the producers of the armaments. Just as Dwight Eisenhower warned about a "military-industrial complex," we now have a money-and-media election complex, with a revenue base measured in the many billions of dollars annually. This complex has effectively become the basis of electoral politics in the United States.

In Chapters 2 and 3 we describe who is providing the lion's share of the money for political campaigns and the legal and political structures that have been put in place to encourage their shenanigans. The next logical question is: What does all this money buy? The short answer is that the majority of the money goes to political advertising, and within political advertising the vast majority goes to television ads. The percentage of campaign spending that goes to TV ads has increased sharply over the past forty years. As a rule, the closer a race, the more money will be spent on the campaigns, and the higher the proportion will go to paid TV political advertisements. "We spent the vast majority of our money last time on broadcast television," Obama campaign advisor David Axelrod told attendees at a 2011 cable convention. "It's still the nuclear weapon."[8]

This chapter chronicles the rise and nature of TV political advertising and explains why, under the commercial model that dominates U.S. television, it was destined to assume the forms it has taken.

THE RISE OF TV POLITICAL ADVERTISING

For Americans born after 1950, and for those born before 1950 but with faltering memories, the televised commercial deluge that now defines American political campaigns is the "natural order."[9] But American campaigns were significantly different in the 175 years before political advertising, specifically television political advertising, came to dominate the discourse. Indeed, for politicians and much of the public, the initial response to the use of broadcast candidate advertising was hostile, even contemptuous, regarding the practice as antithetical to American democratic political traditions.

The story has a history going back to the 1930s and 1940s, when moneyed interests learned they could effectively use motion pictures, radio broadcasting, and, what was then used in a nonpejorative sense, propaganda techniques to win elections they might not otherwise.[10] But political advertising only begins to be considered at midcentury when academic researchers like Paul Lazarsfeld and David Riesman observed that advertising and marketing techniques could be successfully applied to political campaigns and that voters shared many attributes with consumers.[11] Legendary Madison Avenue ad man Rosser Reeves approached Republican presidential candidate Thomas Dewey in 1948 and proposed a series of radio spots. Dewey rejected the idea as "undignified." Reeves was later convinced that Dewey's decision cost him the election.[12]

By 1950, advertising people were brought formally into congressional campaigns, at least on the Republican side. This led the Republican-leaning *New York World-Telegram* to bemoan in a large headline the way in which "The Hucksters" had taken over the GOP campaign.[13] Despite the *World-Telegram*'s dignified dissent, Republicans tended to be more open to employing the evolving talents of Madison Avenue, if only because the major advertising agencies were well known for their Republican sympathies at the time. By the early 1950s, the party had the huge Batten, Barton, Durstine & Osborn firm on retainer as its permanent agency.[14]

The 1952 Eisenhower presidential campaign was the turning point. For the first time, television political ads were deployed in a meaningful, attention-grabbing manner. Reeves took a six-week unpaid leave to develop what would become a series of forty TV spots for the campaign. He conducted market research to determine Eisenhower's strengths and weaknesses with uncommitted voters and what issues they were most concerned with. The top issue was the war in Korea, so the campaign slogan became "Eisenhower, Man of Peace." Reeves then developed a campaign whereby in each ad spot Eisenhower would appear to be answering a question from a voter. In fact, Reeves had scripted both the question and the answer.

Eisenhower was reluctant to participate and not at all happy to spend time recording his "answers." "Why don't you just get an actor. That's what you really want," he protested. But he went along with the advice of his campaign advisors.[15] As Lizabeth Cohen put it, "Ironically, it was the campaigns of down-home, grandfatherly Dwight Eisenhower in 1952 and again in 1956 that brought mass marketing fully into the political arena."[16]

Some Democrats protested mightily. Republicans "have created a new kind of campaign," a speechwriter for 1952 and 1956 presidential candidate Adlai Stevenson said, "conceived not by men who want us to face the crucial issues of the day, but by the high-power hucksters of Madison Avenue." Stevenson "hated the idea of using advertising in the political process," David Halberstam noted. "This is the worst idea I have ever heard of," Stevenson told a CBS executive.[17] "The idea that you can merchandise candidates for high office like breakfast cereal . . . is the ultimate indignity to the democratic process."[18]

Former president Harry S. Truman went before the New York Advertising Club in 1958 to implore "the advertising profession" not to "take over the profession of politics."[19] By then it may have been too late. "Both parties will merchandise their candidates and issues by the same methods business has developed to sell goods," *Nation's Business* observed.[20] As Cohen wrote, the 1960 Kennedy campaign embraced commercial marketing tools in a manner Stevenson never could and advanced the use of market segmentation.[21]

Nonetheless, political campaigns in the 1950s and much of the 1960s appear positively anticommercial compared to what would soon follow. The emerging role of television is a recurring theme in Theodore White's epic *The Making of the President* series, especially for 1960 and 1964, but TV political advertising is barely present in either volume. By White's account, Nixon paid virtually no attention to his Madison Avenue advisors throughout his unsuccessful 1960 presidential campaign.[22] In 1964, the campaign of Republican candidate Barry Goldwater spent money on TV political ads, but campaign managers "rejected the counsel of their advertising agency" for short, stylish spots with modish production values in favor of ads that had all the flair of an old ad from the early 1950s.[23] According to Joe Klein's research, in the 1950s and 1960s candidates routinely hired advertising experts and pollsters, "but these were peripheral advisers; they didn't run the campaigns."[24]

This quickly changed. The success of Lyndon Johnson's 1964 "Daisy" ad—which was broadcast only once—took the understanding of how powerful televised political commercials could be to a new level. The spot was put together by Doyle Dane Bernbach, the agency that developed the legendary Volkswagen campaigns that made it a major automobile in the United States by the 1960s. The spot simply had an innocent young girl picking the petals off of a daisy until she was engulfed in a mushroom cloud. It was followed by a voiceover of LBJ saying, "These are the stakes! To make a world in which all of God's children can live, or to go into the dark. We must either love each other, or we must die."

It was unprecedented and extraordinarily powerful, conveying the concern that Goldwater was far more comfortable with nuclear war than any sane person should be. As one scholar noted, "It was the first presidential television spot to contain no real information and no rational argument." David Broder interviewed Johnson staffers after the landslide election victory and noted the "lip-smacking glee" they exhibited for "the way in which they had foisted on the American public a picture of Barry Goldwater as the nuclear-mad bomber who was going to saw off the eastern seaboard of the United States." "The only thing that worries me, Dave," one of the staffers told Broder, "is that some year an outfit as good as ours might go to work for the wrong candidate."[25]

The 1968 presidential election proved to be a watershed. In 1969, Joe McGinniss published his groundbreaking *The Selling of the President* to chronicle what he termed "a striking new phenomenon—the marketing of political candidates as if they were consumer products." The book, which involved McGinniss spending time with Nixon's television advertising advisors, including current Fox News chief Roger Ailes, during the 1968 presidential campaign, seemed a shocking and sharp departure from the political-driven campaign narratives provided by the likes of White. McGinniss documented how Nixon came to rely upon TV political commercials, based on Madison Avenue marketing principles, as the foundation of his campaign. In the book, Ailes presciently concluded immediately after Nixon's November victory, "This is the beginning of a whole new concept. This is it. This is the way they'll be elected forevermore."[26]

It is ironic that when read today, the book's description of Nixon's campaign seems downright quaint, even homespun, by comparison to subsequent elections. The liberal McGinniss was able to wander through the corridors of power in Nixon's campaign like a serendipitous hippie roaming around at Woodstock looking for a roach clip. Similarly *The Candidate,* a sober 1972 film about a young idealistic California candidate for a U.S. Senate seat, starring Robert Redford, seems Atlantean today. The film, with a screenplay by a former Eugene McCarthy speechwriter, dealt with the phoniness and superficiality that marketing and television had brought to political campaigns. At the time, it was provocative and controversial, and it contributed to subsequent debates about the role of money in politics. TV political advertising plays an important role in the film and is cast in a negative light. But what is ironic is that the TV ads Redford's character airs in the fictional campaign are not nearly as bad in tone and substantive content as the dreck that typifies political ads of more recent vintage. Ads of that caliber today would have political scientists and pundits shouting from the mountaintops that we have nothing to fear. But in 1972, such ads were considered highly suspect and part of the problem.

As it was, by 1972 the total amount spent on television political advertising for all races—from the presidency and House and Senate to governorships, mayoralties, state legislatures, referendums, initiatives, and city councils, the works!—had increased threefold from 1960 to reach $37 million.[27] That would amount to approximately $200 million in 2012 dollars, so when we factor in inflation, *the 1972 election spent around 3 percent of what was spent on TV political ads in the 2012 election cycle.*

Even at those 1972 levels, the American public seemed to have had enough. Research in 1973 by the ad agency Foote, Cone & Belding (FCB) determined that Americans "continued to be disenchanted with political advertising," and found it less credible than commercial advertising, which was not exactly a high bar to meet. An FCB 1971 poll determined that three-quarters of Americans wanted controls to reduce the amount of TV political advertising. Only 19 percent of Americans wanted to keep the amount of TV political advertising at then-existing levels. The notion that anyone might want *more* TV political advertising was so laughable that it was not even an option in the survey.[28]

As the Watergate scandal unfolded, the demand for campaign-finance reform grew so intense that by 1974 candidates for the Senate as diverse as Democratic former attorney general Ramsey Clark, who was running in New York that year, and Maryland senator Charles Mathias, a Republican stalwart, were refusing contributions of more than $100 and talking about the "crisis" of campaigns defined by thirty-second attacks ads. Mathias said he wanted to "avoid the curse of big money that has led to so much trouble."[29]

POLITICAL ADVERTISING AND TRADITIONAL ADVERTISING

The "curse" had actually been recognized decades earlier. As television political advertising became prominent in American campaigns, the common refrain was that political advertising was bad because it was advertising, that it substituted the hustle and chicanery of a Madison Avenue sales job for the meat and potatoes of political debate and democratic governance. Lincoln and Douglas were replaced by Procter & Gamble. "Madison Avenue sells politicians like soap," the lament went. The very term "Madison Avenue" provided a shorthand critique of advertising's lack of ethics, sincerity, and integrity, and it encapsulated much of what people felt they were subjected to with TV political commercials. In 1960, for example, Richard Nixon so feared the tag Madison Avenue that he moved his campaign's television advisers—according to White, "the finest brains of New York's advertising agencies"—from their ad agency offices on that (in)famous street to new offices on nearby Vanderbilt Avenue.[30]

Despite the warm embrace of political advertising by Rosser Reeves and numerous other major figures on Madison Avenue, there was also a dissident element of the advertising industry offended by the comparison of political advertising to commercial advertising, as these admen regarded the latter as having vastly greater integrity and social value. The towering Madison Avenue opponent to political advertising was David Ogilvy, founder of Ogilvy & Mather, and, ironically enough, the brother-in-law of Reeves. Ogilvy thought political advertising "represented the worst abuse imaginable of the advertising man's skills," as Halberstam put it. When Reeves showed his brother-in-law his TV spots for Eisenhower in 1952, Ogilvy wished him luck but remarked that he hoped "for the country's sake it goes terribly."[31] Years later, Ogilvy called political spots "the most deceptive, misleading, unfair and untruthful of all advertising."[32] At another point, he stated, "Political advertising ought to be stopped. It's the only really dishonest kind of advertising that's left. It's totally dishonest."[33]

Ogilvy & Mather's creative head, Robert Spero, shared his boss's stance toward political ads. When told that TV political advertising sold politicians like soap, he responded that unfortunately that was not the case, because soap advertising was markedly superior as a source of useful information. Spero was so appalled by political advertising that he took leave from his position at Oglivy & Mather in the late 1970s to do a comprehensive analysis of every available presidential television political commercial from 1952 through the 1976 election. In Spero's mind, the key distinction between commercial ads and political ads was that political advertising, unlike commercial advertising, had First Amendment protection from regulation for fraud and misleading content. This point is indeed crucial and cannot be exaggerated: political advertising can pretty much say whatever it wants without fear of regulatory reprisal.

Spero's subsequent book, *The Duping of the American Voter*, demonstrated in a meticulous and engaging case-by-case study that political ads for all varieties of presidential candidates routinely had fraudulent traits that would have been impossible for a commercial advertiser facing the Federal Trade Commission and other forms of government regulation at that time. "Corporations and their advertising advisers have not become simon-pure in their evolvement from street hucksters. Historically, bending the truth has been inseparable from selling," Spero wrote. "What has prevented the truth from being bent out of all proportion by corporations and their advertising agents is the phenomenal growth of advertising regulation over the past decade."[34] (It is worth noting that the 1970s was the high-water mark for regulation of commercial advertising.)

Industry dissidents remain, such as creative whiz Claudia Caplan, who in *Advertising Age* dismissed political advertising as "hectoring, polemical dreck" and argued that it was smart business for ad agencies to avoid it altogether.[35] And then there is Burt Manning, the former chairman of the American Association of Advertising Agencies and chairman emeritus of J. Walter Thompson (JWT). Channeling Ogilvy, Manning warned on the eve of the 2012 election that "I relate the decline in Americans' trust and acceptance of general advertising to their violent dislike of mudslinging political advertising. It's more of a problem now, because there is more of it."[36]

This sentiment is countered by the emergence of the money-and-media election complex, which means Madison Avenue still gets a piece of the action—even if much of the political ad business goes to consultants and their specialized agencies—so there is incentive to accept the status quo and go with the flow.[37] After all, can political advertising really be that much worse than junk food, insurance, oil company, pharmaceutical, alcohol, or tobacco advertising? Bob

Jeffrey, who has followed Manning as CEO of JWT Worldwide, noted that election cycles "for the advertising business, these are very profitable seasons."[38] What is clear is that any change of heart from Madison Avenue had little or nothing to do with the integrity or quality of the political ads themselves. Jeffrey was beside himself describing their imbecility.[39] A study in the early 2000s of political spots cited by reputable sources found "roughly half of all ads to be unfair, misleading or deceptive."[40] Preliminary examinations of 2012's political ads suggest that percentage has only grown, perhaps a great deal.

In fact, Ogilvy and Spero were too quick to regard political advertising and product advertising as being distant relations, though their approach has been widely internalized among scholars. Political scientists and political communication scholars generally understand political advertising first and foremost as an outgrowth of political campaigning—understandably, as that is the tradition scholars come from—and they pay particular attention to identifying the common themes that link the present to earlier eras. And because blarney, bluster, deception, character assassination, showmanship, manipulation, idiocy, baby-kissing, superficiality, overstatement, ridicule, hypocrisy, and hyperbole have always been present to varying degrees in popular politics, the argument goes, Americans should not be so alarmed that these traits now come packaged as candidate TV ads. Because in the past the American democratic system always ended up working effectively, and voters were able to cut through the crap and use the system to adequately convey their core political values and concerns, there is little reason to think that will not remain the case in the era of political advertising. The system works; the more things change, the more they stay the same.

This approach underplays or misses the decisive differences in the current nature of political campaigns wrought by TV political advertising. There is the matter of the enormous increase in funds necessary to successfully participate as a candidate and the strings that come attached to these funds. There is also the matter of the power, sophistication, and ubiquity of televised political advertising; it now replaces virtually everything else in the campaign, including all the forces that in theory could counteract the power of money and advertising. There is also the matter that people—to a significant extent and for rational reasons—detest political advertising in a manner that has no apparent precedent in American political campaigns.

In our view, our current political campaigns can be more accurately appreciated by understanding political advertising as a subset of commercial advertising. This approach has received too little attention from scholars, probably because so few of them have given much consideration to the matter, or seem to know much about it. Modern commercial advertising is not a function of what economists term "competitive markets," meaning new businesses can easily enter existing profitable markets, increase output, lower prices, and make the consumer live happily ever after. Such markets tend to have relatively little advertising, if only because producers can sell all that they produce at the market price, over which they have little or no control. (Think of a wheat farmer in 1875.) This is why the largely local and competitive U.S. economy prior to the late nineteenth century had little advertising by the standards of the past one hundred years.

Modern persuasion advertising blossomed as a function of markets that were less competitive by economists' standards. Generally described as oligopolies, these markets are characterized by a handful of firms dominating output or sales in the industry and having sufficient market power to set the price at which their product sells. The key to an oligopoly is that it is very difficult for newcomers to enter the market, no matter how profitable it may be, because of the power of the existing players. Under oligopoly, there is strong disincentive to engage in price warfare to expand market share, because all the main players are large enough to survive a price war and all it would do is shrink the size of the industry revenue pie that the firms are fighting over. Indeed, the price in an oligopolistic industry will tend to gravitate toward what it would be in a pure monopoly, so the contenders are fighting for slices of the largest possible revenue pie.[41]

At first blush, this is a pretty accurate picture of the U.S. economy of the twentieth and twenty-first centuries. Under Dollarocracy, the economy has become far more monopolistic over the past thirty years.[42] It is also a good way, though by no means the only way, to understand the emergence and dominance of advertising. Although firms are not in competitive markets, they are most definitely competing with each other to maximize their profits. Advertising emerges front and center as a major way to increase market share (and protect market share) without engaging in destructive profit-damaging price competition.

The election realm is similar to the economy in that it tends to be a duopoly in general elections, meaning there are usually only two options that could conceivably win, and, as in an oligopoly, they have used their "market power"—in this case control over election laws—to make it all but impossible for a third party to successfully establish itself as a legitimate contender. Nice work if you can get it. Even primary elections are almost always a matter of no more than two or three viable entrants except in a very small number of races.

The great political theorist C. B. Macpherson was among the first to understand modern electoral politics—the two-party system—in terms of oligopolistic and duopolistic market practices. "Where there are so few sellers," Macpherson wrote concerning political parties, "they need not and do not respond to buyers' demands as they must do in a fully competitive system." This means the parties, like oligopolistic firms, can "create the demand for political goods" and largely dictate the "demand schedule for political goods."

In Macpherson's argument, a duopolistic party system in a modern capitalist society like the United States will tend to gravitate to providing a "competition between elites," who are the driving force and "formulate the issues."[43] The basics in the political economy are agreed upon by the two parties and are off the table for public debate or discussion. In Macpherson's view, the two-party system produces citizen apathy and depoliticization—especially among those at the bottom end of the economic spectrum—and maintains elite rule, or what would be called a "weak democracy." For supporting evidence, political scientist V. O. Key's trailblazing research in the 1950s demonstrated the class bias in voting turnout—rich people often voted at nearly twice the rate of poor people—in the first half of the twentieth century.[44]

Macpherson provided these insights in the 1970s, before Dollarocracy and before political advertising nudged the Richter scale in political science. If anything, the linkage of the two parties to elite economic interests is stronger today than it was in his era. But the economic analogy is good only for a broad brushstroke, because elections are not commercial marketplaces and duopolistic elections existed a very long time before the emergence of political advertising. For political advertising to emerge as a major factor required a number of developments, first and foremost the establishment of commercial television broadcasting. Those nations with limited or seriously regulated commercial broadcasting have less political advertising and little political pressure to encourage it.

Where the oligopoly/persuasive advertising analogy is crucial to understanding political advertising—indeed the money-and-media election complex—is when we look at the *content* of the ads. Under conditions of oligopoly, firms tend to produce similar products and sell them at similar prices. Therefore, advertising that emphasizes price and product information can be ineffectual, if not counterproductive. (That type of price and product information advertising can be found in more competitive retail markets or in classified advertising.) An ad campaign based on "Hey, buy our soft drink because it costs the same and tastes the same as our competitor" probably won't lead to awards, a promotion, or a long career. Firms put inordinate effort into creating brands that are perceived as different from competitors, and advertising is crucial in creating the aura surrounding these brands.

Perhaps it is not entirely coincidental that Rosser Reeves, the pioneer of modern TV political advertising, is also generally considered one of the great visionaries of product advertising. He was reputed to have repeated the same presentation for years for newly hired copywriters at his Ted Bates advertising agency in the 1960s. He would hold up two identical shiny silver dollars, one in each hand, and would tell his audience in effect, "Never forget that your job is very simple. It is to make people think the silver dollar in my left hand is much more desirable than the silver dollar in my right hand."[45]

Reeves advocated packaging as new and unique what was actually old and ordinary in a given product. Reeves specialized in making claims for his products that were not always true, but they were not entirely untrue either. His specialty was "the uncheckable claim."[46] It was an ideal approach to selling products in oligopolistic markets. "Since most brands are basically not that different," William Greider wrote, "advertising's fantasies provide as good a reason as any to choose one brand over another."[47]

There is an endless search by advertisers for ways to capture attention and differentiate products that exploit possibilities that may have little or nothing to do with the actual product and the utility it might render to the consumer. This search also leads to ads that attempt to make a product virtue out of something that is insignificant or not specific to the product or irrelevant.

Television advertising, in particular, made it possible to develop this aspect far beyond what Reeves only began to imagine. It uses cultural cues to communicate fairly complex messages in less than thirty seconds, exploiting stereotypes and cultural references to pack a lot of meaning into a few fleeting seconds. It is expert at playing on emotions. TV advertising uses visuals in such a way that anyone only reading the text or listening to the words will miss the heart of what is being communicated.[48] In short, television advertising is the highest grade and most sophisticated system of applied propaganda in the world.

"All advertisers know this," former advertising executive Jerry Mander wrote. "They know that even the dumbest products and ideas can gain acceptance because advertising imagery does not appeal to intellect but exploits a human, genetic, sensory predisposition to believe what we see. That's the way premodern humans protected themselves. In that sense, we are all still premodern."[49] On television, Mander noted, "even auto ads, which we would expect to have something concrete to say, are far more focused on glamorous curves, or speed, or good-looking people."[50]

The nature of oligopolistic advertising leads to two paradoxes. First, the more products are alike and the more their prices are similar, the more the firms must advertise to convince people these products are different. Second, the more firms advertise to distinguish themselves from their competition, the more commercial "clutter" is created in the media and in the general culture. As a result, firms are forced to increase their advertising that much more to pierce through the clutter and reach the public.[51] If there is anything close to an iron law in advertising, it is this: repetition works; the more exposure to a brand's advertising, the better. This follows from the conclusion drawn from social science research: people are more inclined to believe what they have heard before.[52] Repetition doesn't guarantee success, but it increases the odds considerably.

This, we submit, is a good and necessary way to understand the practices of the money-and-media election complex and the content of much of political advertising. It flows from the approach Reeves laid out nearly six decades ago: "I think of a man in a voting booth who hesitates between two levers as if he were pausing between competing tubes of tooth paste in a drugstore. The brand that has made the highest penetration on his brain will win his choice."[53]

Television provides a superpowerful mechanism to penetrate that brain. As TV political advertising's role has grown, an industry has emerged with experts who refine its use strategically and tactically. Research is done to determine what appeals will work with the target audience to get the desired results, and advertising is produced to generate the appeal.[54] The way to success is to relentlessly pound the message home. The more exposure to the ad, the greater the likelihood of brain penetration. As the president of a polling firm put it in 2012, "After the 5th, 6th, 7th, or 8th or 20th time—that's when the ad may start to resonate with people." Research shows that even if you say you are appalled by the repetition, it "probably won't make you vote against someone."[55]

In true Reevesian fashion, that the issues selected may be inconsequential, or that the positions presented in the ads may be misleading, or that the politician's performance in office if elected will have no connection to the position in the ads is just built into the process. The basics of how the corporate economy is structured or how U.S. foreign policy is made are pretty much off the table, much like price and product information in beer advertising, because the two parties largely concur on the most important matters of governance. As Glenn Greenwald observed during the 2012 presidential campaign, the "propaganda orgy" promotes the notion of "vibrant political debate and stark democratic choice, even as many of the policies that are most consequential . . . —the 'war on drugs,' the supremacy of the covert national security and surveillance states, vast inequalities in the justice system, crony capitalism that rapidly bolsters the oligarchy that owns the political process—are steadfastly ignored because both parties on those issues have exactly the same position and serve the same interests."[56]

To the extent that those subjects are broached, it is largely done in an opportunistic and manipulative manner, based upon buzzwords fire-tested by research on the target audience. So it was in the 2012 presidential campaign that fully 10 percent of campaign ads by both parties between June and September singled out the financial sector for criticism. These messages appealed to a population with serious concerns about the role of big banks in the American political economy, but they were mostly bogus, as both parties were soliciting massive contributions from the same sector and were demonstrated advocates of Wall Street's interests.[57] As Peter Baker of the *New York Times* politely put it, "The relationship between what the presidential candidates say on the campaign trail and what they do once elected can be tenuous."[58]

Let's start then with the premise that the content of political advertising will have all the value of a commercial for beer or soft drinks. That the material in the ads may be factually inaccurate or, more likely, may be decontextualized half-truths or quarter-truths is not a surprise, or a pressing concern to those producing the ads. Romney's creative director in 2012 was Jim Ferguson, former president of Young & Rubicam, the nation's largest agency. Ferguson had produced some of TV's most memorable campaigns, such as "Beef: It's What's for Dinner" and "Nothing but Net," a Super Bowl commercial for McDonald's featuring Michael Jordan and Larry Bird.[59] Ferguson made two hundred spots for Romney in 2012. "We were making commercials every day. We would test everything. We'd see what resonated with people and would pick a commercial or two to get ready for broadcast."[60] Vinny Minchillo, a Madison Avenue veteran who also worked for Romney, bragged that they had "an in-house ad team that could turn a gaffe into a spot in 90 minutes."[61]

According to the most comprehensive research on the topic, nearly all political ads "make at least a limited appeal to emotions," particularly enthusiasm and fear, "and a substantial majority make a strong emotional appeal."[62] Julian Kanter, curator of the Political Commercial Archive of the University of Oklahoma, observed that in TV political ads "the most important messages are those that are contained in the visual imagery." That imagery, he pointed out, "can be used to create impressions that are untrue." Through such visual tricks, campaigns duck the scrutiny they might face when only the words in the script are read.[63] That the material in the ads may not be pertinent to the real issues the candidates will be addressing once in office or the actions they might take on those issues is beside the point. The point is to win elections by any means necessary.

No one understood this better than Lee Atwater, the political mastermind who guided George H. W. Bush's successful 1988 presidential campaign. Atwater explained that the battle between the two parties was always about winning the "populist vote." "It is always the swing vote," he said. This was all done through political marketing and, as Atwater conceded, had little to do with how either party would actually govern.[64] By the 1990s, research demonstrated that most candidates had little or nothing to do with the marketing of their campaigns and the content of the advertising. This became the domain of the professional consultant, whose job is to win elections, period.[65]

Moreover, the two paradoxes of commercial advertising apply as well. First, candidates with less tangible records to distinguish themselves from their opponents have to spend more to create the sense that there is a meaningful difference. Ron Paul and Dennis Kucinich, for example, need to spend less to make clear they stand in fundamental opposition to their competition even within their own party. Second, when the competition spends a great deal on advertising, that puts extreme pressure on a candidate to match the advertising and, ideally, up the ante. This applies to the Pauls and Kuciniches as well as everyone else if they are serious about winning.

As the clutter increases, the only course is to push down harder on the political advertising accelerator, not hit the brakes. There is also a certain desperation to break through the clutter and create an ad that will be noticed. So it was in 2012 that outside groups supporting the Romney campaign began using cute babies in attack ads on Obama. "Scare tactics are nothing new," one ad industry executive with experience in politics said, "but with babies? This goes to new extremes."[66]

Importantly, recent research confirms that, even though TV ads are clearly effective, the positive effect of ads decays quickly, so it is important once one goes on the air, to stay at full speed until Election Day.[67] Everything else being relatively equal, the candidate with a decisive TV advertising war chest will win. "Advertising effects emerge most clearly," political scientist John Sides wrote, "when one side can out-spend the other—and by a lot."[68]

This pattern has been confirmed in recent political science research examining whether voters in presidential elections vote "correctly." Drawing from exhaustive research to determine voters' political ideology, Sean Richey of Georgia State University then determined whether voters vote for the candidate who best represents their politics. He found that between 1972 and 2004, where his research ends, as many as 20 percent of voters voted "incorrectly." What is important for our purposes is that the research suggests that if a campaign significantly outspends its opponents "to do more persuasive manipulation than the other campaign," it can increase the number of "incorrect" voters it gets compared to its opponent. "Generally," Richey put it, "voters do not have the knowledge skills to overcome manipulation." By Richey's calculation, the spending imbalance in favor of Republicans was sufficient for George W. Bush to purchase enough incorrect votes to change the 2000 and 2004 elections from defeats to victories.[69]

Perhaps no campaign better exemplifies the logic of commercial advertising than that of Barack Obama's presidential run in 2007–2008. "I serve as a blank screen," he wrote presciently in his 2006 *The Audacity of Hope,* "on which people of vastly different political stripes project their own views."[70] "By the time he won the presidential election, the Barack Obama brand had become a worldwide wonder," media scholar Leonard Steinhorn noted. "He had become an icon, someone who seemed to embody our most personal aspirations and hopes, a larger-than-life figure who exceeded the powers and abilities of any mere mortal."[71] Obama's marketing team put together such an extraordinary advertising campaign—"Change You Can Believe In"— that it was awarded *Advertising Age*'s "Marketer of the Year" for 2008. To win the award, Team Obama needed to get the most votes from the attendees at the annual conference of the Association of National Advertisers, people who know a good sales pitch when they see one. The runners-up included Nike and Coors beer.[72]

In retrospect, Obama's advertising campaign was ambiguous, if not vacuous or deceptive, in terms of governance and policy—though that is now accepted as par for the course. Everyone else does it, the conventional wisdom goes, so why hold Obama to a higher standard? McCain's campaign slogan was "Country First." The candidates could have easily swapped campaign slogans in the summer of 2007, and it would have had no effect on their actual policy positions. This isn't a bull market for nothing.

The Obama campaign underlined another aspect of commercial advertising that applies full force to political advertising: it works! Back in the 1970s, there was a branch of academic scholarship arguing that political advertising was not especially effective or even necessary for electoral success. Today those arguments can be filed away with the claims that cigarette smoking has no connection to lung cancer. "We can say confidently that ads are persuasive, especially if you have more ads than your competitor," Travis Ridout and Michael Franz, two leading researchers who have devoted careers to the subject, wrote in 2011, noting that leading research confirmed "ad effects were also more widespread than we had predicted." "We have found that televised political advertising influences people's voting choices, and more specifically, we have shown that ads are having their greatest influence on those who are the least informed about politics." "Ads have greater influence," they added, "in highly competitive races."[73]

The most comprehensive examination of the 2008 presidential race—Kate Kenski, Bruce Hardy, and Kathleen Hall Jamieson's award-winning *The*

Obama Victory—confirms that Obama's ability to greatly outspend McCain for television political advertising in battleground states as well as nationally was significant. Controlling for other variables in evaluating daily tracking polls, the authors determined "that weeks in which Obama outspent McCain on national ads are significantly related to an Obama vote 'if the election were held today.'" Specifically, the research determined that in battleground states Obama's ability to put far more advertising on the air all but destroyed McCain's hopes for victory.

"Whenever we grabbed a lead, a little toehold in a state," a McCain media person stated, Obama would dump in a wave of new TV advertising "and explode the whole thing out for us." The authors did not claim that Obama's advertising necessarily won him the election, but at the very least, it may well have been decisive in traditionally Republican-leaning states such as Indiana, North Carolina, Florida, and Virginia, where the spending advantage was large and the vote tally was close.[74] Likewise in 2010, the new wave of Republican outside groups outspent Democratic ones 2 to 1, largely in tight battleground races, and, as one commentator noted, accordingly "annihilated them at the polls."[75]

Crucially, research also suggests that television political advertising is even *more* effective in House and Senate races, not to mention other races further down the political food chain. "In presidential campaigns, voters may be influenced by news coverage, debates, or objective economic or international events," Darrell M. West wrote in a book for the Congressional Quarterly Press in 2010. "These other forces restrain the power of advertisements and empower a variety of alternative forces. In congressional contests, some of these constraining factors are absent, making advertisements potentially more important. If candidates have the money to advertise in a congressional contest, it can be a very powerful force for electoral success."[76]

Of course, not all advertising works, which has driven business executives crazy for a century. "I know half of my advertising does not work," goes the urban legend of an exasperated businessman, "but I do not know which half." In the commercial world, only on the rarest of occasions have major advertisers actually curtailed their practices sharply absent their competitors doing the same, and this move has been met with declining sales and no enthusiasm by their competitors to pursue a similar course.

The same is true with political advertising. "So much of presidential advertising is wasted money," noted Mark McKinnon, who made ads for George W. Bush in 2000 and 2004 and worked for McCain in the 2008 primaries. "The ads become just background to a broad architecture the campaigns are trying to create. . . . Easily half of the money spent on TV ads in presidential campaigns is a complete waste and would be better spent online or on other activities."[77] The fact remains, though, that TV political spending is not optional; it is necessary for political survival, not to mention success, in the contemporary United States as much as it is for a commercial advertiser like Coca-Cola or Coors beer or Nike shoes in an oligopolistic industry. Indeed, because of the nature of elections, it is arguably more imperative to maintain a foot all the way down on the TV advertising accelerator.

This point emerged in the 2012 campaign. As the airwaves were flooded with political ads, numerous observers noted that there had to be a declining effectiveness for the money being spent. Nothing short of a fortune was being spent to influence the votes of a sliver of uncommitted voters in a handful of swing states. Why isn't there a better use of resources? According to Kathleen Hall Jamieson, the research is clear that voters are more likely to change their minds if they live in "swing states" marinated in political ads than they are if they live in states without much political advertising. Political advertising may not be especially efficient, its impact may be only "marginal," but as Daniel Adler put it, "it's probably more efficient than any alternative." And in a "market" where the difference between having a 49.9 and a 50.1 market share is life or death, one scholar noted, "that marginal impact is worth it."[78]

Back in the 1990s, there were a handful of major candidates in statewide races who made a virtue of their unwillingness to accept large campaign donations, which meant they could not run anywhere near as many television ads as their opponents. Ed Garvey's 1998 race for Wisconsin governor and Russ Feingold's 1998 Senate reelection campaign in Wisconsin are the most recent and striking examples. The consequences of those campaigns—Garvey lost in a landslide, and Feingold barely won a race he, by all rights, should have won handily—sent a loud and clear message that such a course greatly increases chances of electoral failure. Since then, no major party candidate, not a single solitary one, has dared to emulate them with what is known derisively as "unilateral disarmament."

NEGATIVE ADVERTISING

There is one crucial area where political advertising differs sharply from commercial advertising, and it is here that the blood pressure rises for the likes of Ogilvy and Spero and their modern-day heirs Caplan and Manning. This is negative advertising, where the purpose is to attack and denigrate the competition. In a commercial marketplace such advertising is of little value. The point of commercial advertising is to protect and promote sales for the advertiser's product and ultimately increase profitability. There are no bonus points for simply decreasing a competitor's sales, and in fact it might just take consumers away from the product category altogether, which would be counterproductive. "Tide could attack Cheer to get a little market bump," Carter Eskew wrote, "but Cheer would respond, and soon nobody would be buying detergent because things would be, well, a little dirty."[79] Or as one clean election advocate put it, "If car companies did this to each other, people would be nervous about getting behind a wheel."[80]

Not so with political advertising. Negative advertising can be tremendously effective, even if it does not generate a single new voter for the candidate (or supportive "independent" group) placing the ad. If it simply takes voters leaning toward the opponent and makes them less likely to vote for the opponent, maybe not vote at all, that is a victory. After all, the point is to get the most votes; lowering an opponent's numbers has the same effect as increasing a candidate's own total.

Moreover, negative advertising can have the delicious side effect of forcing an opponent to respond to charges, no matter how spurious. Negative advertising can amplify spectacularly the classic political move captured by the story of the politician who told his campaign manager to start a rumor that his opponent was a child molester. "But he isn't a child molester, is he?" responded the aide. "Of course not," said the candidate, "but I want to hear him deny it."

Perhaps because of this, negative ads have always been a staple of TV political ads. Over the years, though, they have grown in such prominence that they now account for the vast majority of all TV political ads.[81] The most comprehensive research to date concludes that between 2000 and 2008 the overall percentage of negative TV political ads rose from 50 percent to 60 percent.[82] Two years later, the percentage increased again for a simple reason: the new independent groups formed with anonymous money following *Citizens United*—unencumbered by identification with candidate, party, or even funding source—devoted their resources primarily to negative attack ads.[83] "We're seeing a lot more negativity," said political advertising researcher Travis Ridout. "When the outside groups are advertising, we're finding that they are predominantly negative."[84]

The definition of a negative ad is open to interpretation, so the data are hardly uniform. What all research shows is that the amount of negative TV advertising increased sharply in 2012 and the more competitive the race, the more negative the advertising. A disproportionate amount of the so-called positive ads were run by candidates who were not facing a serious challenge and, using their ample campaign contributions, wanted to keep their name before voters.

In October 2012, Kantar Media's Campaign Media Analysis Group, whose research is held in high regard by the ad industry, calculated that 84 percent of the broadcast TV ads for the 2012 presidential race were negative.[85] A similarly respected operation, the Wesleyan Media Project, determined 86 percent of Obama's and 79 percent of Romney's advertising was negative, compared to a combined negative rate in 2008 for Obama and John McCain of 69 percent and a combined negative rate in 2004 of 58 percent for John Kerry and George W. Bush.[86]

Yet even that seems to understate the situation, perhaps because the notorious third-party ads are undercounted. When a number of ad buyers analyzed all the political spots aired in all the swing states on July 12, 2012, they determined that every ad was an attack ad.[87] When National Public Radio commissioned Kantar Media to assess all the TV political spots in Colorado Springs, Colorado, for a week in September 2012, it determined that only 50 of the 1,500 spots were positive.[88]

If political advertising is effective, negative political advertising can be especially effective. Obviously, campaigns have to take into careful account tactical and strategic considerations as there is always a risk that negative advertising could backfire.[89] Some research suggests that negative ads work best in moderation, that overexposure can become counterproductive.[90] Even then, research from the 2008 primary campaigns suggests that negative ads that are widely regarded in exit polls as having been unfair can still be effective, and candidates can still win the votes of the people regarding their ads as unfair. Such advertising can sow doubt in people's "guts," and that can determine how a person votes.[91] So it is not clear how damaging an "unfair" negative ad campaign, or "excessive" exposure, can be to a campaign. The ones usually cited, like Jack Conway's accusation in Kentucky's 2010 U.S. Senate race that Rand Paul acted weirdly as a college student, come from candidates who are almost hopelessly behind in the polls, and these accusations are akin to a "Hail Mary" pass in football.

But when done smartly and when fueled by piles of cash, negative advertising can drive the talking points in a campaign like nothing else. Defenders of political advertising twist themselves into pretzels to demonstrate the value they see negative ads providing. Some argue the ads mention legitimate issues, like jobs or deficits, while avoiding the fact that the actual statement about the legitimate issues is mostly inaccurate, decontextualized, and/or misleading.[92] Some emphasize that voters can learn from these ads and that they often provide citations for their charges. We find this line of reasoning unconvincing, but this much we do concede: negative attack ads are more memorable and entertaining than the standard issue "positive" ad featuring a politician playing Frisbee with his dog and holding hands with his granddaughter, or the endless empty "issue" ads where the candidate says she is for jobs and education and health care and veterans and clean government and against crime, corruption, and terrorism. We understand why people in the money-and-media election complex favor them and why viewers would remember them. "In the final analysis everyone complains" about negative ads, Stanford's Shanto Iyengar noted, "but that doesn't mean they don't listen."[93]

So negative ads tend to work, even when people say they despise them. Drew Westen showed a group of voters an anti-McCain ad by Obama and an anti-Obama ad by McCain from the 2008 presidential campaign.

> The voters we surveyed claimed to despise both ads, describing them in focus groups as "pandering." They insisted the ads would backfire with them. But using a well-established method for assessing which words the commercials activated unconsciously, we discovered that although voters consciously disliked both commercials, the ads were nevertheless highly effective. Both "stuck," triggering negative associations of Obama and McCain in the minds of most voters, including those who thought they were unaffected.[94]

Researcher Dianne Bystrom of Iowa State University reported, "What we find is, even when they say they hate them (ads), there's a movement in the needle."[95] "When asked in focus groups about what they think about candidates," veteran North Carolina political reporter Rob Christensen noted, the same people who "almost universally say they hate negative ads" will "often play back the negative messages they have subconsciously absorbed in commercials."[96]

The recent political ads that have caused electoral upsets have usually been negative and more often than not entirely bogus. In Wisconsin, the 1986 U.S. Senate race provided a chilling example. Democratic challenger Ed Garvey had a solid lead over incumbent Republican senator Robert Kasten two weeks out from Election Day. Kasten then ran a series of TV ads charging Garvey with embezzling money from his days as head of the National Football League Players Association. Garvey was low on money and could not afford TV spots, so he never effectively responded—even as the news media emphasized the charges were unproven and probably bogus. Garvey lost the election by a hair, and shortly thereafter Kasten's campaign apologized for the misleading and inaccurate ads. But Kasten, not Garvey, went to Washington for a six-year term.

Arguably the most famous example came two years later in the 1988 presidential race between Democrat Michael Dukakis, the governor of Massachusetts, and George H. W. Bush, the vice president. In late summer, Dukakis held a seventeen-point lead and was doing especially well with women voters and traditional Democrats. Under the aegis of Lee Atwater, who worked with a staff that included soon-to-be Fox News chief Roger Ailes, the Republicans test-marketed attack ad ideas with a focus group of "Reagan Democrats"— traditional white working-class Democrats who could be pried away if the discussion got away from economics and core government programs like Social Security and Medicare. Atwater was legendary for his conviction that exploiting white racism was the best way to appeal to such voters.[97] The research hit the mother lode when Atwater saw how negatively the focus group responded to the story of how Governor Dukakis had provided a weekend furlough to Willie Horton, a black man, who jumped his furlough and went on to rape a white woman. Atwater boasted, "By the time this election is over, Willie Horton will be a household name."[98] "The only question," remarked

Ailes during the campaign, "is whether we depict Willie Horton with a knife in his hand or without it."[99]

Willie Horton did indeed become a household name.[100] It is unclear how decisive the Willie Horton TV ad was in sandbagging the Dukakis campaign, but by all accounts it played an important role. What is also noteworthy is that the story about Dukakis was entirely decontextualized. The story conveyed nothing distinct about Dukakis that would have bearing on his conduct as president and the policies he would have pursued. What came through was a scary black guy was raping white women and Dukakis seemed to be his un-apologetic wingman. The message was directly out of Rosser Reeves's play-book, and it worked. (Shortly before the forty-year old Atwater died of brain cancer in 1991, he is reported to have apologized for the Horton ad and the racist flames it so triumphantly stoked.)

A more recent example comes from the 2004 presidential race between Senator John Kerry and President George W. Bush. Kerry held a lead over Bush in the polls coming out of the conventions. Kerry made a big deal out of his record as a decorated soldier in Vietnam and campaigned with his "band of brothers," the term for his fellow Vietnam veterans. The contrast with Bush, who had ducked military combat in the Vietnam era, was expected to work to Kerry's advantage. Then a shadowy independent group—Swift Boat Vet-erans for Truth—ran a series of TV ads asserting that Kerry was actually a coward who had betrayed his "brothers" while in Vietnam. The ads were bogus and repudiated by the likes of Senator John McCain, but the issue be-came the hot topic of the campaign for weeks. The Kerry campaign was stag-gered by the charges and eventually lost a nail-biter in November. "For Republicans a swift boat was a very good thing," columnist Robert Novak stated about the 2004 election. It "kept John Kerry from being president."[101]

The 2008 presidential race certainly featured a fair share of slash-and-burn television. Toward the bitter end of a Democratic primary contest, Hillary Clinton's campaign took a swipe at Barack Obama's perceived inexperience on the international stage with a television ad that featured a ringing phone at 3 AM and the question "It's 3 AM and your children are safe and asleep. Who do you want answering the phone?" That fall, the Republican National Committee doubled down on the theme, airing ads that asked, "Would you get on a plane with someone who has never flown? . . . Would you go under with a surgeon who has never operated? Can you hand your nation to a man who has never been in charge of anything? Can you wait while he learns?"[102] But the 2008 campaign, still operating under the old, pre-*Citizens United* rules—and influenced at least in part by the mutual regard Obama and Republican presidential nominee John McCain had for each other—was gentle compared with what was to come.

Almost a year before the actual vote, in a December 2011 *New York Times* column, Paul Krugman wrote, "Welcome to post-truth politics," and he predicted that if Mitt Romney were the Republican nominee, America would witness a campaign "based . . . around a strategy of attacking Mr. Obama for doing things that the president hasn't done and believing things he doesn't believe."[103] Romney delivered just that, with a campaign slathered in money and untethered from fact. To be sure, Democrats and their super-PAC supporters made outrageous statements during the course of the 2012 campaign; and it is appropriate that they were fact-checked and called out.

But nothing rivaled the remarkable closing claim by Romney that Obama had somehow paved the way for the shuttering of America's Jeep plants. Jeeps are made in Toledo, Ohio, where the iconic American vehicle has been produced since 1941, and Romney needed to win Toledo and the rest of northwest Ohio if he were to stand a chance of securing the battleground state that was key to the presidency. Two weeks before the election, Romney went to the region and shocked voters by suggesting, "I saw a story today that one of the great manufacturers in this state, Jeep, now owned by the Italians, is thinking of moving all production to China."[104] The story, an October 22, 2012, report by Bloomberg News, had specifically stated that "Chrysler currently builds all Jeep SUV models at plants in Michigan, Illinois and Ohio. [Fiat/Chrysler executive Mike] Manley referred to adding Jeep production sites rather than shifting output from North America to China." Yet Romney spoke of the company that manufactures Jeeps moving all its production to China.

The statement stirred fundamental fears in a region that had been battered by plant closings. So much so that Jeep's parent company, Chrysler, rushed to explain that Romney was completely, totally, incredibly wrong. "Let's set the record straight: Jeep has no intention of shifting production of its Jeep models out of North America to China," announced Chrysler. Company spokesman Gualberto Ranieri said that Romney had remade the facts so aggressively that "it is a leap that would be difficult even for professional circus acrobats."[105]

It was front-page news, nightly television news.

In the old days, a chastened Romney would have apologized and moved on. But in the new age of commercial carpet-bombing, Romney's response to being caught in a lie was to lie even more. The Romney campaign began airing an ad on Ohio television stations that claimed President Obama had, with the auto bailout that saved domestic vehicle production, "sold Chrysler to Italians who are going to build Jeeps in China." The ad concluded that Romney—whose Bain Capital enterprise was identified as "a pioneer of outsourcing"—"will fight for every American job." Jamieson, the director of the Annenberg Public Policy Center at the University of Pennsylvania, said of the Romney campaign's attempt to suggest that Obama had engineered a change in Jeep's status that would see the Toledo plant shuttered and its more than 3,500 workers idled, "They are inviting a false inference." The *Washington Post* "Fact Checker" site reviewed Romney's ad and declared, "The overall message of the ad is clearly misleading—especially since it appears to have been designed to piggyback off of Romney's gross misstatement that Chrysler was moving Ohio factory jobs to China." The pushback from Obama's backers and his campaign was even more aggressive. Former president Bill Clinton flew to Ohio and decried Romney's claim as "the biggest load of bull in the world." Vice President Joe Biden said, "I have never seen anything like that. It's an absolutely, patently false assertion. It's such an outrageous assertion that, one of the few times in my memory, a major American corporation, Chrysler, has felt obliged to go public and say, there is no truth."[106]

But, ultimately, the Obama campaign recognized that simply correcting the record was not enough. Romney had unleashed his nuclear arsenal. Obama had to return fire. An Obama campaign ad announced that "now, after Romney's false claim of Jeep outsourcing to China, Chrysler itself has refuted Romney's lie." What was Romney's response? His campaign upped the television ad buy and went on radio with an even more aggressive message.

And the Obama campaign upped its ad buy.

Mutually assured destruction framed around the lie that an American president was trying to shutter the American automobile industry. Obama ultimately won the Toledo area and Ohio and the presidency. But at enormous cost.

THE DOWNWARD SPIRAL

Most false advertising, like political advertising in general, is done on television. But TV is, remarkably enough, a milder political battleground than radio. And if you want to see the real dark side, open your mailbox and read the targeted direct-mail attacks that Rove most favors. Or pick up your phone and listen to the most toxic form of negative advertising: push polling. "A push poll," as a leading political science book defines it, "is essentially political advertising masquerading in the guise of legitimate scientific research, and it spreads lies, rumors, and innuendos about candidates."[107] The campaign attempts to influence or alter the view of selected respondents under the guise of conducting a poll, usually through telephone calls, and thereby facilitate entree to unsuspecting voters.[108] Phony "pollsters" ask a bogus question meant to promote suspicion about the opposition candidate.

Lee Atwater was one of the first to champion the use of push polling in the 1980s. And Karl Rove was not far behind. Rove's most famous candidate, George W. Bush, used push polls in his 1994 bid for Texas governor against incumbent Ann Richards. Callers asked voters "whether they would be more or less likely to vote for Governor Richards if they knew that lesbians dominated on her staff."[109]

Perhaps the most famous use of push polls was in 2000 when it was alleged that George W. Bush's campaign used push polling to torpedo the campaign of Senator John McCain. South Carolina primary voters reportedly were asked, "Would you be more likely or less likely to vote for John McCain for president if you knew he had fathered an illegitimate black child?" The poll's allegation had no substance but was heard by thousands of primary voters.[110] In the 2008 general election, Jewish voters in Florida and Pittsburgh were targeted by a push poll attempting to disparage Barack Obama by linking him with the Palestine Liberation Organization.

Push polling is the poison gas warfare of political campaigns, and in some respects it can be seen as simply taking negative advertising to its logical conclusion. But it is controversial for self-evident reasons and is always done surreptitiously. (In each of the 1994 and 1996 election cycles, there were credible reports of push polling in at least three dozen races.)[111] Campaigns that get caught with their fingerprints on a push poll can suffer blowback . . . if the discovery is made before Election Day and if there is a news media hawking the situation. That is why push polling, like the Kerry Swift Boat ads, is best done by third-party groups formally independent of the campaign so that campaigns have plausible deniability. Push polling is most effective when it is compatible with softer messages being done in the campaign's own attacks on the opposition, creating an echo effect and a sense that where there is smoke, there must be fire. The current environment is ideally suited to this caliber of campaigning.

Defenders of negative TV political advertising—no one defends push polling, to our knowledge—acknowledge it has a seamy underside. Their response, however, has been that the solution is to return fire with fire. "Responding to ads with ads," Glenn Richardson wrote, "is perhaps the most appropriate redress to distorted charges."[112] "Any ad from one candidate or party can always be countered with an ad by the opposing candidate or party," Ridout and Franz stated, adding, "This is a particular strength of television compared with other forms of campaigning."[113] "Advertising provides a visible and relatively effective way to respond to attacks," another team of researchers led by Franz argued. "For every thirty-second distortion, there can be a thirty-second clarification; every accusation can be met, every charge responded to in an effective, efficient way." These researchers chastised John Kerry for failing to respond to the Swift Boat attack ads right away and with full fire, much as others criticized Dukakis for failing to answer the Willie Horton charges in 1988.[114]

In 2012, serious candidates took this advice to heart. Both presidential campaigns were prepared to respond almost instantly to attacks against them and to return fire. Ads could travel from their "edit suites" to TV stations for immediate airing within hours. During September, the Obama campaign was rotating twenty unique ads among sixty markets and had the capacity to shift those ads at a moment's notice.[115] One account said that the campaigns could get a fresh ad on the air "within an hour" if need be.[116]

Franz and his colleagues, to their credit, acknowledged that the amount of money it takes to respond to attack ads has become more than a little daunting. It allows those with the most money to set the agenda for the campaign with bogus and/or irrelevant negative charges and forces the opponent to respond with gobs of money or let the charges appear legitimate. Psychological research indicates that there is a great advantage to playing offense, not defense, and to be the first to levy charges against an opponent.[117]

By this logic, the offended party would be wise to shoot first and force the other candidate to respond to the negative ad blitz. "Even principled politicians are under enormous competitive pressure to succumb to a manipulative politics of unreason," Bruce Ackerman wrote. "After all, if your opponents will batter you with hot-button sound bites, it won't do your principle much good if you lose the election. The only good defense is a sound-bite offense!"[118] In our view, that is more than a minor drawback to an otherwise functional democratic election system. It is absurd and disastrous. For fear of being repetitive, we want to say that playing offense is eerily close to embracing the mutually assured destruction of nuclear war games. But it is American electoral politics.

And, tragically, that is not the worst aspect of negative political advertising.

What is most striking about negative television political advertising is that it accentuates the tendency toward depoliticization. Countering the legitimate concerns people have that the great problems facing the nation require political solutions by a democratic state is an immense and overwhelming centrifugal force driving rational people away from the political system. It logically follows from the clear purpose of negative advertising: to turn prospective voters off from the candidates they are most likely to support.

Instead of being a "struggle of ideas," Franz maintained, attack-ad-based "elections are now about convincing people that the other guy is dangerous for America."[119] All ads seem idiotic and deceptive, so the wise course is to just abandon politics altogether. As one observer put it, "The only practical course for now is to believe nothing."[120] Even appealing candidates spend what seems like nearly all their time hassling their supporters for even more donations to pay for their own arsenal of negative ads or for responses to their opponent's negative ads. Why make a donation if the money is to pay for such slobbering nonsense? Let the billionaires cough up for such idiocy. They will win in the end anyway.

Depoliticization is an eminently rational, if ultimately self-defeating, response to a political universe where negative political advertising is the lingua franca. The trailblazing experimental research of Stephen Ansolabehere and Shanto Iyengar has been invaluable in this regard. They have demonstrated that the main consequence of negative ads is that it demobilizes citizens and turns them off from electoral politics, if not public and civic life altogether. As they put it, "The demobilizing impact of negative advertising has been a well-kept secret, and a tacit assumption among political consultants." The trend is toward "a political implosion of apathy and withdrawal."[121] Even those scholars who otherwise defend TV political advertising acknowledge the research establishes that "exposure to negativity is likely to increase cynicism, especially among nonpartisans."[122]

Depoliticization is cancerous to any credible notion of democratic self-government. Subsequent research by professors at Rutgers University and George Washington University "linked negative campaigning with reduced public trust and satisfaction with government." Richard Lau, Lee Sigelman, and Ivy Brown noted that negative advertising "has the potential to do damage to the political system itself."[123]

From 2008 to 2012, voter turnout fell from 58 percent to 52 percent, one of the larger such declines in consecutive presidential elections in recent American history. The explosion in negative advertising was not solely, or even necessarily primarily, responsible for such a drop-off, but it likely played a role. If nothing else, the correlation is striking. America's chattering classes and punditocracy were too entangled in their political junkiedom to see the forest for the trees.

So why does the United States have so much TV political advertising compared to nearly all other democracies? A seasoned observer of American life might ask if the reason such a dubious practice as political advertising is playing such a large and definitional role is because someone is getting very rich from it. It is time to follow the money. Where it leads is the subject of the next chapter.

5

MEDIA CORPORATIONS

Where the Bucks Stop

Don't Hate Political Advertising—Profit from It.

INVESTMENT ANALYST SCOTT EYMER, 2012

Americans may recognize political ads as an annoyance, or even an entertainment, but the general managers of television network affiliates in communities across the United States understand them as something else
altogether: a massive revenue stream. They are now such an important cash
cow that television stations in early caucus and primary states and fall swing
states plan presidential election years—and the years leading up to presidential election years—around the anticipated windfall. Political ads are no
longer a quadrennial bonus; they are essential to the bottom line for old-school
broadcast stations that have been hard hit by changing consumer tastes and
digital challenges.

When confusion about the date for the Iowa Republican caucuses held
up the flow of advertising dollars in the fall of 2011, the general managers
and national ad sales directors of stations in Des Moines and Cedar Rapids
and Mason City panicked. "We saw a little before the (summer) straw poll
and then nothing till late November," said Anne Marie Caudron, national
sales manager of KCCI, the CBS affiliate in Des Moines. "We were"—long
pause—"concerned."[1]

Over at the ABC affiliate, WOI, general manager Russ Hamilton was more than concerned. When the ads did not come, he said, "We were all dumbfounded. I've been in this a long number of years, and we were like, 'You've got to be kidding me.'" Then the money spigots opened. Hundreds of thousands, then millions of dollars flowed into the accounts of Iowa stations— $1.4 million in the week before Christmas alone. "It feels like they combined November and December into one month of spending," a gleeful Hamilton told the *Washington Post*.[2]

The money was moving so quickly—it would eventually add up to $102.20 per caucus goer—that some local managers grumbled about having to work over the holidays. Not Hamilton. The *Post* reported, "To minimize the chaos before a holiday weekend, affiliates closed their books on the purchases by Friday afternoon—except WOI. Hamilton said he would interrupt his steak dinner on New Year's Eve and upload some more commercials if it meant more dollars."[3]

It meant more dollars. A lot more.

In the 2011–2012 election cycle, $10 billion overall was spent on campaigns in the United States. Most of this spending went to pay for millions of television political ads.[4] Some of that TV ad money went to advertising professionals and campaign consultants. But the lion's share of the spending for TV political ads—90 percent, according to one report—went to purchase airtime on commercial television stations.[5] The airtime was a scarce commodity, and if candidates wanted it, they had to be willing to pay commercial broadcasters . . . a fortune. For the broadcasters, this was manna: a massive infusion of income that required virtually no labor on their part other than to make a bank run to deposit checks. They were like Jed Clampett striking oil in the Ozarks.

Well, not exactly like Jed Clampett. Jed was hunting on his own land when he struck it rich. Local television stations hunt on our land.

Commercial broadcasters receive monopoly licenses to sections of the publicly owned broadcast spectrum at no charge. The law states that the fortunate few who are recipients of these monopoly licenses get them on a temporary basis as long as they serve the public interest. The law is based on the assumption that the primary public interest the citizenry has is seeing that the airwaves are used to promote fair and free democratic life with informed public participation. The foundation of an effective democracy is credible elections, and broadcasting on the publicly owned airwaves is singularly positioned to make outstanding elections possible.

In many countries, public and private broadcasters make real contributions to the process. But not in the United States, where the civic and democratic values imagined when the licensing system was developed have been trumped by commercial excess. The robust democracy imagined by Progressive reformers who sought to update the founding principles of the American experiment for the modern age seems less attainable than at any time in a century. Where once a poet like Whitman wrote glowingly of presidential elections as America's "powerfulest scene and show," our ablest interpreters of the national Zeitgeist now suggest that the process does "damage . . . to the American psyche."[6]

"What we Americans go through to pick a president is not only crazy and unnecessary but genuinely abusive. Hundreds of millions of dollars are spent in a craven, cynical effort to stir up hatred and anger on both sides," wrote journalist Matt Taibbi on the eve of the 2012 election. "A decision that in reality takes one or two days of careful research to make is somehow stretched out into a process that involves two years of relentless, suffocating mind-warfare, an onslaught of toxic media messaging directed at liberals, conservatives and everyone in between that by Election Day makes every dinner conversation dangerous and literally divides families."[7]

But it wasn't all doom and gloom. As the election approached, newspaper business pages and broadcast industry trade journals were running celebratory headlines, proclaiming:

"E.W. Scripps Posts Profit on Political Ad Spend"[8]
"Political Boon Leads Gray to Up Estimates"[9]
"Election Money Fuels Big Gains for Scripps"[10]
"CBS Profit Climbs 16% as Political Advertising Boosts Radio, TV"[11]
"Sinclair Broadcast Earnings Rise in 3Q on Political Spending "[12]
"Politics Ads, Olympics Lift Belo 3Q Profit 81 Pct"[13]

Stock analysts noticed, counseling investors, "Don't Hate Political Advertising— Profit from It."

"Who will benefit the most from record setting political revenue?" asked investment analyst Scott Eymer in a fall 2012 column that ran beneath that headline. The answer: "A wide array of businesses profit from political spending, from advertising agencies and marketing companies to media outlets. But especially in 2012 and for the next several weeks, those publicly traded television groups with a coverage footprint which include local markets in battleground states will achieve spectacular political revenue. This is a one-time shot of significant cash flow, all paid in advance."[14]

Station owners and investors pocket most of the "spectacular political revenue." But a portion is diverted to lobbying against campaign-finance reforms that might affect the "significant cash flow." So it is that while thoughtful Americans fret about the damage done to our national psyche by media excess in the election season, media companies aggressively lobby for more, much more, of the same.

In many other democracies, where commercial broadcasting plays a smaller role and public broadcasting is relatively large, paid TV political advertising plays little or no role in the campaign process. There is no great commercial lobby that so greatly profits by ever-increasing amounts of TV political ad spending. Not so here. "In one of the great perversions of the Constitution foisted on its subjects by its overlords," Bill Moyers and Bernard Weisberger wrote, "the public airwaves where free speech should reign have become private enclosures to which access must be bought."[15]

This chapter follows the money and goes where the bucks stop. It is here, arguably, that the corruption and cynicism of the money-and-media election complex are most revealing.

THE MONEY TRAIN

In contrast to the rest of the democratic world, the United States adopted a commercial—for-profit, advertising-supported—radio broadcasting system in the late 1920s and 1930s. There was strong opposition to the commercialization of the airwaves at the time—a heterogeneous array of Americans fought diligently but unsuccessfully for a significant nonprofit and noncommercial broadcast sector in the 1930s. But not even the harshest opponent of commercial broadcasting could imagine our airwaves being used for political advertising.[16] Indeed, during the 1930s when Congress routinely considered radio regulation, the commercial broadcasters were lavish with free airtime for politicians and candidates from both major parties. Even socialists like Norman Thomas received airtime from NBC. And Franklin Delano Roosevelt, never a favorite of the media owners, broadcast thirty "fireside chats," ranging in length from fifteen to forty-five minutes, on the nation's new radio networks between 1933 and 1944.[17]

During this period, when their control over the system was under review, the commercial broadcasters went out of their way to establish that they could be trusted with a central role in the modern political process. For the next two decades, the commercial stations were careful not to appear to favor either political party and equally careful to give a sense that providing access to candidates was a key part of their public-service obligations. There was considerable criticism of how halfhearted the commercial broadcasters' election activities actually were during these years, especially by the late 1940s and 1950s, but by twenty-first-century standards the radio and later television networks might look as if they were being managed by the League of Women Voters.

When the radio networks were granted control over television by the Federal Communications Commission, candidate advertising began in earnest, but it took a long time to get to where the system is today. In the 1950s, political advertising had almost no impact on broadcasters' profit margins. In the 1960s and 1970s, TV candidate advertising was still a minuscule slice of total TV advertising revenues. By the early 1990s, the revenue numbers nudged up to where political ads accounted for around 2 percent of local TV station revenues, and a decade later TV political advertising was between 5 and 8 percent of total local station TV ad revenues.[18] In 2012, political advertising accounted for around 20 percent of TV station revenues.[19] In some key markets in swing states, local TV stations gained as much as 35 percent of their revenues from political advertising. Confirming a line from former New Jersey senator Bill Bradley, election campaigns were indeed beginning to "function as collection agencies for broadcasters. You simply transfer money from contributors to television stations."[20]

Political advertising has become a staple of the commercial broadcasting industry and the indispensable basis for its profitability. It is a dream business as it requires little or no sales force to shake the tree, and the money is paid in advance. Even before the 2012 campaign was under way, Wall Street stock analysts could barely contain themselves as they envisioned the growing cash flow. "Voters are going to be inundated with more campaign advertising than ever," one investor service wrote. "While this may fray the already frazzled nerves of the American people, it is great news for media companies."[21] As Carl Salas of Moody's Investors Service put it, "Virtually all U.S. broadcasters will benefit from spending on political ads in 2012."[22]

The matter was probably put best by Eric Greenberg, a partner of Paul Hastings Janofsky & Walker LLP, who regularly represents broadcasters in the buying and selling of television stations. A twenty-year veteran industry insider, Greenberg was blunt about the business model of commercial television: "Political advertising and elections are to TV what Christmas is to retail."[23] Keeping with the holiday motif, one public-interest advocate said, "Election season has turned into Black Friday for broadcasters. . . . It's just a huge bonanza."[24]

The 2012 election exceeded even the loftiest forecasts. As Election Day approached, Erika Franklin Fowler, codirector of the Wesleyan Media Project, said, "2012 will go down as a record pulverizing year for political advertising."[25] The advertising manager at Iowa's KCRG-TV9 could barely contain himself. "It's just light years different" compared with 2008, said Steve Lake.[26]

Ironically, years earlier Congress tried to stop price gouging of candidates by commercial broadcasters. It passed legislation requiring that in the sixty days before Election Day, presidential and Senate candidates had to be given the lowest rate the station had charged for similar spots in the previous year. That proved entirely ineffectual in 2012. First, much of the action took place before the fall: prior to the 2012 party conventions, political candidates and groups already accounted for half of the top twenty TV advertisers.[27] Indeed, the early advertising was central to Obama's reelection strategy, as postelection reviews of the campaign revealed.

"(Obama) framed the race in the summer as a choice between fairness versus tax cuts for the rich," explained a Brookings Institution analysis. "Using attacks on Romney's finance background at Bain Capital and failure to disclose tax returns, and GOP proposals to cut income taxes by 20 percent, Democrats characterized Romney as a rich and out-of-touch businessman who had little understanding of the economic plight of ordinary Americans. By the fall, many voters believed Romney would protect the rich while Obama would help the middle class."[28]

Second, at least half the TV political ads came from third-party groups, which were not eligible for the low rates. A majority of pro–Mitt Romney ads came not from the Romney campaign but from supposedly "independent" groups. As a result, ad rates at local TV stations, especially those in swing states, shot through the roof. "Stations can and will charge outside groups as much as they dare," Kantar Media's Elizabeth Wilner noted. These groups have "a willingness to pay whatever it takes."[29]

This meant commercial advertisers were then faced with vastly higher rates for the same amount of advertising. One station in Bismarck, North Dakota, for example, estimated its rates were fully three times greater in 2012 than they would have been had it not been an election year.[30] The giant Sinclair Broadcast Group announced that its political ad revenues *tripled* its expectations. "The political business . . . is an ever-expanding business," Sinclair's giddy CEO David Smith proclaimed. "I don't see any evidence that it's ever going to go away."[31]

There are three important consequences of the tidal wave of political advertising money that has flowed into the coffers of commercial broadcasters. The first consequence is that all of this spending means TV viewers were absolutely drenched in political commercials, especially in swing states for presidential ads and wherever there was a contested Senate race. "For people in those battleground states and battleground markets," Kenneth Goldstein of the Campaign Media Analysis Group said, it was "all campaign ads all the time."[32] One Boston advertising agency executive termed it "a snowstorm on TV of commercials like we've never seen."[33] The 2012 campaign saw nearly 4 million spots on local TV stations, almost double the 2008 level of 2.3 million local spots, and there would have been many more if there had been additional time available.[34] In the critical battleground state of Ohio, 207,518 presidential campaign spots ran during the course of the Obama-Romney race.[35]

"So many political ads. So little time. What's a TV station to do?" That was how the *Washington Post*'s Paul Farhi framed the dilemma facing stations across the nation, especially in battleground states.[36] Longstanding policies not to show competing political ads back to back and not to air political ads during news programs—a standard that had been established in order to defend the integrity of newscasts—were abandoned everywhere. Indeed, local news programs became among the most desired slots in the schedule.[37]

One study of the Columbus, Ohio, CBS-TV affiliate's evening newscast found twenty-two consecutive political ads in one half hour; another observer counted forty-five consecutive political ads on another evening's newscast on the same station.[38] The Washington, DC, Fox affiliate went so far as to temporarily add a half hour to its 6 PM newscast simply to accommodate the flood of political ads eager to be on a local news program. The ABC affiliate in our nation's capital shaved time from some of its shows to create more space for political ads.[39] But political ads quickly filled all day parts, and cable TV channels and cable TV systems saw large increases in their political ad sales as well. Comcast's vice president for political advertising—yes, now an executive position!—said many of the major cable TV channels reached "maximum density" thanks to the surge in political ads.[40]

Even this analysis barely conveys what it felt like to countless Americans in the summer and fall of 2012. Research by Kantar Media comparing the number of presidential TV political ads for one week in August in 2004, 2008, and 2012 in several American cities was revealing. The Las Vegas market had 867 such ads in 2004, 925 in 2008, and 2,870 in 2012. Orlando had 153 spot ads in 2008 and 1,863 in 2012. What about 2004 in Orlando? *Zero* ads, and that was during a competitive year for Florida as well. Columbus, Ohio, in arguably the most contested swing state of modern times, had 608 spots during the same week in August 2004. In 2008, the number was 832. In 2012, the total was 1,842. And these figures were just for presidential ads. According to Wilner, the increase in the number of presidential ads in swing states ranged from three to twelve times greater than the levels in 2004 and 2008.[41] As one reporter put it, people were "drowning" in ads.[42] But the ultimate confirmation of how bad things had become came from the man who won the presidential race, Barack Obama. More than two months before the election, Obama joked, "If you're sick of hearing me approve this message, believe me, so am I."[43]

The second consequence is that the popular antagonism toward political advertising, which has always been significant going back to the 1960s, absolutely exploded in 2012. And it wasn't just in Iowa and other battleground states that the revulsion was rising. Polling data, anecdotal statements—the works—all confirmed that voters across the country had by Election Day reached the conclusion expressed by Sheree Dierdorff, a Maryland voter who said of the advertising onslaught, "It's such a waste of time and money."[44] Dierdorff was interviewed while waiting in line to vote on a gambling referendum. But what she wanted to talk about on Election Day was the nightmare of political advertising. Her proposal: "a law that limits politicians and political action committees to broadcasting ads only in the three weeks leading up to Election Day."[45] Our bet: Americans of all political views would leap to approve Sheree Dierdorff's fix.

Evidence suggests that disdain for the political carpet-bombing of America with commercials in the run-up to elections transcends partisan and ideological lines. Indeed, it may well be that in this extraordinarily diverse nation, the one thing that unites all Americans more than anything else is their unanimous contempt for TV political advertising. (The other possible candidate: the deeply held conviction by most Americans that their local TV news is the worst in the nation.) As one New York State newspaper editor put it in the heat of the campaign, "I never thought I would look forward to seeing erectile dysfunction ads return to my living room."[46] Two frustrated Omaha pharmacists became local cult heroes when they sprung for and produced a parody of a TV political ad suggesting that "getting your teeth drilled is preferable to one more political commercial."[47] When Prime Minister of Britain David Cameron appeared on David Letterman's CBS show in September 2012, he received his loudest applause when he explained that Britain did not permit paid political advertising.[48]

But it is no laughing matter, especially to the commercial broadcasters. This overwhelming antipathy to what campaigns have become provides broadcasters' one great concern: that public anger might provide enough ammunition to get reform measures passed that would slow down or end the gonzo profits they are making.

The third consequence of this flood of ad dollars is that it could affect the structure of the industry. Broadcast analyst Greenberg expects that due to political advertising being so "huge," there will likely be another wave of mergers and acquisitions among TV stations.[49] This enhances a core concern in democratic theory: that media ownership should be diverse and competitive so as to prevent bottlenecks over the flow of information. Indeed, the one form of broadcast regulation that had real teeth from the 1940s to the 1980s was a commitment to strict broadcast station ownership limits. For most of that period, even the mightiest firms were permitted to own only five TV stations. The majority of local TV station revenues was controlled by a large number of relatively small regionally based firms. In the 1980s and 1990s, ownership regulations began to be relaxed under pressure from the largest media firms, the ones that owned the broadcast networks. By 2012, a single company was permitted to own as many TV stations as it could afford until that ownership extended to audiences accounting for 39 percent of the American population. But that's an official fantasy. The system is riddled with corporation-induced loopholes and waivers, such that Rupert Murdoch's News Corporation–owned TV stations actually reached 45 percent of Americans by 2007.[50] A handful of other giants have emerged to build similarly expansive TV empires. Some of these firms—News Corporation, Comcast, Disney—are media conglomerates with vast interests in film, newspapers, digital ventures, and publishing. They rank among the one hundred largest companies in the nation.

This is of particular importance because as the dominant television-owning firms get larger, their lobbying prowess only increases. And it is not as if commercial broadcasters were ever laggards in that department. The industry trade association, the National Association of Broadcasters (NAB), has been renowned as far back as the 1930s for its obsession with and near-total dominance over Congress in legislative matters. After all, commercial broadcasting is a government-created system of monopoly licenses granted at no charge to publicly owned property; controlling the various branches of government is central to the business model. The extent of competition is set by government policy; there is nothing "free market" in the equation at all. In addition to traditional business power, however, commercial broadcasters also controlled how politicians were covered on radio and TV, and how debates over broadcast policy issues were covered in the broadcast media. Consequently, few, if any, politicians wished to tangle with them.

Merge this traditional strength with the conglomerate power of a Comcast, a News Corporation, or a Disney, and the result is a political leviathan. The commercial broadcasting lobby determined decades ago that nothing would interfere with the golden spigot of TV political advertising. Today the matter is foundational to the industry's very existence. Yet its influence is rarely noted. Whole discussions about the barriers to campaign-finance reform can play out without mention of the most powerful force agitating against reform. We have a permanent lobby for a broken status quo. These "deformers," as clean politics advocate Ellen Miller referred to them, actually argue, "We need more corporate spending—not less."[51] And they tell us that what has developed is a natural state of affairs for American democracy. They are wrong.

IT DID NOT HAVE TO BE THIS WAY

America does not have a political process built on mounds of money and millions of negative commercials because Americans chose this circumstance, and certainly not because it developed organically from the founding of the Republic to the airing of the last attack ad. The politics we have today is the result of choices made over many decades. Much of the analysis of these choices focuses on campaign-finance reform legislation and judicial rulings, but choices with regard to how a media system develops are equally important. And equally definitional.

Research demonstrates that in those democratic nations with well-funded and prominent nonprofit and noncommercial broadcasting systems, political knowledge tends to be relatively higher than in nations without substantial public broadcasting, and that the information gap between the rich and the working class and poor is much smaller.[52] Stephen Cushion's recent research confirmed this pattern and noted that public-service broadcasters tend to do far more campaign reporting than their commercial counterparts. One of Cushion's conclusions is especially striking: those nations that have maintained strong public broadcasting continue to have better campaign coverage (e.g., news about policy that can help inform citizens about the relative merits of a political party or a particular politician). Moreover, the effect of strong public broadcasting is that commercial broadcasters tend to maintain higher standards than they have in nations where public broadcasting has fallen off in resources and campaign coverage.[53]

As with their global counterparts, U.S. public and community broadcasters have routinely done a better job of covering political campaigns than the commercial news media do. It is there that viewers are most likely to see debates or see in-depth interviews with candidates, even obscure candidates. But here the marginal status of American public media, combined with budgets that are microscopic on a per capita basis compared to those of nearly all other advanced democratic nations, means that the public media election coverage has considerably less substance and influence than it might otherwise. And the serious budget cuts public media have taken in recent years make their ability to do even rudimentary coverage far more difficult. But it is worth noting that in the recent past, leading American politicians understood that public broadcasting was a key to credible democratic politics in the United States, as elsewhere.

The time was 1967, a period of great tumult, and President Lyndon Johnson was vexed by a concern that had troubled him for more than a decade: a sense that American democracy needed to be repurposed to meet the new economic and technical demands of the television age. So it was that the most powerful man in the world devoted long hours to assuring that, instead of having American politics defined by commercial broadcasting, Americans would define the intersection of media and politics so as to reinforce "the bedrock of democracy."[54]

To that end, Johnson became determined to return to the fight that had been lost in the 1930s and establish a muscular public and community broadcasting system that would "be free . . . be independent and . . . belong to all of our people." We already discuss in Chapter 1 the remarkable campaign-finance initiatives of the Kennedy and Johnson eras and how close the United States came to a bipartisan consensus in favor of clean politics. For the purposes of this chapter, and the broader discussion about the role television plays in our politics, we focus briefly on the thirty-sixth president's equally remarkable attempt to create an "American BBC."

Johnson was a man of politics and media, a veteran of more than twenty-five years in the U.S. House, the U.S. Senate, the vice presidency, and the presidency. His family controlled a Texas radio and television empire that began with an Austin radio station that would eventually be dubbed "KLBJ." Readers of the epic biographical series penned by Robert Caro are well aware that Johnson used his political influence to build that broadcast network and his media influence to build his political career. But Caro readers are also aware that Johnson was a far more complex thinker—and doer—than might be suggested by the stereotype of the uncouth powerbroker stealing elections or threatening reporters.[55]

Like a striking number of world leaders in his moment, Johnson understood that at a point where developed nations were forging their futures in "the white heat of [a technological] revolution"—to borrow of a phrase from British prime minister Harold Wilson—governments were called upon to frame and shape the role those technologies would play in future societies.[56] And technologies that could define the political debates of a great nation—be they broadcast or digital (and both Wilson and Johnson were fascinated by the emergence of the computer)—were a particular concern.

Johnson put it another way in his speech ushering in a new era of public and community broadcasting:

> It was in 1844 that Congress authorized $30,000 for the first telegraph line between Washington and Baltimore. Soon afterward, Samuel Morse sent a stream of dots and dashes over that line to a friend who was waiting. His message was brief and prophetic and it read: "What hath God wrought?"
>
> Every one of us should feel the same awe and wonderment here today.
>
> For today, miracles in communication are our daily routine. Every minute, billions of telegraph messages chatter around the world. They interrupt law enforcement conferences and discussions of morality. Billions of signals rush over the ocean floor and fly above the clouds. Radio and television fill the air with sound. Satellites hurl messages thousands of miles in a matter of seconds.
>
> Today our problem is not making miracles—but managing miracles. We might well ponder a different question: What hath man wrought—and how will man use his inventions?[57]

Bill Moyers, LBJ's press secretary and confidant on public broadcasting matters, argued that as someone who had "become wealthy through a virtual family monopoly on media in Austin, Texas," Johnson "knew that something was missing from American television. There was more to what the medium could be if it were not measured by ratings and the bottom line." Presidents are often the last to know where a policy proposal is headed, but Johnson, said Moyers, knew exactly where he wanted this one to go:

> We thought democracy deserved better. It was one thing for information to be commercialized, privatized, and devoted exclusively to profit. But democracy doesn't live by bread alone; it lives on ideas, too, and occasionally it needs a full-course banquet of truth. Once television became the tool of commerce, only the price tag mattered. Contrary ideas, critical journalism, public debates, and programs that served the tastes, interests, and needs of significant but less than mass

audiences were rare items in the inventory of the marketplace. In only a few years television had become, in the words of the FCC chairman "a vast wasteland," a phrase that quickly entered the lexicon of lost opportunities.

We talked about how television could be much more of an open marketplace of ideas, available to everyone.

We talked about how instead of merely offering predigested views of current events or defining "debate" as the off-setting opinions of two politicians with vested interest in the issue, television could be more of a real battle of ideas, where one person might actually change another's mind.

We talked about how television could be more of a storyteller, providing people with some coherent sense of the broader social forces that affect their everyday world—portraits of the world and not just snapshots.

We talked about how television could be more diverse, exposing us to the experiences and thoughts of people living on the other side of the country or the other side of the globe, including thoughts that might rattle the cage of our own settled opinions.

We talked about how television could be more independent and how it could encourage journalism that would help check the corruption and abuse of power—something that was very much on the minds of our founding fathers when they provided for the constitutional freedom of the press.

We talked about how television could be more of a mirror held up to America, revealing that we are not all white, or male, or tall, or blonde, or blue-eyed, or brave, or Protestant, or rich, or powerful.

We talked about how television could be more than the boss' stenographer—how it would convey the interests and opinions of more people than the economic and political elites; how it could in fact help those elites understand the questions regular people asked every day—how to get a job, how to pay the doctor, how to put food on the table, how to get the kids through school, how to afford old age—the very questions corporate media scarcely valued.

All this talk led to something. It led us to believe that what democracy needed was a truly free and independent broadcasting service—free of both state and commerce. The President sat in on some of these meetings. He liked what he heard, and when he sent to Congress what became the Public Broadcasting Act of 1967, it was with a ringing request that "the public interest be fully served through the public airwaves."[58]

Bill Moyers well recalled how close they came. The Carnegie Commission prepared a report that LBJ used as the basis for his legislation; it coined the phrase "public television" in calling for "a broadcasting system that would be publicly funded but not government run, an important distinction to keep in mind."[59] U.S. public broadcasting was seen as providing cutting-edge political and creative programming that commercial broadcasting found unprofitable, and as serving poor and marginalized audiences of little interest to the commercial networks.[60] As Pennsylvania Republican senator Hugh Scott said during the congressional debates on the matter in 1967, "I want to see things on public television that I hate—things that make me think!"[61] The vision was bold: in the *New York Times* James Reston compared the Carnegie Report to the 1862 Morrill Act creating land-grant colleges and universities. Public broadcasting would change media, journalism, and politics just as land-grant colleges had begun "the great experiment of mass higher education in the United States."[62]

To the view of the Carnegie Corporation, this would be a well-funded service, based on an excise tax on the sale of television sets eventually reaching 5 percent and placed in a trust fund where politicians would not have direct control.[63] When the Public Broadcasting Act of 1967 was passed, this was the one key element of the Carnegie plan that was dropped. "It was a bold idea," recalled Moyers, "and it went nowhere."[64] Had it been fully implemented, public broadcasting would enjoy an annual budget that would be approaching the $4 billion range in 2012 dollars.[65] That is almost ten times more than the present federal budget for public radio and television.

What happened to put the kibosh on the crucial funding mechanism? Unfortunately, the men who controlled the congressional purse strings did not share Johnson's enthusiasm for "rededicating a part of the airwaves, which belong to all the people . . . for the enlightenment of all the people." House Ways and Means Committee chairman Wilbur Mills, a wily Arkansas Democrat whose committee developed and advanced legislation dealing with taxes, was called to the White House, poked and prodded by Johnson. But Mills, who despite initial reservations had helped the president establish a funding stream for Johnson's Medicare program, was not going along this time. "Well, that's all well and good, Lyndon," he told Johnson. "But you were up there long enough [in Congress] to know we ain't gonna give money to folks without some strings attached. We don't work that way."[66] Mills was in those days known as "the most powerful man in Washington."[67] And he refused to use that power to create an independent public broadcasting system robust enough to hold men like him to account. "That was that," recalled Moyers. "It meant a life on the dole for this new enterprise. And it left us vulnerable."[68]

Vulnerable—not just to bad television, but also to bad politics. Johnson's and the Carnegie Commission's vision of a dissident, edgy, and provocative broadcasting service to drive American culture and democracy to ever-greater heights was doomed from the start because the independent funding mechanism had been sabotaged. Before 1967 ended, nascent public broadcasting journalism was in the midst of controversy for programming it did on racism and for examining the dubious claims in television advertising.[69] When the newly formed Public Broadcasting Service (PBS) aired muckraking programs such as *Banks and the Poor,* it sent some politicians into a tizzy. President Nixon vetoed the public broadcasting budget authorization in 1972 to express his displeasure.[70] The Democratic platform that year, arguably the most left-wing Democratic platform since the New Deal, stated, "We should support long-range financing for public broadcasting, insulated from political pressures. We deplore the Nixon Administration's crude efforts to starve and muzzle public broadcasting, which has become a vital supplement to commercial television." PBS eventually did get its funding, but the message was made very clear to public broadcasters: be very careful in the coverage of political and social issues, and expect unwanted controversy if you proceed outside the political boundaries that exist in commercial broadcast journalism.

Although the Carnegie report and all the related documents surrounding the creation of public broadcasting emphasized the importance of the service to extending and deepening democratic citizenship and participation to the great mass of Americans, its importance for election campaigns was never directly stated; it was implicit. The importance became explicit with a revealing episode during the 1968 election campaign. The Carnegie Corporation gave a two-year $300,000 grant to Thomas P. F. Hoving to launch the National Citizens Committee for Public Broadcasting in 1967 to push the government to get the public system funded and operational.[71] Hoving, a Princeton PhD, had served as New York City parks commissioner before becoming director of the Metropolitan Museum of Art in 1967, his job at the time, all before turning forty.[72] Hoving assembled an impressive membership, a veritable who's who, of intellectuals including John Kenneth Galbraith, artists such as Harry Belafonte, civic leader Walter Sandbach of the Consumers Union and other leaders like him, and some business leaders and heads of nonprofit organizations. This group's purpose was to create a "people's lobby" that would pressure Congress to "pay off" on its "public broadcasting pledge."[73] Not only was Hoving frustrated that Congress was dragging its heels; he also thought the commercial TV networks and AT&T, which controlled the necessary wires to make a national network possible, were in no particular hurry to launch a fourth network.

In the summer of 1968, the National Citizens Committee for Public Broadcasting issued a report on the state of public broadcasting, and Hoving, a talented publicist, went on a media blitz for the next six months to push the cause of public broadcasting.[74] In the midst of the 1968 election campaigns, Hoving quickly gravitated to the issues that provoked an enthusiastic response: the horrible coverage of campaigns by the commercial broadcasters, the inundation of the airwaves by political advertising, and the desperate need for a noncommercial alternative. Commercial networks are premiering "new season trivia when our times literally scream out for relevancy," Hoving proclaimed. Candidates "are being seen primarily in paid political announcements—commercials—where they are shown to their best advantage. . . . The institution of free elections in this country is being reduced to the level of selling soap ads and dog food."[75]

The networks refused to air presidential debates unless they could get a waiver to prevent third-party candidates from participating. Hoving dismissed this as "an artificial issue and a stalling tactic." He noted that the existing public broadcasters had already announced their willingness to air presidential debates with all the candidates on the ballot participating.[76] The solution was obvious: "a fourth, noncommercial network" that could go toe-to-toe with the commercial players and raise the standards for everyone.

To judge by press accounts, with his emphasis on campaign coverage, Hoving struck a powerful nerve. "Mr. Hoving has a point. The debates should be held, even at the risk of including other than major party candidates," the *Boston Globe* wrote.[77] "It is unrealistic to think that a fourth, noncommercial network could be set up in time for the election," the *Christian Science Monitor* editorialized. "But the current lightweight electorate-information efforts of the commercial networks argue that one is needed as soon as possible."[78] The National Citizens Committee for Public Broadcasting's campaign floundered thereafter. Hoving committed the unforgiveable political sin of "arousing the wrath . . . of the commercial broadcasting lobby," something proponents of public broadcasting had steadfastly avoided doing at all costs.[79] The blowback was intense—from the fearful noncommercial broadcasters as well as from commercial interests—and effectively ended the campaign. He soon left the group, which was reformed as a public-interest group based in Washington to push for more public-interest work by the commercial broadcasters. The brief moment for fundamental reform, for muscular independent public broadcasting, to the extent it existed, had passed.

Almost since its inception, public broadcasting has been in the crosshairs of Dollarocracy. Conservatives in Congress use what little money it does provide as leverage to continually badger public broadcasters to stay within the same ideological range found on the commercial networks.[80] Conservatives are obsessed with public broadcasting because the traditional sources of control in commercial media—owners and advertisers—are not in place, and that means there is a greater possibility that the public system might produce critical work.

Milton Friedman wanted public broadcasting to be subject to "market discipline," while Rush Limbaugh characterized PBS as "an elitist group of politically correct millionaires."[81] In 1995, following the Republican takeover of Congress in the 1994 elections, Speaker of the House Newt Gingrich announced his plan to "zero out" federal support for public broadcasting. In 2012, Mitt Romney returned to this idea in the first presidential debate. Over the years, Democrats have proved timid in their defenses of the institution, and after LBJ none of their leaders ever expended political capital to elevate it from its marginal status, especially on the television side. At best, Democrats defended the status quo.

Ironically, while the conservative attacks on public media have created a rallying cry among the loud, hellfire elements of the right, they have never been embraced by the general population. Many conservatives actually *like* public broadcasting. And conservatives who value supporting a quality political culture over gaming the system to increase the odds of victory regardless of the consequences want no part of this battle. In 1984, no less a conservative icon than Barry Goldwater decried cutting any government funding to public broadcasting. Goldwater argued that the rise of commercialism on public broadcasting "marks the end of the only decent source of broadcasting in this country."[82] The Republicans dropped their plan to zero out public broadcasting in the 1990s when Congress was flooded with public opposition, much of it from conservatives who, presumably, enjoyed watching Bill Buckley chat with Ronald Reagan and Margaret Thatcher on the PBS program *Firing Line*.[83]

Without muscular public broadcasting serving the public interest, without commitments to replace advertising that sold candidates like toothpaste—as Adlai Stevenson had complained—without free airtime, and without the real campaign-finance reforms that would guard against the buying of elections, America met the high wave of the electronic age without adequate break-waters against abuse. The extent of the abuse would become increasingly evident as television evolved from its initial role as a campaign tool to become the defining force in American politics.

THE WASHINGTON BATTLEFIELD

In the 1970s and 1980s, there was continual grousing about political advertising and its perceived deleterious effects on the electoral process. There were also a number of reform efforts, though none led to anything that would change the system in any substantive sense. By the mid-1990s, however, the connection between money and politics was widely recognized as a very serious issue and as a threat to credible elections and governance. Warren Beatty's acclaimed 1998 political satire *Bulworth* addressed squarely the very issues that drive this book. Foundations devoted many millions of dollars to create organizations that would rally support for campaign-finance reform at the state and national levels. There was a concerted effort by top Democrats and Republicans—among them Senators Russ Feingold and John McCain—to require commercial broadcasters to provide free time to candidates so as to deemphasize the role of Big Money in corrupting the election system. This effort had widespread popular support. Yet it got so little attention that media analyst Howard Kurtz would note in an interview with McCain, "Now the major networks as best as I can determine have devoted zero airtime to this provision of yours."[84]

Kurtz and McCain established where the challenge lay:

KURTZ: In pushing this bill for free airtime, you are taking on the National Association of Broadcasters. Let me ask you a serious political question. What are you, nuts?

MCCAIN: They are the most powerful lobby in Washington.

KURTZ: Why is that?

MCCAIN: I think one of the reasons is, is because they can say we'd like for you to meet with the general managers of every television station in your state. You go into a room, hear the people that carry your message, and they never—they're very sophisticated. They're not saying do what we want done. Don't get me wrong, it's not that kind of a scenario, but it's very clear that these are the people that shape the opinion to a large degree of the people who are your constituents.

KURTZ: It's going to be awfully hard to beat in both Houses of Congress . . .

MCCAIN: Yes.[85]

Free airtime for candidates was a reasonable and modest demand; the commercial broadcasters received their monopoly licenses and rights to the scarce air channels at no charge in return for serving the public interest. The pertinent law assumes that these are firms that must go beyond just maximizing their own profits to justify their getting these lucrative monopoly licenses over other prospective licensees. Those broadcasters that refused to make concessions to the public interest would see their monopoly licenses turned over to a different firm when the term expired. (That this was the case in the letter and spirit of the law, but not in the application of the law, attests to the power of the commercial broadcasting lobby over the years.)[86]

In legislation and rulings, both Congress and the Supreme Court explicitly stated that providing campaign coverage was a definitional component of the public-service requirements for a broadcaster. The FCC even has a formal expectation that local broadcasters would cover state and local races, and until 1991 candidates in such races had an affirmative right of access to the extent the race could be considered significant.[87] As political advertising and the costs of campaigns mushroomed in the 1980s and 1990s, the amount and quality of commercial television's campaign coverage seemed woefully inadequate, and, on the whole, television's contribution to electoral democracy was regarded by more than a few Americans as increasingly destructive.

By 1997, the matter reached its apogee as a viable public issue. President Bill Clinton came out publicly for free airtime with the formation of the Gore

Commission. This was a body recommended by the FCC and appointed by the White House in 1997 to determine the public-service obligations of commercial broadcasters in exchange for their having received lucrative digital broadcasting spectrum for free—valued by some as worth $70 billion—in the 1996 Telecommunications Act. The president noted upon forming the Gore Commission that, although the move from analog to digital signals would give broadcasters "much more signal capacity than they have today," broadcasters had "asked Congress to be given this new access to the public airwaves without charge"—an end result the president found inadequate. "I believe, therefore, it is time to update broadcasters' public interest obligations to meet the demands of the new times and the new technological realities. I believe broadcasters who receive digital licenses should provide free air time for candidates, and I believe the FCC should act to require free airtime for candidates."[88]

The FCC chair at the time, William Kennard, was an ardent supporter of free airtime. No radical—he followed the FCC pattern and went on to a lucrative career as a wheeler-dealer in the telecommunication industry following his tenure—Kennard hoped that the Gore Commission would adhere to the president's wishes. But with several commercial broadcasters among its members, the Gore Commission proved next to worthless.

"At the end of the day," Kennard said, "the broadcast industry was fundamentally unwilling to accept any requirements that they broadcast more public interest programming."[89] "When President Clinton asked that broadcasters set aside free television time for candidates," columnist Jeff Cohen wrote at the time, the "NAB reacted with the indignation one might expect from the National Rifle Association if the president had proposed banning not only assault weapons, but hunting rifles, handguns and toy guns."[90] Kennard understood the core problem. "The Gore Commission report came after the spectrum had been given away. And so the leverage was lost."[91]

Clinton would eventually let the matter drop, but Kennard persisted in his efforts to secure free airtime for political candidates. He knew from getting out on the road that the idea was popular everywhere, across the political spectrum. "I'd go out to talk to groups, grassroots groups, and I'd say, 'Well, what about breaking some of this dependency of politicians on money by requiring broadcasters to give away some of their time for free?' and people would say 'Yeah, that's a great idea,' and we'd talk about how to do it." He quickly learned that popular sentiment notwithstanding, the range of discussion was far narrower in Washington. "You say the same thing at a cocktail party in Washington and people would look at you like you were crazy."[92]

Congress was certainly not listening to Kennard, or the people, on this one. In fact, when Kennard broached the idea of free airtime for candidates, key members of Congress made it clear that Kennard should drop the matter or risk seeing the FCC's budget cut severely. "The job has been made much harder because of the influence of money in politics." Kennard explained what happened behind the scenes:

> When I first started talking to people about free airtime for political candidates, some of my oldest and closest friends in Washington took me to breakfast, and they said, "Bill, don't do this; it's political suicide, you know. You're just going to kill yourself." And, you know, they were right. I thought it was so sad that we have so distorted the concept of what it means to be a public trustee that you can't even talk about these issues as an independent regulator without people castigating you. It's really sort of outrageous.[93]

No regulator or politician close to the levers of power has dared to expend political capital advancing Kennard's cause subsequently. The issue has all but evaporated since 2000, even among staunch progressives on the FCC such as Michael Copps. The various campaign-finance groups either folded their tents or reconciled themselves to the distant margins of polite society. The U.S. Supreme Court's *Citizens United* decision of 2010 seemed to lock in unlimited political spending and TV commercialism for all time, or until a constitutional amendment could be passed.

Nonetheless, there were two revealing incidents in 2012. By law, commercial broadcasters have to keep records of political ad buys, including their cost, and show them to anyone who asks. With the massive growth of super-PACs and overall political advertising spending, many people had a newfound interest in seeing who was paying for all the political ads on their local stations. Traditionally, that has meant that citizens had to trek to a local TV station's office and stay there to peruse the files. "The notion of someone walking in and looking at pieces of paper—in the 21st century—it's ridiculous on its face," public interest advocate Meredith McGehee said.[94] The majority opinion in the *Citizens United* decision had stated that transparency on the Internet was essential if the unlimited campaign spending it countenanced was not to be damaging to the electoral process.

FCC chairman Julius Genachowski, a Democrat, supported regulation requiring stations to post the material online so that citizens could more readily access it. But the broadcasters responded negatively, in part for fear that increased publicity might dampen the enthusiasm of some political advertisers to purchase spots. It "would ultimately lead to a Soviet-style standardization of the way advertising should be sold," one executive stated. They also claimed the cost of transferring the material to digital form was onerous and could lead to annual expenses of between $120,000 and $140,000 per station.[95]

The FCC voted on party lines for an Internet political advertising database in April. Beginning August 2, television stations affiliated with the top four networks (ABC, CBS, Fox, and NBC) in the nation's top fifty television markets were required to upload new political ad purchases to a *public database*. But as a Sunlight Foundation report noted, that left out "some 160 television markets, some of which are in battleground states." Sunlight's research concluded, "In four of the nine states considered key in this year's general election—Colorado, Florida, Virginia, Ohio, Nevada, New Hampshire, North Carolina, Virginia and Wisconsin—less than half of presidential ads would be disclosed on the FCC database."[96]

The NAB attempted unsuccessfully in the U.S. Court of Appeals to stay the rule in July and then announced it was proceeding to court to have the rule formally overturned.[97] The matter is to be taken up in 2013 if the NAB proceeds with the case. To the extent the matter received any digital or print news media attention, the commercial broadcasters were flame-broiled, not that it had any effect. "The hypocrisy of the media conglomerates, which (occasionally) insist on transparency in government but resist it themselves," Dan Gillmor wrote for Britain's *The Guardian,* "is unsurprising."[98]

The second incident concerned the massive influx of political advertising placed by third-party groups unaffiliated with candidates' campaigns. This posed a new dilemma for broadcasters. With regard to candidate ads, broadcasters could not check them for factual accuracy; they were protected political speech that had to run as they were. The news divisions of the stations could then criticize the content of the advertising if they found the material misleading or fraudulent. Not so with third-party political ads. Similar to commercial advertisements, broadcasters could reject them or require them to provide evidence that they were accurate. And it wasn't really an "option."

According to a 1971 ruling, the FCC should assure that stations must take "reasonable steps" to satisfy themselves "as to the reliability and reputation of every prospective advertiser." If stations fail to comply, a 1978 court ruling determined, it might be grounds for a broadcaster losing its broadcast license. Viewers have a right to view ads on publicly owned airwaves that broadcasters believe are accurate and not deceptive. "The FCC has a long history of expecting stations, as part of their overall obligation to operate in the public interest, to avoid knowingly airing false claims in commercial advertising," broadcast industry attorney Michael Berg wrote in *TVNewsCheck*.[99]

In part because much of the funding for these ads was anonymous, the third-party spots tended to be blatantly bogus. "The level of inaccuracy in the third-party presidential ads has been high," scholar Kathleen Hall Jamieson observed during the course of the campaign. One study showed that 57 percent of the money spent by the four biggest-spending third-party groups in Iowa was for ads containing misleading claims, the likes of which fast-food and automobile advertisers would have a hard time getting away with.[100] The Annenberg Public Policy Center determined that 85 percent of the money spent on ads by the four biggest-spending third-party groups between December 2011 and June 2012 contained deceptive information.[101]

Nevertheless, the commercial broadcasters punted when they were approached on the matter. FactCheck.org found not a single case of TV stations rejecting a third-party political ad or requiring third-party groups to verify the claims they were making in their ads.[102] As the head of the Iowa Broadcast News Association concluded, "The test for accepting an ad is whether the check that pays for it is good."[103] The FCC punted, too, apparently not wanting to tangle with the broadcast lobby. "They're not going to touch that until after the elections, if then," one activist on the issue informed us in the summer of 2012. FCC chairman Julius "Genachowski is afraid of his own shadow right now, especially when it comes to appearing to be too political in an election season."[104]

With only minor exceptions, the general sense emanating from the 2012 experience was that, while just about everyone else thought the entire system was breaking down, commercial broadcasters were cashing in. And the responsible regulators were watching from the sidelines. The Federal Election Commission was so ineffectual that there was virtually no significant penalty for breaking the rules. "The Federal Election Commission is a national scandal," said Fred Wertheimer, president of the campaign-finance reform group Democracy 21. "We have no enforcement of the campaign-finance laws."[105] "The enforcement system is so weak, nonfunctional," political advertising scholar Michael Franz put it, "that pretty much anybody can do whatever they want."[106]

As we discuss in Chapter 2, the term used in much of the commentary was that it was a "wild west" environment. "We're no longer arguing what standards we should apply to political advertising," *Washington Post* columnist Michael Gerson said. "We're starting to argue whether there are any standards whatsoever for political advertising."[107] *Rolling Stone*'s political correspondent Tim Dickinson concluded his examination of TV political advertising by noting, "The dirtier the system, the better for the bottom line at TV stations."[108] With the immediate stakes of winning an election, or making big bucks as a commercial broadcaster, hanging in the balance, the rational course is to shoot first and let the lawyers and lobbyists worry about any legal niceties later.

SERVING THE PUBLIC INTEREST

The corruption goes far beyond the flexing of lobbying muscle. Perhaps coincidentally, precisely as political advertising began to mushroom for commercial broadcasters, they began to lessen or even discontinue the manners in which they had covered political campaigns previously. The average number of free messages fifteen minutes or longer that broadcasters gave to presidential candidates, for example, fell from sixty in 1952 to twenty in 1972 to five in 1988 and, as far as we can tell, to zero thereafter.[109] Party convention coverage has shrunk; what were from the 1950s to the 1970s major civics lessons for Americans have become vacuous, scripted events. Candidate debates are rarely shown on commercial television, and commercial stations increasingly do not carry *any* debates except for three presidential and one vice presidential debates.[110]

Consider the 2010 U.S. Senate race in Wisconsin. Incumbent Russ Feingold offered to debate his millionaire opponent in forums across the state. It sounded like a great opportunity for Republican Ron Johnson, who had never sought or held public office and had little record in public life. Johnson could have had equal footing with the three-term senator he was trying to unseat—an opening that challengers historically have sought. But Johnson, who scrupulously avoided interviews with newspaper editorial boards that might have given a sense of where he stood, refused the debate offer.

Instead, he let his advertisements and those paid for by the Chamber of Commerce, American Action Network, and sundry organizations that flooded the state with anti-Feingold ads do his talking. Even when Johnson did participate in the three traditional candidate debates available for broadcast by the state's TV stations, some stations avoided airing them in prime time. These same stations were broadcasting Johnson ads around the clock, including the period when the debate was taking place. Wisconsin lawyer Ed Garvey, a former Democratic nominee for governor, tried to tune in to a much-anticipated Feingold-Johnson debate, only to find it was not being aired. He called the station and was told he could track it down on a Web site. "As a citizen, I was left with no option but the ads. I got nothing of substance from television stations," griped Garvey. "I thought they were supposed to operate in the public interest."[111]

Most ominously, the amount of news coverage of political campaigns on commercial television, never much to write home about, has fallen precipitously over the past three decades.[112] Thomas Patterson noted that the amount of network TV news coverage of campaigns plummeted from 1992 to 2000 alone.[113] By the new century, the average commercial television station had long been providing far more political advertising during a political campaign than it did news coverage of the campaign.

In a hotly contested U.S. Senate primary race in New Jersey in 2000, $21 million was spent on TV ads, but the stations receiving the ads averaged only thirteen seconds per day in news time on the race.[114] One study showed that in states with competitive Senate races in 2004, four times as many hours were given to ads for the race as were given to news coverage of the race. Another study of the 2006 election found a similar pattern.[115] "Local television news in most communities is unashamedly show business, not journalism," communication scholar Michael Schudson wrote in 1995, "and devotes only the slightest amount of airtime to local electoral candidates and issues."[116]

A study of eleven local media markets in 2004 determined that only 8 percent of the 4,333 news broadcasts in the month preceding the election had even mentioned a single local race. The same newscasts had eight times as many stories about accidental injuries as they did local races during this month.[117]

Indeed, the pathetic and appalling state of broadcast campaign coverage no longer requires academic research to be established; it is on a par with stating that people no longer tend to use the telegraph to communicate. One acquaintance we know who was running for governor of a Midwest state as a Democrat in a general election complained to a TV station manager that his campaign was not getting any news coverage. "You want to get on the air?" the broadcaster replied. "Buy an ad." Whether intentional or not, commercial broadcasters have little incentive to give away for free what has become a major source of profit for them.

In 2010, the Pew Research Center reported that broadcast news remained the most important source of news for Americans, with 78 percent of Americans turning to local TV on a typical day.[118] If there is a public-service component in commercial broadcasting, this is likely where it is to be found. How well are the broadcasters converting their revenues from political ads into quality campaign journalism?

By 2012, the ongoing tragedy was now a farce. The amount of resources going to broadcast journalism fell sharply in recent years. A *Columbia Journalism Review* study of a "hard-fought congressional primary near Scranton, PA, found that six local stations aired some 28 hours of political ads, and only a half-dozen news reports, over nearly eight weeks."[119] And it is not just the quantity, but the quality as well. Much of what little local TV broadcast news campaign coverage remains is superficial, focusing on polls, predications, and spin. Actual hard reporting is increasingly rare.

Some of TV coverage of campaigns actually uses political ads as the basis of news stories. "Releasing a single ad often drives millions of dollars in publicity," Wilner wrote. "A provocative ad can accomplish its mission without a single dollar behind it. Compare that with product marketing, where there's no free lunch."[120] Vanderbilt political scientist John Geer noted, "Ads now are not just aimed at voters. They are aimed at journalists."[121] TV news embraces this role, publicizing TV ads, especially negative ones, and assessing how much political impact the ads are having as the basis of the shows' political journalism.

Whole cable programs are devoted to "deep, searching" discussions of particular ads; television loves the visual and the chance to "cover" campaigns without ever leaving the studio. This is an ideal way for corporate broadcasters to cover politics: it is cheap and easy to do, takes no particular skill or intelligence, reaffirms that the Commercial is King, and reminds candidates that the path to news coverage goes through the ad sales department. Each of the examples of negative presidential ads in Chapter 4—from the Daisy ad and Willie Horton to Swift Boats—gained far more attention from the TV news coverage of the ads than the ads themselves generated. It is now part of the strategy in the money-and-media election complex to use ads strategically to drive or shift news coverage.

So where has local TV news been in covering some of the great political stories of our times, the ones that directly involve them? How has TV news fared in examining the massive influx of cash into the election process, as well as the veracity of the TV political ads broadcast? As the *Columbia Journalism Review* noted, local TV stations have an "obligation, given the ad saturation . . . to stay on top of this spending spree." They must also cover "when and how the ads mislead."[122]

Research during the 2012 campaigns provided comprehensive answers to these questions, and, to be sure, they took no one who ever watched television by surprise. The media reform group Free Press conducted comprehensive examinations in several swing states of how local TV news covered the role of outside third-party money in the states' political campaigns. These were all stations flooded with political spots from such groups, much to the dismay of their viewers. In Milwaukee, for example, there were no stories on any of the seventeen groups buying massive amounts of airtime before the recall election of Governor Scott Walker. But in the same two-week period, local news programs aired fifty-three stories on Justin Bieber. In Cleveland, the four network affiliates did no stories on the Koch-brothers–funded Americans for Prosperity, although that group placed five hundred anti-Obama attack ads on the same stations. In Charlotte, between January and August 2012, the three top-spending third-party groups spent $4 million for their ads at the network-affiliated stations. Those stations did zero stories on these three groups.[123]

Another Free Press study, this time in Denver, compared the amount of coverage local news shows gave to the five biggest-spending third-party groups with the amount of time those groups' ads ran on the same stations. The conclusion: for every 1 minute Denver TV news reported on these outside groups and their ads, the same stations ran 162 minutes of ads from these groups.[124] "In other words," journalist Edward Wasserman wrote, "the funders of political advertising appear to have purchased not just air time, but immunity from media scrutiny."[125] As the Sunlight Foundation's Bill Allison noted, local TV news has a "huge conflict of interest" when it comes to examining these subjects. "Broadcasters have an incentive not to see the system changed."[126]

Deep into the campaign, the Pew Research Center determined that only one in four Americans had heard "a lot" about outside third parties involved in the 2012 election, and that the balance of Americans had heard little or nothing on the subject. (A mere 2 percent of Americans thought the outside money had a positive effect on the election process.)[127]

WHO NEEDS FACT-CHECKING?

Even if third-party money was a new development in American politics by 2012, the notion of TV news (or news media more broadly) fact-checking ads has a longer pedigree. By the early 1990s, leading scholars like Jamieson argued elegantly that the news media could do a decent job policing TV political advertising to prevent candidates from misleading voters. Jamieson acknowledged that was a tall order in view of the pervasiveness and persuasiveness of the spots.[128] But, Jamieson argued, "fact-checking matters. The act of fact-checking does tend to improve accuracy in political ads and it helps voters learn."[129]

In the past decade, the bottom dropped out of that cup. To some extent, it was due to the shrinkage of traditional print media newsrooms. It was also due to the explosion in the number of ads, which were far beyond what even a large reporting crew could monitor effectively. "With a literal flood of advertising expenditures in contested battleground states," Darrell West wrote in 2010, "the ability of journalists to oversee candidate and group claims plummeted. . . . Journalists have relinquished that traditional role and left candidates to police themselves."[130]

As the 2012 campaign came to a close, Jamieson was reduced to pleading with television and radio outlets that "benefited from unprecedented levels of political ad spending this year to "increase their scrutiny of every non-candidate ad they are offered, rejecting those containing deceptions and protecting the public by using the power of their newsrooms to inform, contextualize, and debunk."[131]

Local TV news, conflicted as it is, gave an especially deplorable performance in fact-checking ads in 2012. In the examination of Denver, Free Press determined that there was more TV news fact-checking of political ads there than in any of the other communities it examined. The Fox affiliate, for example, ran a "Fact or Fiction" segment once or twice per week on the local news in the summer and fall anchored by veteran reporter Eli Stokols. But Stokols had no illusions about this periodic examination of political ads. "While campaigns are quick to cite such fact-checking spots in their effort to discredit opposition advertising," he wrote,

> the campaigns we call out for blatant falsehoods don't seem to care at all. And why should they? In a campaign that could see close to $1 billion in campaign spending, it's inevitable that any TV ad, however false or misleading, will air hundreds of times, overwhelming any news outlet's fact-check that might air a couple of times. . . . The fact-check itself becomes part of a countering ad, just more noise in a never-ending echo chamber of allegations and attacks.[132]

At every one of the Denver stations that did do fact-checking in their news of the ads, Free Press found that the stations nonetheless "kept airing ads that their reporters found were false or misleading." Free Press concluded that the "sheer amount of advertising has drowned out the few attempts to evaluate the ads' veracity."[133]

The same thing happened at WTSP in Tampa, where the station's reporters teamed up with PolitiFact to assess the credibility of TV political ads airing in the community. They gave an attack ad from Americans for Prosperity their lowest "Pants on Fire" rating. They did so, PolitiFact's Angie Holan said, "because it's so misleading, and it's ridiculously false." Nonetheless, WTSP aired the spot 150 times in the month following the report. "If the station's own news team says it is false, and they keep running it, you have to question the station's commitment to the audience," Free Press policy director Matt Wood said.[134]

Indeed.

It is difficult to review the commercial broadcasters' performance and not react like Dan Gillmor, who said one of the "great scandals" is how "television is complicit in this thoroughly corrupt system."[135] Or Bill Moyers and Bernard Weisberger, who asked, "When was the last time you heard one of the millionaire anchors of the Sunday morning talk shows aggressively pursue a beltway poohbah demanding to learn about the perfidious sources of secret money that is poisoning our politics?"[136]

Americans now take their predicament for granted, and many wade though the sludge of election campaigns in a state of despondence and depression, if they are paying any attention at all. How refreshing to hear words like these of Marty Kaplan: "Imagine what democracy would be like if elections were more than cash cows for local TV stations selling ads, if they were more than profit centers for conglomerates whose business model is monetizing the attention of—that is, entertaining—audiences. Imagine if campaigns really were what we deserved: great national conversations about issues and choices."[137]

Just imagine.

THE DISCUSSION IN this chapter leads to several questions: First, why does television get the preponderance of political advertising in an era when people are spending more and more time online? Put another way, has the system of television political advertising already reached its peak, and is it facing an inevitable decline? In 2012, the answer was clear: "Online is how you preach to the converted," Goldstein explained. "TV is how you reach the undecided, the passive viewers of politics."[138] "When it comes to political advertising," *AdWeek* wrote, "digital is still just a sideshow."[139] As Eli Pariser put it with regard to the Internet, "The state of the art in political advertising is half a decade behind the state of the art in commercial advertising."[140] Goldstein said one of digital's main functions at present is for "fundraising so that a lot of money can be spent on TV."[141]

At some point, however, the audience for television almost certainly will decline sufficiently that the money will begin to flow in different directions. By Election Day, more than a few politicos were wondering if "voters [might] become so tired of the messages, most of them negative, that they begin to tune them out."[142] The transition from television to digital appears inevitable; it is only a matter of time. Whether this will lead to a weakening of the money-and-media election complex or, as with commercial advertising, the money will simply flood whatever new arena emerges, possibly in a more insidious manner, is another matter altogether. In Chapter 8 we assess the extent to which the Internet has altered the system to date and what the indications are for it to do so in the visible future.

Second, nearly every scholarly treatment of political advertising and commercial broadcasting acknowledges the defects we highlight in this chapter and in Chapter 4. Indeed, we draw much of our critique from this research—and from the very public crack-up that was the 2012 campaign. Some of these scholars, however, are sanguine about political advertising's role in American democracy. Their defense of political advertising invariably assumes there will be a credible political journalism—a viable Fourth Estate if you will—that will provide an effective counterbalance to political advertising, if not provide the preponderance of political information to the citizenry. After all, research repeatedly confirms that political ads "are most effective with less-engaged voters."[143] If the United States has a high-quality political journalism, the ability of bogus and destructive TV spots to dominate campaign discourse will be sharply reduced, if not eliminated.

But television journalism has all but abandoned its duty to provide fact-checking and thorough reporting as a corrective to political advertising. This puts increased pressure on the balance of the news media to do yeoman's work to protect the integrity and vitality of the political culture. Are the news media doing their job satisfactorily? To the extent they are not, where does that leave matters?

These are the questions we turn to in Chapters 6 and 7. We will not keep you in suspense: the news is not good.

6

THE RISE AND FALL OF PROFESSIONAL JOURNALISM

There are in the body politic, economic and social, many and grave evils, and there is urgent necessity for the sternest war upon them. There should be relentless exposure of and attack upon every evil man, whether politician or business man, every evil practice, whether in politics, business, or social life. I hail as a benefactor every writer or speaker, every man who, on the platform or in a book, magazine, or newspaper, with merciless severity makes such attack.

THEODORE ROOSEVELT, "THE MAN WITH THE MUCK RAKE," APRIL 15, 1906

On the eve of the critical CBS News/*National Journal* debate among the candidates for the Republican nomination for president in the fall of 2011, CBS News' political director, John Dickerson, was notified that Congresswoman Michele Bachmann of Minnesota, a conservative firebrand who had won the Iowa straw poll and continued to mount a credible if not front-running campaign for the party's nod, would be available to join an online discussion following the debate. Dickerson indicated that he would prefer to "get someone else" because Bachmann's poll numbers had dropped "nearly off the charts."[1] Fair enough. Journalists get to choose whom they want to talk with. In an e-mail sent to his colleagues, Dickerson announced that the congresswoman was "not going to get many questions" in that evening's debate.[2]

Sure enough, when the eight Republican contenders took the stage in Spartanburg, South Carolina, that night, Bachmann was passed over by the moderators, again and again and again. Instead, attention was lavished on the front-runner of the moment, Herman Cain, whose candidacy would crash and burn before the lights were flipped on for the first Iowa caucus, and on the best-funded if least-loved candidate, Mitt Romney. It was fifteen minutes into the debate before Bachmann got a question. She never got any follow-up questions. Indeed, she was so marginalized that press reports from the high-profile event barely mentioned her presence. And she wasn't alone on the sidelines. Former Utah governor Jon Huntsman, who as a former U.S. ambassador to China brought unique skills and qualifications to the race, was so neglected that night that when a question finally came his way, Huntsman expressed relief, saying, "It gets a little lonely over here in Siberia."

But in the high-stakes game of presidential politics, this was no laughing matter. It's devastating for credible candidates who, though they might be down in the polls at the moment, are denied an opening to reintroduce themselves at a point in the race when voters are beginning to focus seriously on the contest. Bachmann complained about the neglect, and she had no trouble making the case that it was intentional. Why? Dickerson had mistakenly hit "reply to all" when sending his "not going to get many questions" e-mail, and "all" included Bachmann's communications director. The Bachmann team went apoplectic, with the candidate declaring, "Clearly this was an example of media bias." Her aides complained that their candidate had been victimized by the dreaded "liberal mainstream media elites[, who] are manipulating the Republican debates by purposely suppressing our conservative message and limiting Michele's questions."[3] We're not so sure about that. There were plenty of conservatives on the stage at the CBS/*National Journal* debate, and they got plenty of opportunities to mouth right-wing talking points.

Yet with regard to which candidates got questions, and with them the attention that makes or breaks a campaign, there is no debating that the fix was in. When Dickerson's e-mail was revealed, his defenders argued that the network's political director had no say with regard to the character, content, and quantity of questions asked in the network's big political debate. Dickerson, they said, was just spouting "his punditristic [*sic*] expectations of the event," and Bachmann was a "second-tier" candidate who got the coverage she deserved. Perhaps. But isn't that a much more serious issue, and a much more fundamental problem for democracy? When consensus punditry trumps curiosity, when it is clear before a debate even begins that candidates who have qualified to participate in that debate are not going to get questions, then we have reached a point where the media are deciding who gets a chance to break out of the pack and, indeed, who gets a chance to win or lose. This bias can shape a race every bit as thoroughly as a negative ad or a grassroots mobilization. Indeed, given the omnipresent role and influence of media in the shaping of our discourse at the early stages of campaigns, they often set the field before a single ad is aired, before a single field office is opened.

Yet for the most part, while most observers increasingly grasp the defining influence of money on American election campaigns, they do not similarly appreciate the defining role of media. Most election coverage is not just inadequate but also inaccurate. It warps our understanding not just of particular elections but also of the changing dynamics in our politics. It preserves and even enhances a dysfunctional status quo while narrowing prospects for real reform. Only when we consider the interplay of money and media influences can we begin to identify not just symptoms but also disease. And until the disease is diagnosed, there can be no sufficient cure.

There is reasonably broad recognition today of a symptom: the hijacking of American elections to the point where they have lost much of their capacity to provide a popular check on entrenched corporate power and the wealthy over the government and the broader political economy. But as much as anything, the disease that afflicts American elections is a media crisis, and it reflects the disintegration of a credible journalism system. Indeed, if the United States had a sufficient journalism, the ability of the wealthy and corporations to dominate politics and elections would be considerably weakened. Political advertising would have less effect; the need for gobs of money would be less pressing. For that reason, the path to rejuvenating elections and democracy goes through media policies as much as anything else. There can be no question, in a modern society with increasingly sophisticated communications, that credible journalism is a necessary precondition for effective elections and for self-government.

"Elections are also proxies for democracy," Herbert Gans wrote, "because they are virtually the only occasion in which citizens play a major [role] in government."[4] There is arguably no greater test of the quality of a press system than how it prepares voters for elections. If media outlets flunk this test, it really doesn't matter how good a job they do analyzing some celebrity's love life or reporting on a car crash.

Until rather recently, the matter of having a sufficient journalism for elections was a fairly straightforward proposition. There were reporters who worked for news media, and their job was to accurately convey what the issues were, where the candidates stood on those issues, and what the pertinent characteristics, records, and qualifications of the candidates were. The calculus, never quite as simple as it seemed but always well understood, went like this: journalists would give the voters the straight news, without bias or a political agenda, and let those voters come to their own conclusions.

Equipped with that information, voters could successfully participate in elections, and democracy worked. As one great newspaper's motto put it, "Let the people have the truth and the freedom to discuss it and all will go well."[5] Popular information, broadly available and easily accessible for all, was essential to the calculation. Were the news media to fail to fill the void, voters would be left adrift in the middle of the ocean on a raft, while political and economic elites sailed by on their ocean liners. But failure could be averted by scholars and analysts, whose role it was to admonish news media for foibles and limitations in covering campaigns—or, when appropriate, praise them for their accomplishments—in an effort to make the system work more effectively.

These are the broad outlines of a media system built around the premise of "professionalism."

To most Americans today, including many reporters, a commitment to professionalism and objectivity remains the hallmark of the First Amendment and of our constitutional system. They assume it has always been the American way and no other way is possible for a democracy. To the extent our news media fail today—in election coverage or otherwise—it is, the theory goes, because they have strayed from the professional path. And as Americans are now experiencing the unprecedented disintegration of the profession and institutions of journalism—to the point where they barely exist in a meaningful sense—people are at a loss to comprehend why it is happening and what, if anything, can be done to reverse the situation. Because rejuvenating journalism is one of the crucial reforms that must be enacted to make elections meaningful and democracy functional, this book argues that a misunderstanding of American journalism proves to be a major barrier to policy debates and eventual action.

In this chapter we chronicle the rise and fall of professional journalism. To do so, we assess the role of journalism from the beginning of the Republic, several generations before contemporary theories of professionalism and objectivity in the news existed. What we find is that at all times the connection among news media systems, journalism, and the caliber of elections has been a primary political concern in this country. Although there is much to value in professional journalism, the knee-jerk embrace of it as the be-all and end-all fails to convey that some of the most successful periods of American electoral democracy, not to mention other successful democracies, had news media systems that operated under premises and with purposes substantially different from what nostalgic admirers of Watergate-era journalism pine for. Although there are no perfect systems for creating and disseminating political news, some, on balance, are far more conducive to popular sovereignty than others. And Americans who would shape a democracy-sustaining and -enhancing media are fortunate to have a very rich press tradition from which to draw.

THE PARTISAN ROOTS OF AMERICAN JOURNALISM

America was called into being by a journalist, Tom Paine, whose writings for the radical weekly newspapers of the colonial era framed the arguments that would be collected in his seminal works of American revolution, the pamphlets *Common Sense* and *The Crisis*.[6] After their revolution against the British Empire had succeeded, the founders outlined a "freedom of the press" provision in the First Amendment to their Constitution not as a protection for the Rupert Murdochs who were to come but as a necessary defense against the excess of elites.

The singular importance of a broad-based newspaper system that provided citizens with the resources to effectively participate in politics was foundational to the American experiment. As Thomas Jefferson put it, this was the only way people without considerable property could ever be politically equal to the wealthy who traditionally ruled societies. There was no sense in the first decades of the Republic that entrepreneurs pursuing maximum profit through the "market" would generate a satisfactory quantity and quality of journalism to achieve the Jeffersonian standard. The wealthy would certainly have a commercially driven journalism to meet their needs, but everyone else would be out of luck.

To create the circumstance necessary for a popular journalism to flourish, the federal government instituted extraordinary postal and printing subsidies to spawn an independent press. To give some sense of the commitment, if the federal government subsidized journalism as a percentage of GDP today at the same level it did in the 1840s, it would have to spend in the range of $30–35 billion annually.[7] When Alexis de Tocqueville came to America in the 1830s, he was astounded by the prevalence of newspapers far beyond that to be found anywhere else in the world. "The number of periodicals," he wrote, "exceeds all belief." He was also impressed by the inextricable relationship of newspapers to political equality and to democratic governance. "The power of newspapers must therefore increase as men become equal."[8] It was no accident; it was the result of explicit government policies and subsidies.

Journalism, the newspaper system, the Fourth Estate, effectively became synonymous with the party system that dominated American politics through the nineteenth century. Readers defined a party or a political movement by its newspapers; if a party or movement did not have a newspaper, it effectively did not exist. Virtually all newspapers were explicitly partisan, usually linked to a party or even a faction within a party. Sometimes newspapers received direct subsidies from parties. Newspaper editors—generally also the newspaper owners—were important partisan political figures. Andrew Jackson, for example, appointed fifty-nine editors to government positions upon taking office in 1829. The measure of a newspaper's success was to some extent commercial—few publishers were generating fortunes in a competitive market. But it was arguably as much political: Did the newspaper's party win elections and control government policy-making? The competition for voters put a check on outlandish propaganda for the most part. Likewise, the ability to launch new newspapers, and take advantage of the huge postal subsidies, meant that newspapers could not take their readership for granted.[9] A democratic partisan press system with genuine competition and no censorship was a far cry from what is often associated with partisan press systems today, such as the totalitarian propaganda systems of Nazi Germany or Soviet Russia, where only one party was permitted to have a voice and everyone else either shut up or was locked up, or worse.

At the same time, it would be inaccurate to read back to the antebellum United States our contemporary obsession with elections as the essence of politics and political journalism. Politics was very much about parties and policies, like slavery, tariffs, the economy, and expansion. Newspapers often engaged in serious expositions on policy matters, sometimes in debate with other papers. Elections and voting were important, of course, but they tended to be more the entrée to political life and citizenry than the epitome. To provide some sense of partisan journalism, Karl Marx was the European correspondent for Horace Greeley's *New York Tribune* in the 1850s and considered one of the great reporters of the era. It can fairly be argued that the Republican Party would not have come into being had it not been for Greeley's *Tribune,* which circulated nationally in the form of a weekly edition that in the late 1840s and early 1850s linked the network of disappointed Whigs, dissenting Democrats, and radical reformers that would form the infrastructure of the new party.

Among the regular readers of Greeley and Marx, as well as the leading advocates for ending slavery, distributing land to the poor, welcoming immigrants, and extending popular democracy, was an Illinois lawyer named Abraham Lincoln, who devoured the *Tribune* when it arrived via the mails at Springfield.[10]

At the same time, Walt Whitman was editing the *Brooklyn Eagle,* a rigidly Democratic paper. And the most prominent print proponent of the 1852 presidential candidacy of Franklin Pierce was Nathaniel Hawthorne, who in the previous two years had risen to national prominence as the author of *The Scarlet Letter* (1850) and *The House of the Seven Gables* (1851). It is not surprising that some scholars have argued the partisan press of the first half or so of the nineteenth century produced the highest caliber of journalism in our nation's history. After all, the partisan press attracted the finest literary voices of the era to the work of writing articles, pamphlets, and campaign biographies that Hawthorne said were "intended to operate on the minds of multitudes during a presidential canvass."[11]

The strength of the partisan system of journalism is that it generally puts politics in context and attempts to make sense of political issues and events, which is very attractive. Facts are not presented unconnected to other issues or to political values. "Unlike our contemporary papers," Richard Kaplan, one of the leading scholars on the matter, observed, "the partisan paper was thus authorized to explore systematically and repeatedly the various social implications of governmental policies in editorials and in feature articles."[12] The partisan press made elections come to life with a vibrancy few living Americans have ever experienced. Not surprisingly, the system contributed to far higher rates of turnout among eligible voters, especially in the northern states, than has been the case for the past century. "Political participation," one scholar noted, "skyrocketed during an era of partisan press."[13]

This is not to say that the partisan system was perfect, or necessarily superior to what would follow it. The system produced extreme attacks on enemies and its share of nonsense. But elements of the partisan system remained central to some of the most vibrant democracies in the world throughout the twentieth century. Even those who were often at the receiving end of its strongest criticism, like Jefferson and Lincoln, were among its strongest proponents. In a manner that would likely surprise most contemporary observers, nineteenth-century Americans thought the partisan press system was ideal for spawning diversity, getting at the truth, and making democracy effective. It *was* the free press, and it worked. "I am a firm believer in the people," Lincoln said. "If given the truth, they can be depended upon to meet any national crisis."[14]

The political and media landscape began to change in the final third of the nineteenth century, in the era following the Civil War that saw the rise of manufacturing and the transition of America from an agrarian economy to the industrial economy that would characterize much of the twentieth century. The population exploded, cities grew from outposts to metropolitan centers, advertising rapidly became a major economic force, and printing costs plummeted; newspapers truly became a ubiquitous mass medium. Printing subsidies ended, and postal subsidies became far less important as daily newspapers were distributed increasingly by their own circulation networks. This was an extraordinarily competitive market—with new entrants routinely appearing, other papers falling by the wayside, and chain ownership being all but nonexistent—typified by numerous daily newspapers in any cities of consequence and often ten or more daily newspapers in major cities. Newspaper publishing was booming and in the process becoming very lucrative.

Newspaper journalism in this period remained stridently partisan, and all newspapers were identified by party affiliation. Election coverage would invariably focus almost exclusively on the party's candidates and neglect altogether the opposition. To some extent, the partisan status was a carryover from earlier years, and Americans expected their newspapers to be active political agents. In the late nineteenth century, most Americans explicitly identified with a specific political party. As Kaplan put it, in this period "partisan identification was so pervasive that political independents were likened to some impossible third sex, a hermaphrodite species."[15] Newspapers needed to do the same to attract readers. Moreover, in markets where no newspaper had more than a sliver of the total population, each newspaper was wise to distinguish itself by adopting a partisan stance. Newspapers played a critical role in maintaining and even extending the high voter turnout rates until the end of the nineteenth century. In the late nineteenth century, 78.5 percent of eligible voters participated in presidential elections, 84 percent if the South is excluded. In 1896, arguably the most sharply defined election in American history because of the brief Populist takeover of the Democratic Party's national ticket under William Jennings Bryan, fully 95 percent of Michigan's eligible voters went to the polls.[16]

Beneath the surface, however, important changes in American politics and journalism were taking place that would undermine partisan journalism and eventually turn the news on its head. By the 1870s and 1880s, the two main parties had dropped their relatively strong and distinct ideological identities and become increasingly amorphous. Much as C. B. Macpherson argued, this was accompanied by both parties being increasingly comfortable with the big business domination of the emerging industrial political economy. Much of the distinction between the parties was geographical, traditional, ethnic, and familial—much like the religion a person inherited—but the parties hardly took consistent and sharply defined antagonistic positions on the central issues of the day.

This was a period marked by growing inequality and levels of corruption comparable to what the United States is experiencing today. Consequently, the new pressure in American politics in this period and going forward came primarily from social movements, such as the Populists, the labor movement, suffragists, and the Progressive movement, that existed outside the two entrenched parties, which pretty much had a lock on the electoral system. In the case of the Progressives, they infiltrated each of the parties, depending upon geographical location. These movements got short shrift in the daily newspaper press, and they relied as much as possible on their own newspapers and magazines to make their cases. The postal subsidies proved essential for their survival, especially as the emerging advertising-based newspaper economics was hardly conducive to anticorporate and prolabor politics.

At the same time, daily newspaper publishers began to emphasize nonpartisan political news, and so the percentage of the stories outside of editorials that could be considered explicitly partisan fell sharply. In the late nineteenth century, newspapers still rallied the troops for elections, but the intervening political coverage diminished, to be replaced by nonpolitical news. The sort of policy coverage that had been routine through midcentury fell by the wayside. "The reading public had become relevant only as the voting public, and not as a participant in political opinion formation," Kaplan noted. "Into this gap between party and public, corporate interests were able to enter and exercise their influence over governmental decision-making."[17]

In some cases, profit-hungry publishers found that sensationalism, what came to be called "yellow journalism," was a lucrative course. Bribery of journalists, favoritism toward advertisers, and assorted unethical practices were not uncommon. Most importantly, by the 1890s newspaper markets began to shift from being competitive to being oligopolistic, even monopolistic, markets. Although revenues and population continued to increase sharply, the overall number of newspapers began to stagnate and then fall. "The stronger papers are becoming stronger and the weaker papers are having a hard time to exist," one newspaper executive observed in 1902.[18] Newspapers began to serve a larger and larger portion of their community's population—with much less fear of new competition than had been the case—and had considerable power as a result.

In addition, the great chains of Pulitzer, Hearst, and Scripps were being formed almost overnight. The new publishing giants no longer had any need to be closely tied to political parties; in fact as local newspapers grew more monopolistic, partisanship could antagonize part of the market and undermine their commercial prospects. Yet many publishers continued to use their now-monopolistic power to advocate for their political viewpoints, which were generally conservative, probusiness, and antilabor.[19] The great progressive Robert La Follette devoted a chapter of his book on political philosophy to the crisis of the press. "Money power," he wrote, "controls the newspaper press . . . wherever news items bear in any way upon the control of government by business, the news is colored."[20] La Follette argued:

> Except for the subserviency of most of the metropolitan newspapers, the great corporate interests would never have ventured into the impudent, lawless consolidation of business, for the suppression of competition, the control of markets, production and prices.
>
> Except for this monstrous crime, 65 percent of all the wealth of this country would not now be centralized in the hands of two percent of all the people. And we might today be industrially and commercially a free people, enjoying the blessings of a real democracy.[21]

So frustrated was La Follette that he forged his own publication, initially *La Follette's Weekly,* now *The Progressive,* with the stated purpose of "winning back for the people the complete power over government—national, state, and municipal—which has been lost to them."[22]

La Follette and his kind were raging against the dying of the light, and they would fight with some success during what was known as the Progressive Era. But the forces arrayed against them were more financially powerful and more determined to consolidate the power of the press for the purpose of consolidating the power of the economy in the service of what would come in 2011 and 2012 to be known as "the 1 Percent."

ENTER PROFESSIONAL JOURNALISM

The reshaping of American journalism as a steady defender of a corporate-defined and -dominated status quo did not happen immediately. These changes never play out with that sort of precision. But the arc of history was bending in the direction La Follette and other Progressives feared, toward a place where the press was no longer inclined to attack the politically and economically powerful with the "merciless severity" that Teddy Roosevelt declared in 1906 to be an "urgent necessity."[23]

A crisis in journalism lasted from the 1890s until the 1920s. Party-driven journalism had disintegrated, the increasingly lucrative and powerful newspaper magnates ruled their independent empires and exercised considerable political power, and the pursuit of profit sometimes led to an incredible, even appalling, journalism. Mounting public anger and dissatisfaction with the journalism of this era produced what became the first great existential crisis for journalism.[24] The problem at its core was that a relatively small number of very powerful newspaper owners dominated their communities and states, and a handful of them had national empires. Market economics was pushing toward more concentration and ever less competition. As even the publisher of the Scripps-owned *Detroit News* argued, in private, in 1913, the corrosive influence of commercial ownership and the pursuit of profit were such that the rational democratic solution would be to have municipal ownership of newspapers.[25] In view of the explicitly political nature of newspapers in American history, this was not as absurd a notion as it may appear today. Scripps, always the most working-class-oriented of the major chains, even launched an ad-less daily newspaper in the 1910s, because it saw how commercialism undermined the integrity of the news.[26] By 1912, three of the four candidates for president— Woodrow Wilson, Theodore Roosevelt, and Eugene Debs, all but President William Howard Taft—made the irresponsibility and corruption of the daily press a theme of their campaigns. The world of newspapers had turned upside down in three decades.

The major newspaper owners were able to repel any serious threat to their survival, and to do so, they promoted a new sense of journalism, one that saw the press as independent of politics, neutral in stance, and there to provide the facts necessary for citizens to understand the world and participate effectively as citizens. Put crudely, publishers gave up their direct personal control over news content that had been the hallmark of American journalism to create a product that would have legitimacy and allow the increasingly monopolistic commercial system, already generating lovely profits, to remain in place. The more visionary owners, like Joseph Pulitzer, argued that journalists needed to be educated at universities, and that there needed to be a "Chinese Wall" between the newsroom and the business offices. In this way, readers could trust that they were getting straight news that was not playing favorites for owners, advertisers, politicians, or the editors and reporters themselves. There were no schools of journalism in 1900; by the 1920s nearly all of the major schools had been established across the nation. In 1922, the American Society of Newspaper Editors was established and formally adopted its professional code of ethics for reporters forthwith.

For press owners, professionalism was the solution to their problem. As Edward Scripps explained it, once readers "did not care what the editor's views were . . . when it came to news one paper was as good as a dozen."[27] If trained journalists were striving to present an objective report, monopoly would no longer be a pressing concern. Moreover, all attention to understanding news coverage would focus on editors and reporters as the decisive players; publishers and advertisers would drift into the background. This was a striking shift in American journalism. For the first century of the Republic, the vast majority of papers were owned and edited by the same person and the newspaper reflected the owner's partisan viewpoint. Knowing the owner meant knowing the paper.

Americans today often regard independent, nonpartisan, factually accurate reporting conducted by commercial enterprises as the ideal form of democratic journalism, for understandable reasons. But accomplishing such a system without having significant problems proved to be impossible. Scarce resources needed to be deployed, and some topics would therefore receive coverage and others would not. There was no neutral value-free code or algorithm that could make that decision; it would, in the end, be determined by values. And the process of generating professional journalism was done under commercial auspices, where the commitment to professional standards was tempered by commercial considerations. This is not to say that some forms of news cannot be more neutral than others, only that all news has a set of values and assumptions that drive it and determine the broad contours of what is covered, how it is covered, and what is not covered.

The values that would drive professional journalism were determined and occasionally fought over by publishers, editors, and journalists for the first half of the twentieth century. There was a strong reform impulse, attached to the Progressive Era and muckraking, which believed journalism should "afflict the comfortable and comfort the afflicted." This was nonpartisan journalism, and it held politicians of all parties to the same standard, but it was hardly value free. This type of journalism was embraced by the Newspaper Guild (the union for reporters) when it was founded in the 1930s. To protect the integrity of the news, leading elements of the guild wanted to effectively prohibit owners and advertisers from having any influence over the newsroom. Some publishers embraced the spirit of the reform approach—if not their formal banishment from controlling their newsrooms—but the vast majority found the notion of a truly independent journalism far too controversial and adversarial toward the power structure, of which they were most indubitably a part.

The professional journalism that emerged in the 1920s and crystallized by midcentury moved decisively in an establishment direction, where it remains to this day.[28] To take the controversy away from story selection, and to maintain neutrality, political coverage was based primarily on what people in power—official sources—said and did. When they debated an issue, or when they had no particular interest in an issue, it was fair game for journalism. When they agreed on an issue, it was considered inappropriate and "ideological" for a journalist to raise questions challenging the elite consensus, except on the rarest of occasions—as, for instance, when a handful of southern editors such as Hazel Brannon Smith questioned the segregationist consensus in states such as Mississippi.[29] We remember dissenting and dissident editors such as Smith not only because of their courage, but also because of their rarity. For the most part, however, a premium was placed on achieving factual accuracy and on not tilting the coverage toward challenging the powerful and questioning the basic infrastructure of an often corrupt and dysfunctional status quo. So it was that one of the greatest journalists of the age, I. F. Stone, had to create his own small publications to raise big questions about the health risks posed by cigarettes, the military-industrial complex, and McCarthyism. In 2008, the Nieman Foundation for Journalism at Harvard University announced plans to award an annual "I. F. Stone Medal for Journalistic Independence," but in the 1950s and 1960s, when he was in his prime, Stone could not get his writing published in major American newspapers and was given no forum on broadcast television.[30]

That's because the journalists who got the jobs, and the journalism that was rewarded, bent over backward to avoid taking a side not just in the political debate between the two parties but also in the great debates of the era. This approach fostered the illusion of professional impartiality. But it also had the important business benefit of making journalism less expensive: just plant reporters near people in power and have them report.

There were major problems with this style of professional journalism, problems that surround us to this day, especially when it comes to the coverage of politics. It tended to make off-limits and unquestioned those areas that people in power agreed upon, and that not coincidentally tended to be near and dear to press owners. Specifically, when it comes to covering politics, professional journalism has a strong inclination to simply publicize the positions of the leadership of the two parties and regard them invariably as the two legitimate poles of debate—with the rational center between them, the place journalists tend to see themselves and the best people inhabiting. To maintain neutrality, journalists are loath to call out one side for lying. They also do not want to antagonize their sources, upon whom they are dependent. Instead, journalists prefer to report that one side is calling the other side liars and leave it at that. We report; you decide. The problem is that the liars can dismiss the criticism as being driven by their opponents and ignore it, so this becomes a liar's paradise.

This obsession of professional journalism to play it strictly down the middle between the two legitimate parties, to avoid at all costs the charge of favoritism—the "cult of balance" as Paul Krugman termed it—compromises the rigor and integrity of where political analysis would go if it simply followed the evidence "without fear or favor." Krugman defined the cult of balance as "the insistence on portraying both parties as equally wrong and equally at fault on any issue, never mind the facts." "If one party declared that the earth was flat," Krugman stated jokingly, "the headlines would read 'Views Differ on Shape of Planet.'"[31] Ari Melber wrote, "For years, Americans' political press has been stuck in a fact-free model of neutrality, often covering even the most obvious lies as 'one side' of a dispute."[32]

The grave damage of the cult of balance is that it allows dubious players to pollute the political culture and get away with it. After all, if the news media attack them, the media are accused of being partisan and unprofessional. And when the political culture moves sharply in one direction, journalism comfortably and uncritically goes along with it, sticking resolutely to the "center." The center, more than anything in the United States, is determined by where Big Money is located. So-called objectivity on paper can come across as cowardice in the real world. "If a calculus of power determines truth," scholar Lance Bennett observed, "the press has become the handmaiden of power.

There would seem to be little that would hasten the demise of democracy faster than this."[33]

An example of this cult of balance came when in November 2011 Mitt Romney's campaign released its first TV ad attacking President Obama. The ad lifted a quote by Obama from a speech—"If we keep talking about the economy, we're going to lose"—and ridiculed it. But in that speech Obama was directly and unambiguously quoting Republican John McCain. So did the news media report this flat out as a fraudulent ad based on a lie? Not generally. The tenor of the coverage was captured in the *New York Times* headline: "Democrats Crying Foul over a New Romney Ad."[34] When White House press secretary Jay Carney complained on national television that the ad was intended to "deliberately distort what the President said," Romney senior adviser Tom Rath responded with the impossibly lame defense: "[Obama] did say the words. That's his voice."[35] Yet major media continued trying to split the difference with lines like "New Mitt Romney Attack Ad Called 'Deceitful' by Obama Campaign."[36] It is true: the ad had been called deceitful by the Obama campaign. But the broader, more compelling truth was that the ad *was* deceitful. This was the truth that media outlets dared not speak. In so doing, they fostered a fantasy that the fact of the Romney camp's lie was a debatable proposition. That suited the eventual Republican nominee's aides just fine. Indeed, Rath told CBS, the ad and the muted controversy surrounding it were "exactly what we want."[37]

Media outlets do not merely stand down when it comes to calling out political lies. They police the process, identifying debates about critical issues as somehow off topic. As American journalism became "professionalized," two areas of discussion in particular became off-limits, areas that would have almost certainly been more in play under a partisan system. First, the propriety of corporate capitalism itself is not questioned or discussed. As award-winning journalist Ben H. Bagdikian put it, capitalism is almost as off-limits to structural criticism in American journalism as communism was in the Soviet media. It is fitting that when Adolph Ochs purchased the *New York Times* in 1896, he published his oft-cited pronouncement that the *Times* would "give the news impartially, without fear or favor, regardless of party, sect, or interests involved." In the next (rarely quoted) paragraph, Ochs gave a taste of his so-called impartiality, stating that his "non-partisan newspaper" would attempt, "if possible, to intensify its devotion to the cause of sound money and tariff reform, opposition to wastefulness and speculation in administering public affairs, and in its advocacy of the lowest tax consistent with good government, and no more government than is absolutely necessary to protect society."[38]

Second, the U.S. role in the world as a military superpower, with the right to intervene in other nations' affairs like no other nation, is beyond debate. The record of the U.S. news media has been dismal with regard to covering U.S. war making for much of the professional era. As the elites in both parties tend to agree on basics, America time and time again has been led into wars by the news media under dubious and mostly unexamined pretenses.[39] The range of debate in America's partisan media for the nation's nineteenth-century wars was considerably more heated and vociferous by comparison.[40] Indeed, the greatest debates over the U.S. role in the world did not play out during the Vietnam or Iraq wars but in the late nineteenth and early twentieth centuries when the three-time Democratic nominee for president, William Jennings Bryan, declared, "The mission of the [American] flag is to float—not over a conglomeration of commonwealths and colonies—but over 'the land of the free and the home of the brave,' and to that mission it must remain forever true—forever true."[41]

The structure of the economy and the state of militarism are, along with the protection of individual liberties and civil rights, certainly among the most important areas for governance. In stable and prosperous times, the fact that our news media are unquestioning of the status quo is noticed only on the margins; in times of crisis, it converts our professional news media into what appears more like blatant propagandists.

There is spectacular irony in what has become of major media coverage of the issues on which elections should turn. Walter Lippmann, the acclaimed writer generally regarded as the "father of modern journalism" because of his call in the 1920s for trained professionals to be nonpartisan reporters, was adamant about the single most important task of professional journalism: it must not take the pronouncements of government or public officials at face value, especially in matters of foreign affairs where the track record is one of extraordinary lying with disastrous consequences.[42]

So it is that the greatest weakness of professional journalism as it evolved was to commit precisely the journalism failure that most concerned Lippmann in 1920. Lippmann's concern was, more broadly, that propaganda and public relations generated by the powerful—what we today call "spin"—would dominate the news unless skilled and talented journalists prevented them from doing so. In his view, the fate of democracy hung in the balance. Here, too, irony abounds, as the emergence of professional journalism has been accompanied by the rise of the PR industry, which is expert in using professional news standards to plant or influence seemingly independent and credible news stories for their clients. Even at the high point of professional journalism, perhaps as much as 40 or 50 percent of the news came primarily from some sort of PR intervention or from regurgitation of an official source.

When commercial television came along, it adopted the professional code and, if anything, accentuated some of its weaknesses, creating the absurd circumstance of partisan "talking head" guests on "news" shows arguing over who is telling the truth while a highly paid host refuses to make the call as to which side is lying. There has for decades now been a continued de-emphasis on the meat of public policy and a turn toward personalizing politics. On television the commercial basis of journalism was more explicit, and the turn to an entertainment format more transparent. Although the lion's share of original reporting was done by newspaper journalists, TV became the leading source of information for most Americans by the 1970s and remains so to this day. The academic research does not suggest that TV news, or professional news in general, tells us exactly what to think, as in some dystopian novel. Instead, what the news does is tell us what to think about—it sets the agenda—and by omission what not to think about. Professional news then sets the terms for how to think about that agenda.[43]

This is a point that merits elaboration. If, for example, "the news" does not cover the effects of poverty because, for whatever reason, this is not seen as an important issue, it is not going to make the tens of millions of impoverished Americans think they are doing just fine, thank you. As *The Nation*'s Greg Kaufmann illustrated with his groundbreaking "This Week in Poverty" reports, the news media work their effects not on a blank slate but on people who bring their own experiences to the table.[44] But that being said, journalism has considerable influence, even more so in areas where people do not have personal experience to draw from. If it did not, dictators and revolutionaries would not rush to control the press immediately upon taking power. Political communication scholarship demonstrates that when people are exposed to an issue in the news on a regular basis, they will tend to regard it as an important issue—and, conversely, an issue that is downplayed will not be seen as especially pressing.

Lame journalism can therefore have very real effects. Thomas Patterson wrote of how crime news exploded in the early 1990s—for reasons owing mostly to the commercial basis of journalism—and became far more prominent than political news. Polling showed that by 1994, 39 percent of Americans regarded crime as the nation's most pressing problem, compared to only 8 percent of Americans a decade earlier. This fed the frenzy of tough-talking politicians, prison construction, and onerous sentencing that has produced the massive prison-industrial complex. Yet the crime rate throughout this period was actually in decline.[45]

The genius of the system has been that journalists are largely oblivious to the compromises with authority they make by following the professional code. "Journalistic norms and reporting practices," Bennett concluded in 1983, "operate together to create a strong status quo bias in the news—a bias that is well hidden behind a façade of independent journalism." Bennett was one of the first to comprehend and demonstrate that the nature of professional news made "apathy" a rational response to the news environment; professional news therefore encouraged as much as it combated political depoliticization.[46] In general, it not only took fundamental issues off the table and had an establishment cast, but it also avoided contextualizing political stories, as the process of contextualization was fraught with the ideological linkages that professional journalism wished to avoid. Political news tended to be either boring or semi-incoherent. The significance of what was at stake was often unclear or inaccurate, and people understandably tuned the news out as irrelevant. Scholars Joseph N. Capella and Kathleen Hall Jamieson demonstrated persuasively that the manner in which news media covered politics—emphasizing the manipulation involved in the "game of politics," rather than its substance—fed a growing public cynicism toward politics.[47] In short, the news media complemented other aspects of American society that reduced public participation in elections and civic life.

We have used very broad brushstrokes to make our points and have emphasized political journalism. Obviously, professional journalism in practice has produced plenty of quality coverage, done by thousands of reporters committed to their craft. Our news media have been responsible for countless major investigative pieces that have saved lives and stopped corruption and injustice. Even political journalism has been valuable, especially in the examination of scandals and explicit political corruption, despite the limitations built into the professional code. And there is a great deal to be said for news media that strive to be responsible for covering public life by maintaining a strident commitment to factual accuracy and hard evidence.

The professional code is also somewhat malleable, shaped by shifting political winds and the commercial imperatives of media owners. In the 1960s and 1970s, popular movements—civil rights, antiwar, and consumer followed by the feminist and environmental movements—grew large enough that they could force their way into the news even when elites or political leaders were uncomfortable with them.[48] But the playing field was never level, and when popular movements lost their power, they lost their legitimacy as sources. When American politics—Republican and Democratic—made a turn toward the right in the 1980s, journalism followed along, continually replanting the flag of "centrism" until it ended up near what had been the right field foul line.[49] Here the politics dovetailed nicely with the commercial interests of news media owners. American news media all but dropped the labor coverage that had been standard at midcentury, when the labor movement was relatively strong, and replaced it with an exponential increase in business reporting.[50] The shift also provided a lucrative affluent market much desired by advertisers.

ELECTION COVERAGE IN RECENT TIMES

If we begin with the idea that the election coverage in the partisan era tended to be rich and engaging because the broader political journalism was rich and engaging, and that the political journalism of the professional era is rather staid, decontextualized, and establishment-oriented by comparison, we should not expect to have especially useful election campaign journalism today. Put another way, if political journalism does a relatively unsatisfactory job of covering public policy issues and drawing people into civic life, we should not expect campaign journalism to be any different. And it isn't. Most of the main trends and great weaknesses in campaign coverage Americans lament today became dominant only in the last four or five decades.

Most accounts of the postwar era, specifically the 1950s and 1960s, characterize news media coverage as being very much in the professional mode: descriptive and deferential toward officeholders and politicians. That changed as broadcast media began to redefine campaign coverage.[51] By the late 1960s and the 1970s, professional journalism enjoyed its Golden Age, when it had its largest budgets, most autonomy from owners and commercial pressures, and greatest prestige in the twentieth century. The news media also became increasingly important as a factor in determining electoral success. The news media filled some of the void as New Deal party loyalty dissipated and parties became less important as organizing tools in American politics. The number of "independent voters" grew, and straight-ticket party-line voting became less dominant. The importance of news media became especially clear with the emergence of television. As we note in Chapter 4, already by 1960 political campaigns were concerned with getting the best possible TV exposure, and initially the emphasis was on news coverage. Print media remained important, in part because the campaign beat reporters had considerable influence on TV coverage. The tenor of the campaign coverage then underwent a metamorphosis. Patterson's research demonstrated that the framework of election stories in the *New York Times* went from 92 percent descriptive/8 percent interpretive in 1960 to 20 percent descriptive/80 percent interpretive by 1988.[52]

Timothy Crouse captured the emerging role of the news media in his classic account of the working press during the 1972 campaign, *The Boys on the Bus:* "Now the press screened the candidates, usurping the party's old function. By reporting a man's political strengths, they made him a front runner; by mentioning his weaknesses and liabilities, they cut him down. Teddy White, even in his wildest flights of megalomania, had never allowed himself this kind of power. The press was no longer simply guessing who might run and who might win; the press was in some ways determining these things."[53]

Former Democratic senator from Alaska Mike Gravel, whose career in Washington began around this time, described the news media "echo chamber" as the decisive element for political success, especially for the White House. "Before most Americans start paying attention to the presidential race, the echo chamber has already promoted certain candidates over others and given them tremendous advantages that prove extremely difficult for other candidates to overcome."[54] One of the best barometers for understanding which candidates the media deemed legitimate before the first vote had been cast was what Jeff Cohen dubbed "the money primary," meaning who had the biggest war chest.[55]

Because of the news media's newfound importance, since the 1970s a sizable industry of academic scholarship has emerged that examines news media coverage of political campaigns. Much of the research, especially the most highly regarded research upon which our analysis depends, is critical of the problems with political coverage. As a rule, this work aspires to delineate weaknesses and convince editors, producers, and reporters to change their modus operandi and do a better job of serving voters and the political system.[56] We tend to agree with those observers, like Patterson and Marvin Kalb, who recognized two decades ago that the news media were being put in a hopeless position. "With the demise of political parties," Kalb said, "the press has moved into a commanding position as arbitrator of American presidential politics—a position for which it is not prepared, emotionally, professionally, or constitutionally."[57]

A subset of this research addresses one of the primary complaints of both Democrats and Republicans: the notion that campaign coverage has a consistent bias toward one major political party or the other. One meta-analysis of fifty-nine studies of partisan bias toward one of the major political parties in all political journalism found insignificant levels of bias, at most, in the major news media.[58] Specifically with regard to news coverage of election campaigns, we can report that over the years this has not been the major problem—though many political partisans are obsessed with what they regard as their candidate's mistreatment by the news media, and doubtlessly there have been clear instances when it occurred, sometimes with ill-effect.[59] In the end, though, this is one area where professional journalism has been somewhat successful.[60]

But that does not mean there are not all sorts of deleterious tendencies and biases built into how news media cover electoral campaigns, arguably with significant effects. One clear bias is for incumbents. In congressional races incumbents receive far more coverage than challengers, and incumbents win around 90 percent of the time.[61] The other side of the coin is that the system is very much stacked against third-party candidates, and always has been. Ralph Nader, with a record of public service arguably unrivalled in modern American history, was ignored or considered a nuisance by the news media during his 2000 presidential campaign as the Green Party candidate. Back in 1980 when renowned environmentalist Barry Commoner ran as the Citizens Party candidate for president, he was so exasperated by the unwillingness of the news media to cover his campaign that he resorted to using the word "bullshit" in a radio ad to get any sort of press attention.[62]

Even dissidents running within the primaries of the major parties, such as Ohio congressman and two-time Democratic presidential contender Dennis Kucinich, are often treated by the news media as if they were carrying communicable diseases. On the eve of the critical 2008 primary in New Hampshire, where Kucinich had been campaigning for months, hired staff, opened campaign offices, and enjoyed the support of state legislators and prominent activists, the candidate was informed that he would not be included in the last big debate among the Democratic contenders—even though he was the only candidate raising issues of presidential accountability, budget priorities, and trade policy that polls confirmed were most in tune with the sentiments of likely voters.[63] One of us well recalls a conversation with a lead CNN political correspondent in late 1999, when he was already planning how to get rid of marginal candidates like Alan Keyes so that he and the news media could concentrate on the "serious" candidates for the Republican presidential nomination. And we both recall the 2004 media assault on former Vermont governor Howard Dean's antiwar, antiestablishment campaign for the Democratic presidential nod, which culminated in magazine articles speculating on whether a veteran governor of an American state, and a past chairman of the National Governors Association, was too "extreme" or even "crazy" to be president. Notably, this speculation began before the so-called scream speech following the Iowa caucuses, which was so inappropriately and inaccurately covered that CNN would eventually apologize for wrongly portraying Dean as a nut.[64]

This phenomenon was particularly evident in the news media treatment of Ron Paul in his campaign for the 2012 Republican presidential nomination. Paul had usually finished among the top three or four candidates in polling, and sometimes in the top two, but he was routinely ignored or treated in a patronizing manner compared to all the other candidates, even those with less funding and fewer prospects for attaining Republican National Convention delegates. What was Paul's crime? He was outside the elite consensus on militarism, the drug war, and foreign policy. As one British political journalist wrote, "Paul has held his beliefs for years and does not change them to suit a focus group. He has principles and stands by them. This makes Paul admirable even when you disagree with him (as I mostly do). It also makes Paul the one thing that American media and political elites of all stripes can't stand: a genuine outsider. . . . To cast him as a fringe weirdo says far more about the biases and idiocy of the media and his political rivals than it does about Paul."[65]

Americans are so accustomed to this media vetting that it seems natural and appropriate. It is simply a catch-22 that goes with democracy: as one newspaper acknowledged, "It's hard to win without media attention, but it's hard to get attention if no one thinks you can win."[66] Why waste time on candidates who do "not have a chance"? But why exactly do they not have a chance? And why is it that in the modern era the only clear way to get attention as a third-party candidate, or a "marginal" major party candidate, for president is to have a very fat bank account, like Ross Perot, greased up to purchase tens of millions of dollars of TV ads?

Even Donald Trump—whose qualifications for public office are unknown and who became an embarrassment to Republicans as the 2012 campaign evolved—received far more intense and encouraging coverage for a few weeks in the spring of 2011 concerning his possible run for the Republican presidential nomination than consumer activist Ralph Nader received for the whole of his presidential campaigns. Consequently, Trump would show up in polls as a legitimate candidate and justify more coverage. We cannot help but wonder how Nader would have done in the 2000 polls had he received the exact same amount of press attention as Bush and Gore and been afforded equal standing in the debates. Here is a rhetorical question: Wouldn't the news media provide a far better service for our electoral system if they skewed their coverage toward all the candidates on the margins, those without the big campaign contributors? The less money a candidate had, the more coverage she would receive! That way the playing field could be leveled and there would be much more competition.[67]

It is a rhetorical question, because merely asking it demonstrates its absurdity in the face of the entire logic of the money-and-media election complex. If the question is put another way—Who are the news media here to serve anyway?—the answer is obvious. When MSNBC removed Cenk Uygur from his slot hosting an early-evening program, he said he was told by MSNBC officials that the network was a part of "the establishment" and "that you need to act like it." MSNBC disputed the claim, saying disagreements with Uygur were over "style, not substance," and that the network had sought "to develop him into an even bigger television talent."[68] Uygur ultimately moved to another cable network, Current, while the Reverend Al Sharpton took the MSNBC gig and emerged as a major voice in the fight for justice following the shooting of Florida teenager Trayvon Martin.[69] On the narrow spectrum of American discourse, MSNBC may be decried by its critics as "left wing" or even "radical." It may be described by mainstream media outlets as safely "liberal." But MSNBC, owned by Comcast and General Electric, fits very much within the ideological spectrum that most international observers would identify as "mainstream." It is not a dissident voice. And neither, frankly, is Fox, which regularly scrambles on board the bandwagon to support business-friendly initiatives—such as free-trade deals—whether they are promoted by Republican or by Democratic presidents. While much is made of the ideological "extremes" on the cable spectrum, the amount of money a presidential hopeful has, the ability to purchase TV ads, the closer he or she is to power, and the more that candidate buys into the elite consensus on the economy and the U.S. role in the world remain the surest measures of whether a presidential contender is treated as a serious candidate.[70]

This is a change for America. It wasn't this way for much of the nation's first century. Even with electoral laws that encouraged the development and extension of a two-party system, the decentralized and highly competitive newspaper industry made it possible for dissident ideas to be heard and for movements to organize around them. The abolitionist, suffragist, Populist, labor, and socialist movements were built on the backs of their weekly and monthly newspapers, which themselves depended to a large extent upon low postage rates for distribution, if not survival. If nothing else, these movements driven by a very different press system were able to force the two main parties to move in more adventurous and enlightened directions than they otherwise would have. But by the final third of the twentieth century, that tradition was no longer even visible in America's rearview mirror.

The centerpiece of campaign coverage since the 1970s has been squarely in the zone that is fun and easy to cover, and that allows journalists to look and sound smart while avoiding difficult and controversial policy matters: the horse race. One study found that some 80 percent of early campaign coverage now dealt with fund-raising, organizational issues, and tactics—issues related to the candidates rather than the issues affecting voters.[71] Since the 1990s, research shows, political horse-race/money-race coverage constituted a majority of campaign news in general elections across all media, leading policy coverage by a 2-to-1 or even 3-to-1 ratio.[72] The tenor of much of this coverage seemed to be "just how good of a job is the candidate doing manipulating the news media and voters?" The horse-race and money-race obsession reinforced the bias of coverage toward incumbents: by horse-race criteria those leading in the race tended to get favorable coverage for playing the game well and those trailing had all their tactical flaws subject to review. "Horse-race coverage takes the place of substantive coverage," *The Atlantic*'s Conor Friedersdorf wrote, "and the candidate with the lead appears decisive and competent, and the trailing candidate fairly ridiculous."[73] Nor do we mean to exaggerate the quality of so-called policy coverage, as that sometimes entailed reporting of nonresearched decontextualized fatuous claims and charges of dubious value.

Significant research has emphasized the silly nature of much campaign coverage, horse race or otherwise. Len Downie and Robert Kaiser of the *Washington Post* lamented the overall plethora of "pontificating commentators" who represent a dramatic shift from the journalism of their youth and "the substitution of talk, opinion and argument for news."[74] Harvard's Patterson took dead aim at the abundance of stories based around poll results: "A poll story is entirely manufactured. It is pseudo-news created by the media to report on the game: 'They create it, pay for it, and then report on it.'"[75] For James Fallows, election coverage is now filled with the conventions of sports reporting—actually, *bad* sports reporting—especially the endless and mindless predictions, to which no journalist or pundit is ever held accountable.[76]

Political expedience was not the only factor accounting for such nutrition-free fare. Every bit as important was cost: such material was far less expensive to create and produce than hard journalism that might go out and investigate candidates and the issues or bring new candidates and issues to public attention. Stripped-down election campaign journalism, especially on TV, and particularly for the presidency and Congress, could pay for itself, as cable channels came to demonstrate by the 1990s. Some of the "breaking news" of campaigns came when reporters got leaked material from a campaign that was damaging to the candidate's opponent, and then the news media reported on it—sometimes in rumor status and often decontextualized—as if they had conducted a hard investigation. Then the leaking campaign could run a series of negative TV ads using the news coverage as a "citation" for the charges. This contributed to what Patterson observed: the percentage of campaign news stories with a negative framing increased sharply starting in the 1980s and 1990s.[77] It also explains the obsession of campaign journalists with candidate "gaffes" or minor screw-ups, like getting an expensive haircut or making the wrong food choice at a restaurant.

Campaign news stories are now based on political ads to a significant and growing extent—in some cases as much as 20 percent of a newspaper's campaign stories. To be sure, these articles are at times critical of the dubious claims in the ads, but even when they are, the pattern is basically to allow the news coverage to amplify the claims in the ad, with the wildest charges making for attention-getting stories. "Advertising is easy to cover," Travis Ridout and Michael M. Franz wrote. "Writing a story about a new political ad does not require the reporter to do a lot of difficult research or travel to an isolated location."[78] Candidates also use their ads as their way to direct the campaign coverage to where they want it to be, and journalists largely oblige. This creates a sense that campaigns are all about ads, and that activists and voters are mere speculators whose only real role is to donate as much as they can in order to keep favored contenders "on the air." As early as 1968, Joe McGinniss recognized that the power of marketing in general and television ads in particular was such that "the press doesn't matter anymore."[79] He was jumping the gun, as it mattered then far more than it does now. But McGinniss was right that what can only be described as political propaganda, rather than serious news coverage, was beginning to define the discussion in America.

In sum, the logical product of this type of campaign coverage is an amplified version of the popular cynicism scholars have attributed to professional journalism's political news in general. "The audience is left to sift among the images of this power play for conclusions about the political system," Matthew

Kerbel wrote in the conclusion of his 1998 study of election news. "It was not difficult to decide that politics is simply about power, that power is about personal gain, and that the candidate who figures this out and exploits it best is the most likely to prevail. Finding reasons to participate in the election, enthusiastically support a candidate, or feel good about the electoral process was far more problematic."[80] All the tendencies that generated Kerbel's assessment were apparent and thriving in the 1980s and 1990s.

Yet even then, there was still a sense that there were many journalists and much news media covering politics, so the system had rays of light, as few as they may have been. So we were not surprised when we interviewed Americans for this book and discovered that more than a few of them recalled wistfully the election press coverage of just two or three decades ago, warts and all. Something horrible must have happened between then and now. Let's find out what it was.

7

JOURNALISM EXITS, STAGE RIGHT

All the so-called communications industries are primarily concerned
not with communications, but with selling.

I. F. STONE, 1963

Few voters in the United States saw more television political advertisements
in 2012 than those living in Nevada, a presidential "battleground" state that
was also hosting a competitive U.S. Senate race and competition for an open
U.S. House seat and dozens of state and local offices.[1] And if candidates, their
supporters, and the "independent" super-PACs that advertised in their favor
wanted to reach voters in Nevada, they had to buy time on Las Vegas television stations. Lots of it. As the election approached, Las Vegas television stations aired more than 600 ads a day—yes, *more* than 600—from the Obama
and Romney campaigns, their parties, and allied groups seeking to influence
the outcome of the presidential race. Hundreds of additional ads were aired
each day by Senate candidates and their allies, and hundreds more by state
and local contenders. The total number of ads aired on some days surpassed
1,500.[2] At a thirty-second rate, that's twelve full hours of television programming each day. But it was not spread through the day. The campaigns and
their allies wanted to reach the most likely voters. And the most likely voters
watched local news programs.

What to do?

"Local stations are shaving minutes off their news programs to accommo-date the crush," reported the *New York Times* in a mid-October report from Las Vegas.[3]

The calculus cannot get any worse, or any more illustrative, than that. Faced with a flood of campaign commercials that were, in the words of an independent observer, "as caustic as they are ceaseless," essential local media outlets decided to give voters less news in order to make way for more po-litical propaganda.[4]

But that's just how they roll in Vegas, right? Wrong. That's the calculus of American media in a new age when journalism is continually sacrificed on the altar of profit. It is not merely a matter of greed or shortsightedness any longer; the structure of the money-and-media complex, Dollarocracy itself, demands this sacrifice.

The historical problems with campaign coverage we outline in Chapter 6 continue to the present and generally are getting more pronounced. The efforts of scholars to convince journalists to reform their practices have been an abject failure; the structural forces are far too powerful. Two developments, both beginning decades ago but hitting full force more recently, have funda-mentally changed American political journalism and, with that, the most im-portant journalism in a democracy: the coverage of the election campaigns that define federal, state, and local governments. First, after years of trivial-ization and commercialization of the news, the corporate abandonment of journalism as a profitable investment is accelerating. Second, the resulting journalism void has been "filled" by the emergence of substantial explicitly right-wing news media that aggressively promote the talking points of the Republican Party. In combination, these new factors should make some Amer-icans nostalgic for the past, even the recent past, and all Americans very con-cerned about the future. If election coverage has been weak in the past generation, look out below. The power of money and political advertising is greater than ever and is virtually unchecked by any effective institutional force.

THE COLLAPSE OF JOURNALISM

We chronicled the decline in resources to American news media in detail in our 2010 book, *The Death and Life of American Journalism*. On a per capita basis, less than half as much time and money is devoted to journalism today as was the case twenty-five years ago. And the crisis is getting worse, rapidly. Just since 2000, the labor and resources committed by major media to producing the news have dropped by 30 percent. The wheels came off corporate journalism in 2007, and since then the number of newspapers and newsrooms has declined sharply. This was not merely a reflection of broader economic troubles: while other industries edged back toward functionality after the effects of the recession and the 2008 Wall Street meltdown began to ease, newsrooms continued to empty out and once-great newspapers, such as the *New Orleans Times-Picayune,* ended daily publication.[5] By 2012, the situation was grimmer than ever, and news industry veterans spoke openly about the end of the journalism that Americans had known throughout their history and that democratic theory requires for effective self-governance.[6]

Why do corporations no longer find journalism a profitable investment? To some extent, because increasingly monopolistic news media corporations gutted and trivialized the product for decades, this ultimately made the "news" irrelevant.[7] To some extent, the crisis exploded as it did because the Internet destroyed the traditional business model by giving advertisers far superior ways to reach their prospective consumers. But the bottom line was clear and unequivocal: "The independent watchdog function that the Founding Fathers envisioned for journalism—going so far as to call it crucial to a healthy democracy," a 2011 Federal Communications Commission study on the crisis in journalism concluded, "is at risk."[8]

The causes of this decline are not germane to our immediate analysis. We want to focus instead on the devastating implications for political journalism and, with that, campaign journalism. The numbers of foreign correspondents, foreign bureaus, Washington bureaus and correspondents, statehouse bureaus and correspondents, right on down to the local city hall, have all been slashed to the bone, and in some cases the coverage barely exists any longer.[9]

In an era of ever-greater corruption, the watchdog is no longer on the beat. Consider that the biggest political scandals in Washington in the past decade—the ones that brought down Jack Abramoff, Tom DeLay, and Randy "Duke" Cunningham—were all revealed by investigations done by daily newspaper reporters. Those paid reporting positions no longer exist, and those specific reporters no longer draw a paycheck to do such work.[10] This means the next generation of corrupt politicians will have a much easier time fattening their bank accounts while providing their services to the highest corporate bidder.

After we wrote *The Death and Life of American Journalism,* we traveled across the United States for events at universities, churches, and community centers. Everywhere we went during the period leading up to the 2012 election, we heard horror stories about the important stories being missed as the watchdog role of newspapers in particular and media outlets in general was steadily diminished. We heard about a woman who ran the county social services office in an eastern state. Her office, which employed hundreds of people, accidentally screwed up, and as a result a person apparently died. When this happened, this individual freaked out, thinking it would lead to wrongheaded threats to the budget for her department and, though she was not in any way responsible, the possible end to her career. Then after a few weeks, she realized that no one knew anything about the death. It had got no press coverage because there were barely any reporters left at the one daily newspaper in her county, and they were overmatched by the assignments before them. The moral of the story: life and death stories are no longer "news."

The accountability that saves lives—or, at the least, sends up red flares when lives are lost—is no longer demanded of public agencies by a media industry that "afflicts the comfortable and comforts the afflicted." In following up on this report with journalists from the area, we learned that until recently the newspaper in question had been regarded as one of the finest dailies in the region and had won numerous awards. In 2008 and 2009, however, it laid off over 80 percent of its reporters. In 2012, the staff was made smaller again.

Blowing stories of corruption and misconduct, as horrific as they are, may not be the worst symptom of the condition that now defines journalism in America. Even more serious is the lack of coverage of the details of legislation and budgets, what is debated at hearings and buried in official reports, and what regulatory agencies are doing, even when there is no explicit corruption but just politics as usual. This is the stuff of politics; when people talk about wanting a serious issues-based politics, this is precisely what is meant.

But everywhere in the nation most of this government activity is taking place in the dark, certainly compared to two or three or four decades ago. The Wisconsin budget battles of 2011 generated massive protests and, by recent standards, inordinate press coverage from what remained of the state's news media. Yet it was striking that key radical changes in the budget were missed by working reporters. Matt Rothschild, editor of *The Progressive,* stumbled across a major change in the budget in which controversial governor Scott Walker would use a line-item veto "so that state employees are no longer vested in the pension system until they have worked for the state for five years, instead of being partially vested immediately."[11] One or two decades ago, this might have been a front-page scandal and possibly a major news story for weeks; in 2011 it made it into a blog and had no echo effect, because there were so few journalists to follow up these loose ends.

Everywhere the situation is the same: far fewer journalists attempting to cover more and more news on tighter schedules. As the FCC observed, reporters and editors "are spending more time on reactive stories and less on labor-intensive 'enterprise' pieces." Television reporters "who once just reported the news now have many other tasks, and more newscasts to feed, so they have less time to research their stories." The situation is especially disastrous at the local level, where smaller news media and newsrooms have been wiped out in a manner reminiscent of a plague. The *Los Angeles Times* is now the primary news medium for eighty-eight municipalities and 10 million people, but its metro staff has been cut in half since 2000. The staff "is spread thinner and there are fewer people on any given area," Metro editor David Lauter lamented. "We're not there every day, or even every week or every month. Unfortunately, nobody else is either."[12]

At least the Los Angeles region still has a daily newspaper that tries to cover some of the area's diversity. A growing number of American cities that were once served by one or more daily newspapers now have none. In some cases, newspapers have shuttered altogether, but the far more serious trend is one of sweeping consolidation so that a part of the country that once had multiple dailies serving individual communities—such as California's East Bay—now has one paper with dramatically fewer reporters overall.[13] Serious local coverage is disappearing, and often the void is being filled by advertising dressed up as "news." For instance, the venerable *Boston Globe* began allowing advertisers to write their own blog posts on its boston.com Web site, thereby further blurring the distinction between news and advertising with so-called branded content.[14]

Cutbacks in print are the most notable, especially when they occur at the national level—as when *Newsweek* announced in 2012 that after seventy-nine years, it would no longer produce a weekly magazine.[15] Like quality regional dailies that once felt a sense of responsibility to sort through all the news from all the communities under their watch, *Newsweek* and other national publications once performed a similar task for the whole of the United States, producing weekly roundups of the news from cities and states across the country in a form that was, limitations notwithstanding, relatively thorough and accessible. No more. The information is still there, but it comes now in a constant pattern of flash floods that leaves little insight in its wake.

The erstwhile first responders of the media system—radio stations—were the canaries in the commercial news media coal mines. By the end of the 1990s, they had already cut back and consolidated news departments so rapidly that many communities that once got hourly broadcast updates now get nothing but Rush Limbaugh and Sean Hannity ranting from afar. And, as we've noted, local television stations are "shaving" newscasts in order to create more space for political ads.

There may not be much journalism, but there still is plenty of "news." On the surface, at least on cable and satellite television, we seem to be deluged in endless news. Increasingly, though, it is unfiltered public relations generated surreptitiously by corporations and governments. In 1960, there was less than one PR agent for every working journalist, a ratio of 0.75 to 1. By 1990, the ratio was just over 2 to 1. In 2012, the ratio stood at 4 PR people for every 1 working journalist. At the current rates of change, the ratio may well be 6 to 1 within a few years.[16] There are far fewer reporters to interrogate the spin and the press releases, so the likelihood that they get presented as legitimate "news" has become much greater. The Pew Center conducted a comprehensive analysis of what the sources were for original news stories in Baltimore in 2009; it determined that fully 86 percent originated with official sources and press releases. These stories were presented as news based on the labor and judgment of professional journalists, but, as Pew noted, they generally presented the PR position without any alteration.[17]

For the already powerful, this is an ideal circumstance: they can guide the discussion via press releases, press conferences, and manufactured messaging. There's only a one in seven chance that a story not to their liking gets told, and if it does, their PR firm can send out six more press releases. That's not the outline of a functional and democratic media system. It's better understood as a petri dish in which propaganda is nurtured.

But won't the Internet save us?

For a good decade, pundits have argued that digital developments will provide a new system of commercially viable journalism. In fact, as traditional journalism disintegrates, no models for making web journalism—even bad journalism—profitable at anywhere near the level necessary for a credible popular news media to be developed, and there is no reason to expect any in the visible future.[18] Today we have a few thousand paid online news workers, interpreted liberally to include many aggregators who do little or no news gathering or reporting or even writing. As often as not, the best-known bloggers and online journalists are supported by some old medium that provides the resources. When these old media go down, the number of paid digital journalists is likely to shrink, not grow.

That has certainly been the case in cities such as Seattle, where the *Post-Intelligencer* newspaper ceased print publication in 2009 with this announcement: "The thing that should not be missed here is that the P-I is not going away. The P-I is going online." It fell to Washington's governor, Chris Gregoire, to note that with the move, "most of the newspaper's dedicated staff lost their jobs." At the time of its closing, the *P-I* had 150 employees, who maintained a fierce competition in local news with the *Seattle Times.* Just about everyone in town recognized the competition as good not just for journalism but also for the community, for the public's right to know, and for democracy itself. Citizens had organized to try maintaining that competition, and when the *P-I*'s decision was announced, local lawyer Anne Bremner, who cochaired the Committee for a Two-Newspaper Town, responded, "What a terribly sad day this is. Only tomorrow will be worse." She was right. The *P-I*'s newsroom full of beat reporters, columnists, editorial writers, copy editors, photographers, and even a Pulitzer Prize–winning cartoonist would be replaced by "about 20 news gatherers and Web producers." Three years later when we checked, the Web site had eight "news gatherers" (apparently doing a good deal of aggregation) and two "producers" to cover a metropolitan area that was home to 3.5 million people. Most of the space on the front page of the site's "Local" section was dedicated to wire service reports, under the headline "Local News from the Associated Press."

Research concludes that the original journalism provided by the severely underpaid or unpaid contributors to Internet news sites gravitates to what is easy and fun, tending to "focus on lifestyle topics, such as entertainment, retail, and sports—not on hard news."[19] This does not mean the Internet is not affecting political communication significantly (an issue we devote Chapter 8 to examining). It just means that the Internet has not in any way solved the crisis of journalism.

In short, journalism, especially political journalism, is facing an existential crisis in the United States. There has understandably been an increase in the number of people, to nearly one in five, who state they have gone "newsless"— not even glancing at Internet headlines—for the day before the poll. Who can blame them? By 2009, nearly a third of Americans aged eighteen to twenty-four were so self-described.[20] Forty years ago, young Americans consumed news at the same rate that their parents and grandparents did. Similarly, Gallup determined that mistrust in news media hit an all-time high in 2012, with 60 percent of Americans saying "they have little or no trust in the mass media to report the news fully, accurately, and fairly." Gallup polling showed positive trust in media was as high as 72 percent in the 1970s.[21]

CONTEMPORARY ELECTION COVERAGE

The problem that the collapse of journalism has created for election coverage is devastating. As the Gallup report on popular antipathy toward news media concluded, "This is particularly consequential at a time when Americans need to rely on the media to learn about the platforms and perspectives of the two candidates vying to lead the country for the next four years."[22] Thomas Patterson's research showed "a close association between the ups and downs in the amount of coverage and the ups and downs in involvement. As coverage rises, people increasingly think and talk about the campaign."[23]

What coverage remains, even by major news media like CBS News, is being done increasingly by inexpensive and inexperienced reporters in their twenties.[24] Don't get us wrong. Young journalists have in the past contributed mightily to the coverage of American politics, and they are continuing to do so. We think, for instance, of the groundbreaking work of labor journalist Mike Elk, which revealed late in the 2012 campaign that Mitt Romney had urged his business supporters to pressure their employees to back the Republican ticket.[25] That's classic good, and necessary, journalism. But even as Elk was breaking the story, *In These Times* was struggling to figure out how to keep him on the job, as grants for independent journalism dried up.[26] And even though Elk was determined to keep at it, a growing number of veteran journalists—many of whom have contacts and experience that allowed them to provide nuanced news coverage—were closing their notebooks and giving up on the frustrating work of not just covering campaigns but also trying to make ends meet.[27]

The most striking consequence of the exodus of journalists and journalism is that for countless races there is barely any coverage at all. By 2010, a "nearly reporter-free campaign trail" in statewide races across the nation was common.[28] In Wisconsin, where Senator Russ Feingold was in a fight for his political life, he found himself traveling virtually alone during much of his campaign. In his three previous Senate campaigns, especially in the 1990s, Feingold had been trailed by a posse of reporters. In Illinois in 2010, so little attention was paid to the Democratic primary for the state's number 2 job, lieutenant governor, that a pawnbroker who spent heavily on TV ads was nominated. The ads failed to mention that he had been arrested in 2005 for domestic abuse or that he had failed to pay back taxes and child support. When those details were revealed, a scandal developed that would ultimately force Scott Lee Cohen from the ticket. So why didn't voters know about Cohen's problems *before* the election? As Mark Brown of the *Chicago Sun-Times* explained it, "We in the news media failed the voters by missing the story." But the story wasn't really "missed." Like so many political stories these days, it was left uncovered by news media that no longer hire enough reporters to cover all the races, leaving most voters in the dark most of the time.[29]

Fairness & Accuracy in Reporting (FAIR) conducted a comprehensive study of how regional daily newspapers in St. Petersburg; Portland, Oregon; Pittsburgh; Burlington, Vermont; and Madison, Wisconsin, covered campaigns for the House of Representatives in their areas in 2008 and 2010. The study found that the coverage was effectively nonexistent; that only close races or races with scandals connected to one of the candidates received any attention at all—and then not much; and that third parties were ignored. "If you want to cast an informed vote for Congress," FAIR concluded, "local daily newspapers will likely not be much help."[30] Journalist Joe Rothstein added the only consolation for newspapers: "As thin as newspaper coverage is, local TV coverage is virtually invisible."[31] In Bangor, Maine, two weeks after the

2012 election, the news anchors on the local ABC affiliate closed a Tuesday night broadcast by announcing that they were quitting. Citing mounting frustrations with management choices that made it harder to cover the news in general and elections in particular, anchor (and station news director) Cindy Michaels complained, "We were expected to do somewhat unbalanced news, politically, in general." What made the story of her departure notable was not the complaint, but merely that she voiced it on a live newscast.[32]

This elimination of press coverage has had devastating effects on political campaigns. "It's hard to believe," University of Virginia professor Larry Sabato said, "that only five presidents ago, reporter Sam Donaldson and President Ronald Reagan sparred during fairly spontaneous press conferences. And [1984] vice presidential candidate Geraldine Ferraro spent two hours answering reporters' questions about her tax returns."[33]

In 2012, Mitt Romney's refusal to release his tax returns was only briefly a major story—a summer dalliance before the "real" campaign began. And even though Romney's refusal violated recent practice, contradicted a standard established by his father going into the 1968 campaign, contradicted broadly accepted practice in recent campaigns, and left fundamental questions about his personal and business activities unanswered, the Republican nominee for president was essentially allowed to coast through three debates and an intense fall campaign without having to face the tax issue.

The ability of candidates to dodge questions increases exponentially as the focus moves down the ballot. The scrutiny afforded presidential candidates is virtually nonexistent at the regional and local levels, despite the fact that the officials who occupy those positions arguably have more direct and far-reaching influence over the day-to-day lives of Americans.[34] "If you think about what government provides on a day-to-day basis—schools, transit, water supply, waste and sewage disposal, public health surveys of restaurants, fire, police—those things are mostly provided by local government," explained Sarah Elkind, a professor of political history at San Diego State University and the author of the book *How Local Politics Shape Federal Policy*. "If those services are not adequate people have to supplement out of their own pocket."[35]

Yet local reporters are now the first to admit that the job of covering politics is no longer getting done. In part, this is because of the dramatic cutbacks that local newspapers, radio stations, and television stations have experienced and because of the dramatic underfinancing of online news sites. But there is more to it. Politicians are starting to recognize, and enjoy, the political benefits of an absence of accountability. "Political campaigns have changed dramatically since I was a rookie reporter," veteran St. Louis journalist Phill Brooks observed. "Back then most candidates were easily accessible to reporters. They held regular and lengthy news conferences in the statehouse. They issued detailed policy papers that reflected extensive thought and staff research. They seemed truly eager to talk with reporters about their views."[36]

Increasingly during the course of the 2012 campaign, it became evident that candidates, especially incumbents or favorites, were barely even considering journalists a necessary evil they needed to work with any longer. As Patterson noted in the early 1990s, candidates had been angling for awhile toward reducing their reliance on the news media;[37] with the disintegration of journalism, this becomes a plausible strategy to pursue. "With every campaign," *Mother Jones'* Kevin Drum wrote in 2012,

> candidates push the envelope a little more, testing the boundaries of how far they can restrict press access. The answer, I think, is pretty plain: they could literally allow the press no access at all and it wouldn't hurt them. The only reason they still allow the little bit they do is inertia. Despite all the evidence to the contrary, they still find it hard to believe they could get away with shutting out reporters completely. But they could. The mainstream media, by its own rules, isn't really allowed to gripe about access, and anyway, nobody listens when they do.

As Drum noted, the appeal to candidates is obvious.

> Campaigns can reach everyone they need to reach, more safely and with more pinpoint control, via partisan media, television ads, data mining, debates, short hits on local TV, and social media. In those forums they can pretty much say anything they want, without having to field any embarrassing questions about whether they have their facts right and without fear of inadvertent gaffes. The truth is the downside risk of talking to reporters is now greater than the upside benefit of the coverage they give you.[38]

Or as Brooks put it, candidates "can buy all the broadcast time and newspaper advertising they need to communicate without the risk of being forced off message by pesky reporters."[39] The press corps "shadows, but rarely interacts, with the candidates" any longer, the *Washington Post* acknowledged.[40] "I want to be reincarnated as a late-night TV host, for one reason," Walter

Shapiro wrote for the *Columbia Journalism Review*. "It is my one shot at an interview with a presidential candidate during the fall campaign."[41]

A clear example of this calculus came in October 2012 after Republican vice presidential nominee Paul Ryan took some tough questions from Flint, Michigan, television reporter Terry Camp. The journalist from a town that had experienced significant gun violence in hard-hit neighborhoods asked Ryan whether the Republican candidate's one-size-fits-all response to society challenges would be a sufficient response for Flint. "And you can do all that [deal with poverty and violence] by cutting taxes? With a big tax cut?" An agitated Ryan grumbled, "Those are your words, not mine," as an aide rushed to end the interview with shouts from off-screen of "Thank you very much, sir." The camera kept rolling, however, capturing Ryan reprimanding the reporter for putting him on the spot. "That was kind of strange," the vice presidential nominee bellyached.[42] Actually, it wasn't strange at all; in most mature democracies the leading figures in major political parties are familiar with aggressive interview questions and consider it a mark of honor to be able to handle them. Not America. Ryan did not just end that interview; his aides suddenly started turning down local media requests for interviews—and kept doing so until the end of the campaign.[43]

It wasn't just candidates whom the campaigns walled off from the media. Remarkably, in 2012, we even witnessed campaigns restricting reporter access to supporters who were attending rallies, a narrowing of access that left journalists with no option but to stenographically note the remarks of the candidate and perhaps describe the red-white-and-blue bunting.[44] And when reporters were fortunate enough to get candidate interviews, campaigns increasingly insisted on getting control over what quotes were used in the eventual stories and how they were worded.[45]

The effect of the new journalism-free or journalism-lite campaign was apparent in 2012. A comprehensive Pew Research Center study determined that the percentage of campaign themes in the news coverage coming from the press, as opposed to the candidates, fell from 50 percent in 2000 to 27 percent in 2012. The report had one "unavoidable" conclusion: "Journalists to an increasing degree are ceding control of what the public learns in elections to partisan voices."[46] Tom Rosenstiel, director of Pew's Project for Excellence in Journalism, noted that the press coverage "balance has shifted to stenography versus mediating."[47] As Rosenstiel noted, that also explained why press coverage was so much more negative in 2012 than in previous election years. It was often regurgitating the campaigns' talking points. "The media are more an enabler and conduit for partisan rhetoric than we've ever seen before. It's been happening steadily over time, and this year, it really jumped out at us as inexorable. And it helps explain why the campaign feels so negative."[48]

The implications of this new world order are striking: in the absence of journalism, voters must become journalists themselves. One *Orlando Sentinel* reporter put it well:

> Thanks to the confluence of media layoffs, the fracturing of the public sphere and the explosion of partisan research and pseudo-think thanks, voters are being asked to drink from a fire hose of flawed or intentionally misleading information with little to help them to sort out what's true and what isn't about hundreds of candidates. Nobody has time to cast fully-informed votes. Social scientists have known for about 70 years that information has an acquisition cost, which is why we need mechanisms like party systems to help organize and simplify the decision-making process. The build-up of pseudo-information adds to those costs, instead of reducing them, by making it harder for voters to sift through the nonsense.[49]

The absurdity of this process for voters is clear and is confirmed by polling. In the hard-fought race for an open U.S. Senate seat representing Wisconsin in 2012, the advertising by the campaigns of Republican Tommy Thompson and Democrat Tammy Baldwin and their supporters was relentlessly negative; indeed, surveys suggested it was the most negative Senate race in the country.[50] To assess the direction of the race, pollsters barely asked about the positions of the candidates; rather, they inquired about the extent to which voters agreed with the messages of the attack ads.[51] Newspapers in Wisconsin, with no apparent sense of irony, then reported on the fact that the dynamic force in the Baldwin-Thompson campaign was not solid reporting on the positions of the contenders but the ads purchased by the candidates and their out-of-state backers. The *Milwaukee Journal Sentinel*, which announced during the campaign that it was going to stop making endorsements of candidates, threw its hands up in the air editorially and declared, "The truth [is] hard to dig up amid all the attack ads."[52]

There are those who will suggest that this is journalism evolving to respond to the changing dynamics of campaigns. We beg to differ. This is journalism surrendering to the demands of politicians and to the all-important demands of corporate owners. And in our view, it serves as a powerful argument for a rethink by journalists and for a renewal of historic commitments to maintain a strong, independent journalism.

What the 2012 campaign demonstrated as much as anything was that in the postjournalism era, campaigns fully enter a "post-truth" era, as Paul Krugman put it when he coined one of the takeaway phrases of the 2012 campaign.[53] Michael Cooper captured the logical concerns: "Every four years there are lies in campaigns, and at times a blurry line between acceptable political argument and outright sophistry. But recent events—from the misleading statements in convention speeches to television advertisements repeating widely debunked claims—have raised new questions about whether the political culture still holds any penalty for falsehood."[54]

THANK GOODNESS FOR DEBATES!

In Chapter 5 we discuss the central role public media play in girding election coverage in other democracies and the tragedy of the woefully underfunded version in the United States, which has compromised public media's campaign coverage. While avoiding the most moronic and salacious aspects of commercial journalism, public media still follow the same professional code for campaign coverage as the commercial news media. And it was one of public media's most lasting figures, *PBS NewsHour* executive editor Jim Lehrer, whose bizarrely disengaged moderation of the first of 2012's presidential debates allowed Mitt Romney to lie with such impunity. When Romney said something completely inaccurate in a later debate, the Republican nominee was shocked to be corrected by the next moderator, CNN's Candy Crowley.[55]

Beyond the fact of Lehrer's "phone-it-in" presence at the moderator's table, the truly disappointing thing about PBS's role in the debates was the network's willingness to lend public media credibility to the entire charade. It is, sadly, not surprising that the commercial networks buy into schemes managed by the former chairs of the Democratic and Republican national committees. But it is appalling that a network that is supposedly more serious, more thoughtful, and more ethical than the others would foster the fantasy that America *has* presidential debates. The United States does not hold presidential debates in any realistic sense of the word. It holds quadrennial joint appearances by major-party candidates who have been schooled in the art of saying little of consequence in the most absurdly aggressive ways. In 2012, as in every presidential election since 1988 when control over presidential debates was taken away from the League of Women Voters by the two parties, America was denied the full debate because major media that *should* demand real debates cooperated with the travesty that is the Commission on Presidential Debates.[56]

Going into the 2012 debates, pundits said much about their importance, and there is no question that the combination of a ridiculous format, Lehrer's fact-free moderation, and Obama's somnambulance, gave Romney a brief leg up in the horse race. But by the standard understood by any and every fourth grader—that the point of any debate should be to enlighten voters with a clash of ideas that accurately reveals the differences between the candidates—the presidential and vice presidential debates of 2012 were massive failures.

It wasn't the fault of Barack Obama or Mitt Romney. American debates fail because, since the commission took over, they have become the political equivalent of a classic rock radio station. You'll hear all the hits and maybe even a few obscure tracks that you'd almost forgotten. But you'll rarely hear anything new—let alone enlightening. The whole point of Barack Obama's debate appearances was to say nothing that harmed himself and everything that harmed Mitt Romney, just as the whole point of Mitt Romney's debate appearances was to say nothing that harmed himself and everything that harmed Obama. Neither man left his comfort zone, except perhaps in the brief moment when a nonplussed Romney took in the fact that Crowley was correcting him. Neither candidate jumped off the narrow track on which the 2012 campaign had been running. The only theater was provided by gaffes, which major media "fact-checkers" were more than happy to identify and repeat ad nauseam. But America deserves better than the journalistic equivalent of drinking games built around the wait for Mitt to be Mitt.

Anyone serious about politics or journalism knows what would make the debates better: more candidates. In most developed nations—from Canada to Britain to France—debates are multicandidate, multiparty affairs. It is not uncommon for five, six, even seven candidates to take the stage. Those countries do not just survive the clashes; they thrive—with higher levels of political engagement than the United States has seen in decades.[57]

Only the most crudely authoritarian states erect the sort of barriers that the United States maintains to entry into the debates by so-called minor-party candidates. And why? The fool's argument against expanding the number of contenders is that debates involving more than the nominees of the two big parties—which, conveniently, control the access to the debates through their joint commission—is that it would somehow confuse the electorate. As if Americans aren't quite as sharp as the French. Adding more candidates would not create confusion. It would add clarity.[58]

In 2012, had Green Party presidential candidate Jill Stein joined Obama and Romney for the debates, it would not have been necessary to listen to a pair of adult men trying to distinguish between Obamacare and Romneycare. The debate could have explored real alternatives, with a working physician explaining why a "Medicare for All" program would be dramatically more efficient, economical, and humane than what either the Democratic president or his Republican challenger was proposing. Had Libertarian Gary Johnson been present for the predictably empty wrangling about whether America is "broke"—as opposed to suffering from broken budget priorities—the former governor of New Mexico would have pushed the parameters of the discourse out to where the American people are thinking. He could have proposed bringing American troops and resources home from policing the world's trouble spots, a wholly sensible fix that would make the United States safer, richer, and more popular.

By the standards of most countries, Stein and Johnson were qualified to join national debates. Both had secured places on enough state ballots to win the electoral votes needed to assume the presidency. No, there was not much chance that the alternative candidates were going to become front-runners; there was every chance, however, that their presence in the debates might have run their numbers up. But, of course, the point of expanding the range of debate is not to help or hurt particular contenders. The value of adding more candidates to the debates is in the quality and diversity of ideas they bring and in the prospect that they might force the candidates to address— perhaps even embrace—those ideas. In 2012 in France, Left Front candidate Jean-Luc Mélenchon in that country's presidential race raised the issue of taxing speculators. Mélenchon won only about 12 percent of the vote, but by the time the campaign was done, both the sitting president, conservative Nicolas Sarkozy, and the man who beat him, Socialist François Hollande, were proposing their own variations on the Robin Hood Tax.[59]

Could Stein, Johnson, or Constitution Party candidate Virgil Goode have added as much to the American debate as an experienced campaigner like France's Mélenchon did? A credible case can be made for each of them. Johnson, former Republican governor of New Mexico, debated Romney during the Republican nomination fight. Goode, a Virginia legislator and member of Congress, served initially as a Democrat and then as a Republican. Stein, as the Green nominee for governor of Massachusetts in 2002, debated Romney several times, with major media outlets declaring her the winner.

So why not let them in? Oh, right, the rules. But the rules that have been adopted by the Commission on Presidential Debates are based on a deal cut by Democratic and Republican powerbrokers. Either major-party candidate could have called for opening up the debates and the other would have a hard time keeping them closed.[60] Unfortunately, neither opted for openness. Why? Because neither Barack Obama nor Mitt Romney was all that excited about getting dragged into a real debate. And thanks to the way in which the big parties have rigged the process, neither Obama nor Romney had to worry about any interesting questions, unexpected issues, or pointed challenges interrupting their joint appearance.

SAME AS IT EVER WAS?

The debates provide a reminder of just how routinized our campaigns have become and of the extent to which traditional media outlets are complicit in the dumbing down of the political process—not merely by excluding the full range of candidates and ideas but by covering even the major-party candidates as predictably as possible. It is regrettable but true that what passes for campaign coverage these days hardly makes anyone wish the media had greater resources. All the patterns that developed over the course of the second half of the twentieth century persist, and they have grown only more severe with less countervailing material. What remains of the coverage is disproportionately concerned with the presidential race.

As Ralph Nader put it, the 2012 election coverage was "a dreary repetition of past coverage. Stuck in a rut and garnished by press cynicism and boredom, media groupthink becomes more ossified every four years."[61] Issues that polls show are of great concern to voters—such as corruption, money in politics, the failed drug war, and America's military adventurism—are nowhere to be found in the press coverage because "legitimate" candidates do not include them among their talking points.[62] And issues that ought to be the concern of independent journalists representing those outside of power, such as the significant levels of poverty, even extreme poverty, that mark the United States as an outlier among advanced economies, are nowhere to be found. FAIR's 2012 examination of campaign coverage by eight elite media—including PBS's *NewsHour* and NPR's *All Things Considered*—found that only 17 of their 10,489 stories covered poverty in any substantive manner. In short, the concerns of the weakest and least powerful 20 percent of the population did not exist.[63]

Glenn Greenwald accurately described the only remaining thread of professionalism guiding election coverage:

> At best, "objectivity" in this world of journalists usually means nothing more than: the absence of obvious and intended favoritism toward either of the two major political parties. As long as a journalist treats Democrats and Republicans more or less equally, they will be hailed—and will hail themselves—as "objective journalists." But that is a conception of objectivity so shallow as to be virtually meaningless, in large part because the two parties so often share highly questionable assumptions and orthodoxies on the most critical issues. One can adhere to steadfast neutrality in the endless bickering between Democrats and Republicans while still having hardcore ideology shape one's journalism.[64]

Bill Moyers and Bernard Weisberger got it exactly right when they observed, "Sacrificed to the ethos of entertainment, political news—instead of getting us as close as possible to the verifiable truth—has been reduced to a pablum of so-called objective analysis which gives equal time to polemicists spouting their party's talking points."[65]

The reigning motif remains the horse race. It is inexpensive and mindless to cover elections in such a manner and gives the illusion of actual reporting. Endless discussions of polls, pointless predictions, and assessments of how well a candidate's spin is working are the order of the day. Maybe struggling candidates need to cook up some better spin? The 2012 election followed the recent pattern: the Pew Research Center determined that "coverage of the two candidates overall was fairly balanced."[66] "A good deal of the difference in treatment of the two contenders," Rosenstiel wrote, "is related to who was perceived to be ahead in the race." Once that factor was eliminated, "the distinctions in the tone of media coverage between the two nominees vanish."[67]

Commercial pressures to hype the campaign like a sporting event are ever present. *Variety*'s Brian Lowry noted how commercial news media are "breathlessly chronicling the campaign's every twist" because they "have a vested interest in ensuring the audience stays engaged, right until the end."[68] "Journalists themselves concede that to maintain daily or hourly tension in the contests they promote, they have little choice but to elevate minor poll shifts into major developments," Sasha Issenberg wrote. "The truth is that we aren't even that good at covering the horse race."[69]

Sabato said reporters become obsessed with what he termed the "Gaffe Game," a singularly poor way to evaluate candidates. "When we tire of Gaffe Game, let's have a POTUS spelling bee. Would be about as revealing," he tweeted.[70] Media outlets obsess about misstatements and missteps—few of which ever move poll numbers—not simply on debate nights; they do so every night. *Politico*'s Dylan Byers wrote that "because of the pace established by Twitter and the Internet, the latest 'gotcha' moment snowballs faster than ever. For a reporter pressed to be ahead of the cycle, assuming conscientious-objector status would be suicide. Once one credible journalist takes the bait, everyone takes the bait."[71] The phenomenon is so common that *Mother Jones'* Adam Serwer coined the term "dumbgeist" to refer to the plethora of "manufactured controversies, substance-free media obsessions" in campaign coverage.[72]

The tidal wave of unabashed lies told by candidates during the 2012 campaign raised hopes there would be a newfound role for news media as aggressive fact-checkers. Jay Rosen thought fact-checking was "something every full-service news operation should do."[73] And indeed this was a golden age for fact-checking, but the news media had nowhere near the resources to make this a significant part of the campaign coverage or the courage to stick to it when politicians ignored them and accused them of being biased.

Even the serious campaign coverage often revolved around horse-race themes. "Some journalists think of themselves as mini-campaign consultants,"

Bob Woodward said.[74] Their work can be sophisticated assessments of campaign strategy and tactics, occasionally it includes reporting on actual substantive issues, but it is generally about how well candidates can manipulate voters.

We admit to being political junkies who have spent countless hours assessing the minutiae and trivia of American politics. We can devour and enjoy horse-race coverage as much as any other political junkie. But by 2012, even we found ourselves agreeing with the Ohio journalist who wrote, "I love politics, but I hate campaigns—this year's especially."[75] The degeneration of all political coverage into horse-race minutiae that never got beyond a slurry of polls and inane partisan talking points was too much for us to stomach. For the vast majority of Americans, who are not political junkies to begin with but who retain a stake in having a news media and a government that actually address the crucial issues of our times, elections become a chore. They know they should pay attention, but they aren't given much of consequence to pay attention to.

In truth, they might be better off if they did not try. Horse-race coverage is not just bad for journalism. It's bad for democracy. As Jonathan Chait noted in the final weeks of the 2012 campaign, "Rampant horse race coverage affects the outcome of the race. . . . Campaign coverage devotes far too much attention to which candidate is winning, and far too little time to conveying information that voters might use to make up their minds. Instead, the horse race coverage takes the place of the substantive coverage, and the candidate with the lead appears decisive and competent, and the trailing candidate faintly ridiculous."[76] So even though journalists may claim that horse-race coverage is a clinical examination of the contest and thus wholly nonpartisan, it ends up shaping the pattern of the campaign and perhaps even the result. That's not good for journalism or for democracy.

The decline of campaign coverage has been masked to a certain extent because the gutting of newsrooms has also encouraged what Herbert Gans described as the conversion of all political news into campaign coverage. As political campaigns have become permanent, so has campaign coverage. Political journalism has been subsumed into campaign coverage. So what journalism resources do remain are disproportionately devoted to either campaign coverage or the increasingly cynical assessment of public policy from a campaign angle, in the worst horse-race mode described above. "At times," Gans wrote, "it appears as if no government decision is ever made if it does not support White House campaign strategy."[77] Strategy coverage is cheap and easy to do, lends itself to gossip and endless chatter, and provides the impression that the public is being duly served and serious affairs of state are under journalistic scrutiny.

The nature of 2012 campaign coverage was not really a surprise. "The 2012 presidential election is 15 months away. The first primary vote will not be cast until almost *six months from now,*" Greenwald wrote in August 2011.

> Despite that, the political media are obsessed—to the exclusion of most other issues—with the cast of characters vying for the presidency and, most of all, with the soap opera dynamic among them. It is not a new observation that the American media covers presidential elections exactly like a reality TV show pageant: deeply Serious political commentators spent the last week mulling whether Tim P. would be voted off the island, bathing in the excitement of Rick P. joining the cast, and dramatically contemplating what would happen if Sarah P. enters the house. But there are some serious implications from this prolonged fixation that are worth noting.
>
> First, the fact that presidential campaigns dominate news coverage for so long is significant in itself. From now until *next* November, chatter, gossip and worthless speculation about the candidates' prospects will drown out most other political matters. That's what happened in 2008: essentially from mid-2007 through the November 2008 election, very little of what George Bush and Dick Cheney did with the vast power they wielded—and very little of what Wall Street was doing—received any attention at all. Instead, media outlets endlessly obsessed on the *Hillary v. Giuliani* showdown, then on the *Hillary v. Barack* psycho-drama, and then finally on the actual candidates nominated by their parties.[78]

Perhaps the only surprise was how much the doubling of spending on the campaigns compared to 2008 reduced the already low standards beneath what Greenwald anticipated in 2011. Someone watching the twenty-four-hour cable news channels might think presidential races have never been so thoroughly exhumed by reporters. But the coverage was as nutritionless as the cardboard box that packages a fast-food hamburger. After a diet of "experts" discussing whether Joe Biden was a windbag or if Mitt Romney needed to make himself seem more likeable, and another group of experts assessing the meaning of the latest poll numbers, political ads didn't look that bad.

DOLLAROCRACY'S MIGHTIEST MEGAPHONE

The other factor that has altered campaign coverage comes from the corporate right in the form of "conservative" media. If there has been a vacuum created by the downsizing of newsrooms, conservative media have filled it with an insistent partisanship unseen in commercial news media for nearly a century. As we discussed in Chapter 3, the conservative media program has been a cornerstone of the Dollarocracy's political program since at least Lewis Powell's 1971 memo. Initially, the work was largely about criticizing the news media for being unfair to conservative Republicans and having a liberal Democratic bias. Although the actual research to support these claims was, to be generous, thin—one major book edited by Brent Bozell actually claimed corporations such as General Electric were "liberal" companies with an interest in antibusiness journalism because they had made small donations to groups like the NAACP and the Audubon Society—the point was not to win academic arguments.[79] The point of bashing the "liberal media," as Republican National Committee chairman Rich Bond conceded in 1992, was to "work the refs" like a basketball coach does so that "maybe the ref will cut you a little slack" on the next play.[80]

The ultimate aim of Dollarocracy was, as James Brian McPherson put it, "to destroy the professionalism that has defined journalism since the mid-twentieth century."[81] The core problem was that professional journalism, to the extent it allowed editors and reporters some autonomy from the political and commercial values of owners, opened space for the legitimate presentation of news and perspectives beyond the range preferred by conservatives. That professional journalism basically conveyed the debates and consensus of official sources and remained steadfastly within the ideological range of the leadership of the two main political parties—it never was sympathetic to the political left—was of no concern. It still gave coverage to policy positions on issues such as unions, public education, civil rights, progressive taxation, social security, and the environment that were thoroughly mainstream but anathema to the right. Key to moving the political center of gravity to the right was getting the news media on the train, and that meant getting them to have a worldview more decidedly sympathetic to the needs of society's owners. Newt Gingrich was blunt when he told media owners in 1995 that they needed to crack the whip on their newsrooms and have the news support the corporation's politics. "Get your children to behave," he demanded in a private meeting with media CEOs.[82]

In the late 1980s, conservatives moved from criticism to participation with the aggressive creation of right-wing partisan media. The first decisive move came with AM talk radio. The elimination of the Fairness Doctrine (which required that a broadcaster provide two sides to controversial political issues) and the relaxation of ownership rules such that a handful of companies established vast empires opened the door to a tidal wave of hard-core right-wing talk-show hosts. By the first decade of the century, the 257 talk stations owned by the five largest companies were airing over 2,500 hours of political talk weekly and well over 90 percent was decidedly right wing.[83]

This isn't your grandfather's conservatism either. Although some conservative hosts, such as Michael Medved, can be quite thoughtful, just as conservative writers such as William Kristol will sometimes acknowledge when the movement has gone off the rails, the realists are in the minority. For a huge portion of contemporary conservative media, the broadcast begins and ends with the fear card, and it is often played in extraordinarily incendiary ways. Sure, some of the radio ranting comes from lightweights who are only trying to fill the three hours on the all-talk affiliate in St. Louis or Minneapolis. But the most effective purveyors of the venom are gifted and charismatic figures, such as Glenn Beck and Michael Levin, whose fire-and-brimstone moralizing is matched only by their willingness to bend the truth to support whatever argument they've decided to make that day.[84] Across large swatches of America, and most rural areas where little journalism remains, right-wing talk radio is arguably the leading source of political information.

The undisputed heavyweight champion was and is Rush Limbaugh, who emerged as a national radio force by 1990 and who by 1993 was already recognized by the bible of modern conservatism, William F. Buckley Jr.'s *National Review* magazine, as an unmatched political power in Republican circles; the *Review* dubbed him the "Leader of the Opposition."[85] Limbaugh and his cohorts have the power to make or break Republican politicians, and all who wish successful national careers have to pray at his far-right altar or suffer the consequences. As Kathleen Hall Jamieson and Joseph Cappella put it, in many respects Limbaugh came to play the role party leaders had played in earlier times.[86]

In the late 1990s, Rupert Murdoch launched the Fox News cable channel, and because television is such a ubiquitous and powerful medium, that put right-wing news media in the center of the mainstream.[87] Michael Wolff characterized Fox News as "the ultimate Murdoch product," because it brought tabloid journalism to American television.[88] What has been missed in the analysis of Fox News is the business model of tabloid journalism: dispense with actual reporting, which costs a lot of money to do well, and replace it with far less expensive pontificating that will attract audiences. For a tabloid news channel, that means the value added is a colorful partisan take on the news; otherwise the channel has no reason to attract viewers. Former CNN head Rick Kaplan told the story of how he was confronted by Time Warner executives in 1999 or 2000 who were dissatisfied with CNN's profits despite what had been record revenues and a solid return. "But Fox News made just as much profit," Kaplan was informed, "and did so with just half the revenues of CNN, because it does not carry so many reporters on its staff." The message to Kaplan was clear: close bureaus and fire reporters, lots of them.[89] In short, Fox News is the logical business product for an era where corporations deem journalism an unprofitable undertaking.

Fox News and the conservative media sector (including the conservative blogosphere) provide a "self-protective enclave" for conservatives to cocoon themselves. Research demonstrates that the more a person consumes conservative media, the more likely she is to dismiss any news or arguments that contradict the conservative position as liberal propaganda and lies.[90] Tom Frank argued that the point of conservative media is to facilitate a "deliberate cognitive withdrawal from the shared world" by their adherents.[91] Conservative media also, to a remarkable extent, stay on message, and the message is largely that of the Republican Party; these media, at least Fox News and Limbaugh, seem to march in lockstep with the same talking points, the same issues, and even the same terminology deployed across the board. They apply the core principles of advertising and propaganda.

Although Fox News and today's conservative media might look at first glance like descendants of the partisan media of the nineteenth century, there are crucial differences. The old partisan media were far smaller in scale, and they operated in very competitive markets where it was not difficult for newcomers to effectively enter the field, hence giving readers/voters/citizens considerable leverage and a greater diversity of views. A partisan newspaper had difficulty avoiding periodic serious engagement with contrary policy positions in its pages if it wished to remain credible. Chains and corporate empires did not exist. In partisan systems, everyone is partisan and behavior is thus understood.

Moreover, nineteenth-century newspapers, while often aligned with parties, tended also to be ideologically driven, which meant that they frequently fought inside parties and in the broader political landscape for a set of ideals. In the twenty-first century, ideals are invariably sacrificed by corporate right-wing media outlets that are, first and foremost, profit machines owned by some of the largest multinational conglomerates on the planet. They make their profits by selling advertising to other large corporations. They have considerable monopoly power and receive valuable licenses and privileges from the government, which they are adamant to protect. They are at the pinnacle of the corporate establishment as much as the political establishment.

The single most important difference, however, is the shell-game premise of the entire conservative media shtick: that the mainstream news media have a distinct liberal bias that is deeply hostile to the right and big business and therefore that conservatives are simply offering either straight unbiased news by contrast or, more to the point, are justifiably bending the stick in the conservative direction to balance the liberal propaganda.[92] In the current system, mainstream journalism works formally to not favor either major party and to prove at every turn its lack of bias toward either party. Reporters have to answer for such a bias if it is exposed. Conservative media do not have to play by those rules. The irony, of course, is that Fox News insists that it is "Fair and Balanced" and that "We Report, You Decide," so it assumes the mantle and prerogatives of professional journalism while going about its partisan business.

Being a partisan player in the world of professional journalism has provided the right with considerable power to set the news agenda. Traditional journalists get their cues about what to cover from official sources and can dismiss some as ludicrous if they fail to meet an evidentiary standard and are opposed by other official sources. Fox and the conservative media, on the other hand, can reduce complex issues to one-word battle cries—"ACORN!" "Solyndra!" "Benghazi!"—which Republican politicians gleefully echo. Then those same politicians and right-wing media "watchdogs" badger traditional media for having a "liberal bias" if they do not cover the stories as well. By the time a hyperpartisan congressman like House Oversight and Government Reform Committee chairman Darrell Issa, a Republican from California, is gaveling hearings into session, the Washington press corps is not about to say, "Hold it! This is ridiculous."[93] So it is that the nonstories that come to dominate news cycles invariably benefit the right.

But the right is never satisfied. Because they believe they are in an uphill battle with liberal propagandists, conservative media can have an unabashed and breathtaking double standard: they have very different evidentiary standards for stories that support, rather than damage, their politics. If facts prove inconvenient for the preferred narrative, ignore them. Republican officials are treated entirely differently from Democrats, even when the facts of a story are virtually identical. It is this opportunistic and unprincipled nature of conservative "journalism" that draws widespread analysis and consternation from outside the political right and from those remaining thoughtful conservatives willing to brave the wrath of Limbaugh.[94]

Between the cocoon effect and the shameless disregard for consistency and intellectual honesty, it is not surprising that professional surveys tend to find regular viewers of Fox News to be more ignorant about what is actually happening in the world compared to those who watch other networks. In November 2011, Fairleigh Dickinson University's PublicMind Poll examined how New Jerseyans watched television news, and the poll concluded that "some outlets, especially Fox News, lead people to be even less informed than those who say they don't watch any news at all."[95] In some surveys, to be accurate, Fox News does not rank at rock bottom in terms of audience knowledge.[96] But on balance, it is the clown dunce of TV news. No other network ever comes close to getting the sort of assessment Fox News received from World Public Opinion, a project managed by the Program on International Policy Attitudes (PIPA) at the University of Maryland, in 2010. As one reporter summarized it, PIPA conducted a "survey of American voters that shows that Fox News viewers are significantly more misinformed than consumers of news from other sources. What's more, the study shows that greater exposure to Fox News increases misinformation. So the more you watch, the less you know. Or to be precise, the more you think you know that is actually false."[97] As Theda Skocpol and Vanessa Williamson concluded in their study

JOURNALISM EXITS, STAGE RIGHT | 215

of the Tea Party, "Fox News makes viewers both more conservative and less informed."[98] What may be most revealing is that there is no evidence that this finding bothers the management of Fox News in the least.

In private moments, conservatives concede they have won the battle to control the news, though to justify their modus operandi, they have to maintain and ceaselessly hype the shtick of being the abused outsiders battling entrenched liberal dominance. The mainstream of journalism has indeed moved to the right, in part because it has followed official sources to the right. Also the corporate news media owners, as Newt Gingrich understood, were certainly open to the idea of more probusiness journalism. The news media have made concerted efforts to appear welcoming to the right, unlike any similar welcome to the left. As Jeff Cohen, who has spent time in all the major cable TV newsrooms, observed, the greatest fear of working journalists is to be accused of being a liberal. "Nearly all of the Clinton scandals," McPherson noted, "were set in motion by right-wing groups, floated through conservative media organs."[99] Rick Kaplan acknowledged as much and said he sometimes covered stories at CNN for fear of right-wing attack, not because they were legitimate stories.[100] If professional journalism was resolute in splitting the difference between the two parties, there has been a greater price to pay for antagonizing Republicans in recent years.[101]

The unraveling of media over the past two decades has driven many liberals, not to mention those to their left, to the brink of madness. Many are frustrated that traditional journalism has proven so incapable of resisting the right. With the success of Keith Olbermann's on-air commentaries condemning the Bush-Cheney administration, MSNBC began to recognize that a lucrative market for low-expense, high-revenue programming was being underserved; it gradually put a few explicitly liberal programs on its schedule, which now includes boundary-breaking shows hosted by Rachel Maddow, Lawrence O'Donnell, Chris Hayes, and Ed Schultz.

Some have equated these programs with Fox News in style, imagining MSNBC as just a left-wing variant on Rupert Murdoch's network, but the comparison fails upon inspection. Although these programs are expressly liberal, they are more independent of the Democratic Party than Fox has been of the Republican—as was amply evident when MSNBC hosts were quick to decry Obama's weak performance in the first of 2012's three presidential debates.[102] They also have a commitment to factual accuracy and intellectual consistency that is rare on the right. At the same time, as Olbermann and Cenk Uygur learned as they were shown the door, the corporate management has little sympathy with the politics of these shows if it veers too often outside the mainstream Democratic Party, even when the shows are profitable. There is an implicit pressure to rein in the politics.

Most striking is this: the explicitly liberal programs tend to spend considerable time fact-checking, debunking, and ridiculing the material on Fox and conservative talk radio. Right-wing media seem far less interested in what the liberals are saying. Why should they be? In the overall calculus, they are still calling the shots, and the liberals spend inordinate amounts of their time responding to the right. This call and response is a logical commercial manifestation of the postjournalism moment. Neither Fox News nor MSNBC has its own teams of reporters to send out to break news stories. Slogans like "We Report, You Decide" are rooted in fantasy. Cable channels have program hosts, producers, and guest bookers. They look at what others are reporting, and then they invite people to talk about the politics of the day. At their best, they invite interesting and diverse guests who might even disagree with one another—as happened on Ed Schultz's MSNBC show during the debate about whether to include a public option in the Affordable Care Act. At their worst, they feature Sean Hannity and Karl Rove abandoning all the touchstones of realism and engaging in extended preelection discussions about how all the polls are wrong and Mitt Romney will win by a landslide.[103]

VOTE THIS WAY

If the rise of conservative media aggressively pushing Dollarocracy policies has strongly shaped political journalism, it has had a similar effect on election coverage. Conservative media are obsessed with elections and with winning power. They aggressively promote Republican candidates, push their issues, and amplify the charges made in TV political ads.[104] They can provide a launching pad for charges against Democrats or progressive organizations and use their influence to demand mainstream coverage. Consider how the group ACORN, which was instrumental in registering poor people to vote, was destroyed in 2009–2010, based on a largely bogus video hatchet job. The stalwarts of conservative media are by their own admission expressly committed to Republican electoral success—as anyone who has heard the whistle of Sean Hannity's "Stop Obama Express" well understands—by any means necessary.[105]

During the 2012 presidential campaign, Fox News steadfastly refused to address *any* significant Romney campaign falsehoods that had been exposed in the balance of the media. It routinely announced that the "mainstream" media were "in the bag" for Obama, all the while giving the Romney campaign an enormous advantage on the amount and tenor of coverage. In the final week before the election, Fox News gave coverage of Romney's campaign speeches eighty-four minutes of airtime, compared to eighteen minutes for Obama. In contrast, the coverage elsewhere was only slightly greater timewise for Obama: forty-nine minutes to forty-two at MSNBC and fifty-three minutes to forty-two at CNN.[106]

Fox News is now a singular force in Republican politics. "The introduction of Fox News into the cable roster has been shown to have coincided with an uptick in voting for Republican presidential candidates," Skocpol and Williamson noted. "The capacity to shift U.S. voting patterns suggests that Fox News has a very real persuasive power."[107] Fox News almost singlehandedly made the Tea Party a powerful force in American politics in 2009–2010, as Tom Frank put it, by presenting "the emerging protest campaign as if it was the network's own reality show."[108] Skocpol and Williamson's comprehensive analysis of the media coverage of the Tea Party concluded that Fox News' "assiduous promotional and informational efforts surely made a big difference." They argued that "Tea Partiers' factually inaccurate beliefs about many policy matters are particularly striking given their relatively high levels of education and overall savvy about the political process. It is hard to escape the conclusion that deliberate propagation of falsehoods by Fox and other powerful media outlets is responsible for mis-arming otherwise adept Tea Partiers, feeding them inaccurate facts and falsely hyped fears."[109]

By 2011, observers noted that traditional presidential "retail" campaigning had all but disappeared on the Republican side. "The contenders," the *New York Times* observed, "are far more likely to make their visits on television than to ever drop by in person." "Everything has changed," Kansas Republican governor Sam Brownback stated. "It's like a town hall every day on Fox

News. You hear people talking back to you what you saw yesterday on Fox. I like Fox, and I'm glad we have an outlet, but it is having a major, major effect on what happens."[110]

Fox's first great achievement came in 2000 when it played a foundational role in getting George W. Bush in the White House despite the fact that he lost the vote. At a critical point in the early morning hours of the day after the November 7, 2000, election, Fox analysts—led by a cousin of Bush, John Prescott Ellis (who would later admit to having been in contact with the Bush campaign in the fateful night)—declared that Bush had won Florida. Thinking Fox had simply crunched the numbers more quickly, the other networks quickly followed Fox in making the call and, with it, identifying Bush as the winner of the Electoral College competition that would identify the next president. But Fox had the same numbers that the other networks had, and its analysts could not by any reasonable estimate have found a win for Bush in the available data. The Florida race, as the ensuing weeks of wrangling over recounts would confirm, was too close to call on election night. Indeed, there is an argument to be made that it was still too close to call when, thirty-six days later, a U.S. Supreme Court majority, made up of justices appointed by administrations in which Bush's father had served, called the contest for the Republican nominee. To our view, there is a better argument to be made that Democrat Al Gore had a more credible claim to victory. That Gore was never able to effectively stake that claim, that he was in fact portrayed throughout the recount fight as a sore loser, was a media construct. By making a seemingly impossible election night call for Bush, Fox positioned the Republican as the inevitable winner.[111]

Twelve years later, the mastermind of Bush's campaign, Karl Rove, melted down on Fox's election night broadcast, openly arguing with the network after it called the key swing state of Ohio for Obama. In 2012, however, it wasn't too close to call. A grudging Rove had to accept the will of the people, a circumstance with which he did not seem to be entirely familiar.[112] But only the most naïve commentators presumed that Rove's embarrassment was anything but transitory. The next day, he was on a conference call, explaining how he was recalculating for the next election. And Fox was featuring him once more, as if nothing had happened. For conservatives, Fox means never having to say you're sorry—even when you are massively, publicly wrong.

That's because, like most of the right-wing echo chamber, Fox is not journalism. It's what fills the void when journalism disappears.[113]

The political right is perfectly comfortable with the false construct of a "news" network that has, in the words of Eric Boehlert, "altered the game by unchaining itself from the moral groundings of U.S. journalism."[114] For partisans who do not want to be held to account, the conservative media landscape of the twenty-first century looks like a future in which they could reside quite comfortably. A world with little journalism, where the affairs of the wealthy and corporations receive little scrutiny, especially their dalliances with politicians, and where the political news agenda is dominated by their partisan news media and pundits, is jim-dandy. The conservative media can continue their migration and colonization of the news so that they are indeed the mainstream. It is a world where their ability to win elections is greatly enhanced, even when they are pushing policies opposed by the majority of the population. Even if they lose an election, as happened with the 2012 presidential race, conservative media are there the next day to tell conservatives that they need not accept the will of the people. "Conservatism did not lose last night," shouted Rush Limbaugh on November 7, 2012.[115] Actually, it had lost. Rather badly.

But if there is a basic premise that unites Limbaugh, the folks on Fox, and the vast infrastructure of regional right-wing talkers, it is this: conservatives should never bend to the demands of the voters; voters should be made to bend to the demands of conservatives. To that end, conservative media actively campaign against any proposal that might renew actual journalism. The conservative media and dollarcrats oppose all policy measures to address the journalism crisis, from increasing postal subsidies, enhancing public media, or breaking up monopoly media firms to create more competition. To the conservatives and to Dollarocracy, the status quo is just fine, thank you.

ELECTIONS ARE the tip of the democratic iceberg, the only moment at which everyday citizens are in control of the system. "The presidential election, when the public's attention peaks, should produce a widening public reporting and discussion," Nader wrote. "Imagine twenty presidential debates around the country with tough questioning by informed reporters and engaged citizens."[116] Instead, by 2012 our elections became what Greenwald termed "a tawdry, uber-contrived reality show that has less to do with political reality than the average rant one hears at any randomly chosen corner bar or family dinner. . . . the process is suffocatingly dumb and deceitful, generating the desire to turn away and hope it's over as quickly as possible."[117] Discussing election coverage, Greenwald wrote:

> If there's an afterlife, I feel sorry for the American Founders: imagine how they must feel looking down on all of this, thinking about all the work they did to enact a First Amendment to protect press freedoms, and wondering why they bothered. . . . Actual journalists think that their "careers will be made" if they expose serious wrongdoing on the part of those in power; these people think that their careers will be made if they get to run in front of an MSNBC or CNN camera and announce Mitt Romney's Vice Presidential pick 11 seconds before everyone else announces it. The latter view about what is career-making is probably more accurate than the former, which explains most everything.[118]

Elections traditionally are embraced by the mass of citizens and feared by the privileged. They become farces without journalism, the kind that hold people in power accountable to the citizenry. By 2012, it was widely acknowledged in research and among political professionals that "nearly all citizens have extremely low levels of knowledge about what their various representatives have actually done while in office."[119]

Walter Lippmann famously wrote in 1920 that "in an exact sense the present crisis of western democracy is a crisis of journalism." Unless a credible independent system of journalism were established, Lippmann was despondent about America's future: "Men who have lost their grip upon the relevant facts of their environment are the inevitable victims of agitation and propaganda. The quack, the charlatan, the jingo, and the terrorist, can flourish only where the audience is deprived of independent access to information." The choice was to address the "fundamental task" of creating credible journalism—and become "genuinely self-governing"—or see democracy "degenerate" into something more akin to dictatorship.[120] The words appear prescient, but they simply clarify what always has been true and always will be true about free and democratic societies.

DIGITAL POLITICS

••

There Is No Such Thing as "Too Much Information"

Tom Paine's ideas, the example he set of free expression, the sacrifices he made to preserve the integrity of his work, are being resuscitated by means that hadn't existed or been imagined in his day—via the blinking cursors, clacking keyboards, hissing modems, bits and bytes of another revolution, the digital one. If Paine's vision was aborted by the new technologies of the last century, newer technology has brought his vision full circle. If his values no longer have much relevance for conventional journalism, they fit the Net like a glove.

JON KATZ, "THE AGE OF PAINE," 1995

Web 2.0 is a formula to kill the middle class and undo centuries of social progress.

JARON LANIER, "YET MORE QUESTIONS"

If there was one assessment of the 2012 campaign that the campaign consultants loved above all others, it was the analysis that said, "Thar's gold in them thar iPhones." Even the Republican consultants delighted in the notion that Barack Obama won, at least in part, because his campaign better mastered the new rules of digital politics—and poured twice the resources into the Internet than the Romney camp spent.[1] After two decades of trying to figure out how to monetize bits and bytes, the consulting class is now all in for the digitalization of our politics. Indeed, the final election-season issue of *Campaigns & Elections* ("the magazine for people in politics") featured "10 Bold Ideas for the Future of Consulting."[2] This was the money-and-media election complex talking to itself, and there was no mistaking the message. Yes, of course, there were the calls for more spending: "Money in Politics: Time to Embrace It." And complaints about even the most minimal restraints on campaign donations: "Give Candidates the Ability to Fight Back: With Contribution Limits Intact, What's a Candidate to Do?"[3]

But the primary focus of the "bold proposals" was on spreading the political pathologies of the "old media"—brutal negative campaigning, crude messaging, divisive tactics, and, above all big spending—to the "new media." "Political Technology Is Best Served Partisan," declared one headline, which was sandwiched between "The Future of Direct Mail Is Digital" and "Software Will Revolutionize Local Politics."[4] Any fleeting talk of ideals and values was mostly muffled by the drooling over dollars: "The political technology field is still relatively new and whenever a new industry shows promise and money is being made, venture capitalists are quick to notice and search out promising opportunities for investment," noted one of the more thoughtful commentators. "Some in the political technology space have been quick to meet these new players with a ready grin and an open palm."[5]

There is no question that the towering variable that remains for those seeking to understand American elections and the nature of the money-and-media election complex has to do with the emergence of the Internet and the broader digital revolution.[6] The political players who have mastered television and radio and direct mail, the Karl Roves *and* the David Axelrods, as well as the thousands of consultants you've never heard of, are deep into a process that they believe will allow them to master the Internet. The reality is that the consulting class no longer views the Internet as a "new frontier" or a tool that needs to be understood. Those are the discussions of five, ten, even fifteen years ago.

Where the consultants are now with regard to the Internet is best understood as roughly where they were in the mid-1960s, around the time the Johnson campaign's 1964 Daisy ad highlighted fears about Barry Goldwater's extremism, with regard to television. They do not know *everything* that they will do with a relatively new tool. But they are sure that they will eventually do everything *with* it. The question is whether they will define the future as they did with television, as a constant process of cashing in that ultimately warps the promise of the media to such an extent that it too becomes a "vast wasteland" or "the place where ideas go to die."

We know that some of our friends and readers believe this is impossible, that the Internet is too vast, too uncontrollable, too ripe with opportunity for discourse and dissent to be conquered by new players with a ready grin and an open palm. We respect their hopes, but we would caution that the better part of fifty years ago, critics as wise and worldly as Clive Barnes were saying of television, "It is the first truly democratic culture, the first culture available to everyone and entirely governed by what the people want."[7]

Barnes was wrong about television. It's not "democratic"; it's definitional. And the people who do the defining are, more often than not, the people with the best political connections and the most money. The question now is whether those who maintain faith in the transformative power of the Internet will recognize that there is a competition for that power. And some of the smartest and most innovative, sly and determined, crude and cutthroat players in American politics and media are already in the thick of that competition.

If they prevail, and they surely intend to do so, America will have the digital equivalent of the Daisy ad and all the pathologies of current campaigning coming through our iPhones. That's why it is so very vital to unpack the details of the digital debate.

The place to begin is where everyone agrees, even those more comfortable with the status quo, and that is on the reality that the United States is in the midst of a thoroughgoing digital transformation of election campaigns. "Online communication has increased by orders of magnitude since the last election cycle," Satwant Kaur wrote after the 2012 election. "Internet users have doubled. Facebook users have increased ten times. Tweets have increased 1,000 times."[8] Only the extent of the conquest remains in debate. "JFK is the first television president. [This] year's victor may well be determined by the impact of Facebook and Twitter," Jordan Bittermann of *Digitas* argued early in the fall campaign.[9] To Paul Springer and Mel Carson writing in *Forbes,* the 2012 election "will ultimately be tagged the first full digital election—the first to exploit the spectrum of live, real-time digital media."[10]

The only question in this regard is how far along in the process the digital transformation is. Silicon Valley's Marc Andreessen is not ready to acknowledge the torch has been passed. "There is going to be a national election that is going to be about the Internet the way that 1960 was about TV for the first time with the Kennedy/Nixon debate. That hasn't happened yet. Best guess would be 2016, but could be 2020 or conceivably one of the midterms 2014 or 2018. . . . When it happens, everything changes. The spending will tip, and the campaigning methods will change."[11]

Andreessen is correct: spending did not come close to the tipping point in 2012. Obama's "aggressive Internet strategy" saw the president's campaign spend roughly double what Romney's team allocated to the task: $52 million for the Democrat, $26 million for the Republican.[12] Indeed, in the overall scheme of 2012 political spending, expenses for digital campaigning could have been taken out of the spare change jar.[13] Romney's total spending for online ads was less than what one donor, Sheldon Adelson, gave in the final weeks of the campaign to the Romney-friendly American Crossroads super-PAC.[14] David Banks, managing director of equity research at RBC Capital Markets—and, yes, it is striking that with the tidal wave of corporate and millionaire money into politics, investment advisors have become authorities on election campaigns—observed, "If you had asked someone four years ago would the next election be the game changer for internet and social media, many would have said yes. It hasn't quite played out that way, and if anything, the spending has been remarkable for how unremarkable it's been."[15] In 2012, like 2008, the *Wall Street Journal* concluded that "television remained king. The great digital migration just isn't happening."[16]

Matthew Dowd, who ran polling for George W. Bush's two presidential campaigns, blamed campaign consultants for the slow migration: "Because media consultants are such a powerful part of the campaign team, doing something different is very hard." Like generals, they have the tendency to fight the last war.[17] But the thing to understand about consultants is that their war never ends; they slowly but surely master new tools and tactics. And their professional journals are now packed with ads that scream "Big Data. Bigger Results" and "Canvassing Tools for the Mobile Campaign."[18] The digital tipping point has not been reached, but we can see it from here—and so can the consultants, slow as they may once have been. They are now racing toward it because they have come to understand, thanks to the innovations and successes of the Obama campaign, that there could well be another pot of gold just beyond the tipping point.

Truth be told, there's already a good deal of gold being spread around. By our calculations, the total amount of campaign money spent online for political advertising in 2012 was in the range of $300–350 million.[19] This was a good tenfold increase from 2008, and what was spent on the Internet in 2012 was almost twice what was spent on television candidate ads in the entirety of the 1972 election, even when inflation is factored in. Recall that in 1972 this level of TV advertising was widely considered scandalous and could have had no small number of Americans fantasizing about burning their TV sets in effigy. So 2012 Internet political advertising was hardly chopped liver, and by all accounts its exponential growth rate will continue through election cycles for the foreseeable future.

Online advertising is, of course, the easiest measure of political activity on the Internet. But it is neither the beginning nor the end of the Internet's role in American politics. In our view, the focus on advertising understates the Internet's overall role in campaigns. In 2012, the Pew Research Center determined that 47 percent of voters categorized the Internet as a "main campaign news source," second only to television, well ahead of newspapers and radio, and up from 36 percent in 2008 and 21 percent in 2004.[20] Pew research also determined that 55 percent of registered voters watched political videos online and nearly 25 percent watched live videos online of candidate speeches, press conferences, or debates.[21] Moreover, 45 percent of smartphone owners used their phones to read other people's comments about a campaign or candidate on a social networking site, while 35 percent of smartphone owners actually used their phones to "look up whether something they just heard about a candidate or the campaign in general was true."[22] A Google poll found that 64 percent of battleground-state voters used the Internet to fact-check the candidates.[23] After the first Obama-Romney debates, there were more than 10 million tweets, making it to that point the most tweeted about event ever in U.S. politics.[24] By November 2012, there were 110,000 political Facebook pages in the United States and more than 11,000 pages just for American politicians.[25] Nearly 25 percent of all the time that Americans spend online is spent on Facebook.[26]

In short, these aren't your grandfather's elections, or your father's, or even your older sister's. "Shaking hands and all the traditional campaign stuff has not gone away. You must still do it to win," Alan Rosenblatt of the Center for American Progress put it, "but if you don't have a complementary online strategy you can't win either."[27] Of course, digital political ad spending matters, and, yes, it will matter a whole lot more in the elections to come. But emphasizing digital political ad spending over all other aspects of the Internet as a source of political insight and inspiration does a grave injustice to the digital revolution occurring in political campaigns. The Internet is already in the bone marrow of the American election system. In this chapter we examine how the Internet has evolved and has altered election campaigns. But we are interested in much more than a mere stroll through the digital garden. Our primary concern is with the great question of the digital age: Will the Internet substantively derail the money-and-media election complex and empower people to tackle Dollarocracy, or could the Internet make matters worse?

THE EVOLUTION OF THE INTERNET

When the Internet burst on the scene in the early 1990s, propelled by the World Wide Web, it generated euphoric enthusiasm for its capacity to overcome institutional obstacles and launch an unprecedented—even revolutionary—democratic surge. The early days of the Internet were characterized by a sort of digital utopianism that suggested everything was possible online and that everything would be better: more transparent, more open, more free.[28] The Internet would make it possible for all people to communicate freely with each other and have near-instant access to a treasure trove of information; the bad old days of media monopolies, commercial interests, and politicians—not to mention dictators—controlling the public sphere would soon be gone. People could bypass traditional gatekeepers and organize effectively among themselves. Digital technology could draw everyday people into actual policy formation and governance in a manner that had been unimaginable previously. Authoritarian regimes would be placed on the endangered species list, while weak democracies would get muscled up. The development of Google search, broadband, smartphones, and social media—such as YouTube, Facebook, and Twitter—in the following decade only accentuated the power now in the hands of the many.

In this technological utopianism, the Internet would be a godsend for elections. Voters would be able to get for free in-depth material on candidates and issues online. The digital record would not allow candidates to make one claim to one group and a contradictory claim to another group without it coming back to haunt them. Lying and manipulation would be nowhere near as effective or possibly toxic. Online it would be much easier to spawn dissident challenges within the major parties as well as to the major parties as the costs of participation would be radically lower. In some countries, such as Britain, it appears that the Internet has been a factor in actually lowering the costs of national campaigns while they have skyrocketed in the United States.

Not much of this has come to pass in the United States, primarily because this euphoria was based on an unrealistic and romantic view of the potential for digital technology to trump powerful economic interests.[29] But this line of thinking appeals to a deep-seated American attraction to the romantic idea that technology can produce sweeping positive change and allow Americans to bypass the messy business of making actual political change.[30]

And this line of thinking is directly pertinent to American elections because it fueled perhaps the single most important justification for the 2010 *Citizens United* ruling.[31] The five justices who voted to allow unlimited spending on elections started with the dubious and absurd proposition that "independent expenditures, including those made by corporations, do not give rise to corruption or the appearance of corruption." They acknowledged, however, that for that proposition to be credible, two conditions were imperative: (1) the "third-party" groups unencumbered by much regulation could not coordinate their "independent" spending with the campaigns of the candidates they favored, and (2) all spending had to be reported quickly and fully so that the public could know who was bankrolling the election campaigns.

If those two conditions were not met, the case for unlimited spending not being an open invitation to corruption and a disaster for the electoral system was mortally wounded. In view of the dismal inability of the Federal Election Commission to collect satisfactory and accurate information or enforce its own modest rules—and there being no reason to believe matters would improve once a few billion more dollars entered the fray—what could possibly have possessed the Court to be so sanguine?

The Internet, of course. "With the advent of the Internet, prompt disclosure of expenditures can provide shareholders and citizens with the information needed to hold corporations and elected officials accountable for their positions and supporters," Justice Anthony Kennedy wrote in his majority opinion. "This transparency enables the electorate to make informed decisions and give proper weight to different speakers and messages."[32] If we take the five members of the Supreme Court at their word, their single-handed radical overhaul of the American election system would have been indefensible prior to the Internet. At the very least, no Internet, no *Citizens United*.

Many public interest organizations, like the Sunlight Foundation, have done yeoman's work in using digital technologies to shine as much light as they can on campaign contributions and the ads they pay for. But with so much secrecy, election laws with Swiss-cheese-style loopholes, and a lack of rigorous enforcement of the rules that do exist, the cumulative effect of the public interest community's Internet work has been comparable to the proverbial piss in the ocean.

Why has the Internet failed to live up to the vision of its celebrants, and to its assigned role by the U.S. Supreme Court? Why, in fact, is that premise absurd? There are two core structural factors that were largely unanticipated in the 1990s that have come to significantly undermine the democratic bias of digital communication, its many virtues notwithstanding.

First, the digital revolution has not rendered giant corporations clumsy dinosaurs on their way to extinction with a gigantic asteroid of competition and consumer empowerment. In grand irony, the Internet has arguably become the greatest generator of monopoly power in the history of economics. Everywhere enormous firms all ranking among the most valuable in the world—Google, Apple, Amazon, and Microsoft, with eBay and Facebook not far behind—have monopolistic domination of huge digital markets often equal to or greater than what John D. Rockefeller enjoyed with Standard Oil in the Gilded Age. As *The Economist* put it, the Internet invariably generates "quasi-monopoly" through "winner-take-almost-all markets."[33] The reasons for this development have been spelled out elsewhere and derive from network economics, the capacity of digital communication to collapse space, patents, standards, and, with time, good old barriers to entry with the enormous capital requirements of cloud computing.[34]

The significance of this digital monopoly capitalism for our argument is twofold. There is the general issue of Dollarocracy versus democracy: this much-concentrated economic power and wealth inequality are invariably dangerous for the survival of credible self-government. And then there is the issue of how this new kind of economic power translates into political power. Given the titanic power these firms have in the overall global economy, their political power should soon approach untouchable status under Dollarocracy, if it is not there already. This is especially true for policy debates directly affecting the direction of the Internet, where a number of crucial issues are in play, ranging from copyright law, network neutrality, community broadband, and the digital divide to taxation, antitrust, and, arguably most important of all, privacy. The old saw in politics is that if you're not at the negotiating table when deals are being made, you're what's being served. The main seats at the digital policy negotiating table are occupied by these giants, and few others are in the building or even know the deliberations are occurring. The results will likely be policies that serve their interests—or what they hash out among them when they have conflicts—not necessarily anyone else's.

Specifically, the Internet giants have set their sights on the lucrative political market, and they can imagine much of the $10 billion plus and counting to be spent on forthcoming elections ending up in their coffers. Google, Facebook, Twitter, Microsoft, and Yahoo!, for starters, all have extensive divisions devoted to working with politicians and third-party groups to solicit their business. Moreover, political online spending is seen as an increasingly permanent feature of American life, not just for elections.[35] "Google, and Google's competitors in the advertising market, really see political advertising from both sides of the aisle as a revenue opportunity," said Rob Saliterman, the former George W. Bush White House official who heads Google's Republican political ad team. "The industry, in general, has progressed by leaps and bounds from 2010."[36] These firms are assuming cornerstone positions in the money-and-media election complex; they will likely join and eventually supplant the commercial broadcasters as steadfast foes of any reform that might jeopardize that bloated cash cow.

Second, back in the 1990s the advertising industry feared and most Internet users rejoiced that the Internet appeared impervious to commercialism. Procter & Gamble CEO Edwin Artzt had the "chilling thought that emerging technologies were giving people the opportunity to escape from advertising's grasp altogether."[37] Who on earth would sit through a lame ad on a computer or click on some banner ad? In 1998, Google founders Larry Page and Sergey Brin dismissed the idea that their search engine should be supported by advertising. "We expect that advertising funded search engines will be inherently biased towards the advertisers and away from the needs of consumers," they wrote. "The better the search engine is, the fewer advertisements will be needed by the consumer to find what they want."[38]

It didn't quite work out that way. Traditional TV-style advertising may not work online, but with the development of "cookies," which allowed marketers to surreptitiously track and collect previously unimaginable and unprecedented amounts of data on individual Internet users, a rather new form of targeted, or "smart," advertising has emerged. The era where people could be anonymous on the Internet has ended, though that point has still not been fully appreciated. Internet giants like Google and Facebook collect mountains of data on those who visit their sites and use this data to attract advertisers that can target their advertising with unprecedented precision at consumers with specific demographics.[39] The key development is "real-time bidding," whereby advertisers place ads for their targeted audience that will find them immediately regardless of the Web sites they are on and follow them wherever they may go. Growing by leaps and bounds, this is expected to be a $100 billion global market by 2015 or so—much of it in the United States—and come to account for 34 percent of *all* advertising by 2017. It accounted for 12 percent in 2012.[40] In short, the world is in the midst of a fundamental reformation of advertising.

To address this new world, and to take advantage of cookies themselves, Internet publishers are increasingly "personalizing" their Web sites so that different users get different content at the sites depending upon what their personal data tell about them. Already Google search results for the same entry generate different responses for users depending on their extensive Google profile. Click on a major news site, and different people get different headlines and stories depending upon their demographics. Former Google

CEO Eric Schmidt noted that individual targeting is "so good it will be very hard for people to watch or consume something that has not in some sense been tailored for them."[41] The age of people sharing a similar digital experience or having a serendipitous experience online is fading, with all that loss suggests. We now experience a "filter bubble," as Eli Pariser put it.[42] Jeffrey Rosen wrote that "a world of customized ads, news, and politics is one where advertisers, publishers and politicians rank and differentiate us. They evaluate us not as citizens but as consumers, putting us in different—and often secret—categories, based on the amount of money they predict we'll spend or the votes they predict we'll cast."[43]

DIGITAL JOURNALISM

This leads directly to another core development of the Internet. Recall back in the day when the Internet was going to level the information playing field and provide an almost incomprehensible wealth of political information to people. It was arguably the loudest and single most important claim about the Internet. The truth was out there if people took what would be the little time necessary to look for it. This claim is certainly the basis for the Supreme Court's blasé confidence that the Internet could shine such a powerful light on corruption resulting from campaign contributions that it could render the practice utterly unthinkable to participants. In practice, this requires the existence of truly great democratic journalism to make certain this information is accurately unearthed and made accessible and intelligible.

That there is a wealth of material online of considerable value to a person's political education is undeniable; likewise, that social media like YouTube and Facebook offer extraordinary opportunities for everyday people to distribute material of their choosing is also true. A 2012 Pew Internet and American Life study found that two-thirds of adults using Twitter and Facebook do so in part to conduct civil and political activity.[44] But, regrettably, the record demonstrates that these new opportunities are not sufficient to spawn democratic journalism or vanquish Dollarocracy.

The emerging digital notion that there are different types of journalism for different types of people is problematic to begin with. The idea that one person gets stories about movie stars, another about sports, and a third about a particular ideological take on only those world events that support their ideology is a radical departure from traditional notions that democratic journalism must provide a common understanding for citizens to draw from if there is to be effective self-governance. "As it becomes clear that you click on certain ads when you read certain kinds of articles," Rosen noted, "sites will give viewers different news based on the value of their predicted responses."[45] This commercially driven citizenship is dubious enough, but the problem runs deeper.

The real problem is that the Internet has not solved the existential crisis of journalism discussed in Chapter 7; it has made that crisis worse. The Internet gives the illusion of an information rainforest, with sufficient riches to make any remotely sentient being an informed citizen. But in terms of actual serious reporting—collecting and sifting through information to make sense of it—the Internet is closer to an information desert, at least as far as popular political journalism is concerned. Real democratic journalism means paid working journalists with editors and fact-checkers and competing independent newsrooms that are accountable for their work who exhume matters of public life and governance necessary for self-government. Even the much-vaunted citizen (i.e., unpaid) journalists depend heavily on full-time journalism to be effective. We are sometimes told that a world with no paid journalists is a world where we are all journalists, as if this were some sort of great revolutionary accomplishment. Wrong. It is a world where there are no journalists, or at least none that anyone in power has reason to fear.

The reason journalism does not exist online is simple and returns to the point made in Chapter 7: there is hardly any money to pay for it. It was bad enough when Craigslist took classified advertising away from newspapers and when display advertisers found they had new options beyond journalism in the digital world. But the emerging targeted, personalized, and real-time—aka smart—advertising has all but terminated any notion that journalism can be commercially viable online, at least with advertising support. This is because advertising no longer supports specific Web sites or content. It is increasingly placed through ad networks or exchanges, dominated by the likes of Google and AOL, which place ads for clients to reach specific demographic profiles on thousands of Web sites simultaneously in real time. "Now specific audiences are bought through advertising exchanges," *The Economist* noted, "and the advertising will run anywhere the audience happens to be. This is more effective."[46] "Up to 80% of interactive ads are sold and resold through third parties," one industry source reported, "and advertisers don't always know where their ads have run."[47]

The actual Web site that displays the ads gets only a pittance of the amount spent. In 2003, for example, digital publishers "received most of every dollar advertisers spent on their sites," Pariser reported. In "2010, they only received $.20."[48] The content on the sites is irrelevant as long as they deliver the desired targets. And only the desired targets at the Web site receive the ad in any case. "With a lot of the money being put toward advertising exchanges," one industry trade publication observed, "web publications . . . have simply been bypassed and overlooked."[49]

That is disastrous for the political Web sites that have sprung up online and that political junkies like us devour. It is not just that these sites, like others, cannot get funds from direct purchases by commercial advertisers. It is, ironically enough, that despite the nature of these Web sites, *political* advertising is not much of a source of revenue either. Zac Moffett, digital director of Romney's campaign, explained that most of its online ads were "smart." "We're not buying a site. We're buying an audience. The power of the Internet is targeting." Alex Treadway, COO of the *Daily Caller,* a conservative blog, said smart advertising "will put [the] free press out of business." It is every bit as true for liberals and the left. John Amato, founder of the left-leaning CrooksandLiars.com, wondered why the Obama campaign couldn't give a supportive site like his $100,000 of the $100 million or so it was thought to be spending online. "We're here," he pleaded. "Don't forget about us."[50]

At the same time, because of the sheer desperation of sites to get advertising support—political or otherwise—this gives advertisers implicit and sometimes explicit power over the editorial content in a way that is not healthy. The ballyhooed professional elimination of commercial influence over the content, discussed in Chapter 6, is being undermined to the point where it is all but out the window.

One of the emerging trends is for campaigns or "independent" groups that support a campaign to quietly or even surreptitiously bankroll (and even create) ostensibly independent Web sites or bloggers with clear expectations of getting favorable coverage.[51] This was one of the core cancers that led to the rise of professional journalism a century ago! And even if the intent of a campaign placing ads on a sympathetic Web site is not to get favorable coverage, the practice can lend credence to the notion that the Web sites, all desperate for money, will be less likely to be critical of the campaign, because, after all, they really cannot afford to sacrifice the prospect of future ads. This dynamic can lead, at the least, to the appearance of corruption.[52]

Most importantly, the evolution of Internet advertising may sound the death knell for commercial journalism. The historical record is clear: final consumers, readers, have never been a sufficient source of revenues to support a credible popular journalism. Advertising provided the majority of revenues to bankroll U.S. journalism for most of the past 125 years, but advertising's attachment to supporting the news was always opportunistic. Now that advertising has more efficient ways to accomplish its goals, journalism is in its rearview mirror.

After twenty years of the Internet, it has barely spawned any viable new commercial news operations, and those few it has are small, pitched at niche audiences, and barely growing despite the quantum leap in Web traffic. The number of actual full-time editors and reporters employed at a living wage to do digital journalism is quite small, and stagnant. In December 2012, Rupert Murdoch's News Corporation shuttered *The Daily,* its ambitious attempt to create a digital news service for iPads and tablet computers. Given that two-thirds of tablet and smartphone owners get news from their devices, creating *The Daily* seemed like a smart play.[53] It speaks volumes that Murdoch, with the vast resources of News Corporation to draw from and his unmatched imperial vision and patience, is jumping ship after torching tens of millions of dollars. If he can't pull it off, who can?

Nonprofit groups, like ProPublica, try to fill the void, but they are puny and depend upon foundation grants, a tenuous and limited source of funding. The notion that reader donations could support more than a smidgen of the needed activity online also has no grounds for credibility. The hope that nonprofit journalism could prosper online was dealt a serious blow by the candid revelations of *The Guardian,* the legendary nonprofit newspaper in Britain, which has one of the largest Web presences in the world. By 2012, it conceded that despite its enormous Web traffic and despite winning seemingly every award in the book, it did not know how it could sustain quality popular journalism online once the traditional newspaper revenues dried up and it burned through its cash reserves. If *The Guardian* can't do it, who can?[54]

Indeed, much of online journalism is simply digital versions of news created by the old media of radio, TV, magazines, and, especially, newspapers. (That journalism, as with *The Guardian,* depends upon old media revenues and therefore is in constant jeopardy of shrinking.) This is very much the case in election coverage. A Pew Research Center survey determined that nearly 60 percent of Internet users regularly or sometimes visited "old media" Web sites and applications, far more than any other digital source for election coverage. And much of the remaining election news coverage and commentary relied upon this journalism as the basis for their contributions.[55] This helps explain why so much of digital campaign coverage seems to be more of the dismal horse-race coverage and triviality found in the old media.

It also explains why social media, rather than upending the status quo, have seemingly been incorporated into it as full partners. Consider Twitter. "Virtually all political reporters" are on Twitter, NBC's Bob Sullivan observed, "and they increasingly take their cues from it."[56] "Twitter generates an outsized share of attention among political professionals and helps to form the narratives that pundits, journalists, and candidates will develop during and after big events." It is part of the spin machine.[57]

One study of seventeen well-known U.S. political magazines found they had generated 216,000 tweets to 700,000 followers during October 2012.[58] "For many news organizations, Twitter in particular has become a stand-in for public reaction."[59] Twitter has proven especially good at exposing and amplifying gaffes, one of the central obsessions of contemporary campaign coverage. Campaign press coverage has been degraded to "being on 24-hour gaffe" patrol, and Twitter is ideally suited for that mission.[60] "The old adage used to be 'don't say anything you wouldn't want to see on the front page of a newspaper,'" Republican official James Davis stated. "Now it might as well be 'don't say anything that can be boiled down into 140 characters."[61] Not surprisingly, the Obama and Romney camps had numerous staffers assigned to do nothing but monitor tweets.[62]

The contribution of Twitter, and arguably social media writ large, to date seems as much about reinforcing the cynicism and practices of the money-and-media election complex as challenging them. It is certainly true that Twitter can be a great organizing tool, as the Wisconsin uprising of 2011 and the Occupy Wall Street movements illustrated. But as a tool for educating and informing voters, Twitter falls short (we say this as devoted Tweeters).[63] The Pew Research Center's Project for Excellence in Journalism determined that online presidential campaign coverage was "relentlessly negative" compared to other news media, and that "the tone of conversation was the most negative on Twitter."[64] Meredith Conroy's study of Facebook users concluded that, while much was taking place there politically, it was "ineffective . . . as a forum to learn new political information online." While Facebook "online political group membership is correlated with offline political participation," Conroy wrote, "we do not see an equally significant correlation with levels of political knowledge." People are not getting better informed online.[65]

DATA ÜBER ALLES

"Personal data is the oil of the information age," the *New York Times* observed, and that captures exactly where the most important transformation of election campaigns, digital or otherwise, is occurring.[66] In 2012, digital data collection moved from the margins to the center for the presidential campaigns. "While the media coverage is focused on rallies and the last-minute dash by Obama and Romney through seven swing states," a reporter observed on the eve of the election, "the real work of the first ever billion-dollar campaign is being done behind closed doors."[67]

Some, perhaps much, of the surprising ease with which President Obama won reelection despite historically unfavorable metrics has been attributed to his decided advantage over the Romney campaign in the underpublicized development of data collection and its effective utilization. Although both sides fought to a draw with their carpet-bombing of TV political ads, *Politico* tech reporter Jennifer Martinez wrote, "Obama's treasure trove of data helped give him a notable edge over Republican Mitt Romney."[68] It was striking that when Tim Dickinson did his postmortem of the 2012 presidential campaign, his top six most valuable Obama operatives were the folks in charge of or directly connected to the digital operation; strategist David Axelrod and the traditional TV ad managers and pollsters followed them well down the list.[69]

Obama's Chicago-based campaign offices were dominated by his secretive analytics department, where hundreds of specialists crunched numbers. As one reporter who got an inside look put it, the football-field-sized office "looks like a corporate research and development lab." The "Chief Data Scientist" of the Obama team was Rayid Ghani, an expert in artificial intelligence who came from Accenture Technology Labs, where he was a trailblazer in consumer data mining for retail purposes.[70] Ghani's directive "was to devise algorithms that could sift through the massive amounts of data collected by the campaign," as Dickinson put it. "If you used Facebook to log onto the Obama campaign's Web site, you revealed to them your entire social network."[71]

Among other things, the Obama team consolidated all of its disparate databases from 2008 and placed nearly all of the material on the Amazon Web Services cloud, where Ghani and his staff could slice and dice the data as never before.[72] "The biggest idea we brought to bear," said Dan Wagner, who ran Obama's analytics team, "was integrating data and then acting on what it told us."[73] Obama's campaign also employed Blue State Digital—described as the "digital consultancy behind Obama's campaign" by the *Financial Times*—which also counts Ford and AT&T among its clients. Blue State Digital is a subsidiary of global advertising and public relations powerhouse WPP.[74]

The secrecy of the effort was such that we cannot accurately determine how much money the Obama campaign spent in this area—or what all the campaigns together spent. But we do know the Obama campaign cut no corners here. In 2008, the Obama campaign dominated Republicans on the burgeoning social media platforms, and that dominance on the increasingly ubiquitous Facebook, Twitter, and YouTube continued through 2012.[75] But the campaign's 2012 initiative went much further. Obama campaign manager Jim Messina acknowledged that he made the 2012 analytics staff five times larger than the much-ballyhooed analytics staff in the 2008 campaign, because 2012 was going to be a "totally different, metric-driven kind of campaign." When asked for any specifics about the data work before the election, the campaign clammed up. "They are our nuclear codes," campaign spokesperson Ben LaBolt told reporters.[76] Data accumulation and evaluation were the Obama campaign's Manhattan Project.

The Obama data operation took Schmidt's advice and drew heavily from private sector talent; one operative called the effort a $1 billion "disposable startup."[77] No, it did not cost $1 billion to create or run; but it got that sort of bang for the buck. That is what so intrigued corporate observers. The Obama campaign was not only joined to the corporate data industry at the hip; it also proved to have been the dominant partner in the relationship.[78]

"Until recently, everyone in politics thought the commercial sector knew better how to locate and engage with their customers, and tried to apply that to politics," a reporter for Britain's *Spectator* put it. Experts believe "the Obama campaign has now leapfrogged the commercial world."[79] The morning after the election, Messina said of his high-tech staff, "Corporate America, Silicon Valley were knocking down the door trying to hire these guys."[80] As we note in Chapter 4, the Obama campaign won *Advertising Age*'s "Marketer of the Year" award in 2008; by that logic the 2012 campaign seems a good candidate for marketer of the decade. Romney's campaign engaged in much the same activities. As the *Wall Street Journal* put it, both "presidential campaigns have gone further than commercial advertisers ever have in using online and offline data to target people."[81] Obama's campaign, by most accounts, just did more of it and was better at it.

What, exactly, did the Obama campaign do to win such accolades? It began by using cookies to collect immense amounts of data online. BarackObama.com, for example, included eighty-seven different tracking cookies dropped surreptitiously on visitors; that is even more than on the Best Buy Web site.[82] Cookies were planted, for example, to see if individuals visited religious or erotic Web sites.[83] DSPolitical, a Democratic strategy group, for example, aggregated more than 600 million cookies.[84] "They know everything Google and Facebook know about you," an Obama campaign "data-miner" said about his colleagues. "They know what music you like, which Harry Potter book is your favorite, your voting habits, etc."[85] The Obama team then integrated into the database all the vast information the campaign had assembled on voters from polling, e-mail lists, fund-raisers, mobile contacts, and millions of in-person visits and telephone calls.[86] This included the material from 2 million volunteers who interviewed more than 24 million voters.[87] The database was continually updated in real time.

The campaign then matched these data to publicly available voter rolls that by law have all been digitized.[88] The campaign also spent millions to purchase "data points" from commercial data warehouses, generally offline matters such as voters' shopping histories, financial problems, and dating preferences. (There are seven companies that advertise their ability to help campaigns target specific voters online.)[89] Thanks to digital technology, there is now "unprecedented access to information about voters."[90]

Sasha Issenberg said the great breakthrough in 2012 was "linking a person's offline political identity with their online presence." Both presidential campaigns had on average around one thousand data points on each voter.[91] Strategists affiliated with the campaigns acknowledged they had "access to information about the personal lives of voters never before imagined."[92] Whereas much of commercial online data collection tends to keep the actual identities of computer users anonymous—because advertisers target users by demographic criteria that do not require knowing the precise identity—political campaigns had every incentive to know who exactly was connected to the online profiles and where exactly they lived. There was no such thing as "too much information."

This is where the fun begins. As *The Economist* put it, "The point of all these data is to mine them for insights into the electorate and identify pockets of voters who can be won over—either to vote, spend or volunteer."[93] Ghani's team plumbed the data for "motivations, attitudes, and protestations."[94] As *Bloomberg Businessweek* described it, the "campaign's Orwellian knowledge of the electorate—its deep understanding of precisely what, or whom, would motivate someone to act on Obama's behalf—was such that it could get supporters to appeal to wavering or unreliable friends and acquaintances with individually tailored messages."[95] The Obama team took the data to predict "which types of people would be persuaded by certain kinds of appeals."[96] It created an "optimizer" that was able to crunch all the data to create a new rating system for all Americans based on their likelihood of being an Obama voter.[97] The data-miners created support scores "for every single voter in battleground states," Messina explained after the election, on a scale of "1 to 100, on whether they would support us."[98] This gave them a far superior means to evaluate where and how resources would be best deployed.

Even more importantly, the Obama campaign used its computer power to test and retest and retest again messages to see what worked best with specific sets of individuals and with individuals themselves. It developed the unprecedented "targeted-sharing program"—what Messina termed its "true innovation"—which would determine which person should contact another person to get that person to vote for Obama and precisely what type of message would be most effective. "People really trust their friends, not political advertising," Obama campaign digital director Teddy Goff said. Goff's team provided people with all the "high-quality, shareable content" they needed to be "effective ambassadors for the campaign." The material the campaign gave its workers was basically idiot-proof.[99] The Obama campaign was able to use targeted sharing on 85 percent of its turnout targets aged twenty-nine and under, largely through Facebook, which was used to reach 5 million such prospects. "What businesses find so tantalizing about the Obama campaign is that it has advanced this phenomenon to its next iteration," *Bloomberg Businessweek* noted. "Your friend isn't just raving about Pepsi; he's telling you, in language and images likely to resonate with you, that you should be drinking Pepsi, too."[100]

The significance of this observation cannot be underestimated, as it offers deep perspective on the extent to which the civic and democratic values that ought to underpin our politics are being replaced by commercial and entertainment values—so much so that businesses now emulate campaigns. We have come full circle from the days when Adlai Stevenson said in 1956, "The idea that you can merchandise candidates for high office like breakfast cereal is the ultimate indignity to the democratic process."[101] Now the folks who sell breakfast cereal are taking marketing cues from the folks who do politics.

The Obama campaign also created "Dashboard," a hierarchical social network, which kept the millions of volunteers on the ground in constant touch with the data center via their smartphones. The data was updated in real time, and volunteers were instantly being redirected to better uses of their time and labor. Volunteers could track their performance against that of their peers, "and the campaign could measure the performance of its field operation in real time." As Messina put it, this meant 30,000 volunteer "neighborhood team leaders" had the effectiveness of full-time paid staffers.[102]

In short, as Messina intended, these data drove everything in the campaign. It used the "optimizer" data to drive TV advertising purchases, which is a reason the campaign spent heavily for spots on cable TV entertainment reruns compared to the Romney or any other campaign.[103] These data were also the driving force in the striking success of the Obama fund-raising effort, which floundered through the first half of 2012, at least with the small donors who had provided so much money for the 2008 campaign.[104] Then, as one campaign senior official put it, fund-raising over "the Internet exploded over the summer," blasting through the campaign's already ambitious goals.[105] How did the campaign do this? Mostly through e-mail solicitations that on the surface struck many on the Obama team as far too casual or even creepy. The Obama team was shocked that all its predictions about what would be successful e-mail fund-raising appeals were shown by testing to be so ineffective. Drawing on the banks of data, a staff of twenty e-mail writers tested extensively and then fine-tuned the winning e-mails. "When we saw something that really moved the dial," the campaign's e-mail director said, "we would adopt it."[106] The final tally: "$690 million raised online, up from $500 million in 2008."[107] Likewise, after detailed study and a redesign, the Obama campaign generated 1.5 million "one-click" donors, often through cell phone texts, who gave $115 million, about $75 million more than had been expected.[108]

The campaign database also provided the direction for the get-out-the-vote drive that was so singularly successful.[109] It was able to "train voters to go to the polls through subtle cues, rewards and threats in a manner akin to the marketing efforts of credit card companies and big-box retailers."[110] "We knew exactly who we had to go get," Messina said, "and that's how we got the turnout numbers that mattered." The campaign turned out "key demographic blocks in astonishing numbers." Consider Ohio, where African Americans accounted for 15 percent of the electorate in 2012, compared to 11 percent in 2008. That was 200,000 more new African American voters in a state Obama won with a 165,000-vote margin. Tim Dickinson noted that Romney's digital tool to monitor turnout, Orca, on the other hand, "was never properly tested and failed disastrously in the crunch."[111]

The lesson of 2012 was summed up by reporter Molly McHugh: "No interested candidate is going to see this campaign and not want to replicate what the Obama team was able to do by taking the mountains of information the Internet holds and turn it into deliverables." "Everyone will jump on the data train," ElectNext CEO Keya Dannenbaum said after the election. "Much like Obama pioneered campaigning on social media and now all politicians are there, so too it will be with big data."[112] Or as Kantar Media president Ken Goldstein put it, "Future campaigns ignore the targeting strategy of the

Obama campaign of 2012 at their peril."[113] This is the next stop on the path of the money-and-media election complex.

At this point, the ethical and social implications of the digital transformation of campaigns are still mostly unexplored. It is a world where the guiding principle is, as Ghani put it, "Will it get me more votes? If not, I don't care."[114] For some insiders, the seamy underside of digital data collection and microtargeting may be better left unsaid. "These are the kinds of things that I think smart people would keep to themselves," an interactive political consultant said.[115] The process may be getting to the point where it cannot be ignored. An ad executive with experience on Republican campaigns provided a sober assessment: "They are tactics that are pretty standard in marketing, but they are nonetheless 'Orwellian.' Those of us who've read *1984* look at this and say, 'This is unbelievable.'"[116] Nor should Democrats regard the digital transformation as not especially problematic because their guy won. Recall from Chapter 4 when David Broder interviewed LBJ staffers after their landslide election victory in 1964. Broder noted the "lip-smacking glee" they exhibited at how the revolutionary Daisy TV ad "had foisted on the American public a picture of Barry Goldwater as the nuclear-mad bomber who was going to saw off the eastern seaboard of the United States." "The only thing that worries me, Dave," one of the staffers confided to Broder, "is that some year an outfit as good as ours might go to work for the wrong candidate."[117]

DIGITAL POLITICAL ADVERTISING

Without our even broaching the topic of digital political advertising, the importance of the Internet to the present and future of campaigns is clear. As we turn to it now, the importance mushrooms and the ethical and political problems associated with the Internet also become clearer. In 2012, political advertising gave a taste of what is to come. By Election Day, the ad-search firm Moat determined that Obama had produced 657 digital display ads, whereas Romney had done 112.[118] To some extent, this advertising, and the advertising for other candidates, was simply a posting of the spots (or variations of spots) also shown on television, with the hope of reinforcing the campaign message and enhancing the effect. The idea was to "hammer their message."[119] By 2012, digital was part of the ad mix for a campaign. "You should never do one *or* the other," the chief digital officer at WPP's GroupM media buying unit said.[120] A Nielsen study (sponsored by Google) found that running advertising across TV, computers, tablets, and mobile phones "increased the amount of key information viewers retained from 22 percent with TV-only ads to 39 percent."[121] "The most natural starting point is take your ads . . . and put them online," said Andrew Roos, who worked on political ad sales for Google.[122]

But it was also a lot more than that. Internet political advertising has a different logic. Colin Hanna of the conservative Let Freedom Ring PAC shifted much of its money from television to online. "We're doing it the opposite way," he explained. "We're buying the audience."[123] Issenberg explained what this means: "It's an incredible tool. If I'm a campaign manager in Ohio and have a list of 100,000 voters I want to remind of the auto-bailout, say, in the past I could send direct mail or get volunteers to phone them. Now I can give a list to the person who buys web ads and they will unfurl a small banner ad at just the person you want to see it."[124]

Writer Jeffrey Rosen got a taste of this during the 2012 campaign when he cleared the cookies off his computer and launched two distinct identities on two different Web browsers, one for a "Democratic Jeff" and the other for a "Republican Jeff." He created new distinct partisan digital identities "as heavy-handedly as possible," with Democratic Jeff visiting Obama and liberal sites and Republican Jeff doing the opposite. Then when he returned to what had been his favorite Web sites, he got completely different political advertising on the sites he visited depending upon which browser he was using. And the political ads would follow him wherever he went around the Web.[125]

What Rosen experienced is just the first stage of how campaigns can microtarget spots to specific individuals. By 2012, microtargeting joined the political lexicon as it became the "predominant means of delivering political messages online," according to the Interactive Advertising Bureau (IAB), a trade association for the commercial Internet. The IAB surveyed campaign strategists, and *all* of them said they were using microtargeting. "We didn't set out to ask only about microtargeting—it just came up so much. . . . It popped," said Sherrill Mane of the IAB.[126] "Political campaigns now for the first time can actually reach out to prospective voters with messaging that addresses *each person's* specific interests and causes," the IAB report noted.[127]

This microtargeting also includes the ability to "target advertisements to mobile phones and tablets based on location."[128] "Geo-targeting," as this is termed, "can target by interest, location, mobile access device," Twitter's head of political ad sales explained. "It's pretty remarkable how minutely we can target." Moreover, a campaign can identify how many clicks an ad gets and how long a viewer watches one of its videos.[129] This provides the sort of data that allows a campaign like Obama's with supercomputer firepower at its beck and call to continually refine its messages until it gets to exactly what buttons to push with each individual voter. "So if it sounds like candidates are actually speaking to *you*," digital marketing expert Andy Ellenthal wrote, "well, they are."[130] This also tends to merge with the pattern of a person delivering a specific ad message to a friend on behalf of the campaign, because then the recipient "will take it more seriously."[131] In short, in combination this represents what Kantar Media's Goldstein termed "a sea change in political advertising."[132]

There is one additional aspect of digital political advertising that is particularly delicious to campaigns. A crucial problem for TV political ads in the era of DVRs and remote controls is that people can and do easily avoid them. "The big problem for advertisers these days is that everyone is fast-forwarding through their video," Jim Walsh of the Democratic DSPolitical explained. The digital solution to this problem is the rapid emergence of "pre-roll video ads" that cannot be skipped if users wish to see video clips on popular sites like ESPN, YouTube, or Hulu. Pre-roll "is great stuff," Walsh enthused, because it "forces you to watch it [the ad] before you get your content."[133] "It's those 30 seconds you can't get rid of," a freshman at George Mason University explained to a *Los Angeles Times* reporter.[134]

Let Freedom Ring's 2012 work on behalf of Mitt Romney provides some sense of how all this is beginning to crystallize. Hanna's group created forty video ads that were custom tailored to 16 million swing voters broken into twenty-four groups, such as independent young women, Hispanic business owners, Israel supporters, and affluent seniors. "People who fall into these different categories can open the same Web page and see different pro-Romney ads—or none, if they don't vote or are considered too diehard to be worth persuading," the *Philadelphia Inquirer* reported. "As of today we have served 150 million 30-second videos," Hanna told the *Inquirer* just before the election. Two-thirds of the viewers watched the ads all the way through, because they were mostly pre-roll ads installed at the beginning of popular videos, such as ESPN's NFL replays. Only a person included in the 16 million targets would see a "pre-roll" Romney ad when going to a video at, say, ESPN.com, and which specific ad that person would get would depend upon which of the twenty-four groups he or she was placed in. Visitors to ESPN.com who were not in the Romney target audience would get a commercial ad for a product like Chevy. And in the online world, advertisers pay only for ads that are viewed.[135]

To hear advertising industry representatives talk about it, microtargeting political ads based on surreptitious gathering of data is the greatest thing since sliced bread. "These technologies provide a method for politicians inexpensively to improve our democracy," a lawyer for the Digital Advertising Alliance, an industry group, said. "I would say the founding fathers firmly believed in the ability—and I think our society very much values the ability—to efficiently reach a desired audience with a political message."[136] Who can complain? After all, advertisers will target you only if they think you have an interest in the product, so no more ads for products you have no interest in. Perhaps this explains why a Toluna survey found Internet advertising was ranked by voters as about as "enjoyable" as newspaper and radio political advertising and far more "enjoyable" than TV political ads or the dreaded robocalls. (The survey found, "to no one's surprise, that most respondents do have a negative view of political advertising overall," so this was hardly a ringing endorsement.)[137]

To some extent, this preference for Internet political ads over their TV variant also may be because digital political advertising in 2012 tended to be more positive than the spots found on TV. It was where campaigns spoke to their own voters and attempted to rouse them. The emphasis was "to mine reams of data about constituents to precisely target ads to loyalists and people most likely to be receptive to their messages," Emily Steel wrote in the *Financial Times*. "Women likely to be concerned about abortion rights were likely to see a different set of ads than people worried about global warming, for instance."[138] Obama's digital director Goff said social media, in particular, provided a "whole different campaign," in contrast to the relentless negativity of the TV ad war. The Internet was used for "uplifting stuff"; it was full of positive messages about supporting the middle class and fighting for education. The Internet was the good cop.[139]

In addition, the relatively positive response to Internet political ads may have been due to their being largely voluntary and easy to skip, except for the pre-roll spots. And by the end of the campaign, the pre-rolls were beginning to take their toll. "It's intrusive, it's evasive. It reeks of lies," a college student told reporters. "Every time I try to watch a video on YouTube that has any kind of ad space there is a political ad there."[140] This suggests that as the Internet gets increasingly clogged with mandatory political advertising in coming cycles, the ennui toward it may begin to look like the antipathy TV political advertising generates.

What acceptance, if not enthusiasm, for Internet political advertising does exist is based largely upon the fact that American voters are "mostly in the dark" about the extent and nature of how they are being spied upon as the basis for microtargeting. "Consumers don't really understand what's going on and haven't given their permission," said the University of Pennsylvania's Joseph Turow, perhaps the leading expert on the subject.[141] Ad industry representatives twist themselves into pretzels to demonstrate that surveys show people view their being microtargeted on the Internet by advertisers as a good thing.[142] What those surveys fail to convey to the respondents is that the gathering of this information is surreptitious and being done without the consumer's approval or awareness, or that the targeting might be done by politicians. On both counts, the evidence is in and it is overwhelming: the American people do not like surreptitious microtargeting, and they especially do not like it if it is done by a politician. As one reporter put it after she learned about microtargeting and paid closer attention to what showed up on her screen, and then consulted others who were also made aware of the process, "If this sounds intrusive, it is. Voters get the sense they are being stalked around the Internet."[143]

The most comprehensive research done on the popular understanding of and attitude toward Internet political advertising was conducted by Turow and a team of his colleagues at Penn and published in July 2012. While 61 percent of Americans do not want "ads for products or services that are tailored to your interests," a whopping 86 percent do not want "political advertising tailored to your interests." When Americans learn how exactly politicians get the data to do their microtargeting, support for digital political advertising all but disappears. People do not even support the practice if it is being done to them (or others) by candidates they endorse. Sixty-four percent said their support for their candidate would decrease if they found out a candidate was microtargeting them differently from their neighbor. Seventy-seven percent of respondents would not return to a Web site if they knew "it was sharing information about me with political advertisers." The survey found that "a large number of internet-using Americans—almost two out of five—are so wary of political advertisers' use of people's data that they simply do not want that use to take place under any conditions."[144] The system survives and prospers based upon the ignorance of the general population, which is largely clueless about the total lack of privacy online and, increasingly, everywhere. This system is also fueled, we might add, by the determination of political, consulting, and media players who prefer not to level with the voters they are in the process of manipulating for electoral and economic gain.

To the extent citizens are aware, however, the authors conclude, "What we have is a major attitudinal tug of war—a political class pulling for new ways to divide and address the populace versus a public that appears deeply uncomfortable, even angry, about activities pointing in that direction."[145] What is striking to our eyes is how acutely the public understands and anticipates genuine threats to the political system augured by the emerging system of digital political advertising. The idea of political privacy is a bedrock principle that few Americans are willing to abandon knowingly. "Anonymity has been crucial to our political process," said Chris Calabrese of the American Civil Liberties Union. "It's the reason for the secret ballot, it's the reason the Federalist Papers were anonymous."[146] "A lot of people consider their political identity more private than lots of information," remarked William McGeveran, a data privacy expert at the University of Minnesota Law School. "We make rules about medical privacy. We make rules about financial privacy. So if you think private political beliefs are in that category, maybe you're concerned about having them treated like your favorite brand of toothpaste."[147]

Nor is this a purely theoretical or an abstract matter; there could be real consequences. "There is growing concern," the *New York Times* wrote, "that the campaigns or third-party trackers may later use that voter data for purposes the public never imagined, like excluding someone from a job offer based on his or her past political affiliations."[148] This became a concern in Wisconsin, following the bitter 2012 recall election, which tried to remove antilabor governor Scott Walker. Close to 1 million Wisconsinites signed petitions demanding that Walker face a new election after he attacked collective bargaining rights in the state. Walker backers demanded that officials post the names of petition signers online, which was done. Search tools were developed so that the lists could be reviewed not just by election officials but also by conservative activists with a so-called Verify the Vote movement. So, too, could potential employers, overzealous partisans, and even stalkers.[149] The harassment following the release of the lists became so serious that the group leading the petition drive announced, "In the face of threats and intimidation from Walker supporters throughout the duration of the petition campaign, we strongly encourage anyone who perceives they are being attacked for exercising their democratic right in this process should immediately contact law enforcement. Furthermore, law enforcement should act swiftly to investigate any such allegations."[150] As it happened, employees of media companies, sitting judges, and others were "exposed" as petition signers and attacked by Walker backers.[151] These incidents played out against the backdrop of a large, relatively transparent public campaign. Imagine what will happen, indeed, what is already happening, behind the closed doors of powerful political operations such as Karl Rove's American Crossroads combine or its Democratic equivalents.

The developing patterns of political advertising online should concern Americans. The logic of TV political advertising going back to Rosser Reeves's packaging of Dwight Eisenhower for the 1952 election on through to Lee Atwater's peddling of George Herbert Walker Bush and right up to the present has been to say whatever has to be said to get votes—even if it is irrelevant to the candidate or actual governance, even if it is untrue. This is all about manipulation. Just win, baby. Now provide that modus operandi with infinite data, supercomputer power, mind-boggling digital production technologies, unlimited funds, and microtargeting. There is the increased likelihood "that individuals will receive ads from candidates based on what the campaign's statisticians believe they want to hear," Turow's Penn study noted. "It will be possible for campaigns to virtually envelop households and individuals with candidates created *for them*."[152] *Politico*'s Jon Peha put it like this:

> Imagine that one of your neighbors keeps seeing campaign ads sharply attacking
> current environmental regulations, another sees ads passionately arguing for
> stronger environmental regulations and the campaign ads you see never mention
> the environment.
>   Now imagine that all these ads come from the same candidate.
>   This can't happen on TV—but it's business as usual on the Internet.

As Peha noted, "It's as if a politician could secretly whisper a personalized message to every voter."[153]

Even the most benign interpretation of microtargeting opens the door to a "silo" effect, whereby Americans stay in a self-referencing cocoon with like-minded people, thereby losing the common ground—and mutual respect—with which to join together and engage in effective self-governance. A political culture based on ads (and what remains of journalism) that drive down to personalized messages will necessarily reinforce existing prejudices and potentially extend them. That's hardly the stuff of democratic culture.

One of the remarkable and heartening developments of the American political journey was the transformation of the politics of southern states in the 1970s, when we saw former segregationists such as George Corley Wallace begin courting African American voters. Wallace, who in the 1960s stood in the schoolhouse door and sought the presidency as a third-party segregationist in 1968, was a decade later winning Alabama elections with coalitions of working-class white and working-class African American voters.[154] In the "bad old days" of mass media and campaigns that thought they had to reach all voters, Wallace felt compelled to build those coalitions. And in so doing, he began a process that might have led his state to a higher ground when it came to race relations. He felt compelled to do so, perhaps by guilt but also by practical political motivations. Now, in the new era of microtargeting, there are no such motivations. A contemporary "Wallace" can tell segregationists that he's with them, stirring their resentments and fears, while at the same time suggesting a measure of moderation in wholly separate communications to African American and liberal white voters. Or combining polling data, messaging, and microtargeting, a Wallace could, as too many contemporary southern politicians have, reinforce old divisions and win without ever having to construct multiracial coalitions.[155]

In 2012, much was made of the right-wing bubble created by Fox News and other right-wing media that provided a safe haven for conservatives so that they would never encounter any facts or coherent arguments that would challenge their often factually inaccurate views or respect those outside the bubble. Imagine this process extending so that everyone gets a personalized bubble. "There is no common ground," John Carroll of Boston University declared. "There's not even a foundation for an argument. They're living in parallel universes."[156] A person interviewed by ProPublica's Lois Beckett put it well: "I'm fine with targeted advertising. If I'm going to see ads on the Internet, I'd rather they be something I'm interested in." But that does not extend to politics, he told Beckett. "I'd prefer a world where candidates tried equally hard to reach everyone, present their views rationally, and let the chips fall where they may. Targeting by political viewpoint is 'creepy.' A little too close to propaganda techniques for my comfort."[157]

Then consider this: we have not even begun to discuss what happens when digital advertising goes negative, which is all but certain to increase sharply in coming election cycles. "The darker side" of microtargeting, *The Economist* wrote, "is to scare off voters leaning to the other candidate."[158] The dark money and so-called independent groups stuck their toes into the Internet in 2012, and that will likely become a full plunge going forward. These groups specialize in attack ads, and the Internet, with its veil of secrecy and lack of accountability, is ideal for such clandestine work.[159]

Imagine that the "attack ad" message arrives not in the form of an identifiable advertisement—with at least a bow to some candidate or committee—but as a text wedged between messages from your daughter letting you know when she needs a ride and your pal checking on whether you're going to be watching the big game. Already dark money operatives are using anonymous text messaging for negative attacks, much like the push polling techniques discussed in Chapter 4.[160]

A week before the 2012 election, Reuters reported, "A controversial Virginia marketing and polling firm appears to have used a legal loophole to bombard scores of Americans with unsolicited text messages berating President Barack Obama less than a week before Election Day. More than a dozen different messages landed on the screens of phone users late on Tuesday, originating from mysterious websites instead of phone numbers." The domain names for the Web sites had been registered to mask the identities of the original owners. So the recipients did not know who was telling them, via phone messages, that "if re-elected, Obama will use taxpayer money to fund abortion. Don't let this happen," or "Medicare goes bankrupt in 4000 days while Obama plays politics with senior health."[161]

These "political text spam waves" were what Scott Goodstein feared would happen in 2012. They are what he is even more fearful will become common in future campaigns. Goodstein, a pioneering figure in new media politics who developed the Obama campaign's social networking platforms in 2008, has long championed ethical and regulated approaches to the use of text messaging. He's a guy who has been on the inside, knows how things work, and knows how unethical players can—and do—abuse digital phone communications.[162]

"I was honored to build a text-messaging system for President Obama's campaign that led to an entire new industry of opt-in text message marketing," said Goodstein. "This system used new technology to provide voters information on their early vote locations, issue information, and answer questions in real-time. And within two years, I've watched bad-players manipulate this new technology to spam and harass voters to make a quick buck."[163] Throughout the 2012 campaign, he tracked abuses in major state and national campaigns, constantly alerting the Federal Communications Commission and calling for action to prevent "nefarious operatives [from] taking advantage of loopholes to spam voters."[164]

It was frustrating work. Ultimately, Goodstein got the FCC to take up the issue of the political spamming of cellphones. But he found he was battling an emerging industry, and he worried—appropriately we believe—that if cellphone users were not explicitly protected under the Technology Consumer Protection Act and related regulations, the spamming would increase exponentially. If it does, microtargeting will become an even more precise, and even more destructive, force in our politics.[165]

Goodstein argues that the battle over political phone spamming is one of the critical privacy struggles of the digital age. We think he is right, and we worry that the "nefarious operatives" and *Citizens United* courts will attempt to put First Amendment and Fourth Amendment rights in conflict as this fight evolves. Already, one of the top practitioners of "Internet-to-phone text messaging"—the sort of spamming Goodstein is concerned about—has hired a legal team that includes former FCC chairs and is saying, "If they have to regulate calls to 479 million people then we've got a problem in our country. Am I worried about taking on a free speech case in this era of *Citizens United*? No."[166]

Goodstein, a genuine advocate for the whole Constitution, including its free speech and privacy protections, worries about the fights to come—and, if he fails, about the politics to come. And so do we and not just because the regulatory process is so frequently twisted to favor those who should be regulated but also because the media outlets that should be calling out abuses neither understand nor follow the new political process closely enough to serve as the check and balance that the founders intended.

Turow and his Penn colleagues suggested that a significant part of the protection from rampant abuse must come from "active press coverage of the issue."[167] In view of the collapse of journalism chronicled in this book, that strikes us as wishful thinking. And even if newsrooms were playing with a full deck, the degree of difficulty might stump our mightiest reporters. Indeed, some of the best journalists of our times, like Beckett, have acknowledged that "targeted online ads are harder for news organizations to track, since they are only shown to some users, and will never appear to others."[168]

This is the wild, wild West where anything goes and there is no oversight. It would be hard enough if there were twenty or thirty or fifty such targeted ads in circulation at one time; now imagine what it would be like if there were tens of thousands of them at any point in time. "Narrowly targeted ads with questionable claims may escape a fast rebuttal" not just from news media, but also from other candidates in the race, who will be similarly powerless.[169] As Turow's report acknowledged, "Opposition candidates and even journalists will have a hard time learning what homes get which thousands of messages."[170] This is an invitation to new levels of deception that would be impossible on a more visible medium like television.[171] After the toxic waste dump of TV political ads in 2012, that is a depressing thought.

And even television political advertising will hardly offer much respite. "An evolution that hints at what's to come in future elections" is taking place online, and it is not simply about a "four screens to victory" strategy that links all electronic media together.[172] The future of TV advertising—perhaps the near future—will make it much more like digital advertising, with cable and satellite set-top boxes providing a wealth of information on viewers that is then linked to a campaign's existing mountains of data generated elsewhere. The new buzzword for this development is "addressable ads," and satellite and cable TV companies can barely contain themselves as they wax about the potential revenues to be had by making "the buy smarter."[173] Not surprisingly, Turow's Penn team captured the logic of what is taking place: "It is important to understand that technology already exists to make television sets 'addressable' electronically much as the Internet is today. Technology also exists to create audiovisual commercials on the fly that reflect the demographic makeup and political orientation of a household. When these developments roll out, political marketers will consider today's tailored ads primitive forerunners of their new era."[174] Or as Duke political scientist Sunshine Hillygus put it, "There's no turning back on microtargeting."[175]

MANY AMERICANS continue to be enthralled by the wonders of the Internet and digital communication, for understandable reasons. They allow people such personal power compared to what had always been the case; each new breakthrough is succeeded by yet another one that seems even more revolutionary and intoxicating. Digital technologies are now central to human existence: it is all but impossible to imagine life without them. Yet this romance should not blind us to what has taken place with regard to elections and democratic governance. The expectation that these technologies would radically and almost inevitably democratize our societies has been turned on its head.

"Political campaigning is moving in a direction starkly at odds with what the public believes should take place," Turow's Penn team wrote. "This divide may in coming decades erode citizens' belief in the authority of elections."[176] Or to put the matter in our terms, it will lead to the thoroughgoing triumph of Dollarocracy over democracy.

It doesn't have to be this way. A central argument of this book has been that media policies have been foundational for the caliber of elections and democratic governance Americans have enjoyed. From the postal and printing subsidies that spawned the great democratic journalism of the nineteenth century to the failure to enact credible public broadcasting that could provide the basis for healthy political campaigns in the age of television, media policies and subsidies have been central. The same is true for the Internet, but even more so given the manner in which it permeates every aspect of elections and governance.

The Internet does not have to be the way it is today; what exists is the result of policies, not some inexorable technological path over which humans have no control. Specifically, the manner in which a handful of giant firms dominate cyberspace and set the rules of the game has far more to do with their political power than with any iron laws of economics or technology. A very different type of system is eminently possible.

In the coming years, a number of crucial policy issues will be debated that will determine the future of the Internet and therefore of our society. Several of these in particular—establishing net neutrality, addressing the "digital divide," determining how to provide resources for independent journalism, and providing the meaningful privacy protections savvy activists such as Scott Goodstein propose—will go very far toward shaping election campaigns and governance in the coming years. A lot rides on how they play out.

Consider online privacy, which goes directly at microtargeting and the entire basis for the manner in which political campaigns are transforming. So powerful are the Internet giants that prosper by data collection, it is hard to see how the Obama administration can effectively advocate for the immensely popular "do not track" systems as mandatory on browsers. It would not only jeopardize his ties to the Internet giants, but it would also undermine the data collection tactics that empowered his own campaign.[177] It seems that the power of the few over the interests of the many has never been greater, with such devastating consequences. It is this calculus that must change. And it is in this time that we must act.

Broadcast media became what they are because meaningful interventions on behalf of democracy were proposed but abandoned, first in the 1930s and then in the 1960s and early 1970s. We have been given a new opportunity to make those democratic interventions for the twenty-first century. We dare not squander it.

THE RIGHT TO VOTE

··

Beginning the New Age of Reform

They who have no voice nor vote in the electing of representatives, do not enjoy liberty, but are absolutely enslaved to those who have votes.

BENJAMIN FRANKLIN, 1774

The vote is the most powerful instrument ever devised by man for breaking down injustice and destroying the terrible walls which imprison men because they are different from other men.

LYNDON B. JOHNSON, AUGUST 6, 1965

[American history] is not just a story of expanding the right to vote. It has expanded and contracted.

ERIC FONER, 2012

A popular Government, without popular information, or the means of acquiring it, is but a Prologue to a Farce or a Tragedy; or, perhaps both. Knowledge will forever govern ignorance: And a people who mean to be their own Governors, must arm themselves with the power which knowledge gives.

JAMES MADISON, AUGUST 4, 1822

Dollarocracy is the antithesis of democracy. Whereas democracy has as its purpose the redistribution of power from elites to the great mass of people,

Dollarocracy seeks to take the power back for the elites. Dollarocracy and democracy cannot coexist because, though he used different terminology, Louis Brandeis was right when he wrote a century ago, "We can either have democracy in this country or we can have great wealth concentrated in the hands of a few, but we can't have both."[1]

This is not a complicated construct.

For Dollarocracy to prevail, democracy must not function as anything more than a spectator sport. And voting must be an exercise in futility.

There is no more important takeaway from the last election, from four decades of corporate pushback against the expansion of democracy, and indeed from almost 240 years of struggle to define the American experiment. Dollarocracy, in the final analysis, is all about reducing the effectiveness of the franchise—the capacity of the many to engage in effective self-government—and thereby increasing the power of those few with large amounts of money over those far more numerous without.

The measure of how entrenched Dollarocracy has become is demonstrated by the vast and growing distance between what significant numbers of Americans would like to see done to address the great challenges facing the nation and the feeble range of policy options countenanced in Washington and by government at all levels. What passes for policy "debate" studiously denies the will of the people, except in those cases where popular sentiment happens to coincide with the desires of powerful interests. When it comes to economics, that is rarely the case. So as America moves more and more toward Dollarocracy, America sees more and more inequality, corruption, poverty, stagnation, and decline.

That's not going to change unless the pathologies inherent in Dollarocracy are countered with a great new embrace of democracy. And we propose nothing less.

The effective response to the crisis that afflicts America in an age of $10 billion campaign seasons and news cycles that have become spin cycles ought not to be a tinkering around the edges of the problem. The response should be robust enough to end, once and for all, the whipsawing of our democratic experiment and to realize, finally, Walt Whitman's promise that we might "use the words America and democracy as convertible terms."[2]

In this concluding chapter, we make the case that what is necessary at this point in American history is not a specific reform but a great reform moment in which an array of amendments, laws, rules, and structural and social responses are initiated and implemented. Without a broad popular movement of historic dimensions, no functional reform will be possible. We outline a few proposals and agendas that follow from our critique, highlight movements that have already developed in response to the crisis, and explore ideas that have earned other nations much higher rankings on measures of democracy. We err on the side of flexibility and innovation and of a deeply American faith that this country can meet any challenge.

But in our core conclusion we are inflexible. To generate focus and momentum, this reform moment must have at its heart a deeply democratic enterprise: the clear-eyed commitment to establish for the first time in America that we the people have an explicit right to vote. This must be settled, and accepted, as a preeminent American right. It must be understood that policies governing the electoral process and campaign finance, as well as guarantees of and support for a free press, can and should be structured to assure that voting rights are nurtured and secured. The notion of one person, one vote must become sacrosanct. Not as a public relations slogan but as a reality. This is the democratic response to what Dollarocracy has wrought. Hence this is the argument that guides our conclusion.

There can be no more blurring of the margins. America must establish an affirmative right to vote, explicitly defined in its Constitution. Only by establishing an explicit right to vote after more than two hundred years of American progress toward full enfranchisement do we enshrine that progress. And only then does democracy begin to become constant. This is a worthy goal, a fundamental goal, a goal sufficient around which to build a reform moment and allow the American people to "announce their future will."[3]

A REFORM MOMENT

America has never been a pure or perfect democracy. It began as a plutocracy where wealthy white male property holders could vote while the rest of the population was expected to pay taxes, fight wars, and hope for the best.

The franchise was extended first to the landless, then to some African Americans, to Native Americans, to women, and, eventually, to eighteen- to twenty-year-olds.[4] An African American man born just before the Civil War in a southern state might well have enjoyed the franchise, lost it, and regained it in a long lifetime, only to have his daughter's ability to cast her ballot undermined by restrictive voter ID laws.

There is constant confirmation of Eric Foner's observation that the history of the right to vote in America is one of expansion and contraction, just as there is constant confirmation of why this occurs.[5] As Garrett Epps noted, "Every step forward in human rights has given birth to a desire to 'purify the electorate.' Some Northern Republicans wanted to exclude 'disloyal' pro-southern Democrats and newly arrived immigrants from the ballot; Southern Democrats were adamant that freed slaves should not vote. As democratic devices like the referendum and initiative took hold in the 20th century, the pressure to purify grew." Epps highlighted Foner's conclusion that "the more you enhance the power [of the people], the more [the powerful] want to make sure the right people vote."[6]

In earlier chapters, we examine how the evolution of the right to vote in the 1960s and the 1970s, the federal oversight of redistricting and voting practices in what were once Jim Crow states, and the development of campaign-finance and ethics laws that made elections more genuinely competitive began to pose a serious political threat to the favored position of the contemporary equivalents of the Virginia plantation owners and Boston merchants of 1787. The modern "white male landholders" mustered their resources and organized a response that utilized some of the clumsy tools of old—legal and structural voter suppression, gerrymandering, and deliberately convoluted practices. But they also embraced new tools, establishing "think tanks" to "rebrand" unpopular ideas, buying huge stakes in major media, and lobbying for rule changes that would allow them to buy even more, thereby grabbing control of debates and popular forums away from nonpartisan good-government groups such as the League of Women Voters and using legal strategies and a new understanding of campaign contributions as "corporate investments" to flood the coffers of candidates with the largesse of special interests.

This latest devolution of democracy is different from the fits and starts of the past; it goes further in replacing the authority of the vote with the authority of the dollar. It is more sweeping and far more cynical. And it has been uncharacteristically successful, preventing a reform moment for the better part of four decades, longer than any other stretch in American history. As a result, the American experiment now teeters at a precipice between democracy and Dollarocracy.

Reformers of every stripe will tell you that something must be done. For the most part, they propose a precise fix. The place of beginning, however, ought not to be with a specific amendment, law, statute, or policy. It's not even with a focus on a specific area of concern. What's at stake is bigger than specifics. It's overarching.

But it is not unprecedented.

The United States has from its founding faced unimaginable challenges, profound divisions, and the toughest choices. And it has met them not with cautious measures but with the broad sweeps that come during what can be identified as reform moments. These are the "critical junctures" in the history of a nation where unaddressed maladies and unrealized aspirations combine to make rapid change inevitable.[7] Historian Arthur Schlesinger Jr. argued that there are cycles of history where the United States shifts from periods of private-interest dominance to periods of public-interest response. During times of private domination, government and society neglect the popular will for reform and tend to "constrain democracy," failing to address pathologies for so long that the pressure for progress becomes "inextinguishable."[8]

In such a circumstance, signs and signals emerge, even for elites with a stake in the status quo, that fundamental changes must be made. This understanding ushers in a liberal or progressive period in which America will not only "increase democracy" but also utilize that increased democracy to initiate societal and economic reforms.

This is not, Schlesinger explained, a simplistic "oscillation between two fixed points."[9] It is an unsteady and unstable process that reflects and responds to reforms that have been made—and to human and technological advances— rather than returning regularly to some ancient point of beginning.

America, explained former Supreme Court justice Thurgood Marshall, has sometimes willingly, often grudgingly, accepted the concept of a "living constitution"—and with it an understanding that this country did not start as a perfect union. Asked on the two-hundredth anniversary of the Constitution to deliver an address on the "achievements of our founders," Marshall responded:

> I cannot accept this invitation, for I do not believe that the meaning of the Constitution was forever "fixed" at the Philadelphia Convention. Nor do I find the wisdom, foresight, and sense of justice exhibited by the Framers particularly profound. To the contrary, the government they devised was defective from the start, requiring several amendments, a civil war, and momentous social transformation to attain the system of constitutional government, and its respect for the individual freedoms and human rights, we hold as fundamental today. When contemporary Americans cite "The Constitution," they invoke a concept that is vastly different from what the Framers barely began to construct two centuries ago.[10]

This is why reform moments invariably witness expansions upon the Constitution; these are the historical turning points where a majority of Americans embrace an opportunity to rearrange and improve upon the underpinnings of the American experiment. This is also why reform moments are as painful, as frightening, as overwhelming, as the Civil War, the labor wars of the late nineteenth and early twentieth centuries, the social and economic upheavals of the 1930s, and the civil rights, gender, and generational struggles of the 1960s and early 1970s. Though America was founded with a healthy rebellion against an existing order, it does not have a tradition of easy evolution. This country demands a "fierce urgency of now" to inspire a great mass of citizens to first demand immediate relief—an end to slavery, regulation of the robber barons, a real response to mass unemployment, respect for the basic humanity of people of color—and then, when they realize that it is possible, to make a more perfect union, to go deeper.

Every major reform period in American history, with the exception of the Jacksonian era, has been accompanied by numerous amendments to the Constitution, amendments that were deemed unthinkable until almost the moment they were passed. If the problems faced at this point in the American journey are going to be solved, history suggests constitutional amendments will be a significant part of the process. The measures of the moment are clear because the stakes are so high. If we are not entering into a new age of reform characterized by progress *and* the consolidation of gains, then we are accepting the certainty of an ever-deepening degeneration toward points unknown and unwanted.

Thomas Jefferson, writing not from some higher theoretic plain but in response to the news of an armed insurrection against economic injustice led by Daniel Shays, counseled that Americans should welcome the tension that ushers in fundamental change.[11] Addressing James Madison from Paris in 1787, the principal author of the Declaration of Independence explained that "a little rebellion now and then is a good thing, and as necessary in the political world as storms in the physical."[12] A few months later, in a note to William Stephens Smith, Jefferson extended this point, arguing, "God forbid we should ever be 20 years without such a rebellion. . . . If [the people] remain quiet under such misconceptions it is a lethargy, the forerunner of death to the public liberty."[13]

This talk of "storms" and "rebellions" reflects the reality that reform moments are times of upheaval. But it is a necessary upheaval, a crisis point where the failed policies of the past must give way to a new order, either through a peaceful process of political transformation (e.g. gay rights) or, if reforms are deferred too long, through more turbulent routes of civil conflict.

After the long campaign of 2012 finished with the long lines of Election Day—demanding six, seven, eight, even nine hours from the lives of those seeking a moment at the polling place—Barack Obama claimed his second term with an offhand reference to the most easily observed evidence of our democracy's dysfunction. Said the president, "I want to thank every American who participated in this election, whether you voted for the very first time or waited in line for a very long time."

Obama paused. "By the way, we have to fix that."[14]

We do have to fix that. And just about everything else. One reform won't do it. The time has come for all the reforms. This is why it is wise to seek not a particular "fix" but rather a reform moment—every bit as bold, every bit as expansive as the Progressive Era, the New Deal era, the Great Society, and the upheavals of the 1960s.

The Progressives of a century ago launched their movements with the promise of "a genuine and permanent moral awakening, without which no wisdom of legislation or administration really means anything."[15] We the people of this century should aspire to nothing less. No small measures. No half steps. Not mere reform. But a new age of reform.

THE REFORM AGENDA

The American people recognize that their country's political system is in deep disrepair. A February 2010 CNN survey found that 86 percent of Americans said the system of government was broken.[16] By January 2013 Gallup found that frustration with "government dysfunction" had—by a wide margin—displaced concerns about unemployment and taxes at the top of the list of what troubles Americans.[17]

Presidential candidates, members of the Senate and House, interest-group leaders, activists, and grassroots citizens we interviewed in preparing this book all came to the same conclusion. But frustration in and of itself does not make a reform moment. There has to be some sign that the people are prepared not just to be angry but also to believe that their anger can and should be addressed. Our read of the survey research says that the faith is there. In the same CNN poll that found 86 percent acceptance of the notion that America's system of government is broken, there was another dramatic number. Of the disappointed 86 percent, fully 81 percent expressed faith that it could be fixed. Only 5 percent said the American experiment was "beyond repair."[18]

We are with the majority on this one. But ours is not an optimism of the will. Rather, it is grounded in the cold hard facts of what is happening. As in previous reform moments in American history, the current crisis has caused patterns of upheaval—from Tea Party protests on the right (often managed by corporate interests but still sufficiently substantial and sincere enough to merit attention) to the much larger prolabor and antiausterity protests that swept state capitals from Madison, Wisconsin, to Columbus, Ohio, to Lansing, Michigan, in 2011 and 2012, and that paralleled the rise of the Occupy Wall Street movement.[19] The upheaval is broad based and volatile, and there is clear evidence to suggest that mounting frustration has inspired a determination to cure what ails the politics of America.

With regard to elections, the days of imagining that it is possible to tinker around the edges of America's historically dysfunctional system for funding campaigns with private dollars are over. There is no small reform, no "bright idea," no quick fix that will begin to control against what former U.S. senator Russ Feingold identified as "legalized bribery."[20] And that's made even winners under the current system, led by President Obama, recognize that it must change. And to make that change, proposals once dismissed as too idealist, too bold, or too radical will have to be entertained. Obama has responded to the Supreme Court's 2010 obliteration of limits on corporate interventions in elections with an aggressiveness that may on the surface seem uncharacteristic: After calling out the Court in a State of the Union address in 2010, he acknowledged in 2012, "I think we need to seriously consider mobilizing a constitutional amendment process to overturn *Citizens United* (assuming the Supreme Court doesn't revisit it). Even if the amendment process falls short, it can shine a spotlight of the super-PAC phenomenon and help apply pressure for change."[21]

Obama's evolution toward an embrace of the constitutional remedy that was once considered extreme mirrors a dawning recognition that the work of campaign-finance reformers in America is no longer just about the simple "good-government" project of old. Now it's about building a movement that goes to the heart of the matter of corporate control of elections and governance. That's a significant transformation. And a popular one. In 2010 after the *Citizens United* ruling came down, veteran reformer John Bonifaz cofounded the Free Speech for People movement for a twenty-eighth amendment to the Constitution to address the ruling. "At the time, there were plenty of skeptics who thought an amendment movement would not have any staying power, could not be built and that people around the country would not get engaged with pushing for what is an ambitious goal," he admitted. "But I think what we've found over the past three years is those skeptics have been quieted."[22]

THE SLEEPING GIANT AWAKENS

Campaign-finance reform movements have been around for more than a century in varying forms. They have always had popular support, and America has come close at various points over the past half century to implementing broad public financing of campaigns and replacing the slurry of thirty-second attack ads with the fair, equal, and substantially more responsible "free-air-time" models employed in most developed democracies. But never before have campaign-finance reformers produced the level of specific and sustained popular engagement that is now on display.

According to Free Speech for People, "America is now one quarter of the way to amending the Constitution to overturn *Citizens United*."[23] That's a generous interpretation—as befits movement building—but it points to the popularity of the effort. Three-quarters of the states must approve an amendment before it can be attached to the Constitution; that's thirty-eight states. By the end of 2012, eleven states had moved in the legislature or at the polls to call for an amendment, and the District of Columbia joined the list early in 2013. On November 6, 2012, Colorado (an Obama state) and Montana (a Romney state) both voted by roughly 75–25 margins for proposals urging their congressional delegations to propose and support an amendment to allow Congress and the states to limit campaign contributions and spending.

On the same day, more than 150 communities across the country weighed voter-initiated questions on the issue. Every single referendum won, and won big. We can find no other issue in our nation's history that has had such an outpouring of support, without a single defeat or even any credible popular opposition, in so many initiatives.

In San Francisco 80 percent of the voters backed a Common Cause–endorsed proposal to overturn *Citizens United*. But so, too, did 65 percent of the voters in conservative Pueblo, Colorado. Despite editorial opposition to the resolution by the local newspaper, voters told their congressional representatives not just to back an amendment that declares, "Money is not speech and, therefore, limiting political contributions and spending is not equivalent to limiting political speech," but also to recognize that "the inherent rights of mankind recognized under the United States Constitution belong to natural human beings only, and not to legally created entities, such as corporations."[24] "In each community where Americans have had the opportunity to call for a constitutional amendment to outlaw corporate personhood, they have seized it and voted yes overwhelmingly," noted Move to Amend activist Kaitlin Sopoci-Belknap. "Americans are fed up with large corporations wielding undue influence over our elections and our legal system. *Citizens United* is not the cause, it is a symptom and Americans want to see that case overturned not by simply going back to the politics of 2009 before the case, but rather by removing big money and special interests from the process entirely."[25]

The grassroots movement for constitutional change that has developed since the Supreme Court's *Citizens United* ruling is real, and it crosses partisan, ideological, and regional lines "This is happening because the people want it to happen," said Marge Baker of People for the American Way, one of a number of reform groups that backed "Money Out–Voters In" actions nationwide, held on or around the Martin Luther King Jr. holiday to launch a 2013 round of local and state initiatives. The movement has not yet reached critical mass, but the growing number of states backing an amendment of some sort—many different proposals have been advanced by groups and by elected leaders such as Senator Bernie Sanders (Vermont) and Congresswoman Donna Edwards (Maryland)—is highly significant from both a practical and a political standpoint.

Public Citizen president Robert Weissman, a veteran of many social change movements and an organizer of the ambitious "Democracy Is for People" campaign, explained to us early in 2013 that if the number of states backing an amendment via legislative action or voter initiative doubles in 2013 and 2014—as Weissman argued is entirely possible—then prospects for meaningful reforms that do not require constitutional interventions increase.[26] That's the vital point Obama was getting at when he said, "Even if the amendment process falls short, it can shine a spotlight of the super-PAC phenomenon and help apply pressure for change." Demands for a constitutional response—not "just band-aids," said Sopoci-Belknap, but "a true and lasting solution"— make space for officials to act at the local, state, and national levels to address immediate challenges. And a growing number of elected leaders and grassroots activists are recognizing that what is needed is a reform moment in which every option is taken, every avenue explored.[27]

This is an important piece of the puzzle. Everyone knows constitutional amendments face daunting barriers: in a time of deep partisan and ideological divisions, it's hard to imagine getting the U.S. House and Senate to approve anything by a two-thirds' supermajority, let alone getting three-quarters of the states to embrace the change. But if we have learned anything from conservative movements for a "balanced-budget amendment" or a "right-to-life amendment," or from progressive campaigning on behalf of an "equal rights amendment," it is that the organizing that goes into amending the Constitution gives impetus to presidents, regulators, and legislators to act. "If we are to build a movement big enough to win a constitutional amendment, we are going to need near-term democracy victories that make a difference in people's lives to sustain and expand that movement," said Nick Nyhart, an experienced reform activist who serves as president of Public Campaign.[28]

The role of a powerful executive, a president with a vision and a will to carry it forward, could be definitional. The question is whether the executive is willing to spend political capital. Public Citizen campaigned in 2011 and 2012 to get President Obama to sign an executive order requiring government contractors to reveal political spending. The administration reportedly drafted an order that would have gone a long way toward revealing otherwise unreported "dark money" contributions by corporations. But by the estimates of DC observers, the initiative was "all but abandoned" by Obama and his aides during a 2012 campaign season that saw the president and his supporters raise and spend $1.1 billion, as compared to $1.2 billion in spending by Republican Mitt Romney and his backers.[29] Obama talks a good line. But, clearly, in his second term, he needs to feel more pressure to act, not just by issuing a long-delayed executive order but also by encouraging regulatory agencies such as the Federal Election Commission to use their authority to crack down on corporate campaign abuses.

There is also much that could be done in the near term to address the collapse of responsible media. Noting the 2012 Free Press study, *Left in the Dark: Local Election Coverage in the Age of Big-Money Politics,* which revealed how broadcast and cable outlets make a fortune from campaign commercials but rarely inform voters about who pays for them, former Federal Communications Commission member Michael Copps urged that the agency aggressively enforce Section 317 of the Federal Communications Act. That section requires on-air identification of the sponsors of political ads in a manner that will "fully and fairly disclose the true identity of the person or persons, or corporation, committee, association or other unincorporated group, or other entity."[30]

Likewise, as we discuss in Chapter 5, the FCC should be requiring broadcast stations to establish the veracity of third-party political ads before they air them, as they are supposed to do by law, and hold stations accountable if they do not. It is a national scandal that the Obama FCC snoozed through the 2012 election cycle and allowed stations to air countless hours of blatantly false third-party political ads that their own reporters had exposed as fraudulent.

We have long argued that the president should be appointing FCC commissioners who are prepared to move on these fronts, just as he should use his bully pulpit to advocate for the restoration of reason to the licensing process for broadcasters. Surely, if a media company agrees to broadcast in the public interest, that commitment must be met by providing full and fair coverage of election campaigns. A license should also assure citizens that their local stations will broadcast several candidate debates—for all candidates on the ballot—for all federal and statewide races in their viewing areas.

And, surely, it is time to renew advocacy for a related public-service initiative: the "free-airtime" requirements outlined in the McCain-Feingold campaign-finance reform legislation initially proposed in the mid-1990s—not as a perfect "fix" but as an indication of how, even in the interim, reforms can be crafted that allow Americans who are not billionaires or in the service of billionaires to compete in campaigns for federal offices.[31] The FCC can and should play a central role in addressing the absurdity of campaigns where, in many instances, television stations drown viewers in a slurry of crude thirty-second ads that actually make those viewers less capable of casting an informed vote.

Along the same lines, the president and his FCC commissioners must join with responsible members of Congress to advocate aggressively for dramatic increases in the funding of public and community media and for new funding initiatives and tax policies that will sustain journalism on broadcast, print, and digital platforms. Journalism, renewed and enhanced and freed from a debilitating relationship with the money that pays for campaign ads, is vital to the struggle against the money-and-media election complex.

Likewise, there must be a renewed effort to have strict privacy regulations for the Internet, with citizens having effective control over data collected from them as they are being stalked online by commercial interests, politicians, and national security agencies. This will go a long way toward making the Internet a central forum for America's democratic future, as opposed to the Orwellian hellhole that some of the wisest analysts of the digital experience fear could be its fate.[32] In particular, federal interventions can derail some of the troublesome digital practices—in areas ranging from data collection to political texting—that began to emerge in the 2012 campaign.

At every stage and in every way, reformers must call the bluff of the Roberts Supreme Court and continue to legislate toward a better system—not on the naïve assumption that the High Court will defer to the will of Congress or the American people but with the understanding that the rejection of that will by the chief justice and his narrow majority will make the need for constitutional interventions all the more evident. In the U.S. House, a task force has been developed by Congressman John Larson, a Democrat from Connecticut, and other top Democrats to explore every legislative avenue for challenging Dollarocracy. Members of the task force have renewed the proposal for the sweeping reforms outlined in the federal Fair Elections Now Act. Unfortunately, though that measure has attracted some bipartisan support, few of the members of Congress we interviewed in 2013 expected that it would get far in a Republican-dominated House. Why try then? Because building support for this plan to develop public financing for campaigns shows what could be done if Congress were freed to regulate the Money Power that Teddy Roosevelt, Robert M. La Follette, and the Progressives took on a century ago—and if the Supreme Court, either with a change of personnel or under pressure from a constitutional reform movement, decided to remove the barriers to legislative reforms.

Another prime congressional vehicle is the DISCLOSE Act, which reads like the old bipartisan proposals for basic transparency from donors but is now officially opposed by the Republican Party in its platform. The League of Women Voters and other good-government groups continue to engage in the frustrating work of trying to get Republicans to back even this minor reform, and their prospects ought not to be underestimated. If in the coming years rational Republicans want to reposition themselves after Mitt Romney's "47 percent" debacle, this is a vehicle they could and should embrace. Ultimately, however, it is far more likely that reform breakthroughs on the disclosure front, which the Supreme Court might accept, will come from the states. The same goes for most other immediate reforms.

Public Campaign, Common Cause, and a network of local and regional groups continue to do tremendous work in the states, and they've secured some key allies in the aftermath of the 2012 election. New groups such as CREDO SuperPAC and Friends of Democracy are going into state election fights with an eye toward exposing and challenging Big Money influence on elections and the candidates who bow to that influence. And a new post-2012 project, the Democracy Initiative, has brought together unions such as the

Communications Workers of America with environmental groups such as the Sierra Club and Greenpeace and civil rights groups such as the NAACP to focus financial resources and people-power energy on reform fights in targeted states such as North Carolina, where they are challenging the grip on elections and policy-making that right-wing millionaire Art Pope has purchased with lavish spending in recent years. The genius of the Democracy Initiative is that it will systematically make the linkages between Big Money politics and everything from the assault on labor rights to fracking to privatization of prisons.[33] That's a message that another new group, United Republic, has delivered with particular skill, arguing that it is possible to build "a bold grassroots campaign to get millions of Americans—from Occupy to the Tea Party—actively supporting comprehensive legislation that reshapes American politics."[34] These coalitions are invariably easier to forge at the state and local levels than in the special-interest-driven swamp of Washington.

States such as Vermont, where progressives control the executive and legislative branches, and Montana, which in November elected a governor who has been in the trenches of reform fights, Democrat Steve Bullock, remain, to our view, the most likely locations for serious challenges to a broken status quo. But as we note in Chapter 3, Montana's Bullock, a former attorney general, has already been shot down by the Supreme Court in an effort to defend state-based regulation of corporate campaign money. And that brings the discussion back to the fact of a High Court majority that has moved at every opportunity to expand the influence of corporations and major donors on our politics. Of course, President Obama may have an opportunity to nominate new justices, and campaign-finance and media-reform issues add a measure of urgency to what under any circumstance would be essential confirmation fights. But waiting for the right mix on the Court is not a strategy; it's a gamble. A gamble that could cost democracy dearly. Most Americans don't want to take the risk. Three-quarters of them tell pollsters they favor reforms that take corporate money and big donor influence out of our politics.[35] When there is this much support for fundamental reform, and when the reform impulse is blocked by so much obstruction in Washington, it is not just right but necessary to recognize, as John Bonifaz suggested, that "the people are ready to take their country back. What's necessary now is to build a movement that is big enough and bold enough to renew their faith that money can be beaten."[36]

So Americans are going "the amendment route." We know they are right to do so. And we are encouraged that President Obama, key members of Congress, and millions of voters have indicated a similar enthusiasm. But we are not content with the notion that undoing the *Citizens United* ruling, or predecessor rulings such as *Buckley v. Valeo,* will be sufficient to claw America back onto a democratic course.

To our view, it is necessary to think much bigger, as has happened in previous reform moments. Yes, campaign-finance reforms are necessary. But so, too, are media reforms that recognize the wisdom of John F. Kennedy's observation that "only an educated and informed people will be a free people, that the ignorance of one voter in a democracy impairs the security of all, and that if we can, as Jefferson put it, 'enlighten the people generally and tyranny and the oppressions of mind and body will vanish, like evil spirits at the dawn of day.'"[37] American electoral structures, processes, and practices, many of which date to times when conservative forces sought to constrain, rather than expand, the franchise, represent a democratic disaster—not in the making but already made. And if this is to be a true reform moment, one that marks a genuine embrace of America's democratic promise, we can and must borrow from the best ideas of a world that—inspired by that promise—has often done a better job of implementing it.

LET AMERICA BE AMERICA AGAIN

While it is true that America has in recent decades missed opportunities to define best practices for sustaining and extending democracy—to the immense detriment not just of our electoral politics but also of our governance—those practices have been established and well defined in other lands. We don't suggest that the United States should, or even could, mirror all the practices of other countries. Some models would be hard, perhaps impossible, to replicate in so large and diverse a country as the United States. Constitutional issues and the challenges created by a system where states define so much of our election law will always make the broad reforming of campaign practices and schedules complicated, as will the immense lobbies of the special interests that benefit so mightily from the current system—first and foremost the broadcasters that have staked their futures on the new "cost centers" of multibillion-dollar campaigns.[38] The radical reforms that are necessary to renew American democracy will ultimately be defined by the American circumstance. Yet to our view, Americans are still, as Thomas Paine suggested almost 240 years ago, well benefited by "frequent interchange" with the ideas and ideals of our fellow citizens of the world.

We begin outlining a reform agenda with the premise that underpins the whole of this book: that democracy demands full public financing of elections, a well-funded public broadcasting system, and subsidies to preserve print journalism where it is viable and to promote the development of "new media" journalism sufficiently substantial to fill the void created by the collapse of reporting by so-called old media. Yet recognizing that fresh ideas regarding the scope, character, and content of reforms can and should be entertained, we have looked to evolving democracies around the world for examples of approaches that are valid, transferable, and responsive to the challenges America now faces. They are not hard to identify, as many countries—often newer and more fragile democracies, but some of them rivaling the United States in their well-established structures and histories— have maintained the great tradition of democratic experimentation that must be renewed in America.

Here are four places to begin.

Free Airtime

Free airtime is an essential building block for a functional debate, no matter how a country's media system is constructed and no matter what constitutional, legislative, or political constraints may exist. Whether party campaigns rely on public funding (as is common in countries ranked as healthy democracies), a mix of public and private funding, or primarily private funding, dozens of countries around the world have rules that require public and private broadcasters to make free time available to parties and candidates.[39]

This is not some radical new idea developed in response to the rise of negative political advertising designed to suppress, rather than encourage, voting. Nor is it merely a contemporary strategy to counter spending by well-financed political parties, individuals, or corporations. Its roots go back to the definitional years of the British Broadcasting Corporation in the 1920s.[40]

The provision of free airtime is an old, yet still necessary response to the development of broadcasting. And it is an alternative to "the idea that you can merchandise candidates for high office like breakfast cereal," which two-time Democratic presidential nominee Adlai Stevenson decried when television was on the rise as "the ultimate indignity to the democratic process."[41]

Free airtime has been a part of the democracy calculus from the beginning not just of the television age but even from the dawn of the "voice age," when politicians spoke to crowds using the "enunciators" that would eventually come to be known as "microphones." Though American politicians continue to debate the very idea of providing candidates with free airtime—having rejected it in the early stages of the debate over the McCain-Feingold Campaign Finance Reform Act[42]—politicians in most countries are able to communicate their ideas and their ideals without having to engage in the sort of election season cash grubbing that recalls another Adlai Stevenson one-liner: "The hardest thing about any political campaign is how to win without proving that you are unworthy of winning."[43] It is, to our view, entirely reasonable and appropriate to suggest that when nations make free airtime available and offer it to all candidates with sufficient ballot status to actually win so as to open up and enliven the debate, they create a politics that inspires the 70, 80, or even 90 percent election turnout levels toward which America should aspire.

Muscular Independent Journalism That Guards Against Political Propaganda

Democracies with which the United States would want to compare itself allow and encourage political parties and candidates to take advantage of free airtime in order to communicate their messages. But they do not stop there. One of the key reasons that pluralism flourishes in countries that are rated by *The Economist* Intelligence Unit and Freedom House as the healthiest democracies on the planet is that they provide massive subsidies for public broadcasting and independent media that take as a top responsibility the serious and detailed coverage of election campaigns. Countries that are ranked as more democratic than the United States subsidize media at rates as high as 50 to 1 (in the cases of some small countries, 75 to 1) over what is seen in the United States. And the results are striking.[44]

Around the world, but especially in Europe, nations have developed and maintained democracy-sustaining public broadcasting systems (of the sort Lyndon Johnson and Bill Moyers imagined in the 1960s) and programs of subsidies for print and digital media.[45] These systems and subsidies recognize and embrace the charge from the UN Special Rapporteur on Freedom of Opinion and Expression and other global observers that states aspiring toward democracy must "create an environment in which a pluralistic media sector can flourish." And that an essential obligation of that media sector must be "to ensure that the electorate are informed about election matters, including the role of elections in a democracy, how to exercise one's right to vote, the key electoral issues, and the policy positions of the various parties and candidates contesting the election."[46]

That's a global standard that has been accepted in the modern age by countries that are serious about democracy. But it is not exactly a new idea. Thomas Jefferson observed at the opening of his second presidential term, "Convinced that the people are the only safe depositories of their own liberty, and that they are not safe unless enlightened to a certain degree, I have looked on our present state of liberty as a short-lived possession unless the mass of the people could be informed to a certain degree."[47] Americans like to reference Jefferson on these issues, as President Obama did in a 2010 commencement address at Virginia's Hampton University. Quoting Thomas Jefferson's observation that "if a nation expects to be ignorant and free . . . it expects what never was and never will be," Obama told the graduates, "What Jefferson recognized, like the rest of that gifted founding generation, was that in the long run, their improbable experiment—called America—wouldn't work if its citizens were uninformed, if its citizens were apathetic, if its citizens checked out and left democracy to those who didn't have the best interests of all the people at heart." So Americans "got it," and Americans "get it."[48]

But Americans don't do it. The United States makes a miniscule commitment to public and community broadcasting when compared with other countries, and much of that commitment funds cultural and children's programming rather than election coverage. And America has not begun to implement democracy-sustaining subsidies that might maintain the newsrooms of the old media age in a new media age. The simple truth is that political journalism is a public good, and the market is not supporting it in sufficient quality or quantity. As

Chapter 8 demonstrates, there is no reason to believe the market will in the foreseeable future. Providing independent, competitive news media has to be a high priority going forward; it is an indispensable part of any reform program.

Shorter, Cheaper Elections

Election campaigns in Japan last twelve days. That's right: twelve days. Parties may name their candidates and organize in preparation for an anticipated election—although doing so is always risky, as elections are not held according to strict schedules. Rather, elections are called by the sitting government. Until the call comes, candidates cannot advertise, solicit votes, or otherwise promote themselves. When the call comes, they are still limited to what Western media outlets invariably describe as "old-fashioned campaigning."[49] As the 2009 Japanese campaign kicked off, *Time* magazine's correspondent wrote, "With 12 days to go until national elections, candidates rode in vans, armed with banners, leaflets and loudspeakers for soapbox speeches at train stations and street corners across the nation. But as their names were blared out on the first day of political open season, their campaigns on Twitter and Facebook were silent. One thing that Japanese politicians aren't armed with is the Internet." In fact, they're also strictly limited in their use of broadcast media.[50]

That does not mean there are no political discussions on TV, radio, Web sites, Facebook pages, or Twitter. But those discussions are driven by independent observers charged with examining the stated positions of the candidates and citizens. And the candidates are given more opportunities—not fewer—to address those issues in televised, print, and digital debates and panel discussions. There's no lack of spin, but it can be challenged and examined. It does not simply flow in a slurry of attack ads and what can only be referred to as propaganda.

Short campaigns are common in democracies around the world, including Britain (on average, twenty-two days), Ireland (twenty-three days), Australia (twenty-seven days), and Denmark (twenty-eight days).[51] Credible arguments have been made that longer campaigns allow for more "voter learning," especially with regard to economic issues.[52] But "longer" is a matter of a few more weeks, not a permanent election cycle. For the most part, however, countries with shorter election seasons have higher voter turnout and much less costly campaigns. And we would argue that the "permanent" character of American campaigning leads increasingly to voter burnout, as voters are marinated in negative advertising for months on end.

Direct observation and statistical measures of political engagement suggest that short, well-defined campaigns put elections in perspective and generate an excitement level that can play a role in focusing debates and boosting turnout.[53] That's especially true in countries with strong public media, substantial public financing of campaigns, and controls on the cost of campaigns.[54]

Nonpartisan Election Commissions and International Assessments

The most successful democracies are characterized by a commitment to constant assessment, review, and reform of existing electoral and media systems. There is an acceptance that what worked in the past may not work in the present and almost certainly will not work in a future redefined by new political demands and new media technologies.

In Europe it is common for countries to formally invite "Election Assessment Missions" from the Office for Democratic Institutions and Human Rights of the Organization for Security and Co-operation in Europe (OSCE) to assess how campaigns are conducted.[55] These missions produce detailed reports that include recommendations for how to update and reform electoral procedures and media structures and funding in order to end abuses and to avoid pathologies defining electoral processes. Those recommendations do not always go "on the shelf." European and African states frequently refine and adopt proposals for how to increase the transparency, fairness, and functionality of elections—and of the media that cover them.

It speaks volumes about the way in which Dollarocracy assaults democratic principles that the notion of political parties coming together in earnest agreement to create fair elections with high voter turnout is now considered to be the stuff of pipe dreams. Today Americans are inured to what seem like endless, shameless attempts to suppress voting and rig elections. That must stop, and a culture that tolerates this attitude must change.

How bogus is this situation? President Jimmy Carter has won international acclaim for the work of the Atlanta-based Carter Center, which has monitored ninety-three elections in thirty-seven nations since 1989, "all of them held under contentious, troubled or dangerous conditions," as Carter puts it. Yet Carter, as we have noted, acknowledged some years ago that the Carter Center would be unable to monitor U.S. elections because "some basic international requirements for a fair election are missing," requirements so minimal that they have been met in nations routinely singled out by the United States as extremely dubious in their commitment to fair elections.[56]

One of the Carter Center's core requirements for nations to establish that they are committed to fair elections and the rule of law is to have nonpartisan national election commissions that are constantly refining processes and approaches to voting, counting votes, and managing elections. Countries around the world have developed such commissions, and they have ably, often courageously, administered free and fair elections. Many countries have gone even further, recognizing the need to assure that citizens are provided with the fair mix of information and ideas that allows for the casting of informed votes. Countries such as Britain and Germany have formal media watchdog structures in place to examine how elections are covered—and to take complaints from citizens, candidates, and parties that believe they have been wronged. These watchdogs do not seek to censor or constrain debate. They seek to assure that there is broad and free-ranging debate and that no voices are silenced or shouted down.

Commissions that oversee elections do not merely tinker around the edges of existing electoral systems. Where they see problems for the democratic process, where they recognize openings to make elections freer and fairer, they intervene. Often this leads to fundamental change. It will come as no surprise that some of the steadiest patterns of reform and adjustment are seen in countries that were formerly controlled by oppressive military (Brazil) or civilian (South Africa) regimes. But well-established democracies also reform themselves, often with dramatic results.

In 1994, for instance, Japan completely restructured its system for electing members of its equivalent of the U.S. House of Representatives, developing a hybrid system that allows for the election of 300 members from individual districts and another 180 members via a proportional representation system. This hybrid thereby allows for the election of local representatives who are closely identified with their districts and for votes that reflect broader ideological and partisan goals. At the same time, direct contributions by corporations and unions to parliamentary candidates were banned, and an existing system of public funding of political parties was strengthened—with parties receiving a specific amount of money for each vote won in an election.[57] Since the change, Japan, which had experienced virtual one-party rule by the centrist Liberal Democratic Party's machine-style politics, has seen dramatically competitive elections, with development of new parties and frequent regional and now national shifts in power from traditional leaders and parties to reformers.[58]

In New Zealand in the 1990s, there was widespread frustration with the political system, which was based on individual members of Parliament elected from individual districts—along lines similar to how the U.S. Congress is elected. The frustration stemmed from the fact that governments were frequently formed by a party that won a parliamentary majority but not a majority of votes nationwide. And there was particular dismay over the underrepresentation of the Maori, New Zealand's indigenous Polynesian minority. After 85 percent of New Zealanders backed a 1994 referendum calling for development of a new election system, a second referendum endorsed a hybrid system where voters cast two ballots: one for a national party list and one for a local representative in the home district. Since the change, New Zealand has seen a flourishing of multiparty democracy (seven parties won parliamentary seats in 2011), stable coalition governments, and increased representation of indigenous Polynesian minority groups, women, Asians, and Pacific Islanders.[59]

There will always be those who want to imagine that what the United States or Great Britain or ancient Greece did provides the only model of democracy. But this is a dangerous game. Democracy is not a possession of one nation; it is a goal that all nations should aspire to. America in its history has provided models, shaped strategies, and achieved democratic advances that the rest of the world has followed. America again finds itself in need of "bold, persistent experimentation."[60] Poor choices were made in the past, but they need not define the future. The dissatisfaction that Americans feel with regard to dysfunctional democracy is real, but it need not be constant. Now is a time for trying new methods and for recognizing that there are ideas, there are options— some discarded, unwisely, in recent history, some readily on display in the family of nations—that can remake America.

IT BEGINS WITH A VOTE

There is more than sufficient demand for reform. And there are more than sufficient reforms under consideration. But to our view and that of many of the hundreds of elected officials, academics, journalists, and activists we interviewed while preparing this book, there is an insufficiency of focus. There needs to be a unifying theme that will galvanize the movement and enhance its power. From this enhanced power—and *only* from such enhanced power—can foundational democratic reforms emerge. This is the last great challenge in shaping the current moment for reform into a necessary transformational politics.

To our view, the focus must be on the act of voting that underpins any sincere democratic experiment. Not on the vote as it has been perverted, dumbed down, and diminished into a merely political act, but on the vote as Walt Whitman understood it when he wrote, "Thunder on! Stride on! Democracy. Strike with vengeful strokes."[61] Voting can be made into a bureaucratic act, into something akin to a spectator sport, or into something even less than that: a "privilege" that must be attained at the end of a long line or after many leaps through the hoops erected by partisans seeking to constrain the franchise to include only "the right people." But that is not how voting should be understood or protected. Bill Moyers argued that "the crisis of the times as I see it" is that Americans too frequently "talk about problems, issues, policies, but we don't talk about what democracy means—what it bestows on us—the revolutionary idea that it isn't just about the means of governance but the means of dignifying people so they become fully free to claim their moral and political agency."[62]

It is this uncompromised definition of voting that we begin with in proposing that the reform moment necessary to establish American democracy must have at its heart a deep definition of the vote. That definition has been well established in other countries, often with the assistance of Americans, frequently at the demand of Americans. The theory of voting as a "privilege" is one the United States tends to regard as dangerous when practiced by other countries. The lawyers who were flown to Baghdad by the U.S. commanders occupying Iraq in 2005 scripted a constitution that declared, "Iraqi citizens, men and women, shall have the right to participate in public affairs and to enjoy political rights including the right to vote, elect, and run for office." All citizens of Afghanistan now enjoy the constitutionally defined "right to elect and be elected." General Douglas MacArthur and the U.S. forces that occupied Japan in the years after World War II scripted a constitution that declared, "Universal adult suffrage is guaranteed." Germany's postwar "Basic Law" is even more precise: "Any person who has attained the age of eighteen shall be entitled to vote."[63] Around the world, the right to vote is specifically established in national constitutions. Globally, there are just eleven democracies that do not guarantee the right to vote in their constitutions.[64]

Remarkably, the United States is one of them.

"While there are amendments to the U.S. Constitution that prohibit discrimination based on race (15th), sex (19th) and age (26th), no affirmative right to vote exists," explained FairVote, the advocacy group formerly known as the Center for Voting and Democracy. "Because there is no right to vote in the U.S. Constitution, individual states set their own electoral policies and procedures. This leads to confusing and sometimes contradictory policies regarding ballot design, polling hours, voting equipment, voter registration requirements, and ex-felon voting rights. As a result, our electoral system is divided into 50 states, more than 3,000 counties and approximately 13,000 voting districts, all separate and unequal."[65]

Rob Richie and the voting-rights experts at FairVote argued, "Many reforms are needed to solve the electoral problems we continue to experience every election cycle. The first is providing a solid foundation upon which these reforms can be made. This solid foundation is an amendment that clearly protects an affirmative right to vote for every U.S. citizen."[66]

In 2001, one year after the *Bush v. Gore* debacle concluded the 2000 presidential election with the Supreme Court pronouncement that "the individual citizen has no federal constitutional right to vote for electors for the President of the United States," several civil rights and reform groups proposed a "right-to-vote" amendment to the Constitution. Hailed by constitutional scholar Jamin Raskin as a "comprehensive package of democracy reforms," it was introduced in the U.S. House as a proposal for an amendment that read:

SECTION 1. All citizens of the United States, who are eighteen years of age or older, shall have the right to vote in any public election held in the jurisdiction in which the citizen resides. The right to vote shall not be denied or abridged by the United States, any State, or any other public or private person or entity, except that the United States or any State may establish regulations narrowly tailored to produce efficient and honest elections.

SECTION 2. Each State shall administer public elections in the State in accordance with election performance standards established by the Congress. The Congress shall reconsider such election performance standards at least once every four years to determine if higher standards should be established to reflect improvements in methods and practices regarding the administration of elections.

SECTION 3. Each State shall provide any eligible voter the opportunity to register and vote on the day of any public election.

SECTION 4. Each State and the District constituting the seat of Government of the United States shall establish and abide by rules for appointing its respective number of Electors. Such rules shall provide for the appointment of Electors on the day designated by the Congress for holding an election for President and Vice President and shall ensure that each Elector votes for the candidate for President and Vice President who received a majority of the popular vote in the State or District.

SECTION 5. The Congress shall have power to enforce this article by appropriate legislation.

Despite the fact that there was no concerted campaign for the amendment after it was introduced in the House by Congressman Jesse Jackson Jr., an Illinois Democrat, the measure eventually earned the backing of more than fifty members, including former House Judiciary Committee chairman John Conyers, a Democrat from Michigan. Even though the amendment should have been an easy "sell," House leaders on both sides of the aisle tended to shy away from it. At the time of the amendment's initial introduction, the chamber's Republican majority did not want to entertain any discussion that might reopen the debate about the miscount of votes in Florida. And Democratic leaders, hypercautious in the aftermath of the September 11, 2001, attacks, were not prepared to question the legitimacy not only of a president who had lost the popular vote but also of a broken voting system.[67]

So the proposal went nowhere. And a decade later, the United States was again embroiled in bitter debates about crudely antidemocratic "voter ID" laws, restrictions on same-day registration and early voting, gerrymandering of congressional districts (and potentially of electoral votes), dysfunctional counts and recounts, and all the other aspects of a voting system so ill defined that it invites manipulation.[68] Recognizing this reality, two members of the House were preparing as we completed this book not just to introduce a "right-to-vote" amendment but also to join in building a movement for its enactment. Congressman Keith Ellison, the Minnesota Democrat who cochairs the Congressional Progressive Caucus, and Congressman Mark Pocan, a freshman Democrat from Wisconsin with a long history of working on voting issues as a state legislator, are taking up the gauntlet. Their decision to introduce a right-to-vote amendment is necessary, and it is energizing. "What could be more American than the right to vote?" asked Pocan. "It's the one thing we should all be able to agree on."[69]

Pocan is not naïve. When he says a guaranteed right to vote is "one thing we should all be able to agree on," he knows there are reckless partisans who do not agree. But he and Ellison are right to take the debate to a higher ground, just as they are right to recognize the debate *must* be had.

The headlines of the contemporary moment lead us back to a core understanding: the time has come to end the expansion and contraction of the right to vote in America and to establish it once and for all in the nation's constitution. Voting rights experts are correct when they argue that doing so will provide the clarity that is needed to achieve the following:

- Guarantee the right of every citizen eighteen and older to vote.
- Empower Congress to set national minimum electoral standards for all states to follow.
- Provide protection against attempts to disenfranchise individual voters.
- Eliminate those rules and practices that give some voters more power than other voters.
- Ensure that every vote cast is counted correctly.

But this, to our view, is merely the point of departure. Most rights outlined in the U.S. Constitution are negative rights. They protect against the encroachment of the government on a citizen's right to speak, to assemble, to petition for the redress of grievances, to own a gun, to be secure from official intrusions. The assurance of a "positive liberty" to engage in the choosing of those governments, and by extension the process of defining its direction, ought to be recognized as the most precious of all freedoms.

To establish an affirmative right to vote, we can imagine an even simpler amendment than has been proposed; one that reads: "Every American citizen

18 years of age or older has a right to vote, to the information necessary to cast an informed vote, and to the assurance that their vote will count equally with others toward the formation of local, state, and national governments." From such an assurance could extend protections necessary to establish real democracy and a more perfect union: not just equal access to the polls but equal access to news and opinions about the candidates and parties and issues; not just the assurance of the fair counting of votes for which there is currently no guarantee but also to voting systems and electoral districts that give those votes meaning. The possibilities are, as the poet Langston Hughes might suggest, "explosive."

Judges who have suggested that there ought to be some kind of constitutional protection against gerrymandering would finally have the tool to prevent a party in power from drawing congressional or district lines that prevent meaningful competition and effectively disenfranchise citizens.[70] Citizens might finally find the standing to demand the inclusion of minority parties in debates and the FCC to require broadcasters to provide free airtime to candidates and parties and more thorough coverage of issues and campaigns.[71] Proponents of instant runoff voting, proportional representation, and other approaches that countries around the world have used to ensure diversity and a deeper political discourse would find an avenue for challenging inherently unfair "first-past-the-post" voting systems that saddle states across the country with one-party rule.[72]

Amending the Constitution to include a right to vote will not, in and of itself, establish a more perfect union. It will not even cure all the ailments of our democratic experiment. If the courts do not bar gerrymandering once and for all, then an amendment doing so will be right and necessary. And there is no question of the need to amend the Constitution to eliminate the Electoral College, as was almost done during Richard Nixon's first term and as must be done if America is to achieve democratic stability.[73] "The United States is the only country that elects a politically powerful president via an electoral college," explained Texas A&M political science professor George C. Edwards III, "and the only one in which a candidate can become president without having obtained the highest number of votes in the sole or final round of popular voting."[74] No reform moment that has as its end the achievement of a more democratic United States can neglect the need to do away with the Electoral College. That is an essential democracy amendment.

But it need not be the only one to accompany the guarantee of a right to vote. There is a vital case to be made for additional amendments that also flow logically and necessarily from the right to vote. These include amendments that would pave the way for the District of Columbia and other American territories to seek statehood if they so desire.

To make those voting rights meaningful, we believe, it is absolutely necessary to assure that the people's representatives can establish rules for how campaigns are financed and to establish once and for all—as Congressman Jim McGovern, a Democrat from Massachusetts, has proposed, with the support of Progressive Democrats of America—that "the words people, person, or citizen as used in this Constitution do not include corporations, limited liability companies or other corporate entities established by the laws of any State, the United States, or any foreign state, and such corporate entities are subject to such regulation as the people, through their elected State and Federal representatives, deem reasonable and are otherwise consistent with the powers of Congress and the States under this Constitution."[75]

McGovern understands, as we do, that such an amendment would not limit the First Amendment rights of Americans, just of corporations. But the congressman goes the extra step and explains within his amendment that "nothing contained herein shall be construed to limit the people's rights of freedom of speech, freedom of the press, free exercise of religion, freedom of association and all such other rights of the people, which rights are inalienable."[76]

This is a critical construct for reformers to recognize as they propose and advance constitutional amendments. Nothing about restoring the right of elected officials—or voters via referendums—to govern the financing of elections infringes on the free speech rights of citizens, as historically or currently understood by any but the most partisan political players. And nothing about the extension of a positive liberty, the right to vote, diminishes the American experiment as it was understood by Thomas Jefferson. Indeed, it provides, finally, for the realization of Jefferson's best and final hope for America.

In the summer of his eighty-third year, Jefferson was asked by Roger C. Weightman, the mayor of Washington, DC, to attend a celebration of the fiftieth anniversary of the Declaration of Independence on July 4, 1826. Jefferson declined but sent to Weightman what would be his last testament to the radical endeavor in which he had engaged. Jefferson did not spend much time reflecting on what had been. Rather, he looked forward, across the democratic vistas that would soon be charted by a young poet, Walt Whitman, who would declare his intention to "speak the password primeval . . . to give the sign of democracy."[77]

"May it be to the world what I believe it will be (to some parts sooner, to others later, but finally to all), the Signal of arousing men to burst the chains, under which monkish ignorance and superstition had persuaded them to bind themselves, and to assume the blessings and security of self government," wrote Jefferson in his response to the mayor of the nation's capital city. "All eyes are opened, or opening to the rights of man. The general spread of the light of science has already laid open to every view the palpable truth, that the mass of mankind has not been born, with saddles on their backs, nor a favored few booted and spurred, ready to ride them legitimately, by the grace of God."[78]

If it is true that human beings have not been born with saddles on their backs, if it is true that they can refuse to be ridden by a "booted and spurred" favored few, then surely in a civil society the vote is the tool by which they must assert their equal humanity. This is the essential understanding for which countless Americans marched and organized. For which far too many perished. Surely, it cannot be left to chance. Not any longer.

The favored few have reasserted themselves, via their courts and their fortunes and their political connections. They have forged a Dollarocracy that serves their interest. But that very Dollarocracy strangles the will of the people and the forward progress of a great nation. The time has come, finally, for citizens to burst the chains and to assume the blessings and security of self-government. The time has come, finally, in this great reform moment, to heed the signal of America's founding, to speak Walt Whitman's "password primeval," to give the sign of democracy.

NOTES

Preface

1. Walt Whitman, "Song of Myself," Poetry Foundation, http://www.poetryfoundation.org/poem/174745 (accessed February 15, 2013).

2. From the review of Al Gore, *The Future: Six Drivers of Global Change* (New York: Random House, 2013), by Leonard Gill that appeared in the *Memphis Flyer,* February 14, 2013.

3. Quoted in Robert Gehrke, "Huntsman Bemoans a Broken U.S. Political System," *Salt Lake Tribune,* May 31, 2012; and in Eric Dolan, "Huntsman Calls for Third Party: 'The System Is Broken,'" *Raw Story,* February 23, 2012.

4. Quoted in Bill Barrow, "Jimmy Carter: Citizens United Ruling, 'Financial Corruption' Are Threatening Democracy," Huffington Post, September 12, 2012.

5. Quoted in "Jimmy Carter: Money Ruining Elections," Associated Press, September 12, 2012.

6. Martin Luther King Jr., *Why We Can't Wait* (Boston: Beacon Press, 2011).

7. Barack Obama, "The 2013 State of the Union Address," www.whitehouse.gov (accessed February 12, 2013).

Introduction

1. Martin Luther King Jr., *Where Do We Go from Here?: Chaos or Community?* (Boston: Beacon Press, 2010).

2. Lawrence Lessig, "The Founders Versus the Funders," *The Progressive,* October 2012, 21.

3. Alex Seitz-Wald, "Feingold: Even Worse Than We Expected," http://www.salon.com/2012/09/22/even_worse_than_we_expected/, September 22, 2012. Accessed March 12, 2013.

4. Editorial, "Election Winners and Losers: Americans Voted in Large Numbers, but Voters Need to Be Better Served at the Polls. Meanwhile, Republicans Must Pause to Reflect," *Christian Science Monitor,* November 9, 2012.

5. Nicholas Confessore, "Results Won't Limit Campaign Money Any More Than Ruling Did,*"* *New York Times,* November 11, 2012.

6. Jillian Berman, "Most Americans Say Economic Structure Favors 'Very Small Portion of the Rich': WSJ/NBC Poll," Huffington Post, November 8, 2011.

7. Jeffrey A. Winters, "Democracy and Oligarchy," *The American Interest,* November/December 2011, 18.

8. Robert F. Kennedy Jr., "A Hostile Takeover of Our Country," EcoWatch, October 29, 2012.

9. See Jane Mayer, "The Voter-Fraud Myth," *New Yorker,* October 29, 2012.

10. Martin Luther King Jr., "Give Us the Ballot," address at the Prayer Pilgrimage for Freedom, Washington, DC, May 17, 1957.

11. Quoted in Ron Hayduk, *Democracy for All: Restoring Immigrant Voting Rights in the United States* (New York: Routledge, 2006), 3.

Chapter 1: This Is *Not* What Democracy Looks Like

1. A July 2012 Gallup Poll found the two top issues rated as "extremely important" by voters are creating good jobs and reducing corruption in the federal government. See Jeffrey M. Jones, "Americans Want Next President to Prioritize Jobs, Corruption," gallup.com, July 30, 2012.

2. Rasmussen Reports, "59% Say Election Rules Rigged to Help Congressional Incumbents" (2012), and Rasmussen Reports, "53% Say Elections Are Rigged to Help Incumbents in Congress" (2011), http://www.rasmussenreports.com.

3. Quoted in Selah Hennessy, "Annan Commission Criticizes US Election Financing," voanews.com, September 14, 2012.

4. Sources: Total vote 1948–2008: Voter Turnout, International Institute for Democracy and Electoral Assistance, http://idea.int/vt (accessed November 23, 2012). Total vote 2012: "Elections 2012," *New York Times* (updated November 25, 2012), http://elections.nytimes.com/2012/results/president. Voting-age population 1948–2008: U.S. Census Bureau, "National Estimates by Age, Sex, Race: 1900–1979 (PE-11)," http://www.census.gov/popest/data/national/asrh/pre-1980/PE-11.html, and "Historical Data: 2000s," http://www.census.gov/popest/data/historical/2000s/index.html. Voting-age population 2012: U.S. Census Bureau, "2008 National Population Projections: Table 1. Projected Population by Single Year of Age, Sex, Race, and Hispanic Origin for the United States: July 1, 2000 to July 1, 2050," http://www.census.gov /population/projections/data/national/2008/downloadablefiles.html.

5. Our figures may be somewhat different from others because we include all Americans who are legal residents of the United States. Whether prisoners, ex-prisoners, and legal aliens are entitled to vote in elections is always a political decision, so all of these people belong in the denominator. "Voting-Age Population Turnout" is defined as the percentage of the "Voting-Age Population" (VAP) that actually voted. In this calculation, the VAP is defined as everyone legally residing in the United States, age eighteen and older, which is in accord with the U.S. Census Bureau. This figure includes prisoners and those on probation or parole regardless of whether they are eligible to vote in a given state. It also includes noncitizens, who constituted 8.6 percent of the population in 2010 according to the United States Elections Project, http:// elections.gmu.edu/Turnout_2010G.html. However, according to the American Community Survey, the estimate of noncitizens in 2011 was only 4.7 percent.

Sources: Total vote 2004 and 2008: International Institute for Democracy and Electoral Assistance (International IDEA), Voter Turnout, http://www.idea.int. Total vote 2012: Wikipedia, http://en.wikipedia.org /wiki/United_States_elections,_2012. Total Population: U.S. Census Bureau, "Table 1 Intercensal Estimates of the Resident Population by Sex and Age for the United States." (2004 and 2008) and "2008 National Projections." (2012). We also consult and rely on the University of California at Santa Barbara's American Presidency Project data, found at: http://www.presidency.ucsb.edu/data/turnout.php.

6. See the data of the International IDEA, www.idea.int. The twelve nations are Japan, Germany, France, United Kingdom, Brazil, Italy, India, Canada, Russia, Spain, Australia, and Canada.

7. Bridget Hunter, "2011 U.S. State, Local Elections Important Despite Low Turnout," Bureau of International Information Programs, U.S. Department of State, November 9, 2011.

8. Wendy R. Weiser and Lawrence Norden, "Voting Law Changes in 2012," Brennan Center for Justice at New York University School of Law, October 3, 2011.

9. For an extended discussion of this issue, see Robert W. McChesney, *Digital Disconnect: How Capitalism Is Turning the Internet Against Democracy* (New York: New Press, 2013).

10. Pew Research Center for the People and the Press, "Nonvoters: Who They Are, What They Think," people-press.org, November 1, 2012.

11. We converted the 2008 figures to 2010 dollars and then applied them to 2010 income data. We rounded to the nearest whole number. Income percentile is a rough estimate made by converting mean household income estimates into 2010 dollars and then using a percentile calculator to determine which percentile each group would fall into.

Sources: U.S. Census Bureau, American Community Survey 1-Year Estimates for 2008 and 2010, "Mean Household Income of Quintiles." American FactFinder, http://factfinder2.census.gov (accessed November 27, 2012); Current Population Survey, "Voting and Registration Supplement," 2008 and 2010, DataFerret Microdata.

12. Walter Dean Burnham, "The Appearance and Disappearance of the American Voter," in Thomas Ferguson and Joel Rogers, eds., *The Political Economy* (Armonk, NY: M. E. Sharpe, 1984), 112–137.

13. Jacob S. Hacker and Paul Pierson, *Winner-Take-All Politics: How Washington Made the Rich Richer—and Turned Its Back on the Middle Class* (New York: Simon & Schuster, 2010), chap. 4

14. In 2012, two major studies were published along these lines. See Martin Gilens, *Affluence and Influence: Economic Inequality and Political Power in America* (Princeton, NJ: Princeton University Press, 2012); and Kay Lehman Schlozman, Sidney Verba, and Henry E. Brady, *The Unheavenly Chorus: Unequal Political Voice and the Broken Promise of American Democracy* (Princeton, NJ: Princeton University Press, 2012). See also Larry M. Bartels, *Unequal Democracy* (New York: Russell Sage Foundation, 2008); and Martin Gilens, "Inequality and Democratic Responsiveness," *Public Opinion Quarterly* 69, no. 5 (2005): 778–796. There is a superb discussion of inequality and governance in Hacker and Pierson, *Winner-Take-All Politics,* chap. 4.

15. The manner in which the two parties seized control of presidential debates is striking in this regard. See George Farah, *No Debate: How the Republican and Democratic Parties Secretly Control the Presidential Debates* (New York: Seven Stories Press, 2004).

16. See Gary Johnson, "Breaking the Two-Party Stranglehold That Is Killing American Democracy," *The Guardian,* November 3, 2012.

17. "2012 Congressional Elections Demonstrate Need for Fair Voting," Fair Vote: The Center for Voting and Democracy, November 2012.

18. Emily Bazelon, "It's Appalling That Gerrymandering Is Legal," slate.com, November 9, 2012. Republicans controlled redistricting in twenty-four states, compared to eight for the Democrats. Democratic votes being highly concentrated in urban areas made it much easier to do effective gerrymandering for Republicans as well. See "The No-Wave Election," *The Economist,* November 3, 2012, 29–30.

19. Rob Richie and Devin McCarthy, "FairVote's Unique Methodology Shows That 52% of Voters Wanted a Democratic House," FairVote: The Center for Voting and Democracy, November 13, 2012.

20. Mark Karlin, "Most American Voters Elected a Democratic House, but We Got a Tea Party Congress," Truth-out.org, November 26, 2012.

21. "How to Rig an Election," *The Economist,* April 25, 2002.

22. Adam Liptak, "The Vanishing Battleground," Sunday Review section, *New York Times,* November 4, 2012.

23. Richard K. Matthews, *The Radical Politics of Thomas Jefferson: A Revisionist View* (Lawrence: University Press of Kansas, 1984), 83.

24. Aristotle, *Politics,* trans. Benjamin Jowett (Stilwell, KS: Digireads, 2005), 60. Aristotle of course was no friend of democracy; he was a supporter of an aristocratic constitution. Moreover, even the supporters of the *demos* in ancient Greece had in mind only male citizens, thereby excluding women and slaves. See Ellen Meiksins Wood and Neal Wood, *Class Ideology and Ancient Political Theory* (New York: Oxford University Press, 1978).

25. For an interesting argument that campaign spending led to profligate corruption and the end of the Roman Republic, see Rob Goodman and Jimmy Soni, "How Political Campaign Spending Brought Down the Roman Republic," slate.com, November 26, 2012.

26. See Alexander Keyssar, *The Right to Vote: The Contested History of Democracy in the United States* (New York: Basic Books, 2000), 15, 11.

27. Jack N. Rakove, "James Madison and the Bill of Rights," in *This Constitution: A Bicentennial Chronicle* (Washington, DC: Project '87 of the American Political Science Association and American Historical Association, Fall 1985).

28. There has been much fine writing on the contested presidential election of 1800. We place a high value on Bernard A. Weisberger's *America Afire: Jefferson, Adams, and the First Contested Election* (New York: William Morrow Paperbacks, 2001).

29. Cited in Juan Gonzalez and Joseph Torres, *News for All the People: The Epic Story of Race and the American Media* (New York: Verso, 2011), 37.

30. Sean Wilentz, *The Rise of American Democracy: Jefferson to Lincoln* (New York: Norton, 2005); and Sean Wilentz, *Andrew Jackson* (New York: Times Books, 2005).

31. In exploring the history of campaign finance reform, we relied on many sources, including discussions with Professor Carin Clauss of the University of Wisconsin Law School, whose research on historic initiatives to clean up politics informed this chapter. She participated in the 1997 Heffernan Commission, which sought to develop a comprehensive plan for campaign finance reform in Wisconsin. The commission's work can be reviewed at http://www.fightingbob.com/files/heffernan_commission_report.pdf. We also relied on the terrific work of Robert G. Kaiser, whose "Citizen K Street: How Lobbying Became Washington's Biggest Business" series appeared in the *Washington Post* in April 2007. We also depended on Jill Lepore, "Money Talks: Who's Fighting for Campaign-Finance Reform?" *New Yorker,* July 10, 2012. Jeff Clement, whose work in this area has been groundbreaking and essential, wrote about some of these issues in his book *Corporations Are Not People: Why They Have More Rights Than You Do and What You Can Do About It* (San Francisco: Berrett-Koehler, 2012); as did Thom Hartmann, *Unequal Protection: How Corporations Became "People"—and How You Can Fight Back* (San Francisco: Berrett-Koehler, 2010).

32. Quoted in Robert C. Nesbit, *Wisconsin: A History* (Madison: University of Wisconsin Press, 2004), 364.

33. Both quoted in Timothy Noah, "Mitt Romney: Crybaby Capitalist," *New Republic,* July 16, 2012.

34. Quoted in David D. Kirkpatrick, "Does Corporate Money Lead to Political Corruption?," *New York Times,* January 23, 2010.

35. Quoted in Jack Beatty, *Age of Betrayal: The Triumph of Money in America, 1865–1900* (New York: Knopf, 2007), xv.

36. Theodore Roosevelt, "The Man with the Muck-Rake," April 14, 1906, http://voicesofdemocracy .umd.edu/theodore-roosevelt-the-man-with-the-muck-rake-speech-text/.

37. David P. Thelen, *Robert M. La Follette and the Insurgent Spirit* (Madison: University of Wisconsin Press, 1986), 82.

38. Theodore Roosevelt, "Political Assessments in the Coming Campaign," *The Atlantic,* July 1892, http://www.theatlantic.com/magazine/archive/1892/07/political-assessments-in-the-coming-campaign /306067/?single_page=true; Jack Beatty, "A Sisyphean History of Campaign Finance Reform: A Look at How We Ended Up Back Where We Began," *The Atlantic,* July 2007; Beatty, *Age of Betrayal.*

39. See Beatty, "A Sisyphean History"; and Nancy Unger, *Fighting Bob La Follette: The Righteous Reformer* (Madison: Wisconsin Historical Society Press, 2008).

40. For biographical details and many of the quotes featured in this section, we relied on Wheeler's autobiography, *Yankee from the West: The Candid, Turbulent Life Story of the Yankee-Born U.S. Senator from Montana* (Garden City, NY: Doubleday, 1962); as well as on Richard T. Ruettens, "Burton K. Wheeler, 1905–1925: An Independent Liberal Under Fire" (MA thesis, University of Oregon, Eugene; 1957). Additionally, we relied on the archives of the *New York Times,* which covered Wheeler and the Montana fight extensively.

41. Progressive Party, "Progressive Party Platform of 1924," November 4, 1924, http://www.presidency .ucsb.edu/ws/?pid=29618.

42. Peter Overby, "A Century of U.S. Campaign Finance Law," NPR, Web timeline, January 21, 2010, http://www.npr.org/templates/story/story.php?storyId=121293380; Kurt Hohenstein, *Coining Corruption: The Making of the American Campaign Finance System* (DeKalb: Northern Illinois University Press, 2007).

43. Lyndon Johnson, "Statement by the President upon Signing the Foreign Investors Tax Act and the Presidential Election Fund Act, November 13, 1966," http://www.presidency.ucsb.edu/ws/index.php ?pid=28030.

44. Tom Wicker, "Kennedy Orders Vote-Cost Study," *New York Times,* October 5, 1961.

45. "On Campaign Funds," *New York Times,* April 22, 1962.

46. Frank Church, "Campaign Money—How Much? From Whom?" *New York Times,* August 26, 1962.

47. Ibid.

48. Records of the Commission on Campaign Costs, which operated from October 4, 1961, to September 17, 1962, are contained in the Papers of John F. Kennedy, Presidential Papers, President's Office Files. Extensive coverage of the commission's work appeared in the *New York Times* in 1961 and 1962. Infor-

mation about Truman and Eisenhower can be found in Peter Braestrup, "2 Ex-Presidents Spurn Party Gifts; Tax Incentives to Increase Contributions Backed by Eisenhower and Truman," *New York Times,* May 27, 1962.

49. Kennedy appointed Alexander Heard of the University of North Carolina to chair the commission. See Alexander Heard, *The Costs of Democracy: Financing American Political Campaigns* (Garden City, NY: Anchor Books, 1962).

50. Braestrup, "2 Ex-Presidents."

51. Editorial, *New York Times,* May 24, 1962.

52. Wicker, "Kennedy Orders Vote-Cost Study."

53. Lyndon Johnson, "Special Message to the Congress on Election Reform: The Political Process in America," May 25, 1967, http://www.presidency.ucsb.edu/ws/?pid=28268.

54. "A Pointless Proposal," *Wall Street Journal,* June 9, 1967.

55. See Jefferson Cowie, *Stayin' Alive: The 1970s and the Last Days of the Working Class* (New York: New Press, 2010).

56. Public Citizen, http://www.citizen.org. Still true to its founding principles, Public Citizen is in the forefront of movements to reform media and politics with an eye toward reducing the influence of corporations and increasing the power of citizens.

57. George McGovern, *An American Journey* (New York: Random House, 1974).

58. Ron Dellums, with H. Lee Halterman, *Lying Down with the Lions: A Public Life from the Streets of Oakland to the Halls of Power* (Boston: Beacon Press, 2000); Suzanne Braun Levine and Mary Thom, *Bella Abzug: How One Tough Broad from the Bronx Fought Jim Crow and Joe McCarthy, Pissed Off Jimmy Carter, Battled for the Rights of Women and Workers and for the Planet, and Shook Up Politics Along the Way* (New York: Farrar, Straus and Giroux, 2007); "Biography of Justin Ravitz," Ravitz Mediation Services LLC, http://ravitzmediation.com/id1.html.

59. Federal Election Commission, *Federal Campaign Finance Laws,* http://www.fec.gov/law/feca /feca.shtml. On the FEC and FECA historical background, see http://www.fec.gov/pages/brochures/fecfeca .shtml#Historical_Background.

60. Bob Woodward and Carl Bernstein, *All the President's Men,* 2nd ed. (New York: Simon & Schuster, 1994); Bob Woodward and Carl Bernstein, *The Final Days* (New York: Simon & Schuster, 2004).

61. Ben A. Franklin, "Senate Votes Top on Political Gifts; $3,000 Ceiling on Donations to Candidate Put in Bill—Parties Could Get More Senate Votes Lid on Political Donations; Future Is Uncertain; Disenchantment Clear," *New York Times,* July 27, 1973.

62. Andy Kroll, "Follow the Dark Money," *Mother Jones,* July/August 2012, 19–20.

63. John Gardner, "John W. Gardner Launches Membership Campaign for Common Cause," Common Cause About Us archives, August 18, 1970, http://www.commoncause.org/site/pp.asp?c=dkLNK1MQI wG&b=4860209.

64. David Vogel, *Fluctuating Fortunes: The Political Power of Business in America* (New York: Basic Books, 1989), 59.

65. See, for example, Morton Mintz and Jerry S. Cohen, with an Introduction by Ralph Nader, *America, Inc.: Who Owns and Operates the United States* (New York: Dell, 1971).

66. Michael Crozier, Samuel P. Huntington, and Joji Watanuki, *The Crisis of Democracy: Report on the Governability of Democracies to the Trilateral Commission* (New York: New York University Press, 1975), 74, 75, 79, 83, 113.

67. Ibid., 114.

68. Quoted at http://www.commondreams.org/headline/2010/10/06–5.

69. Lost to history, for example, has been the very impressive burgeoning media reform movement of the 1970s. See Pamela Draves, ed., *Citizens Media Directory* (Washington, DC: National Citizens Committee for Broadcasting, 1977).

70. For an excellent treatment of the transformation of the Republican Party, see Geoffrey Kabaservice, *Rule and Ruin: The Downfall of Moderation in the Republican Party from Eisenhower to the Tea Party* (New York: Oxford University Press, 2012).

71. Norman Ornstein, "Mitch McConnell vs. Himself on Disclosure Issues," *Roll Call,* June 20, 2012.

72. Matthew A. Crenson and Benjamin Ginsberg, *Downsizing Democracy* (Baltimore, MD: Johns Hopkins University Press, 2002), 49.

73. Quoted in John Nichols, "The Secret of Bernie Sanders's Success," *The Nation,* December 4, 2012.

74. Quoted in "What Election 2012 Reveals About America and Its Shifting Racial Faultlines," bill moyers.com, November 9, 2012.

75. See Steven M. Telese, *The Rise of the Conservative Legal Movement* (Princeton, NJ: Princeton University Press, 2008).

76. Quoted in Sebastian Meyer, "Political Parties Are Basically Bank Accounts," InTheseTimes.com, November 1, 2012.

77. "Romney Agrees with Obama . . . on Everything," Huffington Post video, October 23, 2012, http://www.huffingtonpost.com/2012/10/22/romney-obama-debate_n_2004105.html; Ryan Grim and Joshua Hersh, "Presidential Debate: Obama, Romney Agree on Foreign Policy," Huffington Post, October 23, 2012.

78. Alex Seitz-Wald, "Everyone Hates Citizens United: A New Poll Shows the Vast Majority of Americans Think There's Too Much Money in Politics," *Salon,* October 25, 2012. The poll cited here was conducted by the firm Bannon Communications for the Corporate Reform Coalition.

Chapter 2: The $10 Billion Election

1. Jeff Zeleny, "Mogul's Latest Foray Courts Jews for the G.O.P.," *New York Times,* July 25, 2012.

2. Calvin Coolidge, speech to the American Society of Newspaper Editors, Washington, DC, January 17, 1924; Claude Fuess, *Calvin Coolidge: The Man from Vermont* (Boston: Little Brown, 1940), 358.

3. Coolidge speech.

4. Donald Trump, with Tony Schwartz, *The Art of the Deal* (New York: Ballantine Books, 2004).

5. The site's still up: www.TrumpHQ.com.

6. Dean Debnam, "The GOP's Front-Runner Is . . . Donald Trump?," Public Policy Polling, April 14, 2011.

7. Maggie Haberman, "Donald Trump Says He Won't Run in 2012," Politico, May 16, 2011.

8. Sean Hannity transcript, "Trump May Run as Independent if GOP Picks 'Loser,'" www.foxnews.com, June 14, 2011, http://www.foxnews.com/on-air/hannity/transcript/trump-may-run-independent-if-gop-picks-loser.

9. Neil King Jr., "Trump Threatens to Spend Millions on a Presidential Run," *Wall Street Journal,* November 22, 2011.

10. Michael Waldman, "Why Doesn't Mitt Romney Contribute to His Own Campaign?," Reuters, September 25, 2012.

11. www.opensecrets.org (accessed February 6, 2013). Many groups analyze and review campaign spending. We think the Center for Responsive Politics' work stands out. We also like that it named its phone app "Dollarocracy."

12. Ibid.

13. Center for Responsive Politics, "2012 Election Spending Will Reach $6 Billion, Center for Responsive Politics Predicts," www.opensecrets.org, October 31, 2012. See section "Rise of the Wealthy Donor."

14. Lawrence Lessig, "The Founders Versus the Funders," *The Progressive,* October 2012, 20–21; Chris Rickert, "Campaign Fundraising Holds Our Attention," *Wisconsin State Journal,* January 28, 2012.

15. Sundeep Iyer, "Election Spending 2012: 25 Toss-Up House Races," report by the Brennan Center for Justice at New York University Law School, 2012, www.brennancenter.org; Katrina vanden Heuvel, "Is a 'Citizens United' Democracy a Democracy at All?," thenation.com, October 26, 2012.

16. Lessig, "The Founders."

17. Andy Kroll, "Follow the Dark Money," *Mother Jones,* July/August 2012, 22.

18. Felicia Sonmez, "Perry Spent More Than $300 Per Vote in Iowa; Santorum, Only 73 Cents," *Washington Post,* January 4, 2012.

19. "Facing Romney's Funding, Staffing Edge, How Will Santorum Fare in N.H.?," PBS NewsHour, January 4, 2012.

20. Charles Riley, "Romney Campaign Spent $18.50 Per Vote," CNNMoney, April 25, 2012.

21. Dave Levinthal, "President Obama Outspent Mitt Romney in Last Days," Politico, December 6, 2012.

22. Elizabeth Wilner, "Romney and Republicans Outspent Obama, but Couldn't Out-Advertise Him: Targeting and Message-Control Carried the Day," *AdAge,* November 9, 2012.

23. Ibid., 1.

24. Nicholas Confessore and Michael Luo, "Obama Allies Feel Pressure to Raise Cash," *New York Times,* March 14, 2012.

25. Nicholas Confessore, "Obama Grows More Reliant on Big-Money Contributors," *New York Times,* September 13, 2012.

26. Kevin Roose, "Wall St.'s Dinner with Obama: Hold the Scorn," dealbook.nytimes.com, June 23, 2012.

27. Colleen McCain Nelson, "Political Perceptions: Fundraising Habit Hard to Kick," blogs.wsj.com, September 28, 2012.

28. Wilner, "Romney and Republicans Outspent Obama."

29. Conversation between Robert W. McChesney and Seymour Hersh, May 9, 2005.

30. Jennifer Liberto, "Wall Street Set to Break Spending Records This Election," money.cnn.com, September 5, 2012. For a treatment of the power of finance over both parties and the U.S. government, see Charles Ferguson, *Predator Nation: Corporate Criminals, Political Corruption, and the Hijacking of America* (New York: Crown Business, 2012). For a treatment of how the "rule of law" has effectively ended in the United States, with all that suggests about the caliber of American democracy, see Glenn Greenwald, *With Liberty and Justice for Some: How the Law Is Used to Destroy Equality and Protect the Powerful* (New York: Metropolitan Books, 2011).

31. Daniel Fisher, "Inside the Koch Empire," *Forbes,* December 24, 2012, 86.

32. Nick Confessore, "Total Cost of Election Could Be $6 Billion," *New York Times,* October 31, 2012.

33. Jonathan D. Salant, "Election Costs to Exceed $6 Billion in 2012, Research Group Says," *Bloomberg Businessweek,* October 31, 2012.

34. Christopher Matthews, "Explainer: Did That $6 Billion in Campaign Spending at Least Help the Economy?," *Time,* November 9, 2012.

35. Miles Mogulescu, "After $6 Billion Election Campaign, Movement to Get Money Out of Politics Starts a 'Prairie Fire,'" Huffington Post, November 9, 2012.

36. Center for Responsive Politics, "Historical Elections," http://www.opensecrets.org/bigpicture/ (accessed February 6, 2013).

37. "Data Points: Presidential Campaign Spending: Barack Obama's $150 Million September Fundraising Total Is Over a Fifth of the Total Amount of Money All the Presidential Candidates Spent in the 2004 Election," *U.S. News & World Report,* October 21, 2008.

38. Center for Responsive Politics, "2012 Election Spending."

39. Thomas Ferguson, Paul Jorgensen, and Jie Chen, "Revealed: Key Files on Big-Ticket Political Donations Vanish at Federal Election Commission," AlterNet, July 16, 2012.

40. Luke Rosiak, "Toothless, Overwhelmed FEC Is Ignored by Campaigns," *Washington Times,* September 17, 2012.

41. Taylor Lincoln, "Super Connected: Super PACs Devotion to Individual Candidates Undercuts Assumption in Citizens United That Outside Spending Would Be 'Independent,'" Public Citizen, October 24, 2012, www.citizen.org.

42. Jeremy W. Peters, "Conservative 'Super PACs' Synchronize Their Messages," *New York Times,* September 24, 2012.

43. Kenneth P. Vogel and Tarini Parti, "The IRS's 'Feeble' Grip on Big Political Cash," Politico, October 15, 2012.

44. Center for Responsive Politics, "2012 Election Spending."

45. Alison Fitzgerald and Jonathan D. Salant, "Secret Political Cash Moves Through Nonprofit Daisy Chain," businessweek.com, October 15, 2012.

46. Paul Abowd, "Tracking the Secret Money Behind an Anti-Environmental Political Group," open channel.nbcnews.com, October 22, 2012.

47. Brendan Fischer, "Why Don't We Know How Much 'Dark Money' Groups Have Spent on the Election?," Center for Media and Democracy's PRWatch, November 5, 2012, http://www.prwatch.org/news/2012/11/11838/why-dont-we-know-how-much-dark-money-groups-have-spent-election.

48. Ibid.

49. Paul Blumenthal, "Romney Victory Raises $140 Million, Exploits Campaign Finance Loophole," Huffington Post, July 16, 2012.

50. Lisa Graves, "After the $6 Billion Election, Calls for Subpoenas and Amendments," Center for Media and Democracy's PRWatch, November 15, 2012; italics added.

51. Brendan Fischer, "Outside Election Spending Up at Least 400% Since 2008," Center for Media and Democracy's PRWatch, November 2, 2012, www.prwatch.org.

52. Peter H. Stone, "Sheldon Adelson Spent Far More on Campaign Than Previously Known," Huffington Post, December 3, 2012.

53. Interview with Center for Media and Democracy staff, December 4, 2012.

54. Adam Crowther, *Outside Money Takes the Inside Track* (Washington, DC: Public Citizen, 2012).

55. Kim Barker, "In Montana, Dark Money Helped Democrats Hold a Key Senate Seat," talkingpointsmemo.com, December 29, 2012.

56. John Nichols, "ALEC Exposed," *The Nation,* July 12, 2011.

57. SourceWatch, "Betsy DeVos," www.sourcewatch.org, January 12, 2012.

58. Associated Press, "DeVos PAC Fined Record $5.2 Million by Ohio Elections Board," April 5, 2008.

59. Ibid.

60. John Nichols, "Scott Walker's Billionaire Boys Club: Big Money Backs Anti-Labor Agenda," *The Nation,* May 2, 2012, http://www.thenation.com/blog/167664/scott-walkers-billionaire-boys-club-big-money-backs-anti-labor-agenda.

61. Wisconsin Democracy Campaign, "Recall Race for Governor Cost $81 Million: Fifteen Recall Races in 2011 and 2012 Cost $137 Million," www.wisdc.org, July 25, 2012.

62. Ibid.

63. Brendan Fischer, "Wisconsin Newspapers Create False Equivalency on Recall Spending," Center for Media and Democracy's PRWatch, May 24, 2012.

64. Wisconsin Democracy Campaign, "Recall Race."

65. For Washington, see Andrew Garber, "Tab for Governor's Race: $46 million: Republican Gubernatorial Candidate Rob McKenna and Democrat Jay Inslee Have Raised About $25 Million Combined, and an Additional $21 Million Has Been Thrown in by Independent Expenditure Campaigns," *Seattle Times,* November 3, 2012; this report was from the weekend *before* the election. For Missouri, see Chris Jasper, "Campaign Spending Fuels Missouri Races," *MU Maneater,* November 2, 2012. For North Carolina, see John Frank, "Governor: McCrory Becomes First Republican to Win Governor's Race in 20 Years," *News and Observer,* November 7, 2012; Chris Kromm, "Big Money Plays Big Role in North Carolina Elections," Facing South (Institute for Southern Studies), November 14, 2012, http://www.southernstudies.org/2012/11/big-money-plays-big-role-in-north-carolina-elections.html. For New Hampshire, see Brian Wallstin, "Hassan's Win Powered by $11 Million in Outside Spending," New Hampshire Public Radio, November 16, 2012.

66. National Institute on Money in State Politics, "Total Dollars for All Gubernatorial Candidates," December 12, 2012, http://www.followthemoney.org/database/nationalview.phtml?l=0&f=G&y=2012&abbr=0.

67. Alexander Burns, "RSLC Raises $38 Million for the Cycle," Politico, October 31, 2012.

68. John Surico, "NYAG Eric Schneiderman's New Wall Street Fraud Target: Credit Suisse," *Village Voice,* November 21, 2012; and "Republican Attorneys General Association," Center for Media and Democracy's SourceWatch (accessed January 14, 2013).

69. "Republican Attorneys General Association"; R. Jeffrey Smith and Tania Branigan, "GOP Attorneys General Asked for Corporate Contributions," *Washington Post,* July 17, 2003.

70. "RSLC Statement on 2012 Elections," rslc.com, November 07, 2012.

71. Ibid.

72. Chris Dickerson, "Morrisey Files to Run for AG," West Virginia," *West Virginia Record,* January 28, 2012.

73. Associated Press, "Non-Candidate Ad Spending in W.Va. Races Tops $5M," *Huntington (WV) Herald-Dispatch,* October 22, 2012.

74. Ry Rivard, "Huge Out-Of-State Spending in West Virginia Attorney General's Race," *Charleston Daily Mail,* October 18, 2012.

75. West Virginia Secretary of State, "Electioneering Communications & Independent Expenditures," and "Electioneering Communications" listings, http://apps.sos.wv.gov/elections/ecie/ (accessed December 6, 2012).

76. American Future Fund, "The AG Project," http://americanfuturefund.com/agproject/ (accessed December 6, 2012).

77. National Institute on Money in State Politics, "Missouri 2012," http://www.followthemoney.org/database/state_overview.phtml?y=2012&s=MO (accessed December 6, 2012).

78. Riley, "Romney Campaign."

79. California Fair Political Practices Commission, "2012 Independent Spending on Legislative Races," and National Institute on Money in State Politics, "California 2012," http://www.followthemoney.org/database/state_overview.phtml?y=2012&s=CA (both accessed November 20, 2012).

80. National Institute, "California 2012"; Karl Kurtz, "What Role Will Independent PACs Play in State Legislative Races?," "The Thicket" at *State Legislatures,* May 22, 2012; Karen Shanton, "Big Money Making a Big Splash in Some State Legislative Races," "The Thicket" at *State Legislatures,* November 2, 2012.

81. See Diane Ravitch, *The Death and Life and the Great American School System* (New York: Basic Books, 2010).

82. Mayoral Elections Center, U.S. Conference of Mayors, http://www.usmayors.org/elections/display elections2012listing.asp.

83. Lauren Steussy, "Candidates to Break Pattern of Moderate Mayor in San Diego: Republican Carl DeMaio and Democrat Bob Filner Will Both Lead San Diego Down an Unfamiliar Path," NBCSanDiego, Tuesday, November 6, 2012, Source: http://www.nbcsandiego.com/news/local/Candidates-Break-Pattern-of-Moderate-Mayor-in-San-Diego-177175381.html#ixzz2ErdMQUiB.

84. Tracy Seipel and John Woolfolk, "Race for San Jose District 8 Council Seat Awash in Independent Expenditures," *San Jose Mercury News,* October 26, 2012.

85. Lawrence Mower, "Incumbents Attract Big Money in County Commission Races," *Las Vegas Review-Journal,* November 4, 2012.

86. Jon Kuhl, "History-Making Ballot Measures Pass Throughout Country," "The Thicket" at *State Legislatures,* November 7, 2012.

87. Heather Pilatic, "What Matters About California's GE Labeling Fight," Huffington Post, November 8, 2012.

88. "Ballot Measures 2012," iSolon.org; "Voters Edge: Ballot Measures 2012," MapLight.org, http://votersedge.org/.

89. Chad Livengood, "Campaign Spending in Michigan Hits $175M: Ballot Issues Draw Most Cash, but Court, House Races Add to Total," *Detroit News,* November 5, 2012.

90. Laura Myers, "Adelson Political Bankroll to Grow," *Las Vegas Review-Journal,* December 10, 2012.

91. Billy Corriher, "Big Business Taking Over State Supreme Courts," americanprogress.org, August 13, 2012.

92. Susan Saladoff's 2011 documentary *Hot Coffee* analyzes this trend and its implications, http://www.hotcoffeethemovie.com/.

93. Eduardo Porter, "Unleashing the Campaign Contributions of Corporations," *New York Times,* August 28, 2012.

94. Billy Corriher, "Money Undermines Judges' Impartiality," usatoday.com, November 12, 2012.

95. Brennan Center for Justice and Justice at Stake Campaign, "New Data Shows Judicial Election Ad Spending Breaks Record at $29.7 Million: One Outside Group Spent $429,000 in Louisiana Election," www.justiceatstake.org, December 17, 2012.

96. Ibid.

97. Quoted in Peter Hardin, "Toobin: Court Elections the 'Biggest Outrage' in Political Spending," gavel grab.org, August 14, 2012.

98. Corriher, "Money Undermines Judges' Impartiality."

99. Justice at Stake Campaign, "National Poll: Public Rejects Candidates' Attacks on Courts: Voters Want Judges Accountable to the Constitution, Not Congress," December 22, 2011, http://www.justiceat stake.org/newsroom/press_releases.cfm/national_poll_public_rejects_candidates_attacks on courts?show =news&newsID=12282.

100. Erika Eichelberger, "In States with GOP-Dominated Courts, Is Judicial Election Spending Pointless?," motherjones.com, September 20, 2012.

101. Dave Levinthal, "Sheldon Adelson Gave $10 Million to Pro-Romney SuperPAC," Politico, December 6, 2012.

102. Myers, "Adelson Political Bankroll."

103. National Nurses United, "Tele-Press Conference to Demand Deceitful New Ad Be Taken Off the Air," September 27, 2012. http://www.nationalnursesunited.org/news/entry/tele-press-conference-to -demand-that-new-ad-full-of-lies-be-taken-off-the-air.

104. Myers, "Adelson Political Bankroll."

105. Steven Greenhouse, "In Michigan, a Setback for Unions," New York Times, November 8, 2012.

106. Myers, "Adelson Political Bankroll."

107. John Nichols, "GOP, Koch Brothers Sneak Attack Guts Labor Rights in Michigan," The Nation, December 6, 2012.

108. Alicia Mundy, "Adelson to Keep Betting on the GOP," Wall Street Journal, December 4, 2012.

109. Matea Gold, "Outside Groups Changing the Political Game for Good," latimes.com, October 21, 2012.

110. Janet Stilson, "Issue Ads to Go into Overdrive," adweek.com, November 26, 2012.

111. Quoted in Michael Kranish, "Despite '12 losses, Super Pacs May Play Role in Midterm Elections," boston.com, November 15, 2012.

112. Nicholas Confessore, "'Super PACS' Let Strategists Off the Leash," New York Times, May 21, 2012.

113. Quoted in Ted Johnson, "Election's End Doesn't Stop Ads," variety.com, December 1, 2012.

114. Steven Bertoni, "Why Sheldon Adelson's Election Donations Were Millions Well Spent," Forbes, November 8, 2012.

115. Obviously, this is a thought exercise. The Koch brothers and Adelson do not have their assets in liquid form; if they actually sold off assets to generate billions of dollars in cash for political spending, their net worths would likely decline.

116. Porter, "Unleashing the Campaign Contributions."

117. Seth Hanlon, "Sheldon Adelson's Return on Investment: Billionaire Donor Could Turn $100 Million Invested in the 2012 Presidential Race into a $2 Billion Tax Cut If Romney Is Elected," Center for American Progress Action Fund, September 11, 2012.

118. Robert Reich, "Why Billionaires Will Keep Pouring Money into Politics," Robert Reich's Blog, December 12, 2012, http://readersupportednews.org/opinion2/277-75/14986-why-billionaires-will-keep -pouring-money-into-politics.

119. Kenneth P. Vogel and Tarini Parti, "Inside Koch World," Politico, June 15, 2012.

Chapter 3: The Architects of Dollarocracy

1. Ben A. Franklin, "Senate Votes Top on Political Gifts; $3,000 Ceiling on Donations to Candidate Put in Bill—Parties Could Get More, Senate Votes Lid on Political Donations, Future Is Uncertain, Disenchantment Clear," New York Times, July 27, 1973.

2. Dumas Malone, Jefferson and His Time: The Sage of Monticello (Boston: Little, Brown, 1981), 6:473 –481, 488–490, 495–499, 511.

3. James L. Buckley, et al. v. Francis R. Valeo, Secretary of the United States Senate, et al., 96 S.Ct. 612; 46 L. Ed. 2d 659; 1976 U.S. LEXIS 16; 76–1 U.S. Tax Cas. (CCH) P9189. See also Richard Hasen, "The Untold Drafting History of Buckley v. Valeo," Election Law Journal: Rules, Politics, and Policy 2, no. 2 (2003): 241–253.

4. *Buckley v. Valeo.*

5. Ibid.

6. For a superb discussion of Rehnquist and his politics, see John A. Jenkins, *The Partisan: The Life of William Rehnquist* (New York: PublicAffairs, 2013).

7. Chandler Davidson, Tanya Dunlap, Gale Kenny, and Benjamin Wise, "Republican Ballot Security Programs: Vote Protection or Minority Vote Suppression—or Both? A Report to the Center for Voting Rights and Protection" (New York: Center for Voting Rights and Protection, September 2004). See also "As Supreme Court Decides Presidency, Chief Justice Rehnquist Is Accused of Past Harassment of Black Voters at the Polls," Democracy Now, December 12, 2000.

8. Rick Perlstein, *Nixonland: The Rise of a President and the Fracturing of America* (New York: Scribner, 2008), 605.

9. In the "Watergate" election of 1974, Democrats gained 4 U.S. Senate seats and 49 U.S. House seats, sweeping in a generation of young reformers who promised a new era of ethics and campaign finance reforms. See Andrew E. Busch, "1974 Midterms Bolster Liberalism in Congress," Ashbrook Center report (Ashland, OH: Ashland University, August 2006).

10. *Buckley v. Valeo,* Rehnquist concurring in part, dissenting in part.

11. Ibid., Burger dissenting.

12. *First National Bank of Boston, et al. v. Francis X. Bellotti, Attorney General of Massachusetts,* 435 U.S. 765.

13. Bob Woodward and Scott Armstrong, *The Brethren: Inside the Supreme Court* (New York: Simon & Schuster, 1979). See also Linda Greenhouse, "Lewis Powell, Crucial Centrist Justice, Dies at 90," *New York Times,* August 26, 1998.

14. Greenhouse, "Lewis Powell."

15. Jacob S. Hacker and Paul Pierson, *Winner-Take-All Politics: How Washington Made the Rich Richer—and Turned Its Back on the Middle Class* (New York: Simon & Schuster, 2010); Bill Moyers, "The Powell Memo: A Call-to-Arms for Corporations," www.billmoyers.com, September 14, 2012. See also Jeff Clement, *Corporations Are Not People: Why They Have More Rights Than You Do and What You Can Do About It* (San Francisco: Berrett-Koehler, 2012).

16. Clement, *Corporations Are Not People.*

17. Hacker and Pierson, *Winner-Take-All Politics.*

18. Quoted in Joan Biskupic and Fred Barbash, "Retired Justice Lewis Powell Dies at 90," *Washington Post,* August 26, 1998.

19. Richard Lowitt, *Fred Harris: His Journey from Liberalism to Populism* (Lanham, MD: Rowman & Littlefield, 2002), 218.

20. Charlie Cray, "The Lewis Powell Memo—Corporate Blueprint to Dominate Democracy," Greenpeace USA, August 23, 2011.

21. Lewis F. Powell Jr., "Confidential Memorandum: Attack on American Free Enterprise System," http://www.greenpeace.org/.

22. Ibid.

23. Ibid.

24. Ibid. See also Henry A. Giroux, "The Powell Memo and the Teaching Machines of Right-Wing Extremists," TruthOut, October 1, 2009; and the analysis by the San Francisco–based Commonweal Institute, http://commonwealinstitute.org (accessed October 15, 2012).

25. Powell, "Confidential Memorandum."

26. Ibid.

27. M. Stanton Evans, *The Liberal Establishment: Who Runs America . . . and How* (New York: Devin-Adair, 1965). The Goldwater campaign of 1964 incorporated a broad conservative critique of media, business, and government as the lynchpins of a liberal establishment. But the Goldwater camp's complaint tended to be with "Liberal Republicans" of the Nelson Rockefeller and Jacob Javits camp. Powell would extend the complaint dramatically, creating the image of a media and governing establishment, influenced by activists such as Nader and by an expanding electorate, to advance and celebrate supposedly anticorporate policies.

28. A conservative who made a similar case to Powell in the 1970s was President Gerald Ford's secretary of the Treasury, William E. Simon. See William E. Simon, *A Time for Truth* (New York: Reader's Digest Press, 1978).

29. Moyers, "The Powell Memo."

30. Michael Pertschuk, *Revolt Against Regulation* (Berkeley and Los Angeles: University of California Press, 1982), 16.

31. "Business Responds to Consumerism," *Bloomberg Businessweek*, September 6, 1969, 96.

32. Molly Niesen, "Crisis of Consumerism: Advertising, Activism, and the Battle Over the U.S. Federal Trade Commission, 1969–1980" (PhD diss., University of Illinois at Urbana-Champaign, 2012), 70.

33. John Nichols, "The Wisconsin Model," *The Progressive,* July 2011.

34. Clement, *Corporations Are Not People.* See also Tom Hamburger and Melanie Mason, "Chamber of Commerce Getting Early Start with Attack Ads," *Los Angeles Times,* November 16, 2011.

35. Lisa Graves, "A CMD Special Report on ALEC's Funding and Spending," Center for Media and Democracy's PRWatch, July 13, 2011, http://www.prwatch.org/news/2011/07/10887/cmd-special-report-alecs-funding-and-spending.

36. See Steven M. Teles, *The Rise of the Conservative Legal Movement* (Princeton, NJ: Princeton University Press, 2008).

37. Media Research Center, "About the Media Research Center: Bringing Political Balance to the Media," http://archive.mrc.org/about/aboutwelcome.asp. People for the American Way's "Right-Wing Watch" project was an invaluable resource. It can be accessed at http://www.rightwingwatch.org.

38. Hacker and Pierson, *Winner-Take-All Politics,* chap. 5.

39. David Vogel, *Fluctuating Fortunes: The Political Power of Business in America* (Frederick, MD: Beard Books, 1989), 197.

40. Hacker and Pierson, *Winner-Take-All Politics.*

41. Lawrence Lessig, *Republic, Lost: How Money Corrupts Congress—and a Plan to Stop It* (New York: Twelve, 2011), 99, 123.

42. Quoted in David Sirota, "Post-Election, Politicos Cash In," salon.com, November 9, 2012.

43. Quoted in Kevin Bogardus, "K Street Headhunters Enamored with Upcoming Class of Retiring Lawmakers," *The Hill,* January 19, 2012.

44. Karl Taro Greenfeld, "Mr. Dodd Goes to Hollywood," *Bloomberg Businessweek,* November 15, 2012, 80.

45. Quoted in Moyers, "The Powell Memo."

46. Benjy Sarlin, "Jim DeMint Leaving Senate for Heritage Foundation," Talking Points Memo, December 6, 2012.

47. Jack Anderson, "Powell's Advice to Business," syndicated column, September 28, 1972.

48. Powell, "Confidential Memorandum."

49. John Rawls, *Political Liberalism* (New York: Columbia University Press: 1993), 361. For a review of John Rawls's assessment of the decision, see James Fleming, "Securing Deliberative Democracy," *Fordham Law Review* 72 (2004): 1435. See also "Statement in Support of Overturning Buckley v. Valeo," joint statement organized by the Brennan Center for Justice at New York University School of Law, the National Voting Rights Institute, and the U.S. Public Interest Research Group, http://www.brennancenter.org/sites/default/files/legacy/d/buckley.pdf. Rawls was a signer of the statement.

50. *First National Bank of Boston v. Bellotti.*

51. Ibid.

52. Ibid.

53. Hart Research Associates, "Protecting Democracy from Unlimited Corporate Spending," results from a national survey among 1,000 voters on the *Citizens United* decision, conducted June 6–7, 2010.

54. *First National Bank of Boston v. Bellotti,* Rehnquist dissenting, http://caselaw.lp.findlaw.com/cgi-bin/getcase.pl?court=us&vol=435&invol=765.

55. Ibid.

56. Polls continue to show that a wide majority of Americans, including substantial numbers of conservatives, favor restrictions on money in politics. See Kevin Robillard, "Poll: No Unlimited Political Spend-

ing," Politico, July 18, 2012; and Ian Millhiser, "More Americans Believe in Witchcraft Than Agree with Citizens United," Think Progress, April 24, 2012.

57. Sergio Munoz, "John Roberts Is Still a Pro-Corporate Conservative, and the Media Shouldn't Be Fooled," Media Matters, October 1, 2012, http://mediamatters.org/blog/2012/10/01/john-roberts-is-still -a-pro-corporate-conservat/190237.

58. Robert Barnes, "Roberts Court Rulings on Campaign Finance Reveal Shifting Makeup, Forceful Role," *Washington Post*, November 1, 2010.

59. Ibid.

60. *Federal Election Commission v. Wisconsin Right to Life, Inc.*, 551 U.S. 449; Nathaniel Persily, "The Floodgates Were Already Open: What Will the Supreme Court's Campaign Finance Ruling Really Change?," *Slate*, January 25, 2010.

61. Philip Rucker, "Citizens United Used 'Hillary: The Movie' to Take on McCain-Feingold," *Washington Post*, January 22, 2010.

62. Quoted in Adam Liptak, "Justices Turn Minor Movie Case into a Blockbuster," *New York Times*, January 22, 2010.

63. Ibid.

64. *Citizens United, Appellant v. Federal Election Commission*, 558 U.S. 310, 130 S.Ct. 876.

65. Ibid.

66. Stephen R. Weissman, "Campaign Finance Ruling's Likely Impact Overblown: The Supreme Court's Decision Striking Down Limits on Corporate Spending in Election Campaigns Is Unlikely to Change the Political Situation on the Ground," *Los Angeles Times*, January 28, 2010.

67. Jeff Zeleny, "GOP Captures House but Not Senate," *New York Times*, November 2, 2010. See also Evan Mackinder, "A Republican Wave," *OpenSecretsBlog*, November 3, 2010.

68. Quoted in John Nichols and Robert W. McChesney, "The Money and Media Election Complex," *The Nation*, November 10, 2010.

69. John Nichols, "Unions Can't Compete with Corporate Campaign Cash," *The Nation*, January 24, 2010. See also Open Secrets, "Super PACS," http://www.opensecrets.org/pacs/superpacs.php (accessed September 20, 2012).

70. Quoted in Nichols, "Unions Can't Compete."

71. The *New York Times* in a June 22, 2012, editorial, "The Anti-Union Roberts Court," wrote, "The Supreme Court's ruling this week in *Knox v. Service Employees International Union* is one of the most brazen of the Roberts court. It shows how defiantly the five justices act in advancing the aggressive conservatism of their majority on the court. The court's moderate liberals were rightly dismayed by the majority's willingness to breach court rules in pursuit of its agenda. In this labor union case, there is no getting around that the legal approach is indistinguishable from politics. The court's five conservatives ruled that in 2005, Local 1000 of the Service Employees International Union should have sent a notice to all nonmembers it represented when it imposed a temporary 25 percent increase in union dues for public-sector employees in California to fight two anti-union ballot measures."

72. *Knox v. Service Employees Int'l Union, Local 1000*, 132 S.Ct. 2277, 183 L. Ed. 2d 281, 193 LRRM 2641 (2012) [2012 BL 153979].

73. Ibid.

74. "The Court and Citizens United II," *New York Times*, February 22, 2012.

75. Rachel Leven, "Supreme Court Summarily Reverses Montana's Citizens United Case," *The Hill*, June 25, 2012.

76. Ibid.

77. Quoted in Rachel Weiner, "Supreme Court's Montana Decision Strengthens Citizens United," *Washington Post*, June 25, 2012.

78. Jon Tester, "Tester: Citizens United Ruling a Threat to Democracy," statement to Senate Judiciary Committee, September 12, 2012.

79. Bernie Sanders, "Statement on Supreme Court Ruling in Montana Campaign Funding Case," June 25, 2012.

80. Ibid.

Chapter 4: The Bull Market

1. "Meet Bridget," Bridget Mary McCormack for Michigan Supreme Court Web site, www.mccormack forjustice.com.

2. Ibid.

3. Andrew Rosenthal, "Everyone Deserves Legal Representation," *New York Times,* November 1, 2012.

4. Ibid.

5. Dawson Bell, "Michigan Supreme Court Candidate Defends Against Terrorism Claim," *Detroit Free Press,* October 31, 2012.

6. Ibid.

7. Ryan J. Stanton, "Q&A with Ann Arbor's Bridget McCormack on Being Elected to the Michigan Supreme Court," AnnArbor.com, November 11, 2012.

8. Quoted in Meg James, "Cable Television Gaining in Advertising Revenues, but Not Political Dollars," *Los Angeles Times,* June 17, 2011, http://latimesblogs.latimes.com/entertainmentnewsbuzz/2011/06 /cable-television-gaining-in-advertising-revenue-but-not-political-dollars.html.

9. "A long habit of not thinking a thing wrong, gives it a superficial appearance of being right," Thomas Paine wrote at the beginning of *Common Sense,* the book that helped ignite the American Revolution, "and raises at first a formidable outcry in defense of custom." In many respects, this is the case with how Americans have come to regard TV political advertising as the natural form of political communication, and election campaigns appear unimaginable without them.

10. See Greg Mitchell, *The Campaign of the Century: Upton Sinclair's E.P.I.C. Race for Governor of California and the Birth of Media Politics* (New York: Random House, 1992). See also Jill Lepore, "On the Campaign Trail," *New Yorker,* September 19, 2012, http://www.newyorker.com/online/blogs/news desk/2012/09/a-history-of-political-consultants.html#ixzz2BGDZNINh.

11. This point is made in an excellent discussion of this rise of political advertising in Lizabeth Cohen, *A Consumer's Republic: The Politics of Mass Consumption in Postwar America* (New York: Random House, 2003), 332.

12. See David Halberstam, *The Fifties* (New York: Random House, 1993), 227.

13. Vance Packard, *The Hidden Persuaders* (New York: Pocket Books, 1957), 156.

14. Ibid., 161.

15. Quoted in Halberstam, *The Fifties,* 229–230.

16. Cohen, *A Consumer's Republic,* 333.

17. Quoted in Halberstam, *The Fifties,* 231, 232.

18. Packard, *The Hidden Persuaders,* 172.

19. Quoted in "Admen Shouldn't Try to Take Over Politics: Truman," *Advertising Age,* September 22, 1948, 2.

20. Quoted in Packard, *The Hidden Persuaders,* 160.

21. Cohen, *A Consumer's Republic,* 336.

22. Theodore H. White, *The Making of the President 1960* (New York: Atheneum House, 1961), 312. See also W. J. Rorabaugh, *The Real Making of the President: Kennedy, Nixon, and the 1960 Election* (Lawrence: University Press of Kansas, 2009). Television plays a key role in this account, but TV campaign advertising itself plays a small role in comparison to what would soon follow.

23. Robert Mann, *Daisy Petals and Mushroom Clouds: LBJ, Barry Goldwater, and the Ad That Changed American Politics* (Baton Rouge: Louisiana State University Press, 2011), 108.

24. Joe Klein, *Politics Lost* (New York: Broadway Books, 2006), 17.

25. All quoted in Mann, *Daisy Petals,* 111–113.

26. Joe McGinniss, *The Selling of the President* (New York: Penguin, 1988), xv, xxi, xxii. This book was originally published by Simon & Schuster in 1969.

27. There are numerous totals given the TV political spending in 1968. The standard figure immediately after the election was $60 million. See Malachi C. Topping and Lawrence W. Lichty, "Political Programs on National Television Networks: 1968," *Journal of Broadcasting* 15, no. 2 (Spring 1971): 161. After review, we have elected to use the figure provided in the 1997 congressional research report that drew from research by the Federal Communications Commission on the subject: Joseph E. Cantor, Denis Steven

Rutkus, and Kevin B. Greely, "Free and Reduced-Rate Time for Political Candidates," Report prepared for the Congressional Research Service, July 7, 1997, 4–5.

28. "Study Shows Pols' Ads Less Credible Than Product Ads," *Advertising Age,* February 26, 1973, 10.

29. Bill Richards, "Sen. Mathias Re-Election Drive Opens," *Washington Post,* February 3, 1974.

30. White, *The Making of the President,* 312.

31. Quoted in Halberstam, *The Fifties,* 231.

32. Quoted in Michael M. Franz, Paul B. Freedman, Kenneth M. Goldstein, and Travis N. Ridout, *Campaign Advertising and American Democracy* (Philadelphia: Temple University Press, 2008), 3.

33. "David Ogilvy's Timeless Rules for Advertising and Marketing," bighow.com, http://bighow.com/news/david-ogilvys-timeless-rules-for-advertising-and-marketing.

34. Robert Spero, *The Duping of the American Voter* (New York: Lippincott & Crowell, 1980), 4.

35. Claudia Caplan, "We Don't Do Political Advertising—and for Good Reason: The Risks Outweigh the Rewards," adage.com, October 29, 2012.

36. Quoted in Susan Krashinsky, "Veteran Ad Man Reflects on Election Ads' Negativity," theglobeandmail.com, November 11, 2012.

37. Although the trade publication *Advertising Age* notes that with the emergence of consultants to run the modern political campaign, most advertising agencies are not controlling campaigns like they do commercial accounts, there is still plenty of money to go around. See Elizabeth Wilner, "Toothpaste vs. Candidates: Why the Mad Men Approach Doesn't Work in Politics," *Advertising Age,* August 9, 2012.

38. Bob Jeffrey, "A Sense of What Can Be," jwt.com, August 28, 2012.

39. Quoted in Andrew McGill, "Business Booming for Pittsburgh Ad Agency BrabenderCox," *Pittsburgh Post-Gazette,* October 14, 2012.

40. Cited in Glenn W. Richardson Jr., *Pulp Politics: How Political Advertising Tells the Stories of American Politics* (Lanham, MD: Rowman & Littlefield, 2003), 125.

41. Thorstein Veblen, arguably the most original and greatest American economist of all time, was the first to grasp this fundamental change in capitalism, though many of course have followed in his wake. See Thorstein Veblen, *Absentee Ownership and Business Enterprise in Recent Times* (New York: Augustus M. Kelley, 1964). The book, originally published in 1923, was Veblen's final work.

42. See John Bellamy Foster, Robert W. McChesney, and R. Jamil Jonna, "Monopoly and Competition in Twenty-First Century Capitalism," *Monthly Review* 62, no. 11 (April 2011): 1–39.

43. C. B. Macpherson, *The Life and Times of Liberal Democracy* (New York: Oxford University Press, 1977), 89–90.

44. V. O. Key Jr., *Politics, Parties, and Pressure Groups* (New York: Thomas Y. Crowell, 1955), chap. 19.

45. One of us was told this story by a former advertising professional at Reeves's Ted Bates advertising agency. For somewhat different versions of the story, see Reed Hundt, Chairman, Federal Communications Commission, "The Children's Emmy: An Award Worth Winning," November 19, 1996; and Richard S. Tedlow, *The Watson Dynasty* (New York: HarperBusiness, 2003), 118.

46. Halberstam, *The Fifties,* 227.

47. William Greider, *Who Will Tell the People: The Betrayal of American Democracy* (New York: Simon & Schuster, 1992), 271. Greider, to his credit, is one of the few writers on this subject who made the strong link between political and commercial advertising.

48. Darrell M. West, *Air Wars: Television Advertising in Election Campaigns, 1952–2008* (Washington, DC: CQ Press, 2010), 89. For a smart examination of the importance of visuals for TV news coverage of election campaigns, see Maria Elizabeth Grabe and Erik Page Bucy, *Image Bite Politics: News and the Visual Framing of Elections* (New York: Oxford University Press, 2010).

49. Jerry Mander, "Privatization of Consciousness," *Monthly Review* 64, no. 5 (October 2012): 31.

50. Ibid., 29.

51. For a fuller elaboration on these themes, see Hannah Holleman, Inger L. Stole, John Bellamy Foster, and Robert W. McChesney, "The Sales Effort and Monopoly Capital," *Monthly Review* 60, no. 11 (April 2009).

52. Drew Weston, *The Political Brain: The Role of Emotion in Deciding the Fate of the Nation* (New York: PublicAffairs, 2007).

53. Quoted in Packard, *The Hidden Persuaders,* 166.

54. See Shanto Iyengar and Jennifer A. McGrady, *Media Politics: A Citizen's Guide* (New York: Norton, 2007), chap. 6.

55. Stacia Mullaney, "Do Political Ads Work?" wlns.com, October 2012.

56. Glenn Greenwald, "Election 2012 and the Media: A Vast Rightwing Conspiracy of Stupid," *The Guardian,* August 30, 2012.

57. Dan Eggen, "Both Sides Hate Financial Sector—in Ads," washingtonpost.com, October 8, 2012.

58. Peter Baker, "Romney's Foreign Policy Intentions Can Be Tough to Gauge," *New York Times,* August 29, 2012.

59. Tim Madigan, "Texas Native Is Romney Campaign's Top Ad Man," *Fort Worth Star-Telegram,* October 11, 2012.

60. Quoted in Andrew McMains, "Romney's Guy: No Apologies," adweek.com, November 20, 2012.

61. Quoted in Rebecca Greenfield, "Romney Hired Gun Claims He 'Reinvented Political Advertising' with His Losing Ads," the atlanticwire.com, December 3, 2012.

62. Ted Brader, *Campaigning for Hearts and Minds: How Emotional Appeals in Political Ads Work* (Chicago: University of Chicago Press, 2006), 183.

63. Quoted in Daniel Slocum Hinerfeld, "How Political Ads Subtract; It's Not the Negative Ads That Are Perverting Democracy. It's the Deceptive Ones," *Washington Monthly,* May 1990.

64. Greider, *Who Will Tell the People,* 274–276.

65. W. Lance Bennett, *The Governing Crisis: Media, Money, and Marketing in American Elections,* 2nd ed. (New York: St. Martin's Press, 1996), 151.

66. Jeremy W. Peters, "The New Stars in Republican Commercials Attacking Obama: Babies," *New York Times,* September 29, 2012.

67. Ezra Klein, "Rick Perry Loves Science. Political Science," *Washington Post* blog, September 16, 2011, http://www.washingtonpost.com/blogs/ezra-klein/post/rick-perry-loves-science-political-science /2011/08/25/gIQAD27AXK_blog.html. See also Donald P. Green and Alan S. Gerber, *Get Out the Voter: How to Increase Voter Turnout,* 2nd ed. (Washington, DC: Brookings Institution Press, 2008), 161.

68. John Sides, "The Most Important Ads of the Campaign Are Only Airing Now," themonkeycage.org, November 1, 2012.

69. Sean Richey, "Random and Systematic Error in Voting in Presidential Elections," *Political Research Quarterly* 20, no. 10 (2012): 1–13. Quotation from Lee Drutman, "Did Campaign Spending Buy Bush the 2000 and 2004 Elections?," sunlightfoundation.com, October 1, 2012.

70. Quoted in Eli Pariser, The *Filter Bubble: What the Internet Is Hiding from You* (New York: Penguin Press, 2011), 160.

71. Leonard Steinhorn, "The Selling of the President in a Converged Media Age," in James A. Thurber and Candace J. Nelson, eds., *Campaigns and Elections American Style* (Boulder, CO: Westview Press, 2010), 154.

72. Matthew Creamer, "Obama Wins! . . . Ad Age's Marketer of the Year," *Advertising Age,* October 17, 2008, http://adage.com/article/moy-2008/obama-wins-ad-age-s-marketer-year/131810/.

73. Travis N. Ridout and Michael M. Franz, *The Persuasive Power of Campaign Advertising* (Philadelphia: Temple University Press, 2011), viii, 146, 149, 145.

74. Kate Kenski, Bruce Hardy, and Kathleen Hall Jamieson's, *The Obama Victory: How Media, Money, and Message Shaped the 2008 Election* (New York: Oxford University Press, 2010), 267, 268, 284.

75. Julian Brookes, "Why the 2012 Election Will Be the Most Expensive Ever," RollingStone.com, June 7, 2011.

76. West, *Air Wars,* 174.

77. Quoted in Mike Madden, "A Small Group of Savvy Political Operatives Will Control How Billions Will Be Spent in Next Year's Election," *AdWeek,* June 27, 2011.

78. The material in this paragraph all comes from Daniel Adler, "Political Ads: Overpriced, Inefficient, Essential," RollingStone.com, August 14, 2012.

79. Carter Eskew, "Political Advertising Is Dangerous for Democracy," washingtonpost.com, August 16, 2012.

80. Larry Bivins, "Campaigns Bombard Ad-Weary Wisconsinites," greenbaypressgazette.com, October 29, 2012.

81. John G. Geer, *In Defense of Negativity: Attack Ads in Presidential Campaigns* (Chicago: University of Chicago Press, 2006), 36.

82. Research conducted by the Wisconsin Advertising Project, Political Science Department at the University of Wisconsin-Madison. Special thanks to Katherine Cramer Walsh and Sarah Niebler.

83. Erika Franklin Fowler and Travis N. Ridout, "Advertising Trends in 2010," *The Forum* 8, no. 4, art. 4 (2011): 11–13.

84. Quoted in Alina Selyukh, "Study of U.S. Campaign Ads Finds Growing Role of Outside Groups," reuters.com. September 13, 2012.

85. Elizabeth Wilner, "Why Pushing a Politician Isn't Like Selling Soap," *Advertising Age,* October 1, 2012.

86. Donovan Slack, "RIP Positive Ads in 2012," politico.com, November 4, 2012.

87. Kevin Landrigan, "New Hampshire Facing Onslaught of Campaign Ads, as Obama, Romney Spend $1M a Week," *Nashua Telegraph,* August 10, 2012.

88. Ari Shapiro, "Colorado Springs Soaks in Triple the Political Ads," www.capradio.org, September 25, 2012.

89. See David Mark, *Going Dirty: The Art of Negative Campaigning* (Lanham, MD: Rowman & Littlefield, 2006).

90. Marc Caputo, "UM Professor Studies the Goldilocks Spot for Negative Ads," miamihearld.com, October 9, 2012.

91. Westen, *The Political Brain*, 435–436.

92. Jessica Wehrman, "Despite Nastiness of Political Ads, Many Gave Substance," *Daytona Daily News,* October 6, 2012.

93. Quoted in Pauline Arrillaga, "The Mean Season: Negativity in Election 2012," heraldnet.com, October 22, 2012.

94. Drew Westen, "Why Attack Ads? Because They Work," latimes.com, February 19, 2012.

95. Quoted in Belinda Young, "Iowans Can't Avoid Political Ads on TV," kcrg.com, October 21, 2012.

96. Rob Christensen, "Attack Ads Exhausting, Effective," newsobserver.com, October 28, 2012.

97. Rick Perlstein, "Exclusive: Lee Atwater's Infamous 1981 Interview on the Southern Strategy," the nation.com, November 13, 2012.

98. Quoted in West, *Air Wars,* 3.

99. Quoted in Bernard Weinraub, "Campaign Trail: A Beloved Mug Shot for the Bush Forces," *New York Times,* October 3, 1988.

100. One of us had a relative who was a political junkie and an avid right-wing Republican. He defended the Horton ads as not being racist by stating, "Hell, no one even knew Horton was a god-damned [insert n-word here] until the Democrats made such a stink about it."

101. Quoted in Ridout and Franz, *The Persuasive Power of Campaign Advertising,* 2.

102. Kate Phillips, "The Last-Minute, Anti-Obama Ad Blitz," *New York Times,* November 3, 2008.

103. Paul Krugman, "The Post-Truth Campaign," *New York Times,* December 22, 2011.

104. Craig Trudell, "Fiat Says Jeep Output May Return to China as Demand Rises," *Bloomberg News,* October 22, 2012; "ABC Toledo: Auto Workers Slam Romney's False Jeep Claim," http://www.you tube.com/watch?v=ZnY2qbE4d2w.

105. Gualberto Ranieri, "Jeep in China," www.chryslerllc.com, October 25, 2012, http://blog .chryslerllc.com/blog.do?id=1932&p=entry.

106. Quoted in John Nichols, "Yes, Romney's a Liar, but This Is Getting Ridiculous," *The Nation,* October 30, 2012.

107. Larry J. Sabato and Glenn R. Simpson, *Dirty Little Secrets: The Persistence of Corruption in American Politics* (New York: Times Books, 1996), 253.

108. Michael W. Traugott and Mee-Eun Kang, "Push Polls as Negative Persuasive Strategies," in Paul J. Lavrakas and Michael W. Traugott, eds., *Election Polls, the News Media, and Democracy* (New York: Chatham House, 2000), 283.

109. Robert H. Swansbrough, *Test by Fire: The War Presidency of George W. Bush* (New York: Palgrave Macmillan, 2008), 47.

110. Richard H. Davis, "Anatomy of a Smear Campaign," *Boston Globe,* March 21, 2004, http://www .boston.com/news/globe/editorial_opinion/oped/articles/2004/03/21/the_anatomy_of_a_smear_campaign/.

111. Traugott and Kang, "Push Polls," 290–291.

112. Richardson, *Pulp Politics,* 138.

113. Ridout and Franz, *The Persuasive Power of Campaign Advertising,* 17.

114. Franz et al., *Campaign Advertising,* 142.

115. Wilner, "Why Pushing a Politician Isn't Like Selling Soap,"

116. Andy Ellenthal, "7 Political Ad Tactics Every Marketer Should Know," imediaconnection.com, August 15, 2012.

117. Westen, *The Political Brain,* 346.

118. Bruce Ackerman, *The Decline and Fall of the American Republic* (Cambridge, MA: Belknap Press, 2010), 126.

119. Quoted in Alina Seluhk, "Ads Flood Last Weeks of Campaign—and So Does Negativity," chicago tribune.com, September 27, 2012.

120. Dan Gillmor, "A Strategy for Filtering America's Toxic Sludge of Political Advertising," presstv.com, August 19, 2012.

121. Stephen Ansolabehere and Shanto Iyengar, *Going Negative: How Political Advertisements Shrink and Polarize the Electorate* (New York: Free Press, 1995), 11–12.

122. Fowler and Ridout, "Advertising Trends in 2010," 4.

123. Quoted in Pam Rooks, "Society Watch: Is It American Voters or American Politicians Who Need to Wake Up?" Politicalfiber.com, October 4, 2012.

Chapter 5: Media Corporations

1. Ned Martel, "As Iowa Caucuses Near, TV Stations See Ad Buys Boom After Long Lull," *Washington Post,* December 31, 2011.

2. Ibid.

3. Ibid.; D. M. Levine, "Shot in Arm Expected for 2012 Political Ad Spend: MediaVest Sees a 30% Jump Possible in Key States," *AdWeek,* December 27, 2011.

4. Laura Baum, "Presidential Ad War Tops 1M Airings," Wesleyan Media Project, November 2, 2012.

5. Charles McChesney, "What Does All That Campaign Spending Get Spent On?" Syracuse.com, November 12, 2012.

6. Walt Whitman, "Election Day, November 1884," first published in the 1891–1892 edition of *Leaves of Grass,* http://whitmanarchive.org/criticism/reviews/complete_poems/anc.00131.html; Matt Taibbi, "How the Hype Became Bigger Than the Presidential Election: Blame the Media for Making Whole Generations Hate the Process," *Rolling Stone,* October 9, 2012.

7. Ibid.

8. Ben Fox, "E. W. Scripps Posts Profit on Political Ad Spend," *MarketWatch,* November. 9, 2012.

9. "Political Boon Leads Gray to Up Estimates," tvnewscheck.com, November 8, 2012.

10. Wayne Friedman, "Election Money Fuels Big Gains for Scripps," mediapost.com, November 9, 2012.

11. Andy Fixmer, "CBS Profit Climbs 16% as Political Advertising Boosts Radio, TV," Bloomberg, November 8, 2012.

12. Ryan Sharrow, "Sinclair Broadcast Earnings Rise in 3Q on Political Spending," *Baltimore Business Journal,* November 1, 2012.

13. Associated Press, "Politics Ads, Olympics Lift Belo 3Q Profit 81 Pct," October 30, 2012.

14. Scott Eymer, "Don't Hate Political Advertising—Profit from It," *Seeking Alpha,* September 12, 2012. Eymer, a former broadcaster, writes at http://seekingalpha.com.

15. Bill Moyers and Bernard Weisberger, "Money in Politics: Where's the Outrage?," Huffington Post, August 30, 2012.

16. See Robert W. McChesney, *Telecommunications, Mass Media, and Democracy: The Battle for the Control of U.S. Broadcasting, 1928–1935* (New York: Oxford University Press, 1993).

17. Diana Mankowski and Raissa Jose, "Flashback: The 70th Anniversary of FDR's Fireside Chats," Museum of Broadcast History, http://www.museum.tv/exhibitionssection.php?page=79.

18. Joseph E. Cantor, Denis Steven Rutkus, and Kevin B. Greely, "Free and Reduced-Rate Time for Political Candidates," report prepared for the Congressional Research Service, July 7, 1997, 6.

19. This is a preliminary calculation and is therefore a conservative estimate. Andrew Vanacore, "Political Ads Called 'Gigantic Band-Aid' for TV Stations' Bottom Lines," Associated Press dispatch, October 29, 2010, http://cnsnews.com/news/article/political-ads-called-gigantic-band-aid-t.

20. Quoted in Jeff Cohen, "TV Industry Wields Power in D.C.," *Baltimore Sun,* May 4, 1997.

21. "Time Is Right to Buy Media Stocks Like TWX, DIS, NWS, CMCSA," *InvestorPlace,* June 20, 2011, http://www.investorplace.com/46016/twx-nws-dis-cmcsa-cbs-via-sbgi/.

22. Quoted in Catalina Camia, "TV Stations Set to Make Money from 2012 Political Ads," *USA Today,* June 22, 2011.

23. Quoted in Anthony Noto, "For Media M&A, Christmas Comes Early," *Mergers & Acquisitions,* July 13, 2011, http://www.themiddlemarket.com/news/qa_media_ma_poised_for_a_pickup-221486–1.html.

24. Tim Dickinson, "Guess Who's Profiting Most from Super PACS?" RollingStone.com, August 6, 2012.

25. Quoted in Laura Baum, "2012 Shatters 2004 and 2008 Record for Total Ads Aired," mediaproject.wesleyan.edu, October 24, 2012.

26. Quoted in Belinda Yeung, "Iowans Can't Avoid Political Ads on TV," kcrg.com, October 21, 2012.

27. John Shelton, "The 2012 Election Cycle Is Already Costing You Money," *Advertising Age,* August 7, 2012.

28. Darrell M. West, "Communications Lessons from the 2012 Presidential Election," *UpFront* analysis, the Brookings Institution, November 6, 2012.

29. Elizabeth Wilner, "Equal Time for Politicians May Mean Less Ad Time for Other Marketers," *Advertising Age,* August 23, 2012.

30. Marino Eccher, "Political TV Ad Blitz Dominates Airwaves," *Jamestown (North Dakota) Sun,* September 12, 2012.

31. Quoted in Jack Messmer, "Sinclair's Political Shooting Through the Roof," TVNewsCheck.com, August 1, 2012.

32. Quoted in Dan Eggen, "Observers Say Amount Spent on Federal Races Could Hit $6 Billion," *Monterey (California) Herald,* September 2, 2012.

33. Quoted in Erin Ailworth, "Election Spending on Local TV Surges," *Boston Globe,* September 23, 2012.

34. Elizabeth Wilner, "Ad Avalanche: 43,000 Political Spots a Day Until November," *Advertising Age,* September 13, 2012.

35. Felipe Cabrera and Victor Luckerson, "The Numbers: What Fueled the Priciest Election in U.S. History," *Time,* November 18, 2012; "Florida: Congressional Races in 2012," opensecrets.org (accessed November 20, 2012).

36. Paul Farhi, "Dilemma for D.C. Stations: So Many Political Ads, So Little Airtime," washingtonpost.com, October 22, 2012.

37. Luke Rosiak, "In Pursuit of Coveted Independents, Campaign Ads Invade Local TV News," *Washington Times,* September 2, 2012.

38. Jed Lewison, "22 Consecutive Political Ads During Half-Hour Columbus, Ohio, Newscast," dailykos.com, November 1, 2012.

39. Farhi, "Dilemma for D.C. Stations."

40. Ted Johnson, "TV Biz Savors Windfall from Political Ads," variety.com, October 31, 2012.

41. Wilner, "Ad Avalanche."

42. Luke Rosiak, "Political-Ad Tsunami Swamps Southeast Virginia," *Washington Times,* September 11, 2012.

43. Barack Obama, "Transcript of President Obama's Acceptance Speech at the Democratic National Convention, as Delivered," Federal News Service, September 6, 2012.

44. Alex Jackson," Maryland Voters Agree, They're Sick of Ads," *Capital Gazette*, November 7, 2012.

45. Ibid.

46. Ken Tingley, "Political Ads on TV Are a Bad Dream," poststar.com, October 9, 2012.

47. Mike Plews, "Omaha Pharmacists Take on Political Advertising," wowt.com, November 1, 2012.

48. "Cameron v Letterman: A Zero-Sum Equation," guardian.co.uk, September 27, 2012; James Kirkup, "David Cameron Braves David Letterman's US Chat Show—and Leaves Red-Faced," telegraph.co.uk, September 26, 2012.

49. Noto, "For Media M&A."

50. Derek Turner, the research director at Free Press, provided us with the data for this paragraph.

51. Quoted in Michael Beckel, "Big Business Prefers GOP Over Democratic Super PACs," Center for Public Integrity, July 25, 2012.

52. James Curran, Shanto Iyengar, Anker Brink Lund, and Inka Salovaara-Moring, "Media System, Public Knowledge, and Democracy: A Comparative Study," *European Journal of Communication* 24, no. 1 (2009): 5–26.

53. Stephen Cushion, *The Democratic Value of News: Why Public Service Media Matters* (Basingstoke, UK: Palgrave Macmillan, 2012).

54. Lyndon B. Johnson, "Remarks in the Capitol Rotunda at the Signing of the Voting Rights Act," August 6, 1965, in *Public Papers of the Presidents of the United States: Lyndon B. Johnson, 1965,* vol. 2 (Washington, DC: GPO, 1966), entry 394, 811–815. In his speech, Johnson said, "Millions of Americans are denied the right to vote because of their color. This law will ensure them the right to vote. The wrong is one which no American, in his heart, can justify. The right is one which no American, true to our principles, can deny."

55. Robert Caro, *The Passage of Power* (New York: Knopf, 2012).

56. Harold Wilson, speech at Labour Party conference, October 1, 1963, Labour Party Annual Conference Report (London: Labour Party, 1963), 139–140.

57. Lyndon Johnson, "Remarks upon Signing the Public Broadcasting Act of 1967, November 7, 1967," University of California at Santa Barbara (Gerhard Peters and John T. Woolley) American Presidency Project, http://www.presidency.ucsb.edu/ws/?pid=28532.

58. Bill Moyers, "Remarks at PBS Annual Meeting," May 18, 2006. A version of the remarks can be found at http://www.pbs.org/moyers/faithandreason/pbsaddress.html.

59. Ibid.

60. See Carnegie Commission on Public Television, *Public Television: A Program for Action* (New York: Harper & Row, 1967).

61. Quoted in Roger Smith, "Public Broadcasting as State Television," www.tompaine.com, March 11, 2003.

62. James Reston, "A Base for a Milestone: Carnegie Report, Like Land-Grant Act of 1862, May Greatly Influence U.S. Life," *New York Times,* January 26, 1967.

63. Carnegie Commission, *Public Television,* 8.

64. Ibid.; Nichols, McChesney interviews with Moyers. Nichols and McChesney have interviewed Moyers frequently over the years. The conversation cited here took place March 26, 2010, in New York.

65. Aaron Barnhart, "In Public TV We Trust," *Electronic Media,* July 22, 2002, 10.

66. Moyers, "Remarks at PBS Annual Meeting."

67. Dennis Hevesi, "Wilbur Mills, Long a Power in Congress, Is Dead at 82," *New York Times,* May 3, 1992.

68. Moyers, "Remarks at PBS Annual Meeting."

69. Jack Gould, "News Laboratory Experiences Some Birth Pains," *New York Times,* November 3, 1967.

70. Laura R. Linder, *Public Access Television* (Westport, CT: Greenwood Press, 1999), 2.

71. Jack Gould, "Lack of Funds May Shut Down Hoving's Broadcast Improvers," *New York Times,* February 21, 1969.

72. Grace Glueck, "The Total Involvement of Thomas Hoving," *New York Times,* December 8, 1968.

73. Louise Sweeney, "Congress Urged to Pay Off on Public-Broadcasting Pledge," *Christian Science Monitor,* July 16, 1968.

74. National Citizens Committee for Public Broadcasting, *The State of Public Broadcasting* (New York: National Citizens Committee for Public Broadcasting, July 1968).

75. ". . . Soap Suds and Dog Food," *Boston Globe,* October 14, 1968.

76. Lawrence Laurent, "Hoving's Forthright Blast Will Make Powerful Enemies," *Washington Post,* October 1, 1968.

77. ". . . Soap Suds and Dog Food."

78. "TV and the Voter," *Christian Science Monitor,* October 3, 1968.

79. Jack Gould, "A Gadfly Buzzing the Status Quo," *New York Times,* October 27, 1968.

80. Jerry Landay, "Failing the Perception Test," *Current,* June 2001; David Hatch, "PBS Decision Irks Tauzin," *Electronic Media,* May 15, 2000, 4.

81. Quotes from Lawrence Jarvik, *PBS: Behind the Screen* (Rocklin, CA: Forum, 1997), back cover.

82. Quoted in "ANA '84: Washington Update, Cost Concerns," *Broadcasting,* November 19, 1984, 66.

83. Tom McCourt, *Conflicting Communication Interests in America: The Case of National Public Radio* (Westport, CT: Praeger, 1999), 2–3; William F. Buckley, *On the Firing Line: The Public Life of Our Public Figures* (New York: Random House, 1989).

84. Howard Kurtz, "McCain Wants Free Airtime for Candidates; Is Media Fair to Bush on Corporate Scandals?," CNN Reliable Sources, July 6, 2002.

85. Ibid.

86. Some indication of the power of the commercial broadcasting lobby is that since 1934 there have been well over 100,000 license renewals but only four times has a broadcaster had its renewal denied because it failed to meet its public interest programming obligation. The odds are less than 4/1,000 of 1 percent that a broadcaster might lose its license. In short, it is a hollow threat, and broadcasters know they can do exactly as they please to maximize returns. See Steven Waldman and the Working Group on Information Needs of Communities, *The Information Needs of Communities: The Changing Media Landscape in a Broadband Age* (Washington, DC: Federal Communications Commission, June 2011), 26.

87. Waldman et al., *The Information Needs of Communities,* 295–296.

88. Quoted in Cantor et al., "Free and Reduced-Rate Time," 21.

89. Robert W. McChesney interview with William Kennard, February 2001.

90. Jeff Cohen, "TV Industry Wields Power in D.C.," *Baltimore Sun,* May 4, 1997.

91. McChesney interview with Kennard.

92. Ibid.

93. Ibid.

94. Quoted in Todd Shields, "Broadcasters Fight Plan to Post Names of Political Ad Buyers on Web," washingtonpost.com, March 18, 2012.

95. Todd Shields, "Unmasking the Going Rate for Attack Ads," *Bloomberg Businessweek,* March 26–April 1, 2012, 21–32.

96. Jake Harper, "FCC Database Misses Huge Chunk of Ads," sunlightfoundation.com, October 3, 2012.

97. Katy Bachman, "Broadcasters Lose Attempt to Stay Political File Disclosure Rules," adweek.com, July 27, 2012.

98. Dan Gillmor, "A Strategy for Filtering America's Toxic Sludge of Political Advertising," guardian .co.uk, August 18, 2012.

99. For the Berg quotation and a discussion of these cases, see Timothy Karr, *Money, News, and Deception in Denver* (Washington, DC: Free Press, 2012), 8–9.

100. Bill Knight, "Super PACs Spent Big in Peoria," thecommunityword.com, September 4, 2012.

101. Karr, *Money, News, and Deception,* 5.

102. Knight, "Super PACS Spent Big."

103. Quoted in James Q. Lynch, "Broadcasters Urged to Demand Accuracy, Reject Deceptive Political Ads," *Quad-City* (Iowa–Illinois) *Times,* qctimes.org, September 17, 2012.

104. Confidential conversation between public interest advocate and Robert W. McChesney, July 2012.

105. Quoted in Andy Kroll, "What the FEC?," motherjones.com, April 18, 2011, http://motherjones.com /politics/2011/04/fec-cazayoux-citizens-united.

106. Quoted in Charles Babcock, "Secret Election Financing Surges with Evasion of IRS Scrutiny," bloomberg.com, June 16, 2011.

107. Comment on *PBS Newshour*, August 10, 2012.

108. Quoted in Tim Karr, *Left in the Dark: Local Election Coverage in the Age of Big-Money Politics* (Washington, DC: Free Press, September 2012), 6.

109. Kathleen Hall Jamieson, *Dirty Politics: Deception, Distraction, and Democracy* (New York: Oxford University Press, 1992), 279.

110. Martin Kaplan, Ken Goldstein, and Matthew Hale, "Local News Coverage of the 2004 Campaigns: An Analysis of Nightly Broadcasts in 11 Markets" Lear Center Local News Archive, February 15, 2005, 19–20, http://www.localnewsarchive.org/pdf/LCLNAFinal2004.pdf. Moreover, control over the presidential debates has been taken away from the League of Women Voters by the two major parties, and the capacity for debates to work for citizens rather than politicians has been lessened accordingly. See George Farah, *No Debate: How the Republican and Democratic Parties Secretly Control the Presidential Debates* (New York: Seven Stories Press, 2004).

111. John Nichols interview of Ed Garvey, November 2010.

112. Classic research includes Daniel Halin, "Sound Bite News: Television News Coverage of Elections, 1968–88," *Journal of Communication* 42, no. 2 (1991): 5–24; Erik P. Bucy and Maria Elizabeth Grabe, "Taking Television Seriously: A Sound and Image Bite Analysis of Presidential Campaign Coverage, 1992–2004," *Journal of Communication* 57, no. 4 (2007): 652–675; and Kaplan et al., "Local News Coverage."

113. Thomas E. Patterson, *The Vanishing Voter: Public Involvement in an Age of Uncertainty* (New York: Vintage Books, 2003), 90.

114. Leonard Downie Jr. and Robert G. Kaiser, *The News About the News: American Journalism in Peril* (New York: Knopf, 2002), 171.

115. The research is discussed in Waldman et al., *The Information Needs of Communities,* 84–85.

116. Michael Schudson, *The Power of News* (Cambridge, MA: Harvard University Press, 1995), 215.

117. The research is discussed in Waldman et al., *The Information Needs of Communities,* 84–85.

118. Karr, *Left in the Dark,* 12.

119. Editorial, "Tale of the Tape . . . So Far," *Columbia Journalism Review,* September/October 2012.

120. Elizabeth Wilner, "Why Pushing a Politician Isn't Like Pushing Soap," *Advertising Age,* October 1, 2012. See also Elizabeth Wilner, "What Big Bird Teaches Us About Political Advertising," *Advertising Age,* October 11, 2012.

121. Quoted in Daniel Adler, "Political Ads: Overpriced, Inefficient, Essential," RollingStone.com, August 14, 2012.

122. Andria Krewson, "Big Ad Spending, Little Press Scrutiny," cjr.org, July 30, 2012.

123. Karr, *Left in the Dark.*

124. Karr, *Money, News, and Deception,* 3.

125. Edward Wasserman, "TV 'Watchdogs' Quiet as Political Ad Cash Rolls In," *Miami Herald,* October 8, 2012.

126. Quoted in Dickinson, "Guess Who's Profiting."

127. "Little Public Awareness of Outside Campaign Spending Boom," Pew Research Center for People and the Press, www.people-press.org, August 2, 2012.

128. Jamieson, *Dirty Politics,* especially Appendix II.

129. Quoted in Karr, *Money, News, and Deception,* 6.

130. Darrell M. West, *Air Wars: Television Advertising in American Elections, 1952–2008* (Washington, DC: CQ Press, 2010), 94–95.

131. Quoted in "In Election's Closing Days, Ad Campaign Urges Battleground Stations to Reject Deceptive Outside Group Ads and Increase On-Air and Online Fact Checking," Annenberg Public Policy Center of the University of Pennsylvania, October 31, 2012.

132. Quoted in Jason Salzman, "Checking the Facts in Political Ads," Huffington Post, August 27, 2012.

133. Karr, *Money, News, and Deception,* 6.

134. Quoted in Scott Finn, "Should TV Stations Refuse to Air Political Ads That Make False Claims?," npr.org, October 3, 2012.

135. Gillmor, "A Strategy."

136. Moyers and Weisberger, "Money in Politics."

137. Marty Kaplan, "How to Ignore the Campaign," Huffington Post, August 31, 2012.

138. "Yes, Expect Record 2012 Political Spending," *Media Life,* June 23, 2011, http://www.media lifemagazine.com/artman2/publish/AskaMediaLifeexpert/Yes-expect-record-2012-political-spending.asp.

139. Katy Bachman, "Digital Losing Out on Campaign Ad Billions," *AdWeek,* June 22, 2011, http:// www.adweek.com/news/advertising-branding/digital-losing-out-campaign-ad-billions-132676.

140. Eli Pariser, The *Filter Bubble: What the Internet Is Hiding from You* (New York: Penguin Press, 2011), 154.

141. Quoted in Bachman, "Digital Losing Out."

142. Gerald F. Seib, "Political Perceptions: Ad Burnout Ahead?," wsj.com, September 11, 2012.

143. Chris Kromm, "Did Big Money Really Lose This Election? Hardly," truth-out.org, November 12, 2012.

Chapter 6: The Rise and Fall of Professional Journalism

1. Quoted in Jeremy W. Peters, "A Finger Slips, and the Bachmann Camp Pounces," *New York Times,* November 13, 2011.

2. Quoted in ibid.

3. Nina Mandell, "Bachmann's Campaign Manager Calls CBS Exec 'a Piece of Sh—' After Debate," *New York Daily News,* November 14, 2011.

4. Herbert J. Gans, *Democracy and the News* (New York: Oxford University Press, 2003), 54.

5. Mike Miller, "Born Under a Cloud of War," *Capital Times,* September 3, 2009; John Nichols, "Neglecting Candidates with Whom You Disagree Is Ultimate Disrespect for Democracy," *Capital Times,* September 14, 2010. The *Capital Times* newspaper, for which Nichols has written for two decades, was founded by William T. Evjue, a crusading reformer, in 1917. It was Evjue who developed the "Let the people have the truth" motto.

6. John Nichols, "A New Age for Newspapers: Diversity of Voices, Competition, and the Internet," testimony before the House Judiciary Committee, U.S. House of Representatives, April 21, 2009, http:// judiciary.house.gov/hearings/pdf/Nichols090421.pdf.

7. The material in this paragraph and the material that is unattributed otherwise in the next few paragraphs come from Robert W. McChesney and John Nichols, *The Death and Life of American Journalism: The Media Revolution That Will Begin the World Again* (New York: Nation Books, 2011).

8. Alexis de Tocqueville, *Democracy in America* (New York: Penguin, 2003), 215, 604.

9. It also meant that dissident movements found it far easier to launch weeklies and distribute them. See Bob Ostertag, *People's Movements: The Journalism of Social Justice Movements* (Boston: Beacon Press, 2006).

10. See John Nichols, *The "S" Word: A Short History of an American Tradition, Socialism* (New York: Verso, 2011). See also Robin Blackburn, *An Unfinished Revolution: Karl Marx and Abraham Lincoln* (New York: Verso, 2011).

11. Quoted in James M. Lundberg, "Nathaniel Hawthorne, Party Hack: Why Did the Famous Novelist Agree to Write a Campaign Biography for an Infamously Bad President?," *Slate,* September 14, 2012.

12. Richard L. Kaplan, *Politics and the American Press: The Rise of Objectivity, 1865–1920* (New York: Cambridge University Press, 2002), 42.

13. Michael Schudson, quoted in Natalie Jomini Stroud, *Niche News: The Politics of News Choice* (New York: Oxford University Press, 2011), 174.

14. Quoted in Charles Lewis, *The Buying of the President 2000* (New York: Avon Books, 2000), 343.

15. Kaplan, *Politics and the American Press*, 24.

16. Ibid., 24, 149.

17. Ibid., 77, 73.

18. Quoted in ibid., 123–124.

19. For the classic treatment, see Upton Sinclair, *The Brass Check* (Rpt., Urbana: University of Illinois Press, [1919] 2003).

20. Robert M. La Follette, *The Political Philosophy of Robert M. La Follette,* comp. by Ellen Torelle (Madison, WI: Robert M. La Follette Co., 1920), 345–359.

21. Ibid, 349.

22. "History and Mission," *The Progressive,* http://www.progressive.org/mission.

23. Theodore Roosevelt, "The Man with the Muck Rake," speech delivered in Washington, DC, April 14, 1906, http://www.pbs.org/wgbh/americanexperience/features/primary-resources/tr-muckrake/.

24. For a good look at this period and crisis, see Amy Reynolds and Gary Hicks, *Prophets of the Fourth Estate: Broadsides by Press Critics of the Progressive Era* (Los Angeles: Litwin Books, 2011).

25. Cited in Kaplan, *Politics and the American Press,* 166.

26. See Daniel C. S. Stoltzfus, *Freedom from Advertising: E. W. Scripps's Chicago Experiment* (Urbana: University of Illinois Press, 2007).

27. Quoted in Kaplan, *Politics and the American Press,* 126.

28. McCarthyism in the 1950s went a long way toward weeding out and intimidating those journalists who might take an adversarial stance toward management and were prone toward critical examinations of the existing power structure. See Edward Alwood, *Dark Days in the Newsroom: McCarthyism Aimed at the Press* (Philadelphia: Temple University Press, 2007).

29. Unsigned obituary, "Hazel Brannon Smith, 80, Editor Who Crusaded for Civil Rights," *New York Times,* May 16, 1994.

30. D. D. Guttenplan, *American Radical: The Life and Times of I. F. Stone* (New York: Farrar, Straus and Giroux, 2009).

31. Paul Krugman, "The Centrist Cop-Out," *New York Times,* July 29, 2011.

32. Ari Melber, "Why Fact-Checking Has Taken Root in This Year's Election," pbs.org, September 5, 2012.

33. W. Lance Bennett, "Press-Government Relations in a Changing Media Environment," in Kate Kenski and Kathleen Hall Jamieson, eds., *The Oxford Handbook of Political Communication* (New York: Oxford University Press, forthcoming).

34. Michael D. Shear, "Democrats Crying Foul Over a New Romney Ad," *New York Times,* November 23, 2011.

35. Greg Sargent, "Romney Camp: Misrepresenting Opponent's Words Is Completely Fair Game," *Washington Post,* November 22, 2011.

36. Ros Krasny, "New Mitt Romney Attack Ad Called 'Deceitful' by Obama Campaign," Reuters, November 22, 2011.

37. Sargent, "Romney Camp."

38. Adolph S. Ochs, "Business Announcement," *New York Times,* August 19, 1896.

39. See Eugene Secunda and Terence P. Moran, *Selling War to America: From the Spanish American War to the Global War on Terror* (Westport, CT: Praeger, 2007); Norman Solomon, *War Made Easy: How Presidents and Pundits Keep Spinning Us to Death* (Hoboken, NJ: Wiley, 2005).

40. John Nichols, ed., *Against the Beast: A Documentary History of American Opposition to Empire* (New York: Nation Books, 2004), 93–136.

41. Quoted in ibid., 110.

42. Eli Pariser, *The Filter Bubble: What the Internet Is Hiding from You* (New York: Penguin Press, 2011), 50. See Lippmann's two masterpieces on journalism written in 1919 and 1920 in Walter Lippmann, *Liberty and the News* (Rpt., Mineola, NY: Dover, 2010). The second piece in the book, besides "Liberty and the News," is Lippmann's piece with Charles Merz, "A Test of the News," which appeared in the *New Republic* in August 1920. For a lengthy treatment of Lippmann's writings on journalism and democracy, see Robert W. McChesney, "That Was Now and This Is Then: Walter Lippmann and the Crisis of Journalism," in Robert W. McChesney and Victor Pickard, eds., *Will the Last Reporter Please Turn Out the Lights: The Collapse of Journalism and What Can Be Done to Fix It* (New York: New Press, 2011), 151–161.

43. Shanto Iyengar and Donald R. Kinder, *News That Matters: Television and Public Opinion,* updated ed. (Chicago: University of Chicago Press, 2010), 135–138.

44. Greg Kaufmann, "This Week in Poverty," *The Nation,* http://www.thenation.com/blogs/greg-kaufmann.

45. Thomas E. Patterson, *The Vanishing Voter: Public Involvement in an Age of Uncertainty* (New York: Vintage Books, 2003), 89–90.

46. W. Lance Bennett, *News: The Politics of Illusion* (New York: Longman, 1983), 92, 60.

47. Joseph N. Cappella and Kathleen Hall Jamieson, *Spiral of Cynicism: The Press and the Public Good* (New York: Oxford University Press, 1997). Herbert Gans suggested the news media are not the independent variable in the creation of cynicism, but rather they mostly reinforce a rational response to how the political system operates. Either way, the news media are not actively battling cynicism and depoliticization. See Herbert J. Gans, *Democracy and the News* (New York: Oxford University Press, 2003), 54.

48. We do not wish to exaggerate this phenomenon. Like their nineteenth-century predecessors, the dissident movements of the 1960s required their own media to grow and be effective. See John McMillian, *Smoking Typewriters: The Sixties Underground Press and the Rise of Alternative Media in America* (New York: Oxford University Press, 2011); and Peter Richardson, *A Bomb in Every Issue: How the Short, Unruly Life of Ramparts Magazine Changed America* (New York: New Press, 2009).

49. Jeff Cohen, "Mainstream Reporters: Too Close to the Field and Teams to Get the Debt Story," CommonDreams, July 30, 2011, http://www.commondreams.org/view/2011/07/30.

50. See John R. MacArthur, *The Selling of "Free Trade": NAFTA, Washington, and the Subversion of American Democracy* (New York: Hill and Wang, 2000); and Howard Kurtz, *The Fortune Tellers: Inside Wall Street's Game of Money, Media, and Manipulation* (New York: Free Press, 2000).

51. See Jeffrey E. Cohen, *The Presidency in the Era of 24-Hour News* (Princeton, NJ: Princeton University Press, 2008), 14. See also the comments of *USA Today* reporter Richard Benedetto in Elizabeth A. Skewes, *Message Control: How News Is Made on the Presidential Campaign Trail* (Lanham, MD: Rowman & Littlefield, 2007), 51.

52. Thomas E. Patterson, *Out of Order* (New York: Vintage Books, 1994), 82.

53. Timothy Crouse, *The Boys on the Bus* (New York: Random House, 1973), 39. For a brilliant alternative interpretation of the 1972 campaign, see Hunter S. Thompson, *Fear and Loathing: On the Campaign Trail '72* (New York: Grand Central, 1973).

54. Mike Gravel and David Eisenbach, *The Kingmakers: How the Media Threatens Our Security and Our Democracy* (Beverly Hills, CA: Phoenix Books, 2008), 137.

55. Cohen has routinely used the "money primary" concept in his talks over the years, and it seems appropriate to acknowledge his coinage of the term.

56. See, for example, Kenneth Dautrich and Thomas H. Hartley, *How the News Media Fail American Voters: Causes, Consequences, and Remedies* (New York: Columbia University Press, 1999); Jan Pons Vermeer, ed., *Campaigns in the News: Mass Media and Congressional Elections* (New York: Greenwood Press, 1987); Robert Shogan, *Bad News: Where the Press Goes Wrong in the Making of the President* (Chicago: Ivan R. Dee, 2001); and S. Robert Lichter and Richard E. Noyes, *Good Intentions Make Bad News: Why Americans Hate Campaign Journalism* (Lanham, MD: Rowman & Littlefield, 1996).

For books that go beyond campaigns to general political news but make related arguments, see Kathleen Hall Jamieson and Paul Waldman, *The Press Effect: Politicians, Journalists, and the Stories That Shape the Political World* (New York: Oxford University Press, 2003); Jay Rosen, *What Are Journalists For?* (New Haven, CT: Yale University Press, 1999); and W. Lance Bennett, Regina G. Lawrence, and Steven Livingstone, *When the Press Fails: Political Power and the News Media from Iraq to Katrina* (Chicago: University of Chicago Press, 2007).

57. Quoted in Patterson, *Out of Order*, 26.

58. Kathleen Hall Jamieson and Joseph N. Cappella, *Echo Chamber: Rush Limbaugh and the Conservative Media Establishment* (New York: Oxford University Press, 2008), xi.

59. For a nice discussion of this, see Matthew Robert Kerbel, *Edited for Television: CNN, ABC, and American Presidential Elections*, 2nd ed. (Boulder, CO: Westview Press, 1998), 201; and Skewes, *Message Control,* 13.

60. See Kathleen Hall Jamieson, *Everything You Think You Know about Politics . . . and Why You're Wrong* (New York: Basic Books, 2000), chap. 24.

61. Michael Schudson, *The Power of News* (Cambridge, MA: Harvard University Press, 1995), 214–215.

62. Jeffrey Gale, *"Bullshit!": The Media as Power Brokers in Presidential Elections* (Palm Springs, CA: Bold Hawk Press, 1988).

63. John Nichols, "Go-Along Media Ignoring Kucinich," *Capital Times,* December 13, 2003.

64. Jim Naureckas, "The Dean Surge: Fear and Loathing in Campaign Punditry," *Extra!,* October 2003; Mark Shields, "Time for Apologies," CNNPolitics, April 12, 2004, http://www.cnn.com/2004/ALL POLITICS/04/12/iraq.reconsidered/index.html.

65. Paul Harris, "Ron Paul Exposes Media Bias," *The Guardian,* August 16, 2011, http://www .guardian.co.uk/commentisfree/cifamerica/2011/aug/16/ron-paul-media-bias.

66. Clay Barbour, "Also-Rans Caught in Political Catch-22," *Wisconsin State Journal,* August 10, 2012.

67. See John Nichols and Robert W. McChesney, *Tragedy and Farce: How the American Media Sell Wars, Spin Elections, and Destroy Democracy* (New York: New Press, 2006), for a more detailed discussion of these issues.

68. Lucas Shaw, "MSNBC Bids Adieu to Cenk Uygur," Reuters, July 20, 2011; Mark Joyella, "MSNBC Calls Cenk Uygur's Version of Departure 'Completely Baseless,'" *Mediaite,* July 21, 2011.

69. Brian Stelter, "Sharpton Appears to Win Anchor Spot on MSNBC," *New York Times,* July 21, 2011.

70. Andrew Kirell, "Fox & MSNBC Became More Extreme as Election Day Neared," *Mediaite,* November 19, 2012.

71. Skewes, *Message Control,* 13.

72. See Stephen J. Farnsworth and S. Robert Lichter, *The Nightly News Nightmare: Media Coverage of U.S. Presidential Elections, 1988–2008* (Lanham, MD: Rowman & Littlefield, 2011), 45–52.

73. Conor Friedersdorf, "Is Horse-Race Coverage Killing Mitt Romney," nationaljournal.com, September 28, 2012.

74. Leonard Downie Jr. and Robert G. Kaiser, *The News About the News: American Journalism in Peril* (New York: Knopf, 2002), 231.

75. Patterson, *Out of Order,* 82.

76. James Fallows, *Breaking the News: How the Media Undermine American Democracy* (New York: Pantheon, 1996), 170–181.

77. Patterson, *Out of Order,* 20–23.

78. Travis N. Ridout and Michael M. Franz, *The Persuasive Power of Campaign Advertising* (Philadelphia: Temple University Press, 2011), 129.

79. Joe McGinniss, *The Selling of the President 1968* (New York: Simon & Schuster, 1970), 59.

80. Kerbel, *Edited for Television,* 203–204.

Chapter 7: Journalism Exits, Stage Right

1. Andrew Beaujon, "Las Vegas, Orlando, Pittsburgh Saw Most Political Ads Last Week," Poynter Institute, October 17, 2012, www.poynter.org.

2. Brendan Sasso, "Local Television Stations in Swing-States Cash In on Deluge of Political Ads," *The Hill,* October 28, 2012.

3. Jeremy W. Peters, "73,000 Political Ads Test Even a City of Excess," *New York Times,* October 15, 2012.

4. Ibid.

5. Campbell Robertson, "New Orleans Struggles with Latest Storm, Newspaper Layoffs," *New York Times,* June 12, 2012.

6. For a thorough update of the crisis in journalism through 2012, see Robert W. McChesney, *Digital Disconnect: How Capitalism Is Turning the Internet Against Democracy* (New York: New Press, 2013), chap. 6.

7. See James O'Shea, *The Deal from Hell: How Moguls and Wall Street Plundered Great American Newspapers* (New York: PublicAffairs, 2011).

8. Steven Waldman and the Working Group on Information Needs of Communities, *The Information Needs of Communities: The Changing Media Landscape in a Broadband Age* (Washington, DC: Federal Communications Commission, June 2011), 5.

9. For chilling detail, see ibid., 44–45.

10. This point and a few of the others that follow are drawn from McChesney, *Digital Disconnect,* chap. 6.

11. Matthew Rothschild, "Gov. Walker Uses 'Vanna White' Veto to Rob New Public Sector Workers," *The Progressive Blog,* July 6, 2011, http://www.progressive.org/wx070611.html.

12. Waldman et al., *The Information Needs of Communities,* 12, 90, 46, 52.

13. For an accurate accounting of newspaper closures and cutbacks, we rely on two excellent Web sites: http://newspaperdeathwatch.com/; and http://newspaperlayoffs.com/. They are constantly updated, and they put the lie to claims that the industry has stabilized.

14. Nat Ives, "Boston.com Joins Native Advertising Push with Sponsored Posts: Says More Than Half of Small Businesses Are Already Blogging," *AdWeek,* November 13, 2012.

15. Christine Haughney and David Carr, "At Newsweek, Ending Print and a Blend of Two Styles," *New York Times,* October 18, 2012.

16. Robert W. McChesney and John Nichols, *The Death and Life of American Journalism: The Media Revolution That Will Begin the World Again* (New York: Nation Books, 2010). See Appendix 3 and the Preface written specifically for the paperback edition.

17. Pew Research Center's Project for Excellence in Journalism, "The Study of the News Ecosystem of One American City," January 11, 2010, http://www.journalism.org/analysis_report/how_news_happens.

18. For a treatment of the scorched-earth approach of a newspaper publisher who is regarded as a visionary in the move from print to digital, see David Carr, "Newspapers' Digital Apostle," *New York Times,* November 14, 2011. For a treatment of the handful of the most successful new digital newsrooms at the local level, which depend overwhelmingly on donations and foundation grants, see Michele McLellan and Mayur Patel, *Getting Local: How Nonprofit News Ventures Seek Sustainability* (Miami: Knight Foundation, October 2011).

19. Waldman et al., *The Information Needs of Communities,* 16.

20. Ibid., 226.

21. Lymari Morales, "U.S. Distrust in Media Hits New High," gallup.com, September 21, 2012.

22. Ibid.

23. Thomas E. Patterson, *The Vanishing Voter: Public Involvement in an Age of Uncertainty* (New York: Vintage Books, 2002), 90.

24. Jeremy W. Peters, "Covering 2012, Youths on the Bus," *New York Times,* August 31, 2011.

25. Mike Elk, "In Conference Call, Romney Urged Businesses to Tell Their Employees How to Vote," *In These Times,* October 17, 2012.

26. John Nichols discussion with Mike Elk, October 18, 2012.

27. There are, unfortunately, too many stories of great journalists giving up on the craft. Like most followers of media issues, we turn to Jim Romenesko's great blog for insight on the heartbreaking changes in the industry: http://jimromenesko.com/.

28. Waldman et al., *The Information Needs of Communities,* 86.

29. Quoted in Michael Miner, "Whose Fault Is Scott Lee Cohen? The Reporter Who Didn't Pay Enough Attention Is Now the Scapegoat for Everybody Who Paid None at All," *Chicago Reader,* February 11, 2010.

30. Chad Rosenbloom, "Congress's Missing Coverage," *Extra!,* August 2012.

31. Joe Rothstein, "The No-News Media Flunks Coverage of Congressional Campaigns," EINNEWS.com, September 10, 2012.

32. Andrew Neff, "Take This Job and Shove It: Fed-Up Bangor TV Anchors Quit on Air," *Bangor Daily News,* November 20, 2012.

33. Quoted in Bob Sullivan, "Sarcasm Campaigning: Social Media Hones Cynical Edge in Presidential Politics," redtape.nbcnews.com, October 2, 2012.

34. Gretchen Cuda Kroen, "Why Local Elections Matter More to Your Personal Finance," *Marketplace Money (American Public Media),* November 9, 2012.

35. Quoted in ibid.

36. Phill Brooks, "Capitol Perspectives: Campaign 2012, Advertising or Policy?," stlouis.cbslocal.com, August 28, 2012.

37. See Thomas E. Patterson, *Out of Order* (New York: Vintage Books, 1994), 27.

38. Kevin Drum, "Presidential Campaigns Will Soon Be Done Entirely in CGI," motherjones.com, September 3, 2012.

39. Brooks, "Capitol Perspectives."

40. Jason Horowitz, "Campaigns Have Lost Control of Coverage Due to Social Media," washington post.com, October 31, 2012.

41. Walter Shapiro, "Three Questions About Campaign Coverage," cjr.org, November 2, 2012.

42. Kristen A. Lee, "Local Interview with Paul Ryan Ends Abruptly," *New York Daily News,* October 9, 2012.

43. David Ferguson, "Maddow: Is the Romney Campaign Hiding Paul Ryan?," *Raw Story,* October 27, 2012.

44. Dylan Byers, "Reporter 'Not Allowed' to Talk to Voters at Biden Event," Politico, October 22, 2012.

45. "Campaigns in Control," *Extra!,* October 2012, 9.

46. Greg Mitchell, "Pew Report: Candidates and Partisans, Not the Media, Control Campaign Coverage," thenation.com, August 24, 2012.

47. Quoted in David Taintor, "Media's Control Over Campaign Narrative Shrinks," talkingpoints memo.com, August 23, 2012.

48. Quoted in Beth Fouhy, "Study: Coverage of Obama, Romney Highly Negative," Associated Press, August 23, 2012.

49. Aaron Deslatte, "Elections Forecast: More Money Will Equal More Voter Confusion," orlando sentinel.com, August 12, 2012.

50. Craig Gilbert, "Thompson-Baldwin: Most Negative Senate Race in the Country?," *Milwaukee Journal Sentinel,* October 28, 2012.

51. Marquette University Law School Poll, "Results and Data: October 25–28, 2012," https://law .marquette.edu/poll/wp-content/uploads/2012/10/MLSP14_Toplines_LIKELYVOTERS.pdf.

52. Unsigned editorial, "The Truth Hard to Dig Up Amid All the Attack Ads," *Milwaukee Journal Sentinel,* November 1, 2012.

53. Paul Krugman, "The Post-Truth Campaign," *New York Times*, December 23, 2011.

54. Michael Cooper, "Campaigns Play Loose with Truth in a Fact-Check Age," *New York Times,* August 31, 2012.

55. John Nichols, "In a Debate Between Romney and Romney, Obama Was the Spectator," *The Nation,* October 3, 2012, http://www.thenation.com/blog/170349/debate-between-romney-and-romney-obama -was-spectator.

56. John Nichols, "Open the Presidential Debates!," *The Nation,* August 29, 2012.

57. Amy Goodman, "Expand the Debates: This Is What Democracy Sounds Like," syndicated column, October 7, 2012. The Open Debates movement has for a number of years made the case for allowing more candidates into U.S. presidential debates. See www.opendebates.org.

58. John Nichols, "These Debates Could Use Some Jill Stein and Gary Johnson," *The Nation,* October 2, 2012.

59. Angelique Chrisafis, "Jean-Luc Mélenchon: The Poetry-Loving Pitbull Galvanising the French Elections," *The Guardian,* April 6, 2012.

60. Brian Stelter, "Memo Outlines Format and Rules for Candidate Debates," *New York Times,* October 15, 2012.

61. Ralph Nader, "US Media: Examine Thyself," readersupoportednews.org, August 26, 2012.

62. Frank Vogl, "Corruption Dare No Longer Be a Taboo Topic in This Presidential Election," huffington post.com, August 22, 2012.

63. FAIR cited in Jeff Spross, "Study: Media Campaign Coverage Almost Never Addresses Poverty," thinkprogress.org, September 15, 2012.

64. Glenn Greenwald, "Martha Raddatz and the Faux Objectivity of Journalists," *The Guardian,* October 12, 2012.

65. Bill Moyers and Bernard Weisberger, "Money in Politics: Where Is the Outrage?," Huffington Post, August 30, 2012.

66. Charley James, "Deflating Another Balloon: 2012 Candidate Coverage Balanced," ukprogressive,co.uk, November 10, 2012.

67. Tom Rosenstiel, "Winning the Media Campaign 2012," beyondchron.org, November 5, 2012.

68. Brian Lowry, "Is TV Shaving Political Points?," variety.com, September 15, 2012.

69. Sasha Issenberg, "Why Campaign Reporters Are Behind the Curve," nytimes.com, September 1, 2012.

70. Quoted in Sullivan, "Sarcasm Campaigning."

71. Dylan Byers, "Reporters: We Loathe 2012 Campaign," Politico, September 3, 2012.

72. Quoted in Editorial, "Tale of the Tape . . . So Far," *Columbia Journalism Review*, September/October 2012.

73. Quoted in Ari Melber, "Why Fact-Checking Has Taken Root in This Year's Election," pbs.org, September 5, 2012.

74. Quoted in Kevin Cirilli, "Journalists Bemoan Political 'Food Fight' Coverage," politico.com, September 24, 2012.

75. Phillip Morris, "America Needs a Full-Time President—the 2012 Election Cannot Be Over Soon Enough," Cleveland.com, September 29, 2012.

76. Jonathan Chait, "GOP Poll Denialists Totally Crazy, Not Totally Wrong," *New York* magazine's "Daily Intel" column, September 27, 2012.

77. Herbert J. Gans, *Democracy and the News* (New York: Oxford University Press, 2003), 54.

78. Glenn Greenwald, "The Misery of the Protracted Presidential Campaign Season," Salon.com, August 16, 2011, http://www.salon.com/2011/08/16/elections_9/.

79. L. Brent Bozell III and Brent H. Baker, eds., *And That's the Way It Isn't: A Reference Guide to Media Bias* (Alexandria, VA: Media Research Center, 1990), 86–94.

80. Quoted in Lloyd Grove, "Media to the Left! Media to the Right! The GOP, Shooting the Messengers," *Washington Post,* August 20, 1992.

81. James Brian McPherson, *The Conservative Resurgence and the Press: The Media's Role in the Rise of the Right* (Evanston, IL: Northwestern University Press, 2008), xii.

82. Quoted in Mike Mills, "Meeting of the Media Giants," *Washington Post,* January 21, 1995.

83. Rory O'Connor with Aaron Cutler, *Shock Jocks: Hate Speech & Talk Radio* (San Francisco: AlterNet Books, 2008), 2.

84. David Neiwert, *The Eliminationists: How Hate Talk Radicalized the American Right* (Sausalito, CA: PoliPoint Press, 2009).

85. McPherson, *The Conservative Resurgence,* xi.

86. Kathleen Hall Jamieson and Joseph N. Cappella, *Echo Chamber: Rush Limbaugh and the Conservative Media Establishment* (New York: Oxford University Press, 2008), ix.

87. See Doty Lynch, "How the Media Covered the 2008 Election: The Role of Earned Media," in James A. Thurber and Candace J. Nelson, eds., *Campaigns and Elections American Style,* 3rd ed. (Boulder, CO: Westview Press, 2010), 163.

88. Michael Wolff, *The Man Who Owns the News: Inside the Secret World of Rupert Murdoch* (New York: Broadway Books, 2008), 282.

89. Kaplan left CNN soon thereafter. Robert McChesney conversation with Rick Kaplan, March 2002. For a detailed discussion of this period, see Scott Collins, *Crazy Like a Fox: The Inside Story of How Fox News Beat CNN* (New York: Portfolio, 2004), chap. 11.

90. Jamieson and Cappella, *Echo Chamber,* x, 240.

91. Thomas Frank, *Pity the Billionaire* (New York: Metropolitan Books, 2012), 155.

92. Eric Alterman provided a compendium of prominent conservatives, such as Pat Buchanan, William Kristol, and James Baker, acknowledging that the liberal bias of the news is BS. See Eric Alterman, *What Liberal Media?* (New York: Basic Books, 2003), 2. Ralph Reed said the same in Joe Conason, *Big Lies* (New York: St. Martin's Press, 2003), 34.

93. Pete Kasperowicz, "Issa Warns Taxpayers' Loss on Solyndra Loan May Near $850 Million," *The Hill,* October 22, 2012; Neela Banerjee, "Darrell Issa to Probe Government Loan Programs After Solyndra Collapse," *Los Angeles Times,* September 20, 2011. Far rarer were stories such as Brad Plumer "Five Myths About the Solyndra Collapse," *Washington Post,* September 14, 2011. Note that Plumer's

story discrediting the Solyndra scandal appeared a year before the Issa hearing. The facts did not seem to matter.

94. FAIR and Media Matters for America both have done rigorous work fact-checking and analyzing conservative news media, and their mountain of resultant work is fire-tested for credibility. The picture is not pretty. FAIR also applies the exact same standard to mainstream news media and finds much that is flawed there as well.

95. Fairleigh Dickinson University's PublicMind Poll, "Some News Leaves People Knowing Less," press release, November 21, 2011.

96. "Jon Stewart Says Those Who Watch Fox News Are the 'Most Consistently Misinformed Media Viewers,'" PolitiFact.com, June 20, 2011, http://www.politifact.com/truth-o-meter/statements/2011 /jun/20/jon-stewart/jon-stewart-says-those-who-watch-fox-news-are-most/.

97. Mark Howard, "Study Confirms That Fox News Makes You Stupid," AlterNet, December 15, 2010, http://www.alternet.org/story/149193/study_confirms_that_fox_news_makes_you_stupid/.

98. Theda Skocpol and Vanessa Williamson, *The Tea Party and the Remaking of American Conservatism* (New York: Oxford University Press, 2012), 201.

99. McPherson, *The Conservative Resurgence,* xiii.

100. Robert McChesney conversation with Rick Kaplan, March 2002.

101. See Eric Boehlert, *Lap Dogs: How the Press Rolled Over for Bush* (New York: Free Press, 2006).

102. Noah Rothman, "Chris Matthews' Panel Eviscerates Obama's Debate Performance," *Mediaite,* October 7, 2012.

103. Erik Wemple, "Dick Morris 'Landslide' Prediction Too Early to Call," *Washington Post,* November 6, 2012.

104. Simon Maloy, "Sean Hannity: Media Matters' 2008 Misinformer of the Year," mediamatters.org, December 17, 2008.

105. Terry Krepel, "O'Reilly Is Right: Fox's Hannity Is a 'Republican Show,'" mediamatters.org, September 20, 2011.

106. Solange Uwimana, "Fox News Redefines Unbalanced by Giving Romney 366 Percent More Airtime," mediamatters.org, November 3, 2012.

107. Skocpol and Williamson, *The Tea Party,* 201.

108. Frank, *Pity the Billionaire,* 75.

109. Skocpol and Williamson, *The Tea Party,* 132, 202.

110. Quoted in Jeff Zeleny, "The Up-Close-and-Personal Candidate? A Thing of the Past," *New York Times,* December 1, 2011.

111. For a detailed examination of the 2000 *Bush v. Gore* fight, which includes a chapter on the Fox intervention on election night, see John Nichols, *Jews for Buchanan* (New York: New Press, 2001). See also Melinda Wittstock, "Cousin John's Calls Tipped Election Tally: As US News Networks Raced to Declare the Winner, Fox Enjoyed a Natural Advantage," *The Observer,* November 18, 2000.

112. Meredith Blake, "Karl Rove Melts Down After Fox News Calls Ohio for Obama," *Los Angeles Times,* November 7, 2012.

113. Howell Raines, "Why Don't Honest Journalists Take on Roger Ailes and Fox News?," *Washington Post,* March 14, 2010. See also Robert Greenwald, *Outfoxed: Rupert Murdoch's War on Journalism,* http://www.outfoxed.org/.

114. Eric Boehlert, "30 Reasons Why Fox News Is Not Legit," mediamatters.org, October 27, 2009.

115. Quoted in Dylan Byers, "Rush Limbaugh: 'Conservatism Did Not Lose,'" Politico, November 7, 2012.

116. Nader, "US Media."

117. Glenn Greenwald, "Election 2012 and the Media: A Vast Rightwing Conspiracy of Stupid," *The Guardian,* August 30, 2012.

118. Glenn Greenwald, "The Journalistic Mind," salon.com, August 8, 2012.

119. Todd Phillips, "It's the Need for Campaign Contributions That's the Problem," Huffington Post, August 23, 2012.

120. Walter Lippmann, *Liberty and the News* (Rpt., Mineola, NY: Dover, 2010), 1, 2, 18, 35.

Chapter 8: Digital Politics

1. Daily Download, "Obama Spent 10 Times as Much on Social Media as Romney," *PBS NewsHour,* November 16, 2012.

2. "10 Bold Ideas for the Future of Consulting," *Campaigns & Elections,* September/October 2012.

3. Ibid.

4. Ibid.

5. Ibid.

6. See Jason Gainous and Kevin M. Wagner, *Rebooting American Politics: The Internet Revolution* (Lanham, MD: Rowman & Littlefield, 2011), chap. 1.

7. William Grimes, "Clive Barnes, Who Raised Stakes in Dance and Theater Criticism, Dies at 81," *New York Times,* November 19, 2008. The original quote appeared in a December 30, 1969, *New York Times* article. We like that Barnes added this proviso: "The most terrifying thing is what people do want." But his core point regarding the democratic nature of television echoed popular thinking in the 1950s and 1960s.

8. Satwant Kaur, "How Technology Turned the Tide in the Election," Huffington Post, November 12, 2012.

9. Quoted in Inc.com staff, "Who's Winning the 2012 Social Media Election? Take a Look at How the Obama and Romney Social Media Campaigns Measured Up This Summer," *Inc.,* September 8, 2012.

10. Paul Springer and Mel Carson, "2012: The First Digital Election," forbes.com, November 5, 2012.

11. Quoted in Paul Sloan, "Mark 2012 as History's Last 'Social Media' Election," cnet.com, November 6, 2012.

12. T. W. Farnam, "Obama Has Aggressive Internet Strategy to Woo Supporters," *Washington Post,* April 6, 2012.

13. John Hudson, "The Most Expensive Election in History by the Numbers," theatlanticwire.com, November 6, 2012, http://www.theatlanticwire.com/politics/2012/11/most-expensive-election-history -numbers/58745/.

14. Fredreka Schouten and Christopher Schnaars, "Casino CEO Spends $39.6 Million in Late Election Effort," *USA Today,* December 7, 2012.

15. Quoted in Tony Gara, "Election Ads Boom in 2012, but the Online Shift Still Isn't Happening," wsj.com, November 5, 2012.

16. Quoted in Scott Bomboy, "Analysis: Internet Marketing Was Breakout Star of 2012 Campaign," constitutioncenter.org, November 14, 2012.

17. Quoted in Ned Martel, "Could the Campaign Ads Benefit from the Mad Men Touch?," washington post.com, October 24, 2012.

18. *Campaigns & Elections,* July/August 2012; September/October 2012; November/December 2012. We've read *Campaign & Elections* for years and reviewed it closely throughout the 2012 election season to watch the development of digital campaigning.

19. As we discuss in Chapter 2, the estimates for campaign spending vary dramatically, and that applies to Internet ad spending as well. *The Economist* placed it just north of $300 billion, but that was before the late surge in October and before the full extent of the spending levels became clear postelection. Some campaign insiders we consulted said online ad spending was around 10 percent of total ad spending. So we put the range well below 10 percent of total political advertising spending to play it safe. The actual total may well be closer to $500 million, and we hope in time a harder number will be determined. See "Of Mud and Money," *The Economist,* September 8, 2012, http://www.economist.com/node/21562211.

20. Pew Research Center, "Low Marks for the 2012 Election," people-press.org, November 15, 2012.

21. Cited in Aaron Smith, "Online Political Videos and Campaign 2012," pewinternet.org, November 2, 2012.

22. Aaron Smith and Maeve Duggan, "The State of the 2012 Election–Mobile Politics," pewinternet.org, October 9, 2012.

23. Tim Karr, "The Internet as Political Lie Detector," Huffington Post, October 12, 2012.

24. "Facebook, Tweets Key to Victory in US Presidential Elections," economictimes.indiatimes.com, October 14, 2012.

25. Allison Brennan, "Microtargeting: How Campaigns Know You Better Than You Know Yourself," cnn.com, November 5, 2012.

26. Robinson Meyer, "9 Concrete, Specific Things We Actually Know About How Social Media Shape Elections," theatlantic.com, August 22, 2012.

27. Quoted in Rob Lever, "2012 Election Campaign a Digital Battleground," thepresidency.us, October 13, 2012.

28. For a fascinating perspective on this technological utopianism (with useful historical context), consider Howard P. Segal, *Technological Utopianism in American Culture,* 20th anniversary ed. (Syracuse, NY: Syracuse University Press, 2005).

29. This issue and many other related Internet issues are developed in Robert W. McChesney, *Digital Disconnect: How Capitalism Is Turning the Internet Away from Democracy* (New York: New Press, 2013).

30. For a recent discussion of this point, see Evgeny Morozov, *To Save Everything, Click Here: The Folly of Technological Solutionism* (New York: PublicAffairs, 2013).

31. *Citizens United v. Federal Election Commission,* 130 S.Ct. 876.

32. Quoted in Rick Cohen, "How Nonprofits Inadvertently Provide Cover for Political Donor Laundering," campaignlegalcenter.org, September 6, 2012.

33. "Survival of the Biggest," *The Economist,* December 1, 2012, 11.

34. See McChesney, *Digital Disconnect,* chap. 4.

35. Shira Ovide and Evelyn M. Rusli, "How Facebook, Twitter Court Political Campaigns," *Wall Street Journal,* November 2, 2012.

36. Quoted in Craig Timberg, "Web Sites Lose to Google, AOL in Race for Obama, Romney Campaign Ads," *Washington Post,* October 4, 2012.

37. Joseph Turow, *The Daily You: How the New Advertising Industry Is Defining Your Identity and Your Worth* (New Haven, CT: Yale University Press, 2011), 40–41.

38. Quoted in Eli Pariser, *The Filter Bubble: What the Internet Is Hiding from You* (New York: Penguin, 2011), 31.

39. See, for example, Geoffrey A. Fowler, "Facebook Sells More Access to Members," *Wall Street Journal,* October 1, 2012.

40. Material for this paragraph is from Jeffrey Rosen, "Who Do They Think You Are?," *New York Times Sunday Magazine,* December 2, 2012, 42–45. For an extensive development of these points, see McChesney, *Digital Disconnect,* chap. 5.

41. Quoted in Turow, *The Daily You,* 158.

42. Pariser, *The Filter Bubble.*

43. Rosen, "Who Do They Think You Are?," 45.

44. Sloan, "Mark 2012."

45. Rosen, "Who Do They Think You Are?," 45.

46. "Deus ex machine," *The Economist,* November 3, 2012, 32.

47. Alexis Madrigal, "I'm Being Followed: How Google—and 104 Other Companies—Are Tracking Me on the Web," *The Atlantic,* February 2012, http://www.theatlantic.com/technology/archive/2012/02 /im-being-followed-how-google-151-and-104-other-companies-151-are-tracking-me-on-the-web/253758/.

48. Pariser, *The Filter Bubble,* 49.

49. "Websites Lose Out on Election Advertisements," advertisementjournal.com, October 10, 2012.

50. All quoted in Timberg, "Web Sites Lose to Google."

51. Jamie Court, "Political Bloggers Should Reveal Funding," sfgate.com, November 13, 2012.

52. In 2012, the Obama campaign advertised directly on many liberal Web sites, including those of the *Daily Kos,* the *New Republic,* and *The Nation.* See "Websites Lose Out."

53. Pew Research Center's Project for Excellence in Journalism, "The Future of Mobile News," journalism .org, October 1, 2012.

54. For an extensive development of these points, see McChesney, *Digital Disconnect,* chap. 6.

55. Pew Research Center, "Internet Gains Most as Campaign News Source but Cable TV Still Leads: Social Media Doubles, but Remains Limited," journalism.org, October 25, 2012.

56. Bob Sullivan, "Sarcasm Campaigning: Social Media Hones Cynical Edge in Presidential Politics," redtape.nbcnews.com, October 2, 2012.

57. Quoted in Adam Mazmanian, "Selling the Hashtag Election," *National Journal,* September 11, 2012, http://www.nationaljournal.com/tech/selling-the-hashtag-election-20120911.

58. Susan Currie Sivek, "How Political Magazines Use Twitter to Drive 2012 Election Chatter," pbs.org/mediashift, October 31, 2012.

59. Regina McCombs, "How to Keep Social Media Reaction in Perspective When Covering Elections," pointer.org, October 24, 2012.

60. Jason Horowitz, "Campaigns Have Lost Control of Coverage Due to Social Media," standard.net, October 31, 2012.

61. Quoted in Neha Prakash, ""Gaffesplosion: The Unrelenting Hype of Modern Politics," machable.com, October 2, 2012.

62. Horowitz, "Campaigns Have Lost Control of Coverage."

63. See John Nichols, "The Next Media System," in *Uprising: How Wisconsin Renewed the Politics of Protest, from Madison to Wall Street* (New York: Nation Books, 2012).

64. Quoted in Tom Rosenstiel, "Winning the Media Campaign 2012," beyondchron.org, November 5, 2012.

65. Quoted in Meyer, "9 Concrete, Specific Things."

66. Joshua Brustein, "Start-Ups Aim to Help Us Put a Price on Their Personal Data," *New York Times,* February 13, 2012.

67. Christina Lamb, "Is Obama Stalking You?," spectator.co.uk, October 27, 2012.

68. Quoted in Scott Bomboy, "Analysis: Internet Marketing Was Breakout Star of 2012," blog .constitutioncenter.org, November 14, 2012.

69. Tim Dickinson, "The Obama Campaign's Real Heroes," RollingStone.com, December 7, 2012.

70. Jim Rutenberg and Jeff Zeleny, "Obama Mines for Voters with High Tech Tools," *New York Times,* March 8, 2012.

71. Dickinson, "The Obama Campaign's Real Heroes."

72. Michael Scherer, "Inside the Secret World of the Data Crunchers Who Helped Obama Win," swamp land.time.com, November 7, 2012.

73. Joshua Green, "Corporations Want Obama's Winning Formula," *Bloomberg Businessweek,* November 28–December 2, 2012, 37.

74. Emily Steel, "US Election Offers Advertising Lessons," ft.com, November 8, 2012.

75. See, for example, Derrick Harris, "How Obama's Tech Team Helped Deliver the 2012 Election," gigaom.com, November 12, 2012; "Facebook, Tweets key to victory"; Springer and Carson, "2012"; and Bomboy, "Analysis."

76. Quoted in Scherer, "Inside the Secret World."

77. Quoted in Dickinson, "The Obama Campaign's Real Heroes."

78. Mark Milian, "The Quest for More Clicks," *Bloomberg Businessweek,* September 24–30, 2012, 42.

79. Lamb, "Is Obama Stalking You?"

80. Quoted in Green "Corporations Want Obama's Winning Formula," 37.

81. L. Gordon Crovitz, "How Campaigns Hypertarget Voters Online," wsj.com, November 4, 2012.

82. Ibid.

83. Charles Duhigg, "Campaigns Mine Personal Lives to Get Out Vote," *New York Times,* October 14, 2012.

84. David Wells, "Microtargeting: How Campaigns Know You Better Than You Know Yourself," fox13now.com, November 5, 2012.

85. Molly McHugh, "How Social Media, Data Mining, and New-Fangled Technology Tipped the 2012 Election," digitaltrends,com, November 10, 2012.

86. Scherer, "Inside the Secret World."

87. Dickinson, "The Obama Campaign's Real Heroes."

88. Wells, "Microtargeting."

89. Lois Beckett, "Web Cookies Used by Companies to Tailor Political Ads You See Online," Huffington Post, October 23, 2012.

90. Kevin Liptak, "Obama Team: Campaign Was Great, but Candidate More Important," cnn.com, November 8, 2012.

91. Quoted in Lamb, "Is Obama Stalking You?"

92. Duhigg, "Campaigns Mine Personal Lives."

93. "Deus ex machine," 32.

94. Dickinson, "The Obama Campaign's Real Heroes."

95. Green, "Corporations Want Obama's Winning Formula," 38.

96. Scherer, "Inside the Secret World."

97. Jim Rutenberg, "Secret of Obama Victory? Rerun Watchers, for One," *New York Times,* November 12, 2012.

98. Quoted in Dickinson, "The Obama Campaign's Real Heroes."

99. Both quoted in ibid.

100. Green, "Corporations Want Obama's Winning Formula," 38, 39.

101. Living Room Candidate, "Introduction," http://www.livingroomcandidate.org/.

102. Quoted in Dickinson, "The Obama Campaign's Real Heroes."

103. Jim Rutenberg, "Secret of Obama Victory?"

104. Rutenberg and Zeleny, "Obama Mines for Voters."

105. Quoted in Scherer, "Inside the Secret World."

106. Quoted in Joshua Green, "Hey, Read This," *Bloomberg Businessweek*, December 3–December 9, 2012, 31–32.

107. Dickinson, "The Obama Campaign's Real Heroes."

108. Green "Corporations Want Obama's Winning Formula," 38.

109. Harris, "How Obama's Tech Team Helped."

110. Duhigg, "Campaigns Mine Personal Lives."

111. Messina quoted in Dickinson, "The Obama Campaign's Real Heroes."

112. McHugh, "How Social Media . . . Tipped the 2012 Election."

113. Quoted in Rutenberg, "Secret of Obama Victory?"

114. Quoted in Dickinson, "The Obama Campaign's Real Heroes."

115. Quoted in Kate Kaye, "IAB's Big Data Driven Political Ad Push Backs Lobbying Goals," clickz.com, October 2, 2012.

116. Quoted in Molly A. K. Connors, "After a $6 Billion Election, Politicos Say Data Mining Is the Wave of the Future," *Concord (New Hampshire) Monitor,* November 13, 2012.

117. Robert Mann, *Daisy Petals and Mushroom Clouds: LBJ, Barry Goldwater, and the Ad That Changed American Politics* (Baton Rouge: Louisiana State University Press, 2011), 111–113.

118. Cited in Laurie Sullivan, "Obama Beats Romney in Online Political Ad Spend," mediapost.com, November 5, 2012.

119. Alexandra Jaffe, "GOP Groups Turn to Digital Ads in Final Weeks of Campaign," thehill.com, November 4, 2012.

120. Quoted in Steel, "US Election."

121. Quoted in R. Wilson, "Candidates Turn to Geo-Targeting in Ads," thehill.com, October 14, 2012.

122. Quoted in Melanie Mason, "What's the Future of Campaign Advertising? Look to the Four Screens," latimes.com, November 6, 2012.

123. Quoted in Joseph N. DiStefano, "New Political Advertising Targets Voters Via Their Online Habits," philly.com, November 5, 2012.

124. Quoted in Lamb, "Is Obama Stalking You?"

125. Rosen, "Who Do They Think You Are?," 42.

126. Quoted in Kaye, "IAB's Big Data."

127. Quoted in Natasha Singer and Charles Duhigg, "Tracking Voters' Clicks Online to Try to Sway Them," nytimes.com, October 27, 2012.

128. Joseph Turow, Michael X. Delli Carpini, Nora Draper, and Rowan Howard-Williams, "Americans Roundly Reject Tailored Political Advertising" (Philadelphia: Annenberg School for Communication, University of Pennsylvania, July 2012).

129. Quoted in Wilson, "Candidates Turn to Geo-Targeting."

130. Andy Ellenthal, "7 Political Ad Tactics Every Marketer Should Know," imediaconnection.com, August 15, 2012.

131. Jeremy Peters, "With Video, Obama Looks to Expand Campaign's Reach Through Social Media," *New York Times,* March 15, 2012.

132. Quoted in Tanzina Vega, "Online Data Helping Campaigns Customize Ads," *New York Times,* February 21, 2012.

133. Quoted in Wells, "Microtargeting."

134. Mason, "What's the Future?"

135. DiStefano, "New Political Advertising."

136. Quoted in Beckett, "Web Cookies."

137. Adam Lehmann, "Guess What? Online Political Ads Don't Turn Voters Off. They Work," adage.com, October 4, 2012.

138. Steel, "US election."

139. Dickinson, "The Obama Campaign's Real Heroes."

140. Megan Woo and Joe St. George, "Internet Users React to Online Political Ads," wtvr.com, October 22, 2012.

141. Quoted in Beckett, "Web Cookies."

142. Lehmann, "Guess What?"

143. Lamb, "Is Obama Stalking You?"

144. Turow et al., "Americans Roundly Reject Tailored Political Advertising," 25.

145. Ibid., 26.

146. Quoted in Wells, "Microtargeting."

147. Quoted in Beckett, "Web Cookies."

148. Singer and Duhigg, "Tracking Voters' Clicks Online."

149. MacIver Institute Staff, "Stunner: Walker Recall Petitions NOT Available for Online Review," MacIver Institute, January 30, 2012.

150. "United Wisconsin Statement on Gab Decision to Post Recall Petitions Online," PolitiScoop, February 2, 2012, http://www.politiscoop.com/us-politics/wisconsin-politics/704-united-wisconsin-statement-on-gab-decision-to-post-recall-petitions-online.html.

151. Dan Bice, "Judge Draws Flak for Signing Walker Recall Petition," *Milwaukee Journal Sentinel,* March 6, 2012.

152. Turow et al., "Americans Roundly Reject Tailored Political Advertising," 7, 26.

153. Jon Peha, "Making Political Ads Personal," Politico, September 11, 2012.

154. Stephan Lesher, *George Wallace: American Populist* (New York: Da Capo Press, 1995); "George Wallace: Settin' the Woods on Fire," *The American Experience,* Public Broadcasting Service, 1999.

155. See Thomas F. Schaller, *Whistling Past Dixie: How Democrats Can Win Without the South* (New York: Simon & Schuster, 2008); and Tim Noah, "Forget the South, Democrats: Stop Coddling the Spoiled Brat of Presidential Politics," *Slate,* January 27, 2004.

156. Quoted in Patrick Doyle, "The No-Holds Barred, Deception-Filled Campaign," bostonmagazine.com, September 5, 2012.

157. Quoted in Lois Beckett, "Dark Money Political Groups Target Voters Based on Their Internet Habits," ProPublica.org, July 26, 2012.

158. "Deus ex machine," 32.

159. Beckett, "Dark Money Political Groups."

160. Kim Geiger, "Is Political Text Message Spam Legal?," latimes.com, September 26, 2012.

161. Alina Selyukh, "Storm of Anti-Obama Text Messages Linked to Virginia Firm," chicagotribune.com, October 31, 2012.

162. Goodstein is the founder of Revolution Messaging, LLC, and he served as external online director for Obama for America. You can learn more about him at http://revolutionmessaging.com/about-us/.

163. Scott Goodstein, "An Open Letter to FCC Chairman Genachowski—Take Action and Stop Political Text Spam," Huffington Post, May 31, 2012.

164. Ibid.

165. Dave Nyczepir, "FCC Takes Up Text Message Spam: The Legality of Text Message Spam Depends on Who You Ask," *Campaigns & Elections,* October 25 2012, http://www.campaignsandelections.com/campaign-insider/333042/fcc-takes-up-text-message-spam.thtml.

166. Ibid.
167. Turow et al., "Americans Roundly Reject Tailored Political Advertising," 27.
168. Beckett, "Dark Money Political Groups."
169. Peha, "Making Political Ads Personal."
170. Turow et al., "Americans Roundly Reject Tailored Political Advertising," 26.
171. Margaret Rock, "ITTO: How Political Ads Target You," mobiledia.com, August 8, 2012.
172. Mason, "What's the Future?"
173. Mike Farrell, "Advanced Advertising: Data Will Drive Addressable Market," multichannel.com, November 13, 2012.
174. Turow et al., "Americans Roundly Reject Tailored Political Advertising," 26.
175. Quoted in Wells, "Microtargeting."
176. Turow et al., "Americans Roundly Reject Tailored Political Advertising," 4.
177. Kate Kaye, "Obama's Approach to Big Data: Do as I Say, Not as I Do," adage.com, November 16, 2012.

Chapter 9: The Right to Vote

1. Irving Dilliard, ed., *Mr. Justice Brandeis, Great American* (St. Louis: Modern View Press, 1941), 42.
2. John Evan Seery, *A Political Companion to Walt Whitman* (Lexington: University Press of Kentucky, 2011), 298.
3. Thomas Jefferson to Edmund Randolph, 1799, ME 10:126. This letter is found in *The Writings of Thomas Jefferson,* Memorial Edition (Andrew Adgate Lipscomb and Albert Ellery Bergh, eds.), published in 20 volumes in 1903–1904. Washington: Thomas Jefferson Memorial Association of the United States.
4. Alexander Keyssar, *The Right to Vote: The Contested History of Democracy in the United States* (New York: Basic Books, rev. ed. published in 2009).
5. Garrett Epps, "Voting: Right or Privilege?," *The Atlantic,* September 18, 2012.
6. Ibid.
7. See Robert W. McChesney, *Digital Disconnect: How Capitalism Is Turning the Internet Against Democracy* (New York: New Press, 2013), chap. 3.
8. Arthur M. Schlesinger Jr., *The Cycles of American History* (New York: Mariner Books, 1999).
9. Ibid., 24.
10. Thurgood Marshall, "Remarks at the Annual Seminar of the San Francisco Patent and Trademark Law Association," Maui, Hawaii, May 6, 1987, http://www.thurgoodmarshall.com/speeches/constitutional_speech.htm.
11. To understand the scope and significance of Shays' Rebellion, a 1786–1787 revolt by Revolutionary War soldiers in Massachusetts, reread Gore Vidal, "Homage to Daniel Shays," *New York Review of Books,* August 10, 1972; and Howard Zinn, *A People's History of the United States* (New York: HarperCollins, 2005).
12. Darren Staloff, *Hamilton, Adams, Jefferson: The Politics of Enlightenment and the American Founding* (New York: Hill and Wang, 2005). The core discussion of the exchanges can be found on 305–309.
13. Ibid.
14. Brad Plumer, "'We Have to Fix That,' but Will We?," *Washington Post,* November 8, 2012.
15. Teddy Roosevelt, "The New Nationalism," August 31, 1910, http://www.whitehouse.gov/blog/2011/12/06/archives-president-teddy-roosevelts-new-nationalism-speech.
16. Paul Steinhauser et al., "CNN Poll: Majority Think Government Is Broken," CNN, February 21, 2010.
17. Frank Newport, "Debt, Gov't Dysfunction Rise to Top of Americans' Issue List: Fewer Americans Now Cite Unemployment as Most Important Problem," Gallup Politics, January 14, 2013.
18. Steinhauser et al., "CNN Poll."
19. It is important to note the deep democracy component of the Occupy movement. Though undercovered by much of the media, the Occupy Wall Street activism that took form in September 2011 advanced a steady and serious critique of campaign finance and election issues. Occupy activists linked this critique

to the economic concerns that the movement discussed, making the critical point that giving more power to the people is one of the best ways to assure that economic choices are made with an eye toward the needs of all Americans. See William Greider, "The Democratic Promise of Occupy Wall Street," *The Nation,* November 22, 2011.

20. John Nichols, "Feingold Fears 'Lawless' Court Ruling on Corporate Campaigning," *The Nation,* January 13, 2010.

21. Rachel Weiner, "Obama Suggests Constitutional Amendment in Reddit Chat," *Washington Post,* August 29, 2012.

22. John Bonifaz, Steve Cobble, and other coordinators of the Free Speech for People movement spoke regularly with John Nichols about these changes during the period from 2010 to 2013. Bonifaz also addressed the evolution in a fine interview published January 1, 2013, by the Wisdom Voices project. The interview can be found at http://wisdomvoices.com/john-bonifaz-the-face-of-democracy-2013/.

23. Free Speech for People, "Analysis: America Is Now One Quarter of the Way to Amending the Constitution to Overturn Citizens United," November 7, 2012, http://freespeechforpeople.org/sites/default /files/StateProgessPressRelease.pdf.

24. Move to Amend, "Election Results: Move to Amend Initiative Resolutions Win Big," November 7, 2012, https://movetoamend.org/election-results-move-amend-initiative-resolutions-win-big.

25. Ibid.

26. Interview with Robert Weissman, president of Public Citizen, January 23, 2013. Weissman provided details regarding many of the grassroots campaigns described in this section and discussed strategies for advancing constitutional reform and a variety of related initiatives.

27. Move to Amend, "Election Results."

28. Memo prepared by Public Campaign's Nick Nyhart, shared with authors, January 18, 2013. John Nichols wrote about the memo and many of the campaign-finance reforms outlined in this section in "The Election Reform Moment?," *The Nation,* January 30, 2013.

29. Interview with Weissman.

30. Timothy Karr, "Left in the Dark: Local Election Coverage in the Age of Big-Money Politics," *Free Press,* September 2012. We have spoken regularly to Copps about this issue, as he has worked with Free Press and Common Cause in his post-FCC years.

31. Dave Boyer, "Softer Campaign-Finance Bill Offered by McCain, Feingold: McConnell Promises to Defeat Measure Again," *Washington Times,* September 17, 1999.

32. Jaron Lanier, "The False Ideals of the Web," *New York Times,* January 18, 2012.

33. Andy Kroll, "The Massive New Liberal Plan to Remake American Politics: A Month After President Obama Won Reelection, America's Most Powerful Liberal Groups Met to Plan Their Next Moves. Here's What They Talked About," *Mother Jones,* January 9, 2013.

34. Formed by Josh Silver, with whom we worked to create and develop Free Press, United Republic is online at http://unitedrepublic.org.

35. Free Speech for People, "Analysis."

36. John Bonifaz interview with John Nichols, May 22, 2011.

37. John F. Kennedy, "Remarks in Nashville at the 90th Anniversary Convocation of Vanderbilt University," May 18, 1963. Accessed March 11, 2013, at: http://www.jfklibrary.org/Research/Research -Aids/Ready-Reference/JFK-Speeches/Remarks-in-Nashville-at-the-90th-Anniversary-Convocation-of -Vanderbilt-University-May-18-1963.aspx.

38. John Nichols and Robert W. McChesney, "After 'Citizens United': The Attack of the Super PACs," *The Nation,* February 6, 2012.

39. For a detailed assessment of how different countries approach campaign-finance rules and regulations, public financing, and free-airtime issues, see Reginald Austin and Maja Tjernström, eds., *Funding of Political Parties and Election Campaigns* (Stockholm: International Institute for Democracy and Electoral Assistance, 2003). The information in the handbook is regularly updated online at www.idea.int/.

40. Ralph Negrine, Party Election Broadcasts, Sheffield University, http://pebs.group.shef.ac.uk/ (accessed February 8, 2013).

41. Adlai Stevenson, "Speech at the Democratic National Convention," August 18, 1956, http://www .presidency.ucsb.edu/ws/index.php?pid=75172.

42. The original McCain-Feingold legislation, as advanced in the mid-1990s, featured a plan for free airtime. Compromises to advance the legislation scrapped the plan. But McCain and Feingold returned with a new proposal in 2002. Here's a link to background on the "Our Democracy Our Airwaves" campaign that sought to promote it: http://www.wisdc.org/freeair.php.

43. Quoted in Herbert Joseph Muller, *Adlai Stevenson: A Study in Values* (New York: Harper & Row, 1967), 174.

44. See Robert W. McChesney and John Nichols, *The Death and Life of American Journalism: The Media Revolution That Will Begin the World Again* (New York: Nation Books, 2011).

45. Ibid.

46. UN Special Rapporteur on Freedom of Opinion and Expression, the OSCE Representative on Freedom of the Media, the OAS (Organization of American States) Special Rapporteur on Freedom of Expression, and the ACHPR (African Commission on Human and Peoples' Rights) Special Rapporteur on Freedom of Expression and Access to Information, "Joint Declaration on the Media and Elections," May 15, 2009, http://www.osce.org/.

47. Thomas Jefferson letter to Littleton Waller Tazewell, January 5, 1805. Accessed March 9, 2013, from Jefferson, Thomas, and others. Sixty-eight letters to and from Jefferson, 1805–1817, Electronic Text Center, University of Virginia Library.

48. Barack Obama, "Remarks by the President at Hampton University Commencement," May 9, 2010.

49. Chris Hogg, "Japan's Old-Fashioned Campaigning," BBC, July 12, 2007, http://news.bbc.co.uk /2/hi/asia-pacific/6292602.stm; and Coco Masters, "Japan's Twitter-Free Election Campaign," *Time,* August 18, 2009.

50. Masters, "Japan's Twitter-Free Election Campaign."

51. Randolph T. Stevenson and Lynn Vavreck, "Does Campaign Length Matter? Testing for Cross-National Effects," paper delivered at the Midwest Political Science Association meeting, held in Chicago, April 18–20, 1996. A longer version of the argument is found at http://www.sscnet.ucla.edu/polisci /faculty/vavreck/bjps.pdf. We differ with some of the conclusions of this paper, but we respect its review of the arguments for and against short campaigns, the literature on various sides of the issue, and the comparisons provided in terrific charts.

52. Ibid.

53. In regard to direct observation, John Nichols, a commentator for the BBC, RTE-Irish Radio, and Al Jazeera English, has covered politics and elections in more than a dozen countries around the world, with particular focus on Britain, Canada, Ireland, India, Israel, Italy, and South Africa. For statistical measures of political engagement, see Judith Torney-Purta, Carolyn Henry Barber, and Wendy Klandl Richardson, "Trust in Government-Related Institutions and Political Engagement Among Adolescents in Six Countries," *Acta Politica* 39, no. 4 (December 2004): 380–406.

54. International IDEA, Voter Turnout survey, http://www.idea.int/vt/index.cfm. The International IDEA Voter Turnout Website contains the most comprehensive global collection of voter turnout statistics available. Regularly updated voter turnout figures for national presidential and parliamentary elections since 1945, as well as European Parliament elections, are presented country by country using both the number of registered voters and voting age population (VAP) as indicators. Accessed March 9, 2013.

55. The OSCE comprises fifty-six "participating States" from three continents: North America, Europe, and Asia. Its member states are home to more than 1 billion people, including Americans. The United States is a longtime member. An OSCE team was on the ground observing the 2012 elections in the United States. Unfortunately, there is not much history of U.S. officials embracing recommendations from overseas missions observing our elections. After the 2008 presidential election, an OSCE mission recommended thirty-eight significant changes to how the United States runs elections and how media approach elections. They were tepid proposals. Yet for the most part they were ignored.

56. Jimmy Carter, "Still Seeking a Fair Florida Vote," *Washington Post,* September 27, 2004. For a list of elections monitored by the Carter Center, see http://www.cartercenter.org/peace/democracy/observed.html.

57. Thomas Lundberg, "Election Reform in Japan?," in FairVote, "Voting and Democracy Report: 1995." Accessed November 16, 2012. A longer version of Lundberg's report appears in "Illinois Assembly on Political Representation and Alternative Electoral Systems Final Reports and Background Publications," Spring 2002 (Urbana: University of Illinois Institute of Government and Public Affairs), 19.

58. Alex Martin, "Historic Sea Change at Polls Product of Frustrated Public," *Japan Times,* August 30, 2009.

59. For information on election reform in New Zealand, go to the government of New Zealand's Ministry of Justice Web site at http://www.justice.govt.nz/electoral (accessed February 22, 2013).

60. Franklin Roosevelt, "Oglethorpe University Commencement Address, May 22, 1932," in *The Public Papers and Addresses of Franklin D. Roosevelt,* Vol. 1, *The Genesis of the New Deal, 1928–1932* (New York: Random House, 1938), 639.

61. Walt Whitman, "Drum-Taps, Rise O Days from Your Fathomless Deep, No. 3," www. bartleby.com /142/114.html (accessed February 22, 2013).

62. Bill Moyers, "The Power of Democracy," speech accepting the Public Intellectual Award of the Woodrow Wilson National Fellowship Foundation, February 7, 2007, in *Moyers on Democracy* (New York: Anchor Books, 2009), 92.

63. Epps, "Voting."

64. FairVote, "Why We Need the Right to Vote Amendment," www.fairvote.org, http://www.fairvote.org /why-we-need-the-right-to-vote-amendment#.UQ18P7-x_Qg. Accessed March 10, 2013. FairVote has launched a national campaign to promote the right-to-vote amendment. Learn more about it at: http:// www.promoteourvote.com/.

65. Ibid.

66. Ibid.

67. John Nichols, "One Year After Florida Debacle: Jesse Jackson Jr. Presses for Fundamental Election Reforms," *The Nation,* November 7, 2001. John Nichols wrote a number of articles on Jackson's push for a right-to-vote amendment and appeared at numerous academic and political forums with Jackson, Raskin, Cobble, and other proponents of the amendment. Many of these forums were sponsored by Jim Hightower's Chautauqua Project of 2001 and 2002 and later by Progressive Democrats of America. The latter remains a staunch proponent of full voting rights, making it a rare entity on the American political landscape. Fair-Vote and the Brennan Center also deserve high marks for their ongoing advocacy, which extends beyond detailing assaults on democracy to proposing the reforms necessary to prevent future assaults.

68. Ibid.

69. Conversation with Congressman Mark Pocan, February 23, 2013.

70. For more on the thinking of progressive jurists such as former U.S. Supreme Court justice John Paul Stevens regarding the dubious constitutionality of gerrymandering legislative and congressional districts, see John Nichols, "Three Strategies to Block the Gerrymandering of the Electoral College," *The Nation,* January 25, 2013.

71. For more information on the struggle to open up U.S. presidential debates to more parties, more can-didates, and more ideas, see http://www.opendebates.org. See also John Nichols, "Open the Presidential Debates!," *The Nation,* September 17, 2012.

72. For more on instant runoff voting and other democracy reforms, see www.fairvote.org.

73. The Electoral College, a remnant from the compromises with slavery that were the shame of the Con-stitutional Convention of 1787, allows for the "election" of a president who has actually lost the popular vote. This antidemocratic result last occurred in 2000 when George W. Bush became the president despite having lost the contest by more than 560,000 votes. Unlike in most countries, the popular vote was not definitional in 2000. After the close of the 1968 election, President Nixon and top Democrats appeared to be united in their support of a constitutional amendment to eliminate the Electoral College. It was supported by a majority of senators, but a filibuster by southern segregationist Democrats and conservative Republicans blocked the change. Current proposals to eliminate the Electoral College have been advanced in recent years by Florida senator Bill Nelson and others, as well as a number of reform groups, such as FairVote and the Liberty Tree Foundation.

74. George C. Edwards III, *Why the Electoral College Is Bad for America,* 2nd ed. (New Haven, CT: Yale University Press, 2011).

75. Free Speech for People, "Congressman McGovern Introduces the People's Rights Amendment," No-vember 15, 2013, freespeechforpeople.org, http://freespeechforpeople.org/McGovern.

76. Ibid.

77. Whitman, "Drum-Taps."

78. Thomas Jefferson, "Letter to Roger Weightman," June 24–26, 1826, Library of Congress, http://www .loc.gov/exhibits/jefferson/214.html.

INDEX

© Robin Holland

John Nichols is the *Nation* magazine Washington, DC, correspondent. A pioneering political blogger, he has written the magazine's Beat column since 1999. A contributing writer for the *Progressive* and *In These Times*, he is also the associate editor of the *Capital Times*, the daily newspaper in Madison, Wisconsin. His articles have appeared in the *New York Times*, *Chicago Tribune*, and dozens of other newspapers, and he is a frequent guest on radio and television programs as a commentator on politics and media issues. Author Gore Vidal said "Of all the giant slayers now afoot in the great American desert John Nichols's sword is the sharpest." Nichols lives in Madison, Wisconsin, and Washington, DC.

© Brent Nicasio

Robert W. McChesney is the Gutgsell Endowed Professor in the Department of Communication at the University of Illinois at Urbana-Champaign and the author or editor of twenty-three books. His work has been translated into thirty languages. He is the cofounder of Free Press, a national media reform organization. In 2008 the *Utne Reader* listed McChesney among their "Fifty Visionaries Who Are Changing Your World." He lives in Madison, Wisconsin, and Champaign, Illinois.

The Nation Institute

Founded in 2000, **Nation Books** has become a leading voice in American independent publishing. The inspiration for the imprint came from the *Nation* magazine, the oldest independent and continuously published weekly magazine of politics and culture in the United States.

The imprint's mission is to produce authoritative books that break new ground and shed light on current social and political issues. We publish established authors who are leaders in their area of expertise, and endeavor to cultivate a new generation of emerging and talented writers. With each of our books we aim to positively affect cultural and political discourse.

Nation Books is a project of The Nation Institute, a nonprofit media center dedicated to strengthening the independent press and advancing social justice and civil rights. The Nation Institute is home to a dynamic range of programs: the award-winning Investigative Fund, which supports ground-breaking investigative journalism; the widely read and syndicated website TomDispatch; the Victor S. Navasky Internship Program in conjunction with the *Nation* magazine; and Journalism Fellowships that support up to 25 high-profile reporters every year.

For more information on Nation Books, The Nation Institute, and the *Nation* magazine, please visit:

www.nationbooks.org

www.nationinstitute.org

www.thenation.com

www.facebook.com/nationbooks.ny

Twitter: @nationbooks